CRM 2013 Quick Start

JUMPSTART YOUR CRM 2013 LEARNING CURVE

David Yack, Joel Lindstrom, David Berry, Richard Knudson, Dylan Haskins, Jukka Niiranen

CRM 2013 Quick Start

Published by

We Speak You Learn, LLC
2928 Straus Lane Ste 200
Colorado Springs, CO 80907

www.CRM2013QuickStart.com

Copyright 2014 by We Speak You Learn, LLC

Limit of Liability/Disclaimer of Warranty: The author and publisher have taken care in the preparation of this book, but make no expressed or implied warranty of any kind and assume no responsibility for errors or omissions. No liability is assumed for incidental or consequential damages in connection with or arising out of the use of the information or programs contained herein. The advice and strategies contained herein may not be suitable for every situation. This work is sold with the understanding that the publisher is not engaged in rendering legal, accounting, or other professional services. If professional assistance is required, the services of a competent professional person should be sought. Neither the publisher nor the author shall be liable for damages arising herefrom. The fact that an organization or Website is referred to in this work as a citation and/or a potential source of further information does not mean that the author or the publisher endorses the information the organization or Website may provide or recommendations it may make. Further, readers should be aware that Internet Websites listed in this work may have changed or no longer exist between when this work was written and when it is read.

All rights reserved. No part of this publication may be reproduced, stored in a retrieval system, or transmitted, in any form or by any means, electronic, mechanical, photocopying, recording, or otherwise, without the prior written consent of the publisher. Printed in the United States of America.

ISBN-13: 978-0-9815118-7-0

ISBN-10: 0-9815118-7-2

Credits

Editor
Julie Yack

Assistant Editor
Joy Garscadden

Cover Design
David Yack

About the Authors

Joel Lindstrom
Joel Lindstrom is a Solution Architect working at Hitachi Solutions. Joel is a seven-time Microsoft Dynamics CRM MVP. He lives in South Carolina with his beautiful wife Stephanie and two children. Prior to becoming a CRM expert, Joel worked for 10 years in sales, giving him an appreciation for well-designed CRM systems and how poorly designed CRM systems can impact usability.

Richard Knudson
Richard Knudson is a thought-leader in the CRM industry and has been recognized by Microsoft with its Microsoft® Most Valuable Professional (MVP) Award for Dynamics CRM in 2011, 2012, and 2013. He manages the CRM practice for Magenium Solutions, a Wheaton IL based Microsoft partner, which provides planning, consulting, implementation, and customization services to customers on Dynamics CRM and related products. He is a popular presenter at conferences such as Extreme CRM and CRMUG Summit, and is the author of a highly regarded book, Building Business with CRM: Using Processes in Dynamics CRM 2011, and you can get all the details at http://www.crmbizbook.com . He's hard at work on his next book, "No-Code Customizations and Business Processes in Dynamics CRM." Richard hails from Winnetka, IL, and when he's not wearing his CRM hat, he might be skiing, rooting for the White Sox, coaching one of Bridget's sports teams, or rewriting yet another version of his bio.

David Berry
David Berry is employed as a Senior Developer for Avtex, and has developed solutions for Dynamics CRM since version 3.0. He was first awarded as a Microsoft MVP in 2010, and despite renewing every year since, he still gets nervous that he might not. David enjoys playing with his children, and teaching them the finer points of complex videogames.

David Yack
David is the CTO of Colorado Technology Consultants. He is a Microsoft Regional Director and a Microsoft MVP. As a senior hands on technology and business consultant with over 20 years of industry experience, David enjoys developing applications on the Microsoft platforms, specializing in large system architecture and design. David's focus is on helping clients migrate and build new applications on Microsoft technologies, as well as helping to mentor and train

their staffs. David is a frequent speaker/trainer at user groups, industry events and private company events around the world. Antarctica is the only continent David hasn't been on and he is accepting invitations. David has been on the author team of multiple .NET and Dynamics CRM related books. He lives in Colorado Springs with his wife. You can reach David via his website DavidYack.com.

Dylan Haskins
Dylan has been working in the IT Industry since 1994. He started out in the Infrastructure space working both with the Hardware and Software associated with Server and Desktop Deployments, primarily on the Microsoft Stack. In 1999 he transitioned into the CRM space by heading up a Pivotal CRM practice. He subsequently started his own business focusing on Mobile Application Development but quickly moved back into the CRM space focusing his energy this time on the Microsoft Dynamics CRM Platform. Originally from South Africa, he now lives in New Zealand and is a Solution Architect for Intergen across their Dynamics and SharePoint practices and a Co-Founder of Go2Cloud, a South African based Cloud Services Provider. In 2010 he was recognized for his efforts in Microsoft Dynamics CRM by receiving the Microsoft MVP award and is currently celebrating his 4th year as an MVP.

Jukka Niiranen
Jukka is the guy who will turn your business requirements into a CRM system that not only tracks your key processes but also makes the lives of the end users easier. With 10 years of experience from the field of customer relationship management, Jukka is endlessly fascinated by how modern business applications like Dynamics CRM can be used for automating processes and making customer information easily accessible, without requiring expensive custom development efforts.

Acknowledgments

Thank you to the many other people who helped make this book a reality, including Josh Behl, Robert Boyers, Scott Jung, Peter Majer, Jerry Martin, Tash Quinn, Nishant Rana, Blake Scarlavai, and Dale Wilken.

From our Authors

Joel Lindstrom - Thanks to Hitachi Solutions for enabling me to do what I love, and for my wife Stephanie for putting up with me taking time to write about CRM.

David Berry - To my lovely wife, K'Cee, and our children: Kiera, Lee, and Emmett. Y'all probably won't read this book, but I love you anyway.

Dylan Haskins - To my wife Tamara, my daughter Jessica and my son Jonathan, thanks for all your love and support. Love you all.

Introduction

The CRM 2013 Quick Start is a first look at Microsoft Dynamics CRM 2013 and all the new features that have been included.

Who is this book for?

In the CRM 2013 Quick Start you will find details that can help administrators, customizers (functional consultants) and developers; not to mention power business users wanting to know all the details the admin never tells them. If you run CRM in the cloud or sitting in a server room at your office the information is useful.

This book is targeted to someone who has some CRM prior experience. By that we simply don't spend any time explaining the basics of Microsoft Dynamics CRM from a beginner's point of view. That said, the information in this book would still be useful to your journey to become proficient.

How to use this book?

Read it cover to cover or simply skip and jump to the areas you need more details on, there is no single correct way to use this book. You could use it online or carry around the printed book. Write on the pages, fold the corners and make notes of your own ideas. If you end up doing something cool, drop us a note and tell us about it.

Downloads!

Visit our site, www.CRM2013QuickStart.com for special customer-only downloads and extras. If you bought this book from someone other than us, drop us an email, we'll hook you up with access to the site and any updates that are published.

Contents overview

Chapter 1 - Hello I'm CRM 2013 – Microsoft Dynamics CRM 2013 is a major release building on the strong foundation of CRM 2011. From the user experience to platform capabilities CRM 2013 has changes that are targeted for everyone at users, customizers, IT Pros, and developers. In this chapter we give you a 50,000 foot tour of what's new.

Chapter 2 – The User Experience – Before you can build solutions in CRM 2013 you should learn how the new user experience works. In this chapter we will dive into the new experience and break down all the key changes so you are ready to start thinking about customizing it.

Chapter 3 – Customizing CRM Forms – The 2013 user experience requires rethinking how we customize forms. From the new layout options, new controls and even new form types we have a lot to talk about. We also can't forget you might have CRM 2011 forms and want to know how to move them forward into this release.

Chapter 4 – Security Model Changes – Today's global business challenges the traditional organization structure as people form dynamic teams to work on individual opportunities or other data in CRM. CRM 2013 addresses that with Access Teams that challenge past thinking of how to handle these types of needs. In this chapter we will explore the new feature and discuss how and when to use the different CRM security concepts.

Chapter 5 – Building Business Processes – To consistently bake good cookies people often times use their favorite recipe. The Business Process feature of CRM 2013 brings that to CRM allowing you to bake in a business process into the life cycle of a CRM record. In fact you can even blur the lines of multiple CRM entities and have a business process cross the entity boundaries reflecting more real-world business processes. In this chapter we look at the features and how to leverage them to improve user productivity and consistency.

Chapter 6 – No Code Business Rules – Portable Business Rules, or PBL for short, offer a declarative way to define business rules. This new feature represents the start of a journey to a common need of having simple rules like "This field is required". In this chapter we will explore the capability of PBL and when to use it versus other concepts in CRM that can enforce business rules.

Chapter 7 – Real Time Workflows – Workflows offer an easy way to compose flexible business processes that can optionally include custom code created by a developer. Prior to CRM 2013 these had to run asynchronously in the background and never could happen real time. This caused a lot of plug-ins to be built to handle the requirement. New in CRM 2013 is real time workflows that can allow processing of events real time. In this chapter we discuss when and how to use the new feature.

Chapter 8 – Upgrading to CRM 2013 – Next, Next, Next…Done… If it was only that easy it would be an automated upgrade. In this chapter we explore what you should consider before you upgrade and how to prepare.

Chapter 9 – Solutions going forward – As the pace of CRM releases increases, understanding how to package and deploy solutions becomes increasingly important. In this chapter we will discuss changes to the Solution Framework and how to prepare for the bold new world of frequent CRM releases.

Chapter 10 – Mobile, Outlook and Server Sync – There is no question Microsoft was behind in mobile applications for CRM but came back strong with the introduction of the new tablet application for IPad and Windows. Learn how this fits in with the customizations you are doing to CRM and limitations you should be aware of in this first generation release. This chapter will also cover Outlook enhancements and Server Sync that in many scenarios will free the deployment from having an E-mail router.

Chapter 11 – Developers, Developers, and Developers – This release doesn't have huge new API changes but it does have a lot of small useful changes across the different parts of the developer features. In this chapter we will explore from oAuth authentication support to Custom Actions and all the little changes between them.

What about stuff we screwed up…You know Errata

In the process of writing, everyone sure wanted to make sure it was 100% accurate, but since nobody is perfect, we are sure you might find a few typos or other things that aren't correct. We would love to hear your feedback and will do our best to incorporate it into the next printing of the book. You can look at our website, www.CRM2013QuickStart.com for any last minute changes. Feel free to email us as well, info@thecrmbook.com if you find a typo.

Table of Contents

1 Hello I'm CRM 2013 15

    THE ROAD TO CRM 2013 AND BEYOND 16

    THE USER EXPERIENCE IS EVERYTHING 17

    MOVING FROM RECORD TO PROCESS 21

    WORKING AS TEAMS 23

    EVERYTHING IS A "PROCESS" IN CRM 2013 24

    WORKING ON THE GO 27

    SERVER-SIDE SYNCHRONIZATION 27

    OTHER THINGS YOU SHOULD KNOW 28

    YOUR PLAN FOR GETTING STARTED 29

    WRAPPING UP 31

2 Designing a Great User Experience 32

    WHY DESIGNING THE DATA MODEL IS NOT ENOUGH 32

    NAVIGATION 34

    VIEWS 44

    FORMS 56

    FIELDS 62

    GUIDING THE USER 70

3 Customizing Entities and Forms 81

    NEW ENTITY DEFINITION OPTIONS 81

NEW FORM TYPES 84

WHAT'S NEW WITH FIELDS 93

FORM CUSTOMIZATION IN DYNAMICS CRM 2013 102

NEW FORM COMPONENTS 112

UPGRADING FORMS TO DYNAMICS CRM 2013 117

BRINGING IT ALL TOGETHER 119

4 Security Model Changes 120

OWNING TEAMS VS. ACCESS TEAMS 121

MANUAL CREATION OF AN ACCESS TEAM 121

AUTOMATIC CREATION OF ACCESS TEAMS 123

AUTOMATING ACCESS TEAMS WITH CODE 128

WHEN TO USE ACCESS TEAMS? 129

WRAPPING UP 129

5 Building Business Process Flows 130

THE BUSINESS PROCESS FLOW USER EXPERIENCE 133

CUSTOMIZING BUSINESS PROCESS FLOWS 142

BUSINESS PROCESS FLOWS AND WORKFLOW PROCESSES 155

TIPS, TRICKS AND TRAPS 159

MY TAKE ON BUSINESS PROCESS FLOWS 168

6 No Code Business Rules 172

INTRODUCING CRM BUSINESS RULES 173

- Creating and Managing Rules 174
- Business Rule Conditions 181
- Business Rule Actions 185
- When Do Business Rules Run? 189
- Turn it on, Turn it off 189
- Business Rule or Client Script? 190
- Example Scenarios 190
- Deploying Business Rules 193
- Inside Business Rules Architecture 193
- Wrapping Up 195

7 Real Time Workflows 196

- Getting Started 197
- Option to Run Differences 198
- Security Execution Context 199
- Step Differences 200
- New Security Privileges 200
- Monitoring Workflow Execution 201
- Real Time Workflows and AutoSave 202
- Avoiding too many Updates 203
- Mixing with Custom code 203
- Real Time Workflows vs. JavaScript and Business Rules 204

REAL TIME WORKFLOWS VS. PLUG-INS 205

ARE BACKGROUND WORKFLOWS STILL NEEDED? 206

SCENARIOS FOR USING REAL TIME WORKFLOWS 207

WRAPPING UP 213

8 Upgrading to Microsoft Dynamics CRM 2013 214

INTRODUCTION 214

A NEW VERSION 214

HOW LONG CAN I STAY ON CRM 2011? 215

BEFORE YOU UPGRADE 215

THE CRM 2013 UPGRADE PROCESS 217

PLANNING YOUR CRM 2013 ARCHITECTURE 220

INSTALLING CRM 2013 223

IMPORTING AND UPGRADING AN ORGANIZATION 223

POST UPGRADE 232

OTHER POST INITIAL UPGRADE TASKS 243

TAKE PRESSURE OFF OF YOUR PRODUCTION UPGRADE. 245

THE PRODUCTION UPGRADE 246

9 Solutions going forward 248

A BRAVE NEW WORLD 248

DYNAMICS CRM 2013 – THE BEGINNING OF A PARADIGM SHIFT 249

THE FUTURE'S PAST 252

Reaching for the Stars 258

Wrapping Up 261

10 Taking CRM on the Road 262

CRM for Outlook 262

What is new in CRM 2013 for Outlook? 264

Upgrading to CRM 2013 for Outlook 266

CRM for Phones 269

CRM for Tablets 275

11 Developers, developers, developers 291

I, Developer 292

Developing for xRM, Evolved 295

Caution: Fun Times Ahead 315

Wrapping Up 319

1

Hello I'm CRM 2013

Microsoft Dynamics CRM 2013 represents a major upgrade and in this chapter we will explore some of the new features at a high level. For many of these features this chapter will simply set the stage for a much more detailed discussion later in the book where full chapters will be dedicated to a much deeper look at that feature.

Before we dive too deep into the new features it's important to understand the trends and influencers that are driving the new release.

- **Social** – it's a buzzword almost as broad as CRM itself, but it describes customer empowerment to be heard and to communicate even without official channels as well as internal collaboration across teams working with these customers. CRM has been starting to address this space with Activity Feeds, followed by Yammer for internal and Microsoft Dynamics Social Listening for external focused social collaboration.

- **Mobility** – BYOD = Bring Your Own Device. No one wants to carry a personal phone and a business phone, they want their device and use it on their terms. Users want the experience on the devices to be reflective of how they work with the devices.

- **Cloud** – Enterprise customers have been a tough segment for the cloud to conquer, but with increasing capabilities, better transparency, flexible pricing, and almost immediate (perceived) activation it's becoming increasingly hard to ignore. Integrations can also now happen not just to other on premise systems, but include cloud components as well.

- **Aging** – CRM is in its 6th major release, Service scheduling is a great example of a part of CRM that is showing its age. CRM continues to enhance its core components as the release pace increases.

These trends are not just impacting a single release, many provide influence across multiple releases. In some cases the journey to fulfill improved support for a trend might require multiple releases to implement all the changes. Social is a good example that started in CRM 2011 with Activity Feeds, picked up speed in the December 2012 update with Yammer integration and will continue into the upcoming release that will include Microsoft Dynamics Social Listening.

The road to CRM 2013 and beyond

These trends don't just influence a single release, they transcend a few releases. They drive the transformation of Dynamics CRM 2013 from a slow changing product to a more rapid release cadence. The following diagram gives some perspective on the release history and upcoming plans for Dynamics CRM.

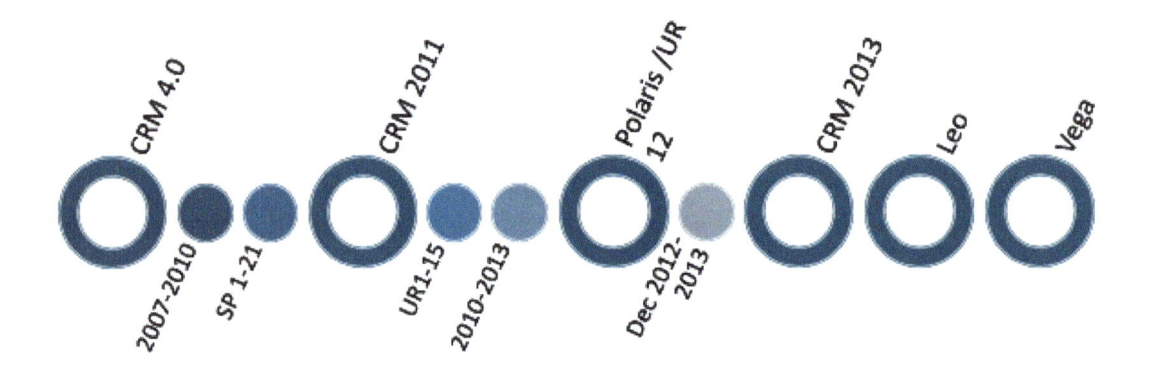

The time between CRM 4.0 to CRM 2011 was 3 to 4 years – in fact there are still some CRM 4.0 deployments today. This slower pace allowed deployments and their administrators to become complacent and in some cases comfortable doing things that might not be supported. Doing this was not a problem because people knew major releases only happened every 3-4 years. From CRM 2011 to CRM 2013 took about 3 years with a pretty major release in December 2012 kicking off the faster pace. This faster pace represents a bold departure for the CRM product. In this model, CRM Online will receive updates twice a year and on premise will be synced up and included in the changes once a year.

Symmetry between Online and on premise used to be a key message of the CRM product. This symmetry is not lost with the new release cycle, but rather aligned roughly once a year instead of all the time. This change makes sense for a couple of reasons. First, deploying changes to CRM Online and patching any issues is all under Microsoft control and doesn't involve distributing service packs and dealing with the variety of end user environments that could be slightly different. Additionally, cloud customers generally are more accepting of change and moving to a new version quicker. A key point in this change in symmetry is you need to be aware that CRM Online may have features that are not yet available in CRM on premise and moving Solutions from Online to on premise might not be possible.

With CRM 2013 in the history books, the CRM team turns to the next upcoming releases. Code-named Leo, this will be an online only release and then Vega will be the next major release for both Online and on premise.

The clear message here is the release cycle is accelerating, this means more rapid change, and it means some things may be works in progress across releases (the new updated forms is a good example). This increased pace requires diligence in making sure unsupported customizations are avoided. In a world where things changed every 3-4 years the likelihood of impact is much less than in a rapidly changing release environment.

The user experience is everything

One of the chief complaints when CRM 2011 was released was that there wasn't enough user experience changes. Having a strong platform foundation is important, in fact arguably most of the changes in CRM 2011 were focused on platform architecture changes the user never saw. Sure there were a few less clicks in the user experience but compared to CRM 2013 the changes would seem insignificant. In CRM 2013 the changes in the user experience are probably the single most significant change. The changes not only impacted style, navigation, but changed the core concept of a form per record to becoming more process focused. In a process focused world the boundaries between records blurs and the user experience incurs less friction. Let's take a tour of some of the major changes to the CRM user experience.

Streamlined Application Navigation

Application navigation is a key aspect of the user experience that allows the user to quickly move around the application. Navigation in CRM 2011 used Navigation Pane ad Ribbon concepts that was always present consuming valuable real estate on the viewing surface. CRM 2013 moves to a Navigation Bar concept that is only visible when the user is interacting. The following image shows the new CRM 2013 Navigation Bar.

Tiles are now used to represent entities that can be navigated to and other navigation sub areas. When the user has made a choice, the Navigation Bar collapses as you can see in the following image freeing up valuable real estate.

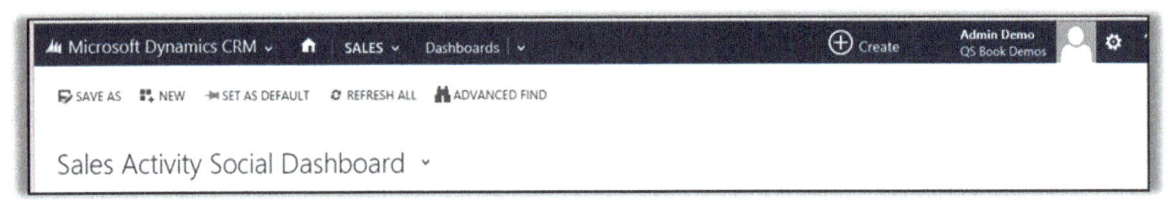

The new navigation still uses the SiteMap to define its contents so existing customizations will migrate. This also means if you knew how to customize Sitemap before, it's the same process for CRM 2013.

Focus on the Task, not the popup

In CRM 2011, just about everything you did on a form would cause a new window or dialog to popup. A key change in CRM 2013 is the move to a more inline form experience. From inline grid editing to changing to inline lookups there are fewer things that popup and surprise the user. Another key change was optimizing the layout of the form to improve use of the real estate to on the form. The following diagram highlights the key elements of CRM 2013 forms and how they layout key information the user needs.

CRM 2013 Quick Start

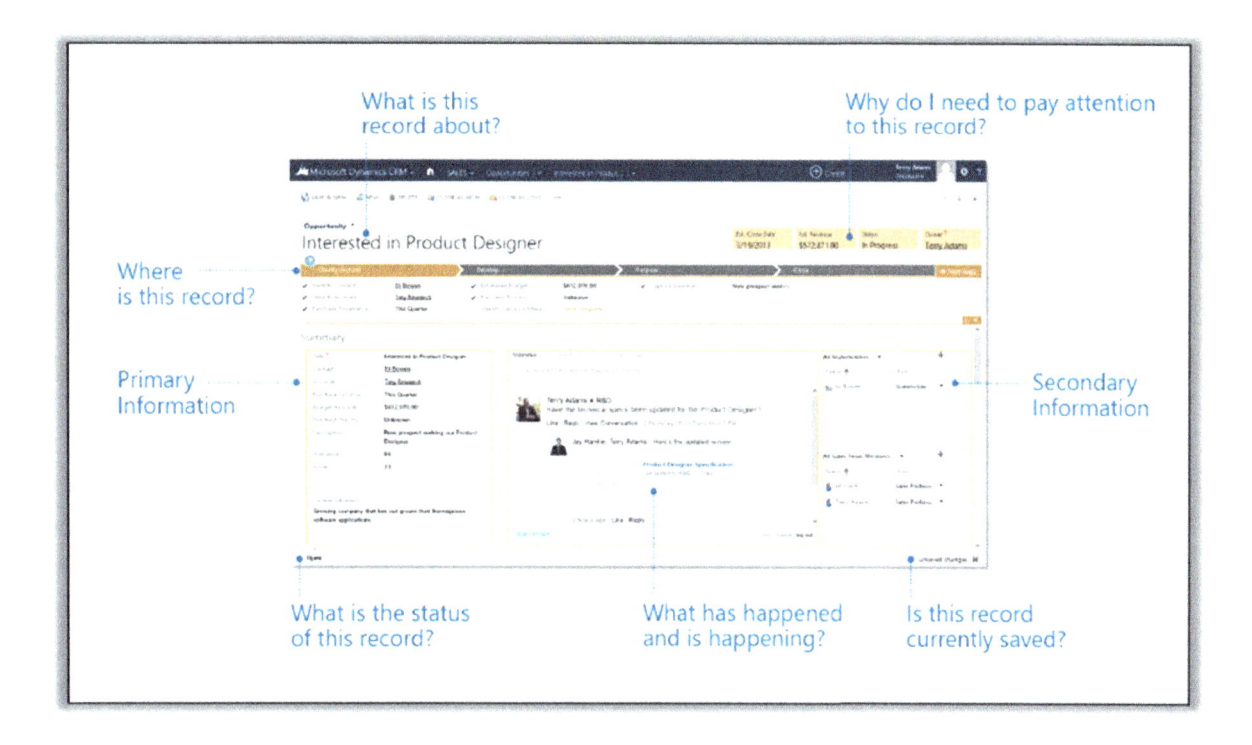

[Screenshot of a Microsoft Dynamics CRM record view with callouts:]
- What is this record about?
- Why do I need to pay attention to this record?
- Where is this record?
- Primary Information
- Secondary Information
- What is the status of this record?
- What has happened and is happening?
- Is this record currently saved?

Auto Saving Data

Are you sure you want to leave this page? Modern applications allow the user to flow without the friction of excessive prompts for obvious decisions. CRM 2013 takes advantage of this concept and implements a new auto save feature anytime a user is editing a record. The following are the key things you need to know about auto save:

- Only applies after the record is created

- Auto Save happens 30 seconds after edit, and every 30 seconds after that

- During Auto Save, any changes to record are retrieved without reload of form

- If a field is being edited (if focus is on a field), it will not be included

- Other Auto Save Triggers

    - Command Bar Actions – New, Close, or Qualify

    - Closing the Form

~ 19 ~

Nervous users can also manually save data at any time using the save button in the lower right corner of the UI.

Not everyone or every situation works well with auto save. For that reason CRM 2013 allows auto save to be turned on/off for all entities by an administrator. Alternatively, using a small amount of client script individual forms can disable auto save.

Quickly Viewing Related Data

A key part of providing the user all the information they need on a single form is the ability to display related data. CRM 2011 only allowed showing the primary attribute value for an item related with an N:1 relationship. Of course you could click on the link for the lookup and it would popup the record but that popup creates user friction. The other way to solve this was to use a Web Resource that a developer built that retrieved and displayed additional fields from the related record. In CRM 2013 a new form type has been introduced called Quick View form. This allows you to create a read only form that contains data to be shown on the primary record. This allows users to see the related fields without requiring a developer to build a custom Web Resource. The following is an example of showing the primary contact information on the Account form.

Creating Data Quickly

Most the time when users create a new record they don't provide all the fields. In fact often times all the fields cause confusion because they don't know what they should really focus on providing and users feel obligated to fill in all the boxes. CRM 2013 introduces a new form type called Quick Create. The Quick Create forms allow creating a special form that is only used for creating that type of entity quickly and on the fly. The following is an example of a streamlined form for Account.

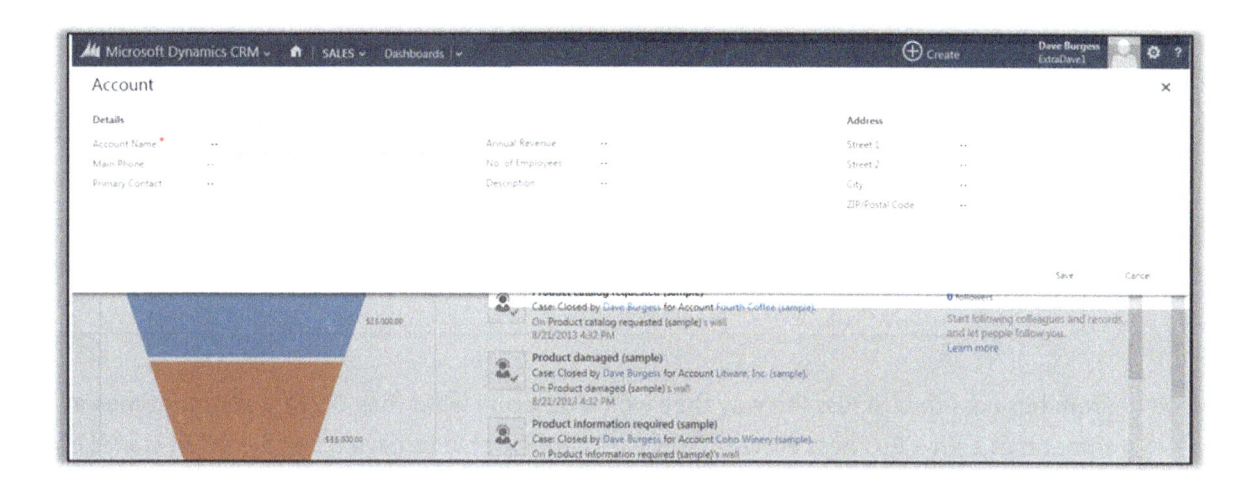

As part of implementing a CRM 2013 project or upgrading you should consider when using a Quick Create form would provide a streamlined process for creating new records.

Moving from Record to Process

Every interaction for users prior to CRM 2013 was based on opening a record and working on it, closing the form then navigating to the next form and so on and so forth. The following illustrates the process from lead to order in CRM 2011.

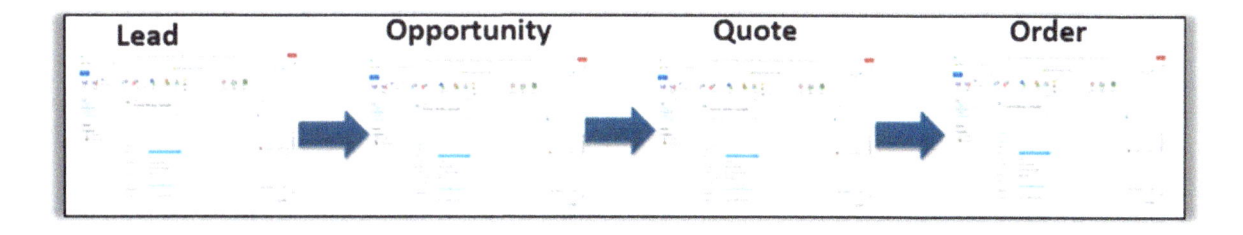

While this was simple for the CRM team to build, it no longer works for the complicated processes and amounts of data business collect and work through to complete a real business transaction. In CRM 2013 with the edition of the new Business Process Flow feature the user can stay on a single form and they are guided through the process.

Business Process flows provide a structured way of thinking about a business process – not about the record but the process. This can be a process on a single record, or a process that spans multiple entities. A process control, as you can see in the following image, guides the user through the steps and stages of the process.

From business to business the way they would describe what they do varies - sometimes a little sometimes a lot – Business Process Flows are configurable to have a flexible set of stages each with steps that need to be accomplished.

The following image is an example of the Business Process Flow editor that we will be exploring later in the book and talking about how to leverage this to build and modify custom business process flows.

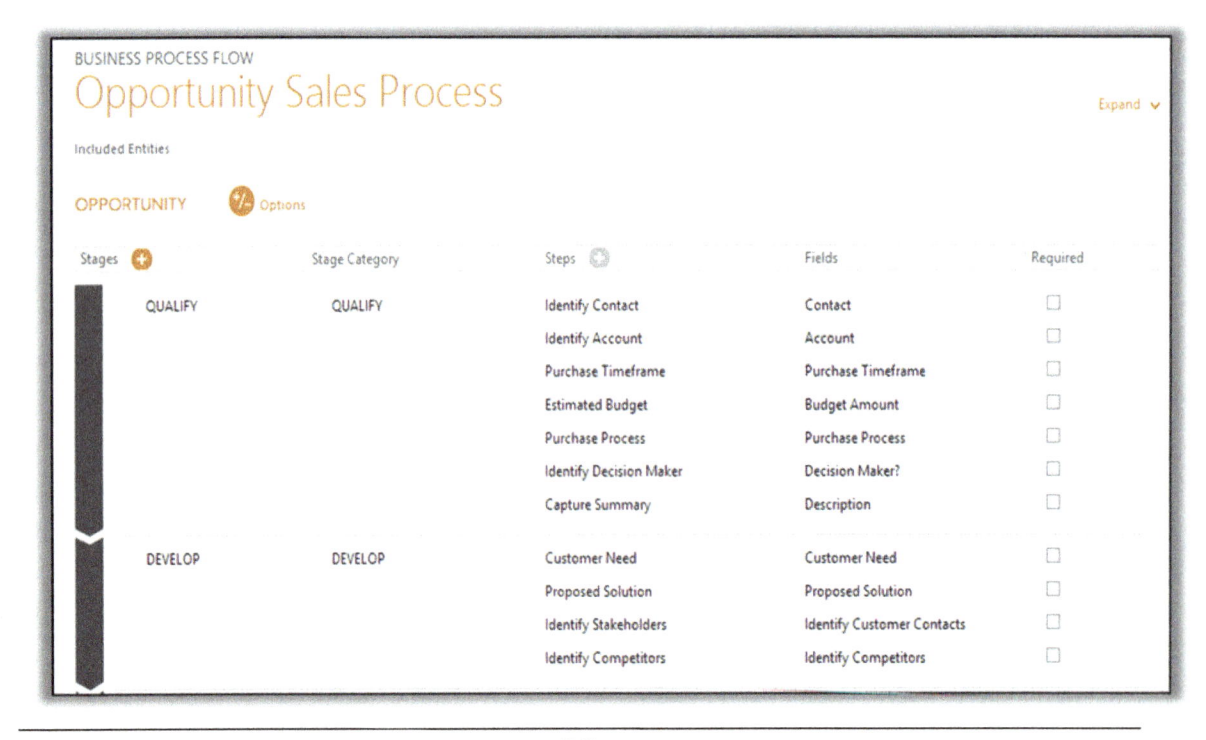

Working as Teams

CRM 2011 introduced the concept that teams could also own data. It made a lot of progress toward modern team collaboration allowing not a single person to be the owner of a record. These teams were really not designed to scale when you started assigning one team per record to represent some very unique collaborative needs of projects.

Access teams are new to CRM 2013, specifically designed to grant one or more teams a set of rights to a record. Access teams can be shared across multiple records simply to grant access or they can be on a per record basis where CRM will create the team the first time you start to add members to it. This is a much more flexible model than owner teams especially in solutions where there are only custom dynamic teams on some records and not all records.

Owning Teams	Access Teams
• Own a record • Can have only one per record • Good when you don't want "a" user owning the record • Membership is centrally administered	• Record Shared with • Can have multiple per record • Access Template defines security rights • Teams can be created per record as needed • Membership can be adjusted on the record

In Chapter 4, Security Modeling, we will dive in deeper into how and when to take advantage of Access Team vs. other CRM security features.

Everything is a "Process" in CRM 2013

Well not really, but it may seem that way when you start hearing "Process" being overloaded to describe several different concepts in CRM 2013. This comes about because under the covers CRM uses the "Process" entity under the covers to store the definition of these various features. The following breaks down the different types of features in CRM 2013 that use the concept of "Processes" and what each one does.

Business Process Flow	Guides a user through steps required to complete a process that involves one or more entities
Workflow	On Demand or triggered by event – runs to perform actions in the background or real time
Action	Allows adding custom messages to CRM, callable by developers, created like a workflow
Dialog	Interactive way of guiding a user through a series of steps, uses workflow steps to complete work

Real Time Workflows

Workflows are a powerful feature of Dynamics CRM. The ability to define a series of steps that can be run on demand or triggered by an event allows automating business processes. By automating, the processes are carried out with a level of consistency that wouldn't always be possible if a human was trying to remember to do them. Another distinct advantage of workflows is that they didn't always require a developer, they could be created and maintained by a functional consultant.

In CRM 2011, workflows always ran in the background after they were started. Most often if the user created a record, a workflow ran and made changes to it, and when the form refreshed after create the results of the workflow wouldn't be immediately visible. Often times if this was required developers would use the plug-in feature where they could get the results real time. CRM 2013 now allows a new option on workflows to allow them to be configured to run real time. When you setup a workflow to be real time it can be run before or after the main operation (e.g. the update of the record) in most cases. Create for example though can only run after the record has been created. In both cases you have the ability to do work before the user sees the result and if necessary abort their request just like plug-ins can. Plug-ins created by developers still have a lot of advantages for complex operations and ability to do things beyond what you can do in workflow steps – however for simple things that in the past would have been written as plug-ins this is an ideal way to handle it

CRM Business Rules

Every CRM project implements a number of rules, if not hundreds of them, to meet, implement and ensure business requirements are enforced. CRM offers a variety of ways to implement business rules. This can be as simple as providing minimum and maximum values on a number field on the entity definition. Or it could be more complex where a developer is creating custom code. This code could be client script that runs on the forms and is visible to the user, or a plug-in that runs behind the scenes doing the heavy lifting. What is missing though is a simple way to specify one or more conditions and provide one or more actions that need to happen when a user is interacting with a record. CRM 2013 introduces a new concept called CRM Business Rules that allows functional consultants to declaratively create rules using the Web Client. These rules are packaged up and deployed with the entity customizations.

The following is an example of using the simple web editor to create one or more conditions that will be checked during loading of the record or when the field values change.

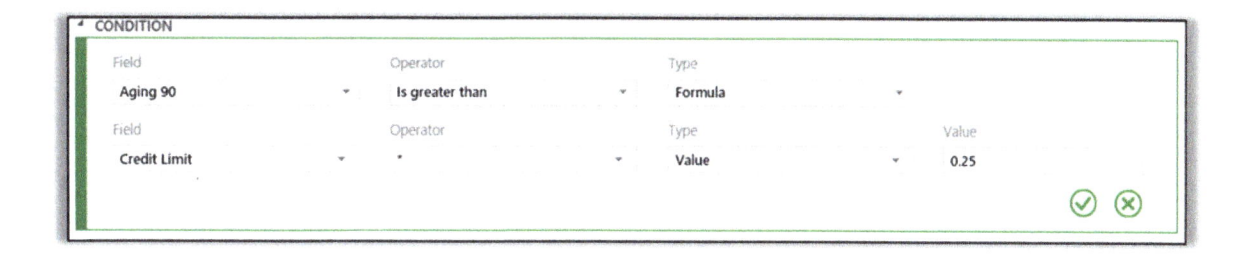

Field	Operator	Type	Value
Aging 90	Is greater than	Formula	
Credit Limit	•	Value	0.25

CONDITION

When the condition is true, one or more actions can be provided to handle things like hiding fields, making them required or other simple actions.

Now before you go fire your developers or if you are a developer don't go job shopping, these aren't a replacement for complex client scripting or plug-ins that implement business rules. CRM 2013 represents version 1 of CRM Business Rules and you don't have to go far to exceed their capabilities. That said, they will solve a number of common challenges and will likely result in more maintainable and better performing code for many implementations. As they continue to evolve, the architecture is in place to support client and server side implementations in the future.

Actions

Another type of new Process supported by CRM 2013 are Actions. Actions are designed to create extensions points in CRM that Developers can invoke to perform custom logic. The implementation of the logic however, doesn't require a developer it can be implemented by a functional consultant or a developer. Unlike Workflows or Dialogs that can be run on demand or triggered by a CRM event, Actions are always invoked by developers using the CRM API. Actions are a type of process that uses custom code and web services to run. Actions are defined using the process editor in a very similar way to defining a CRM Workflow. Unlike a Workflow however, Actions accept input parameters and return output parameters. These parameters are how developers interact with the Action and indicate what work should be done as well as to receive the results of the processing. For example, an action DetermineLeadOwner might take a Lead as the input parameter and return a System User that the developer should use to assign the lead to. The steps in the action might be a series of Check Conditions that determine what user should be assigned.

Developers and Architects should know that under the covers when you create a new Action it also creates a new message in CRM. At its core, CRM is a message driven architecture, when you create a record a Create message flows through the CRM event handling pipeline for processing allowing plug-ins to be attached and do further custom developer work. With Actions, DetermineLeadOwner would also be a message like Create that developers could hookup a plug-in to perform additional work all implemented in code. More on this in Chapter 5, Building Business Process Flows.

Working on the Go

From sales staff to management, users can often be found with two devices and quickly are moving towards a three device lifestyle (desktop or laptop, phone, and tablet). In many cases users are consolidating to just phone and a tablet as these devices become increasingly powerful. Support for this type of on-the-go workforce has been incredibly weak in prior versions of CRM. CRM 2013 however makes a strong down payment with the release of CRM for Tablets specifically designed for iPad and Windows. Additionally, there are now also applications in the respective stores for iPhone, Android and Windows Phone.

CRM for Tablets is focused (in the first release) on the sales professional. Now that doesn't mean that other users wouldn't get benefit from it as well. Non-sales professionals might find things like the Case records being read-only a little limiting. That said it's nice to have native applications. Not only are they native applications, they also honor most of the client side customizations that can be done with CRM including client scripting, business process flows and CRM Business Rules.

In addition to providing out of the box applications that allow users to access CRM and the same Customizations CRM 2013 also offers support for building custom applications. Developers can now use the new oAuth 2.0 support to allow easier authentication of custom client applications. These could be phone or tablet applications or in browser JavaScript applications that interact with the CRM API and take advantage of the new authentication endpoints. Both the CRM OData and SOAP APIs have been updated to allow using this style of authentication.

Server-side Synchronization

It's hard to imagine any part of CRM being higher on the most hated list than the CRM email router. Don't get me wrong, clearly the functionality is a necessity it just always has felt like a bolted-on addition to CRM. CRM 2013 introduces built-in server sync capability with the configuration of the server synchronization built into the CRM web client. CRM server-sync for supported configurations replaces the need for both the email router and Outlook Client synchronization. Now before you shut down your email router and try hard to forget how you configured it, server-sync won't initially at least support all the configurations that the email router and the Outlook Client support.

The primary scenarios in CRM 2013 for the server-side sync are CRM Online to Exchange Online and CRM on premise to Exchange on premise. There is also support SMTP/POP3 email services.

Mixed environment support is not currently available. Additionally, support for email is in all the above supported configurations, but synchronization of appointments, contacts and tasks will be rolled out slowly so check the implementation guide for current status.

Other Things You Should Know

In this section we wanted to highlight a few other things that while not worth a full section probably are things you will want to know.

Duplicate Detection

While duplicate detection is still available it is not active when the user is interacting with the CRM forms. This might cause impact for upgraded projects if duplicate detection is a core part of the implementation. In the SDK you will find an example of how you might consider adding support back into the form. This would however require developer effort to complete.

New User Licensing

CRM now has a new licensing model that now has the following tiers of users

- Basic
- Essential
- Professional

Basic represents a bare bones CRM allowing more focus on using the platform. Many that are looking for building non-CRM or require only custom entity access will find this SKU attractive. The Essential tier is targeted to those that are maintaining accounts and contacts in CRM and don't need the sales and service pre-built business processes. The Professional SKU is targeted towards a user needing full access to CRM. These three roles can be intermixed in a single deployment to balance the needs of different users. Additionally, as of this writing the minimum number of users for an online organization is changing, and will likely remain higher than 1 that we all were used to. A full discussion of licensing is beyond the scope of this book.

Multi Entity Search

Using CRM for Tablets you can configure up to 10 entities to allow searching at the same time. In CRM 2013 this feature is not available via the other clients or the CRM API.

Solutions

At initial release there weren't any major changes to the Solution framework for managing CRM changes. Internally there were some schema changes to the Solution format but that will be upgraded when the Solution is imported. These schema changes are designed to help for future releases to make down leveling solutions easier. CRM 2013 supports importing CRM 2011 Solutions, but you can't take a CRM 2013 Solution and import it into an older version of CRM. The Solution Down-level utility no longer ships with the SDK and in SP1/Spring 2014 update you will be able to specify on export if you want to target RTM of CRM 2013 (6.0) or SP1 (6.1).

Your Plan for Getting Started

It's easy now to look back and say it was easy to get up to speed with CRM 2013, but in reality there are a lot of changes that require exploring. Based on a few of the common roles, we thought it would be good to give a few suggestions on how to get up to speed. Obviously use the rest of this book in addition to the following ideas on how to get up to speed.

- Start with the tour you are offered when CRM loads. It will give you a few basic tips for how things work
- Go through the key CRM modules
    - Create a lead and follow it through to closing an opportunity or even an order
    - Create a case and follow it through to resolution
- Try to find Advanced Find (promise it is there...)
- Open up a Contact and upload an image
- Buy a tablet (ok, all you really need is Windows 8 but it's a good excuse to get a new Surface and give the new CRM for Tablets a try)
- Go to Data Management and turn on the add-on Business Processes – use them along with the Business Process chapter to understand more about how these work (these offer activated processes and coinciding draft workflows)
- Create a few entities and forms and get familiar with customizing
- Add a few Quick View and Quick Create forms to get the hang of using these to speed up viewing and creating data

Fast Path to Try CRM 2013

If you happen to be in an IT shop that takes forever to setup a test environment for new software why wait. Head over to CRM.Dynamics.com and setup a new trial organization to kick the tires.

Locating Reference Information

There have always been two key reference resources for Dynamics CRM the Implementation Planning Guide and the Software Developer Kit (SDK). While both exist for CRM 2013 and you should certainly download them, some of the content has moved around and you should be aware of where to find it. In the past, much of the information on Customizing CRM was spread out with some being in the SDK, and some being in other places. With the new updates all of that information has been consolidated into the Implementation Guide in a new Customization Guide for CRM. You will also find an Administration Guide for CRM in there which is targeted to the person configuring security, data imports and server sync to name a few.

Role	Content	Optional / Required
User	Help is online with CRM	
Business Analyst	Implementation Guide – Customization Section	Good idea
Functional Consultant	Implementation Guide – Customization Section	Required
	Implementation Guide – Administration Section	Optional – good if you are involved in configuring CRM for Security
	SDK	Optional for the curious and those that want to be able to better bridge the gaps
Developer	SDK	Required
	Implementation Guide – Customization Section	Required

	Implementation Guide – Administration Section	Good Idea
Architect	Implementation Guide	Required
	SDK	Required
Infrastructure Admin	Implementation Guide	Required
	SDK	Optional

Wrapping Up

Microsoft Dynamics CRM 2013 is a major release with a big emphasis on the user experience. It is also the first major release on the new, faster update timelines that brings both CRM on premise and CRM Online back in sync from a feature perspective. The faster updates also means that we might see features start and evolve over multiple releases. This has the benefit of allowing early feedback to make a difference before the feature is fully completed. In this chapter, we started your journey to understand more about CRM 2013, in the rest of the book we will dive deeper into each area to help you fully understand what has changed.

2

Designing a Great User Experience

Why designing the data model is not enough

So, you've identified the various entities that your CRM solution will cover, added the necessary fields and created relationships between them – are we now ready to launch the system for all the users to access and start working with? No, we're only about halfway there.

It's far too common to run into Microsoft Dynamics CRM environments that have been built to meet the functional requirements of the organization deploying the system without much consideration on how it feels to use the application. We've all come to know the kind of effortless user experience that modern mobile apps in the consumer space can deliver, yet when we come to our workplace and open the "serious" business apps that we should be using to create value to our customers and colleagues, we're often faced with overwhelming complexity and tedious data entry tasks.

Why do business software and consumer applications appear to originate from different planets? Why shouldn't the same laws of user experience apply to how a user interacts with information, regardless of whether he or she is working with sales opportunity records in a CRM system or status updates shared on a social network?

Sometimes the business applications have merely been built, but they have not been *designed*. The ones defining the business requirements for a CRM system implementation are almost never experts on concepts like usability, yet the ROI of the CRM initiative can be seriously compromised due to shortcomings in that area. It is widely acknowledged that the top challenge with CRM system implementations is gaining user adoption, which means usability is not something optional or "nice to have"; it is a front & center issue to be constantly evaluated during the project.

When discussing user experience design within the context of Microsoft Dynamics CRM, people may be too easily lead into thinking that this would require building expensive custom user interface components to alter the native behavior of CRM. While that is of course an option, it is not what this chapter is about. There is a wealth of opportunities available in the Microsoft Dynamics CRM platform to improve the usability of the system, both in terms of changing its out-of-the-box behavior as well as the design choices you can make when adding customized functionality into the CRM environment of a particular organization.

In order to gain a comprehensive understanding of the available options, we'll start going through the different customization areas in the same order which the user will encounter them while exploring the Dynamics CRM application. The first area will be the navigation structure and menus, which allow the user to reach different entity views. We'll then proceed into looking at individual records by opening up entity forms and from there drill into the lowest level of detail, meaning individual entity fields. To close things off, we'll explore the possibilities of how to guide the user through the processes and actions we are expecting the user to perform in CRM, in order to deliver the business benefits that the system has been implemented for.

CRM user experience design journey

Navigation
- Finding the right area of the application

Views
- Finding the right record to work on

Forms
- Understanding what the record is about

Fields
- Working with the record data

User guidance
- Knowing what to do next

Please note that this chapter refers to the RTM (Release To Manufacturing) version of CRM 2013, meaning a setup that you get if you install CRM without any updates. Service Pack 1 update introduces some enhancements that affect the user experience, one of the most notable ones being the number of menu items shown on the Command Bar. In RTM the limit was five, but SP1 increased the number of visible menu items to seven.

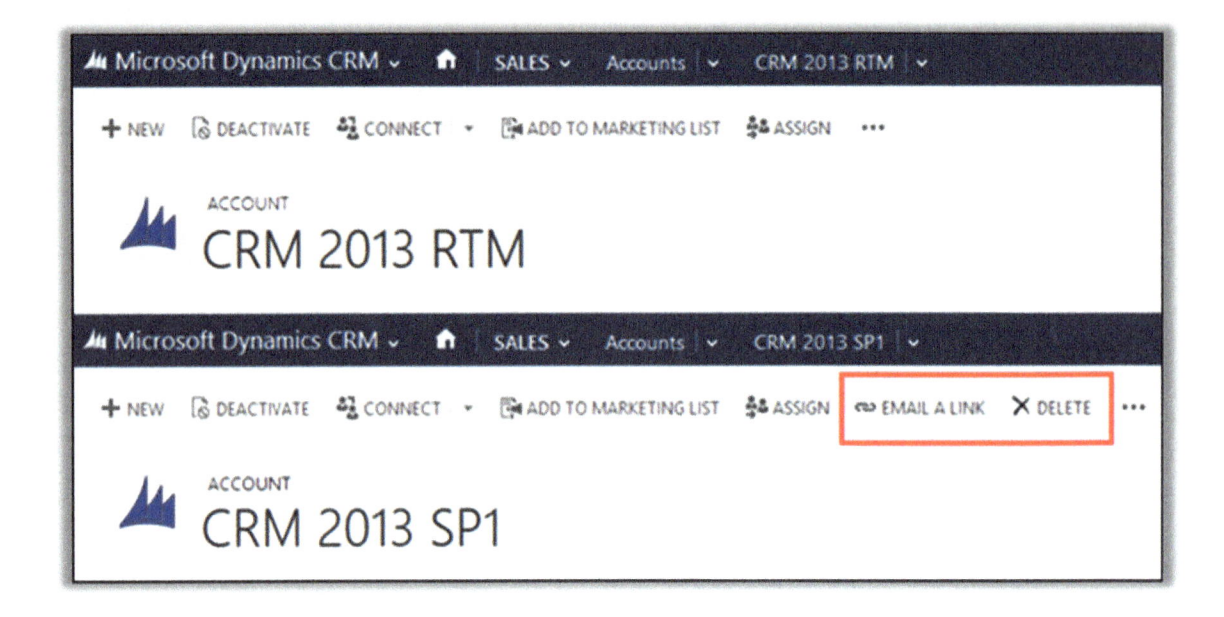

Navigation

Sitemap

Compared to the previous versions, CRM 2013 does a better job of consolidating the menus that a user working within a specific role in sales, marketing or service is likely to need. Previously CRM had the concept of a common Workplace area which was the only module (officially referred to as "pane" in the UI settings dialogs) to contain menu items like Activities, Dashboards or Reports that basically everybody needed. In CRM 2013 the Sales, Marketing and Service modules are self-sustained, meaning a user working within that particular business function does not necessarily need to navigate to any other module (note that if you're upgrading from a previous version, you'll need to manually adjust the sitemap to match this new default navigation design, please see Chapter 8, Upgrading To Microsoft Dynamics CRM 2013 to learn more).

When customizing CRM it's important to adhere to this same principle and avoid creating the need for a user to switch between the modules. When you create a new custom entity, consider for a moment which user groups need to frequently access these records and make sure the entity is added into all their specific modules. This will help especially the casual user who only occasionally needs to dive into CRM, possibly to read information others have put there.

In xRM scenarios where the data model of CRM is heavily expanded to cover a multitude of custom entities, there will of course come a point where trying to cram in all the entities under a single module will decrease system usability. The new Navigation Bar at the top of the screen won't show as many menu items at once as the old left side navigation did. If you're running the risk of having a single module span the width of more than two screens on a typical screen resolution, meaning a user would have to click/swipe two or more times to get to the last menu item, you're probably better off planning the addition of a new custom module in the sitemap.

For example, if your marketing department uses CRM not only for campaign management but also event management and website visitor analytics, you may end up having tens of entities that the marketing user should have access to. Splitting these into dedicated modules could help in organizing the content into more easily accessible menus.

Keep in mind that the modules behave just like the entities contained in them when presented in the Navigation Bar: if you have more items that can fit into the screen, sideways scrolling will again be required. To keep things under control and reduce the clutter in the navigation structure, consider targeting the custom sitemap modules to only specific user groups and hiding them from everyone else.

To manage the visibility of modules, you can't simply declare "show the marketing module only to marketing people" but what you can do is associate privileges to each of the entity nodes contained in that particular module through the sitemap XML. After ensuring that all of the nodes are out of bounds for the user, the module will no longer be rendered on the Navigation Bar.

Let's say that you only want to display the Web Analytics section to marketing users, not the sales or service personnel. As long as there's a certain privilege that only this group of users has, such as deleting marketing campaign records, then you can use it as the criteria that will hide the Web Analytics module from everyone else. Note that it doesn't need to be an entity that is actually presented inside the module itself, so you could even create custom entities like "Web

Analytics Access" meant for only managing the visibility of navigation items to specific user groups.

> **Sitemap Editor**
> CRM does not have a built-in customization UI for editing the menu items shown on the sitemap. Although you can export the sitemap XML and edit it manually, there are free tools available that provide a point & click experience for customizing the CRM navigation structure. One such tool can be found from the XrmToolBox application developed by CRM MVP Tanguy Touzard, available on CodePlex: http://xrmtoolbox.codeplex.com/

Not all entities need to be visible in the end user facing modules of the sitemap. For example, many of the default entities like the line items for opportunity, quote, order and invoice are only accessible through their parent entity form, as they are clearly subordinate entries that primarily exist in the context of the main record. This is a good design principle to keep in mind when adding your own custom entities to model the data structure of the organization. The top level entities can act as the natural gateway to the lower tier by presenting them on the forms rather than the Navigation Bar. Remember that all the entities will nevertheless be accessible through Advanced Find or Dashboards for data analysis and reporting purposes.

Some of your entities may exist purely as dynamic lists of category values or hold configuration information that other parts of the application will consume. There's a common tendency of ticking the box for such entities to show them on the settings module and then just leaving things at that. One thing to keep in mind is that the system administrators and CRM key users are people, too. In the long run you will do everyone a favor by investing a brief moment into considering the logical presentation of the administrative entities of a CRM organization in the UI. In addition to custom configuration entities, you might want to also bring frequently used default menus such as Processes closer to the top in the Settings area to make them easier to access.

The administrative roles of a CRM system are not set in stone and as time goes by it becomes more and more likely that the persons in charge of maintaining the system are not the ones who participated in the design and implementation of it. If the administrators can't keep up with all of the configuration options that they should be maintaining, this will reflect negatively in the overall system usability that the end users experience, which in turn can gradually lower the user adoption of the CRM system.

In CRM 2013 the default setting for new users added into CRM is that they will be taken to the sitemap module corresponding to their security role(s):

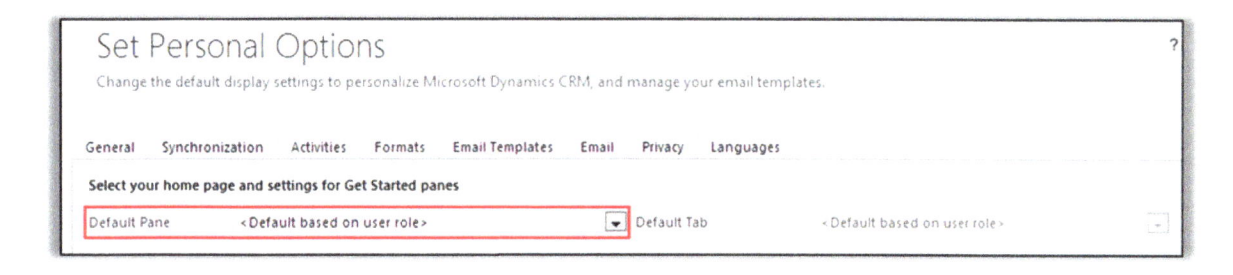

So what exactly is the mapping between the user roles and the default modules (panes)? The process specific security roles that come with CRM are grouped under sales, marketing or service in the following manner:

Module	Security roles
Sales	Sales Manager, Salesperson, Vice President of Sales
Marketing	Marketing Manager, Marketing Professional, Vice President of Marketing
Service	CSR Manager, Customer Service Representative, Scheduler

In case there is more than one default security role per user, the order in which the default pane setting is evaluated is: VP of Sales, VP of Marketing, Sales Manager, CSR Manager, Marketing Manager, Salesperson, Customer Support Rep, Marketing Professional, and Scheduler.

It has previously been a best practice for Dynamics CRM environment configuration to not use the built-in security roles directly but rather to leave them as they are and instead create a copy of the roles to adapt to the security requirements and custom entities of each CRM organization. In CRM 2013 the default pane setting is hard-coded into the built-in security roles, which means the only way to target a particular home page for a user with access to more than one module is to apply one of the aforementioned security roles. Due to this new feature, a better approach in security role management from now on would be to create an "archive" copy of the built-in roles to serve as a future reference point and then proceed with adjusting the contents of the original roles to fit the organization's needs. Although the presentation of navigation options has changed quite fundamentally between CRM 2011 and CRM 2013 web clients, the Outlook client still has the traditional navigation seen in previous versions of CRM. While this hierarchy of folders is well aligned with the native Outlook functionality like email archiving, it's not quite as configurable for the end user who cannot just add or remove folders like they do when managing their own inbox structure. However, the Outlook client does provide one navigation personalization feature that is missing from the web client: the ability to create Shortcut folders.

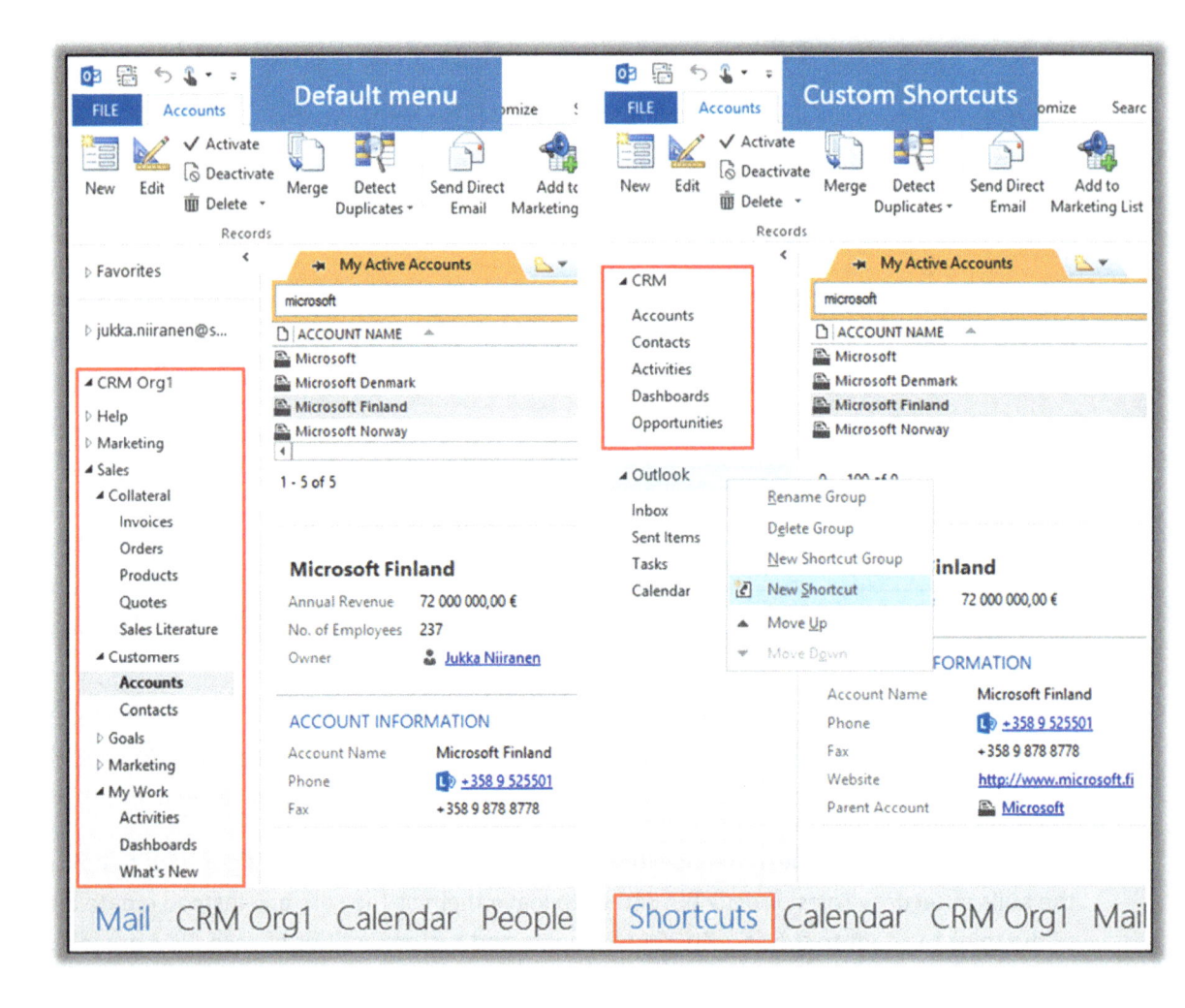

By default the Shortcuts area in the Outlook navigation pane is hidden at the end, but by lifting it up to the beginning and thus making it launch by default when launching Outlook, we can build quite an efficient navigation system to switch between folders from CRM and native Outlook items. The example screen above shows how creating two Shortcut Groups for "CRM" and "Outlook" we can greatly reduce the clutter in the UI while keeping the most frequently accessed items next to each other. No longer is the user forced to expand various folders to reach common menus, instead he or she can simply pin the required items in any desired order next to the top left corner of the Outlook Window. In case any more obscure entities need to be accessed occasionally, they can be reached by opening the full CRM area in the navigation pane.

With CRM 2013 we also need to keep in mind the user experience of accessing the system through a mobile device. The configuration options for the system customizer are somewhat limited in this area, though. We can only define whether a specific entity is available or not in the CRM for Tablets app (for Windows 8 tablets and iPads), the smartphone clients and the Mobile Express browser client. There are currently no tools available for grouping the menu items under modules, nor for modifying the order in which they are presented. We should therefore carefully consider which entities are needed to be present while accessing CRM on the road and only enable those for the mobile clients.

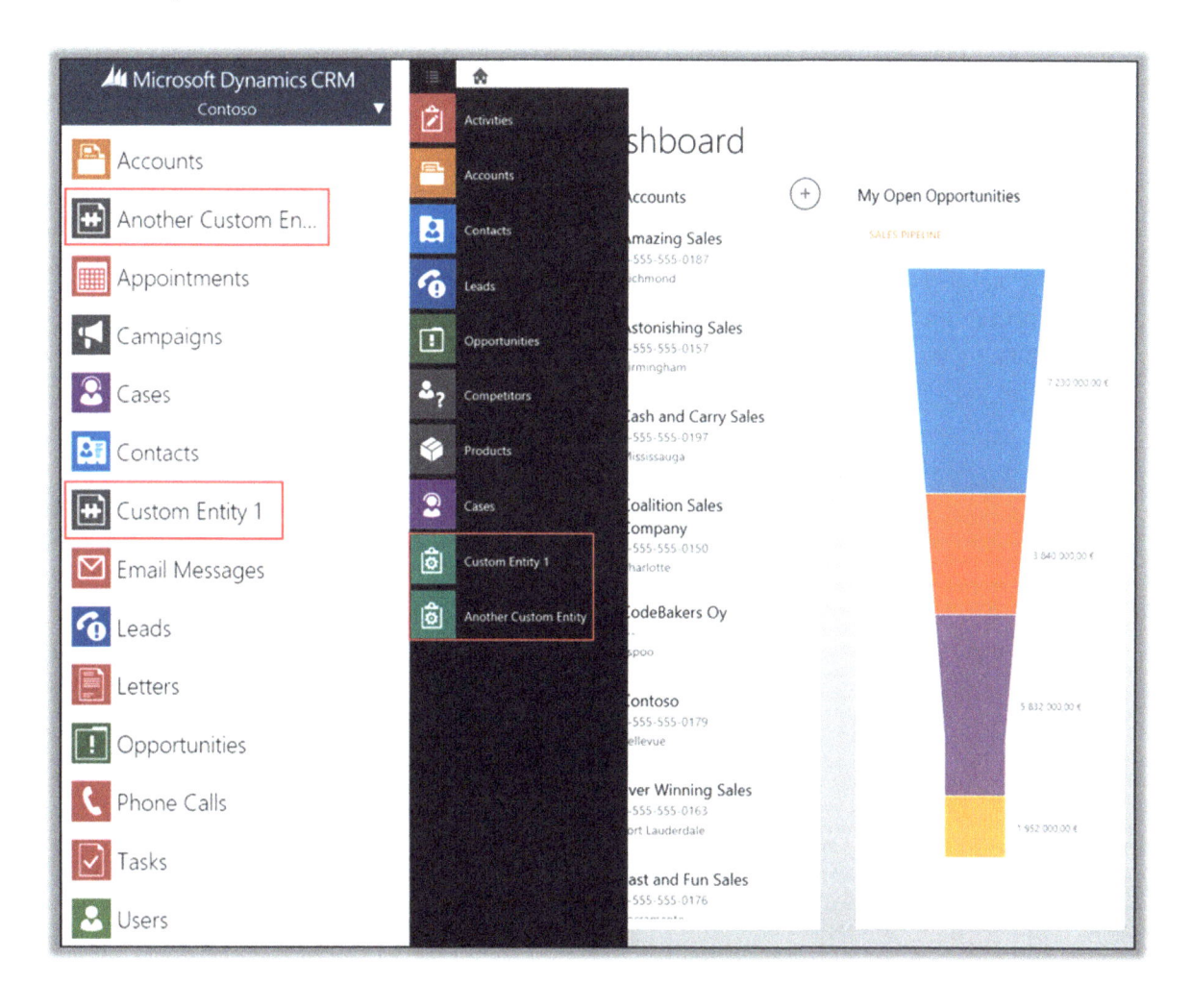

Command Bar

Even before the 2011 version of Dynamics CRM introduced the Ribbon, the contents of the record specific menus in Dynamics CRM were customizable. What the Ribbon really did was bring these menu options front & center in the user interface, which further encouraged system customizers to start adding their own sets of custom buttons alongside the already numerous default actions available on a standard CRM entity. The end result? A lot of options for the end user to look at whenever opening a record in CRM.

Although the Ribbon is visually no longer presented in the CRM 2013 as an actual ribbon (apart from the Outlook client), most of the custom buttons from the previous version will still be carried over into the new Command Bar. Compared to its flashy and loud spoken Ribbon cousin, the Command Bar has a much more toned down personality that doesn't crave for constant attention. He enjoys staying in the corner of the screen, patiently waiting for the moment when interaction with the user is needed.

Similar to the new Navigation Bar, CRM 2013 imposes new constraints on the number of menu options that are presented on the Command Bar at any given time. That number is five, which means that any menu items not included within the Top 5 get pushed behind the "More" button represented by the three dots. Considering that an entity like Account used to have 16 buttons visible on the Ribbon by default in CRM 2011 (not including the different Ribbon tabs), this is obviously quite a significant reduction in the number of possible actions that are promoted to the user.

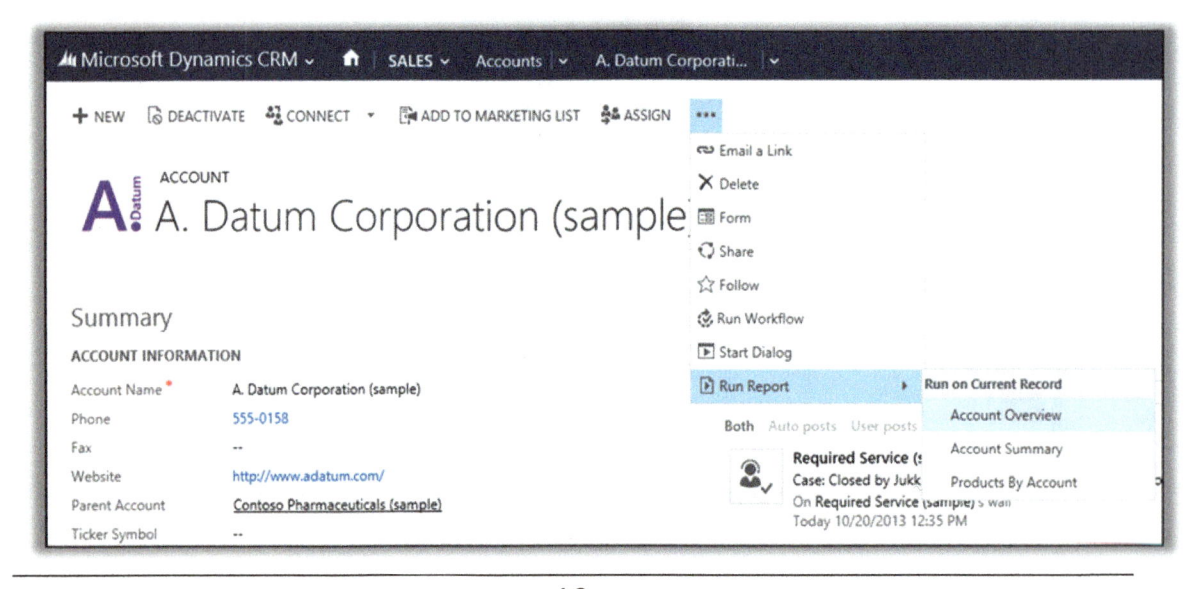

Removing unnecessary options from the application is in general a much more efficient way to improve its usability than introducing additional options. However, if we hide away an option that the user will regularly need to access as a part of their normal workflow, this naturally increases the friction in performing the task and can lead to increased frustration and less user adoption. With this in mind, the question we need to ask is how should the design principles we follow in building custom solutions change as a result of these new limitations imposed by the underlying platform?

In CRM 2011 much of the work done on customizing the Ribbon was about adding new buttons and sometimes hiding existing buttons to replace them with custom commands. In CRM 2013 there is now a great demand for the task of re-ordering the contents of the Command Bar. Obviously the commands chosen in the Top 5 will receive a far larger awareness among the CRM users, so these should be reserved for the actions that are central for the successful completion of the processes the CRM system has been deployed to help in managing.

My recommendation would be to prioritize the "difficult" things when choosing the Command Bar item order. If you're having a hard time teaching the users to always close off their own records as completed/done/approved/etc., ensure this action is one of the first ones they see on the top of the record form. If, on the other hand, we're talking about an action that is typically driven by the needs observed by the users themselves, they will most likely be able to follow the same navigation path that most other applications have taught them, meaning opening the dropdown menu and searching for the action they have in their mind.

Let's look at how we might customize the Account form Command Bar:

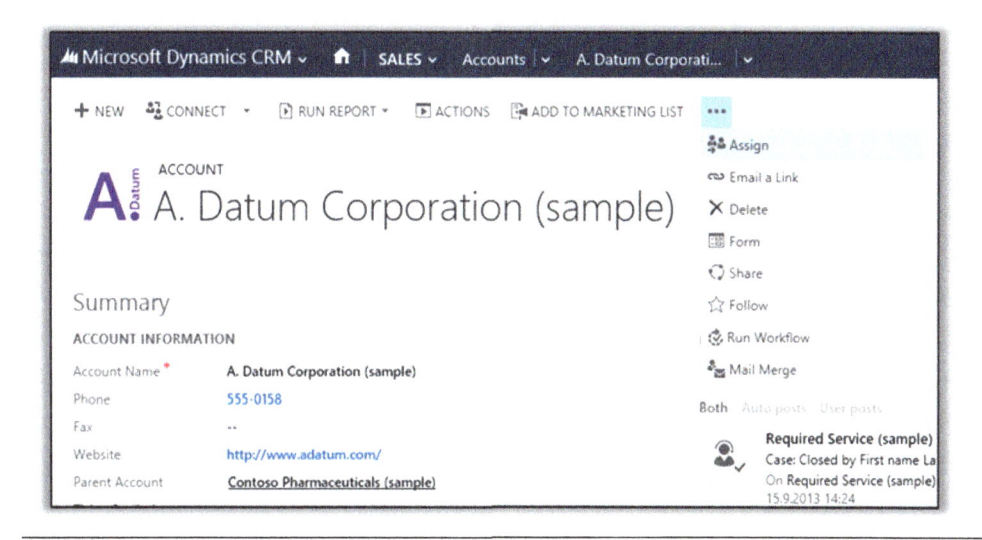

- If we've developed custom reports that the users frequently need to run, promoting them onto the Top 5 buttons makes sense. The flyout menu will now conveniently show all the available reports in a dropdown style menu.
- It's not a very common actions to make an account inactive, so there's no reason to offer it as the second option right after the New Account button. Therefore we've hidden the whole button.
- Since we want to capture the reason of the deactivation of an account record, we've built a custom dialog to perform this action. Due to the fact that the term "Dialog" isn't very meaningful for the end users, we've renamed the Start Dialog button as "Actions" and moved it to the Top 5 buttons on the Command Bar.
- As we've prioritized other commands to be at the start of the list, the Assign button has been automatically pushed onto the More menu. Since this action can also be performed simply by updating a field on the account form, it's not a great loss really.

If we just give enough thought on the actions that user will most often need to access on any given entity type, the constraint of having five menu items visible on the Command Bar shouldn't become an obstacle. You should rather consider it as a method to highlight "promoted actions" that will get the user's attention without having to fight against tens of other possible buttons for them to click on.

> **TIP**
>
> ***Ribbon Workbench 2013***
> *The tool of choice for anyone who's looking into modifying the CRM 2013 Command Bars should be the Ribbon Workbench solution developed by CRM MVP Scott Durow: http://www.develop1.net/public/page/Ribbon-Workbench-for-Dynamics-CRM-2011.aspx*

Quick Create

Quick Create forms are a new way in CRM 2013 to allow the users to add new records into the system without breaking the process which they were carrying out on the current form. This is an excellent way to reduce the cognitive burden associated with adding related child records as the Quick Create form just quickly "peeks" from the top of the page and then disappear once the new record has been created. The amount of fields expecting data entry from the user is most likely going to be more moderate than on the full entity forms.

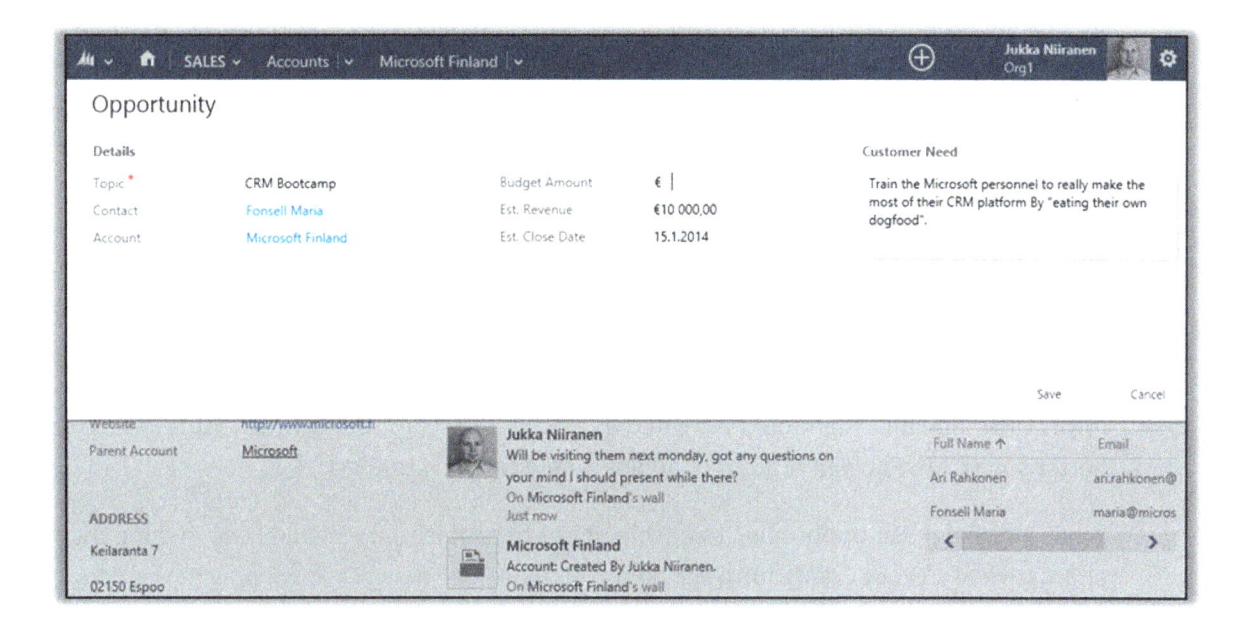

Shouldn't all records be enabled for Quick Form use then if it makes the data entry task more tolerable for the end user? Not necessarily. Here are a few considerations to keep in mind before choosing whether to go Quick or go Full in your choice of forms:

- Is the user likely to want to continue adding related child records to the newly created record, such as notes or activities? Since the new record is not automatically opened after the entry has been added into the CRM database, proceeding with working on the record data will require the user to first figure out a way to navigate onto the full record form. (Notice that if you use the global Quick Create menu for creating the new record, you'll get a menu asking if you want to open the newly created form. If the creation process started from a subgrid, however, no such option is presented after saving the record.)
- Will there be many variations on the requirements of data entry for the same record? Although you can have many Quick Create forms in your system, these will be displayed only based on the security roles of the user. This means neither the user nor you can apply business logic on which form should be shown in which context.
- Does your entity require intelligent forms with business logic to control how fields are presented? You won't be able to add any Business Rules on the Quick Create form to deliver this type of an experience (scripts are supported, though).

As a general rule, if you can cover 90% of the data entry needs with a simple Quick Create form, you'll probably do a service to your users by enabling them. If there will be frequent scenarios where the user will need to go to the full form after using the Quick Create form (which they can't avoid or disable themselves), you may just create more frustration with this feature.

Even with Quick Create enabled, the full form will still be presented if the user clicks "New" on either the entity main grid view or on another record form of the same entity (for example, creating a new account while viewing an existing account record). Since Quick Create is only used in create actions that start from the Global Quick Create menu, a subgrid command bar or a lookup menu you can't force the record creation path to always go through the Quick Create form. They shouldn't therefore be treated as a replacement for the Dialog feature, which can better support the guided process of adding a new record into CRM.

While weighing your options on "to enable or not to enable", you should keep in mind that the alternative of a Quick Create form is a popup window. The new single window navigation paradigm of CRM 2013 relies on the Quick Create functionality to keep things under control when working with related records. If you start the creation of a new record from a subgrid or a related view and the entity has been configured for the full create form experience, at the end of the process the user will have two browser windows that both contain the global Navigation Bar, allowing them to access any part of the system, which may lead to confusion.

> **NOTE**
> *One thing that speaks against the route of enabling Quick Create on each and every entity is that this will cause them to automatically get added into the Create menu on the Navigation Bar. There is currently no supported way for filtering or re-ordering this list of entities.*

Views

Views in CRM shouldn't be considered as just a list of records the user can click on to access the information through the entity form. In fact, what you should strive for in your view design is minimizing the amount of record detail forms that the user will need to click open to reach the outcome they are after. Sometimes the views themselves can offer all the information needed, in which case you've saved one click and screen refresh that the user didn't need to experience in the first place.

Here are some considerations to help you optimize the content of your entity views.

Sort order

Many of the standard entity views as well as automatically created views for custom entities sort the records by their name field. While it may sound like a logical choice for a generic rule of how to present data in the girds, my recommendation is to avoid using this default alphabetic sorting wherever a more logical sort order can be conceived.

During the design phase of your CRM solution, before the database is filled with real data, record sorting may seem like an insignificant detail. You've maybe only entered a few records with titles "Test 1", "Test 2" and "Yet Another Test" into the system, to validate how the data entry process works and plan the fields needed for the entities and entity forms. Those test records line up nicely in the default view of "Active [insert your entity name]", so you may be tempted to just leave it like it is.

Fast forward into a time when the system has been successfully deployed and there are thousands of records in the database. Your view still sorts them alphabetically by name, so whenever a user navigates to the menu of the entity, they are presented with a fairly static list of those records that happen to start with the letter A. At this point you should ask yourself the question: does the fact that a contact's first name is "Abraham" and not "Zachary" serve as a valid reason to always present him at the top of all the contact record views? Or could there be a more logical way to present the data?

The CRM users will hopefully be familiar with how they can utilize Quick Find, click on the view column headers to change sorting or even enable a custom filter if they are real power users. The one problem that remains is that in order to access the records that are relevant to them, the users always need to perform some kind of action on the data. From a purely technical perspective the system does of course work as it enables them to find the record, but could it somehow make the process easier for the user?

If there would be only one design tip that I could give to all the Dynamics CRM customizers in the world, it would be this:

"Show the latest data first."

That's the simple rule that you can apply to any CRM organization and almost instantaneously improve its usability by up to 42%. Yes, I am of course kidding about the statistics, but I'm not kidding about the importance of this design principle. Let's look at our previous example of the contacts view: how about if instead of always presenting Abraham at the top of the list we'd rather sort the view by applying the "latest first" principle:

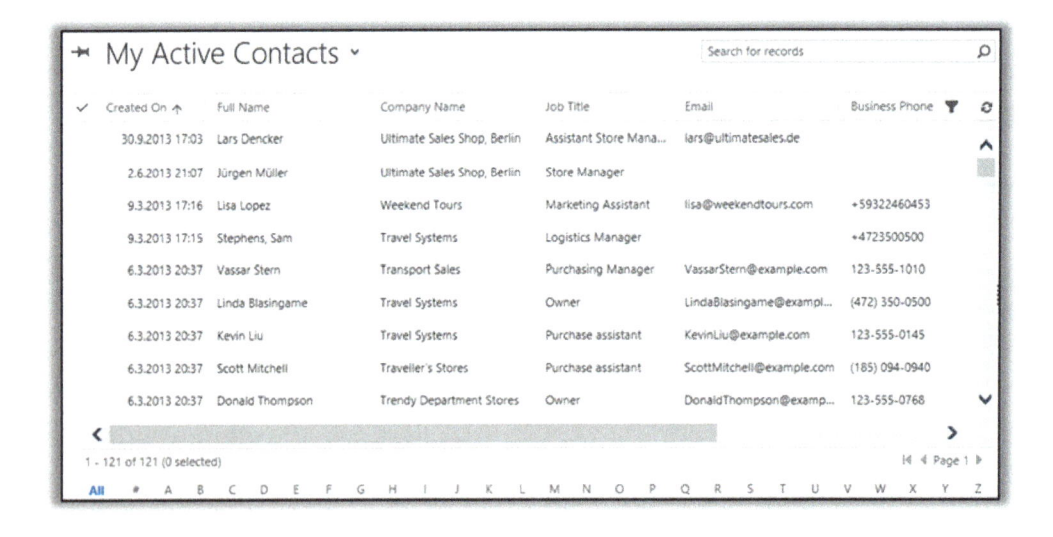

Created On ↑	Full Name	Company Name	Job Title	Email	Business Phone
30.9.2013 17:03	Lars Dencker	Ultimate Sales Shop, Berlin	Assistant Store Mana...	lars@ultimatesales.de	
2.6.2013 21:07	Jürgen Müller	Ultimate Sales Shop, Berlin	Store Manager		
9.3.2013 17:16	Lisa Lopez	Weekend Tours	Marketing Assistant	lisa@weekendtours.com	+59322460453
9.3.2013 17:15	Stephens, Sam	Travel Systems	Logistics Manager		+4723500500
6.3.2013 20:37	Vassar Stern	Transport Sales	Purchasing Manager	VassarStern@example.com	123-555-1010
6.3.2013 20:37	Linda Blasingame	Travel Systems	Owner	LindaBlasingame@exampl...	(472) 350-0500
6.3.2013 20:37	Kevin Liu	Travel Systems	Purchase assistant	KevinLiu@example.com	123-555-0145
6.3.2013 20:37	Scott Mitchell	Traveller's Stores	Purchase assistant	ScottMitchell@example.com	(185) 094-0940
6.3.2013 20:37	Donald Thompson	Trendy Department Stores	Owner	DonaldThompson@examp...	123-555-0768

1 - 121 of 121 (0 selected)

What's the record that's most likely to be of interest to the user? The answer: the one that has had some type of action performed on it most recently. Depending on the business process, these events could be something very specific (like the last change of an opportunity sales stage value), but a great starting point is just the Created On date of a record, because this is an attribute that will be available for each and every CRM entity. By changing your alphabetic view sorting to a descending sort by Created On, you'll be able to present the user with the very latest information entered into the system.

As one more reason on why applying alphabetic sorting to views isn't a sensible option in most cases, I invite you to have a look at the UI control that's present beneath all the entity views (in the web client at least): the Alphabet Index. It's the built-in method for filtering the view contents to those records where the first letter of the entity's primary field matches the selected alphabet. Now, since it's going to be there anyway, why bother setting your view sort criteria to duplicate this functionality?

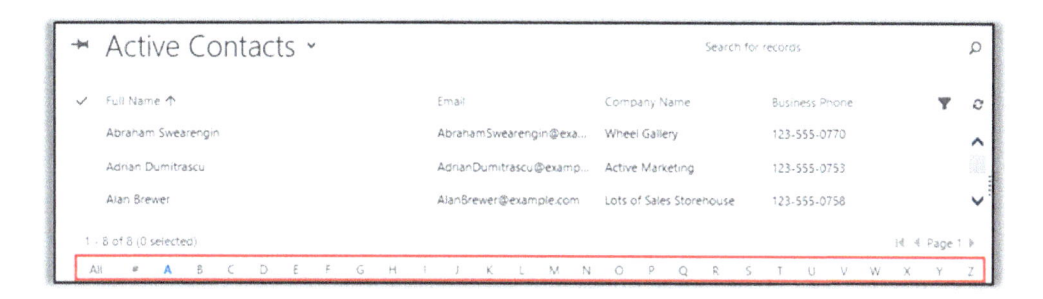

The UI design paradigm of showing the most recent information first has become familiar to all Internet users, thanks to services like Facebook and Twitter, which are built on the concept of an ever updating stream of posts. Applying a date based sorting scheme in your CRM views can certainly help in surfacing the latest actions from the customer database. However, if you really want to provide a rich "ticker" of latest events to your CRM users, it's advisable to look into the Activity Feeds functionality that the platform provides. By configuring workflow rules that create Activity Feed Posts from specific events you'll be able to show a much more vivid stream of data for your CRM users to consume based on their preferences, compared to what you can achieve with entity views alone.

View columns: consistency

Views are a great tool for filtering down the information in your CRM database, which is why the number of views is likely to increase as the usage of your CRM system picks up after the initial deployment. As more specific views are created over time to cater for the information needs of your user groups, switching between views becomes an ever more common action for the user. To make this operation as seamless for the end user as possible, the column set of your views should be as unified as possible.

Often there is no business reason to have a radically different column order or choice of columns between different views. However, if you always create your views from scratch and add columns as necessary, it is likely that the information content of your views will differ considerably, even though the purpose of the views might be very similar. "Accounts EMEA" should obviously have the same columns as "Accounts APAC", right? You'd be surprised how often this is not the case in live Dynamics CRM environments. From a user perspective it can be both confusing and frustrating if the information presented in the application UI comes & goes in a completely arbitrary manner.

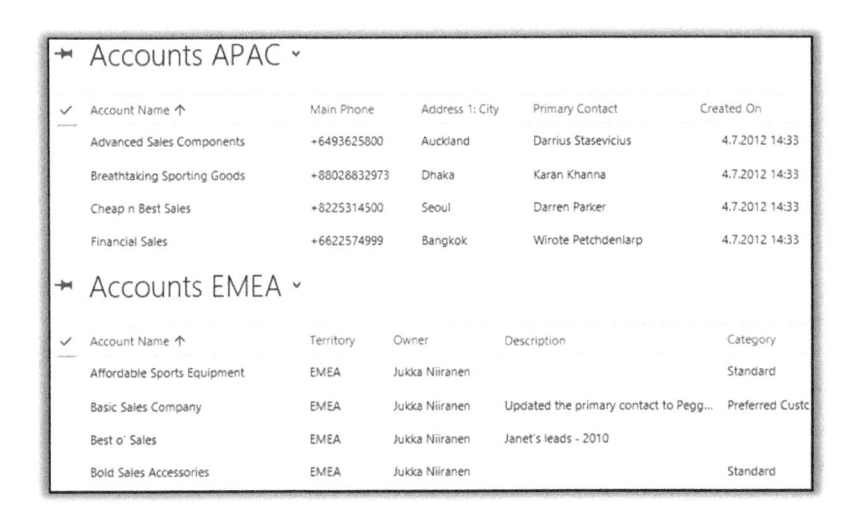

Accounts APAC				
Account Name ↑	Main Phone	Address 1: City	Primary Contact	Created On
Advanced Sales Components	+6493625800	Auckland	Darrius Stasevicius	4.7.2012 14:33
Breathtaking Sporting Goods	+88028832973	Dhaka	Karan Khanna	4.7.2012 14:33
Cheap n Best Sales	+8225314500	Seoul	Darren Parker	4.7.2012 14:33
Financial Sales	+6622574999	Bangkok	Wirote Petchdenlarp	4.7.2012 14:33

Accounts EMEA				
Account Name ↑	Territory	Owner	Description	Category
Affordable Sports Equipment	EMEA	Jukka Niiranen		Standard
Basic Sales Company	EMEA	Jukka Niiranen	Updated the primary contact to Pegg...	Preferred Custo
Best o' Sales	EMEA	Jukka Niiranen	Janet's leads - 2010	
Bold Sales Accessories	EMEA	Jukka Niiranen		Standard

Even if not all views for a particular entity need to be identical (and often probably shouldn't), the core set of fields the user expects to find when browsing through different views should be consistently available. For example, if the ownership of a record is important from the business process perspective, make sure the field is always there (in many out-of-the-box views it is not).

Even better, try to harmonize the location and the relative order of the fields. Put the 300 pixels wide free text description field always at the end of the view, so users can scroll to view it if they need these notes to identify the correct record, regardless of the view filter they are working with.

View columns: relevancy

Nine times out of ten your entity will have more fields than you can comfortably fit in a view. That's quite OK, since that's why we have the record forms to access all the details. What this means, though, is that you'll be faced with the task of choosing which columns are important enough to consume the limited screen real estate of the views. This will obviously a highly case specific decision, but I personally tend to think of relevant view columns as falling into one or more of the following categories:

- Sorting
- Filtering
- Flags

If your typical CRM user might want to sort the records based on the field, it's an obvious candidate to be included in the view. A more advanced user might also be aware of the filtering capability in Dynamics CRM views, in which case having it available in the view is very welcome. The last category would be fields that serve as flags that should draw the attention of the user. These might be alert fields that only contain data when there is a special condition (payment overdue, special requirements etc.) or maybe just free text description fields that help identifying records that contain additional notes to be shared to users.

Avoiding redundancy is generally recommended in CRM view design. If you create a "My Records" view, repeating the owner's name for each and every line of that view doesn't really add value, so feel free to remove it even if you would in general include it as a part of your base columns for the entity's views. In some specific scenarios it might still be justified to include a "static" column in the view, if you want to emphasize things like the cancelled status of a campaign. If you make the view a default for the entity or include it in a dashboard, for example, then it will be less likely for the users to pay attention to the view's name, as he or she did not have to choose it when navigating to the page.

Views and searches

The Advanced Find View of an entity will be quite often used in situations where the user wants to export data from CRM to Excel. A typical scenario would be getting the mailing addresses of contacts exported onto a list that's delivered to a third party mailing service provider. Knowing this, you could do your administrative personnel a favor and design the Advanced Find Views of your entities to serve as this kind of export views, by including a larger set of columns than you would put on a regular view presented in the main application. Since all the personal views that are created by users for their own ad-hoc data analysis should preferably be based on one of your standard system views (to always include the core column set and filters like record status), having the Advanced Find View designed for this export purpose shouldn't adversely affect any other use cases.

The Quick Find View is one of the most important views for any entity. When performing searches in the web client, this is the view that the UI switches to when presenting the results. In conjunction with the view columns you will also need to define the find columns that will be used in Quick Find queries. As a guideline, you should keep the layout of this view as close to the public default view defined for your entity, as that will ensure a consistent experience when a user navigates to that entity, is presented with the default view, enters a search term and then ends up on the Quick Find View. Including all of your find columns as view columns is also very much recommended.

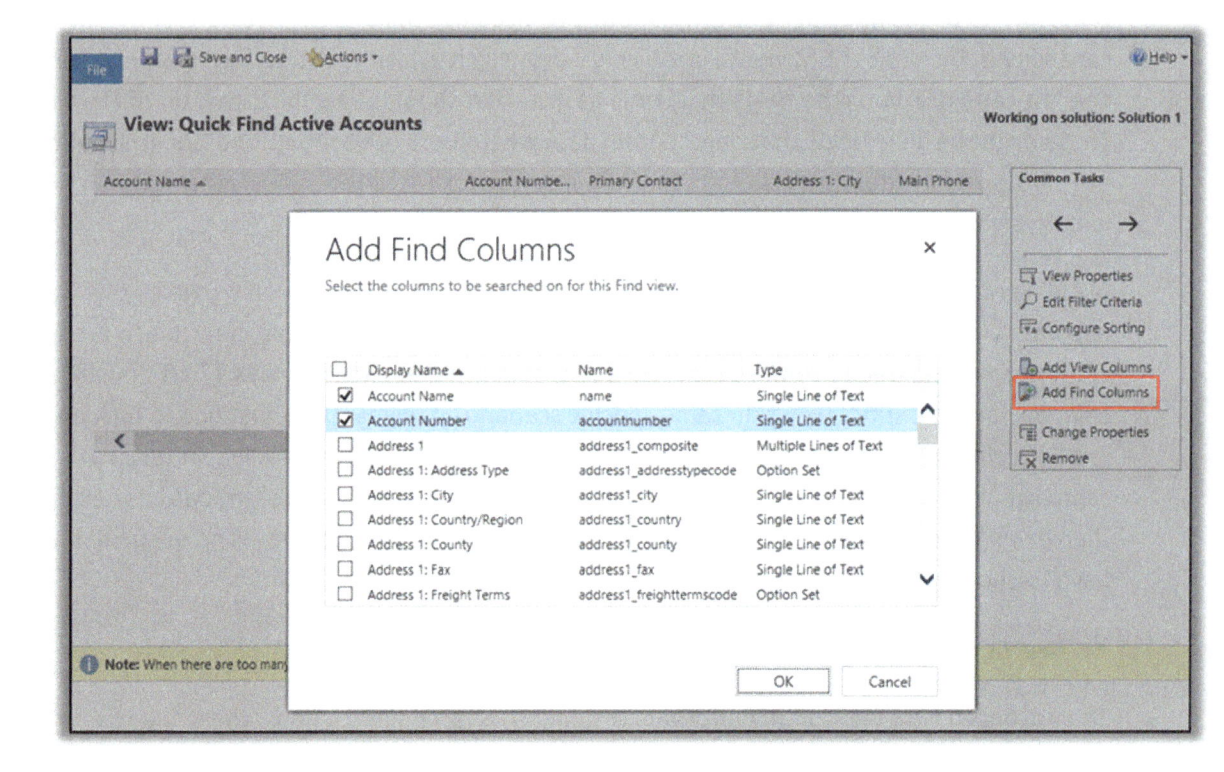

There's one more view related to the search functionality that deserves a more detailed look: the lookup view.

Lookup views

The new CRM 2013 lookup fields on the entity forms provide a much richer view to the related records than before. Not only is the primary field of the related entity shown (typically the name field) but also additional fields that have been configured in the Lookup View of the entity.

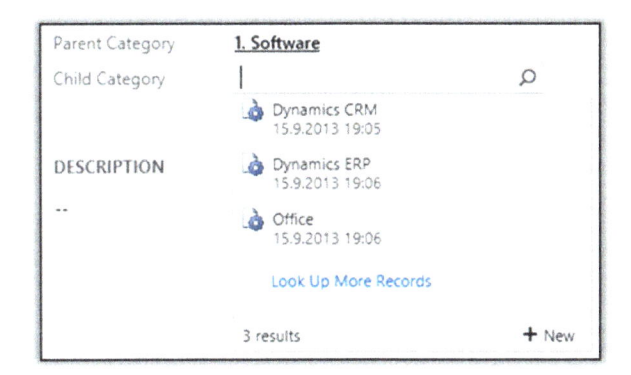

[Screenshot: Lookup view showing Parent Category "1. Software", Child Category lookup with results Dynamics CRM (15.9.2013 19:05), Dynamics ERP (15.9.2013 19:06), Office (15.9.2013 19:06), Look Up More Records, 3 results, + New]

Remember how the date fields were an important component of normal entity views due to the sort options that they enable? Well, here the situation is completely the opposite! By default the lookup views of new entities you create will contain the "Created On" date alongside the primary field of the entity. In the context of an inline lookup view that will be limited to a maximum of 10 records and doesn't provide any user controllable sort options, you'll rarely find such date fields useful.

What you should plan to do instead is to show descriptive fields that will enforce the confidence of the user on that the record he or she is about to select is the correct one. We will want to minimize any need for the user to click on the "Look Up More Records" link to open up a distracting dialog window. In the example here, we've added the description field of our custom category entity into the lookup view, to provide additional details that explain what the category contains. In this scenario, the Office category should be selected if the software in question happens to be Word, Excel, PowerPoint or any of the other products in that family.

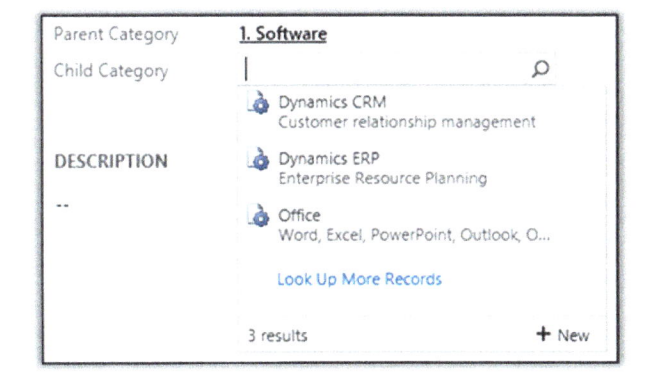

[Screenshot: Lookup view showing Parent Category "1. Software", Child Category lookup with results Dynamics CRM – Customer relationship management, Dynamics ERP – Enterprise Resource Planning, Office – Word, Excel, PowerPoint, Outlook, O…, Look Up More Records, 3 results, + New]

That brings up another important detail: determining the search fields for the lookup view. We'll want to allow the user to perform searches on all of the fields shown in the view. To do this, you'll actually need to configure the Quick Find View and its find columns, because the underlying search is done against this view, although the results are rendered in the lookup view.

Subgrid views

The new form design in CRM 2013 with a three column default layout encourages the usage of more narrow subgrids than the previous forms where a full-width subgrid used to be the norm. Combined with the new fluid forms that have been built to easily scale to different screen resolutions and window sizes this means that most of the time you'll have less space for columns in the subgrid view than before. Avoiding the sideways scroll bar making its appearance under the view is definitely recommended if possible, which means that instead of just recycling the "Active [entityname]" default views you should consider creating dedicated subgrid views with just one or two columns.

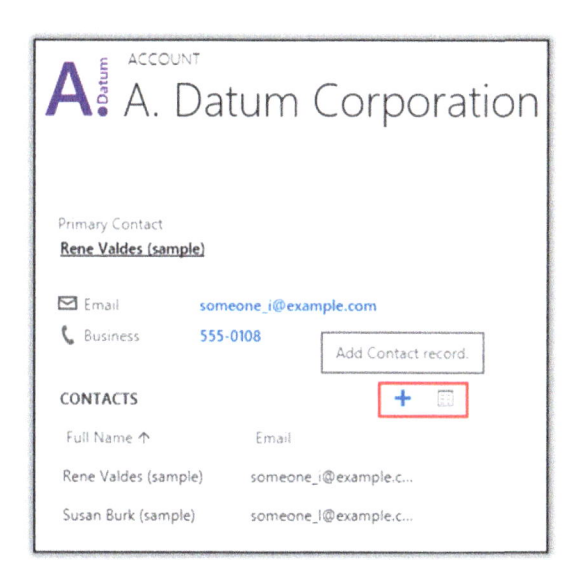

Another noteworthy change related to subgrids is that they no longer have a Ribbon. In fact, they don't even have the Command Bar that is found on top of the entity forms. All that's left is a "mini Command Bar" that allows the user to either add a record through the "+" sign or open the subgrid in a full screen width view that contains the buttons previously found on the subgrid Ribbon. Given how common the use case of adding new related records is compared to performing some data manipulation on the existing records is, this design choice surely does help in streamlining the UI to present just the important commands.

NOTE: *If you don't see the grid icon for opening the full screen subgrid view, your entity may not be present on the form navigation section. To change this setting, open the form editor, go to Select – Navigation and add the required relationship to the navigation section of the form.*

As you work with the subgrids, you may wonder why some subgrid "+" signs present you with the lookup view while others open the Quick Create form directly. For example, if you're on the account form and would like to add a new contact under that account, you won't be able to just click "+" once. In addition, you'll need to click on the magnifying glass icon that appears on top of the first record of the subgrid, after which you're presented with a list of max. 10 records. In this list, you'll then find a "+ New" button that will finally let you open the Quick Create form for entering the details of the new contact record. Not as quick as you might have initially thought, now is it?

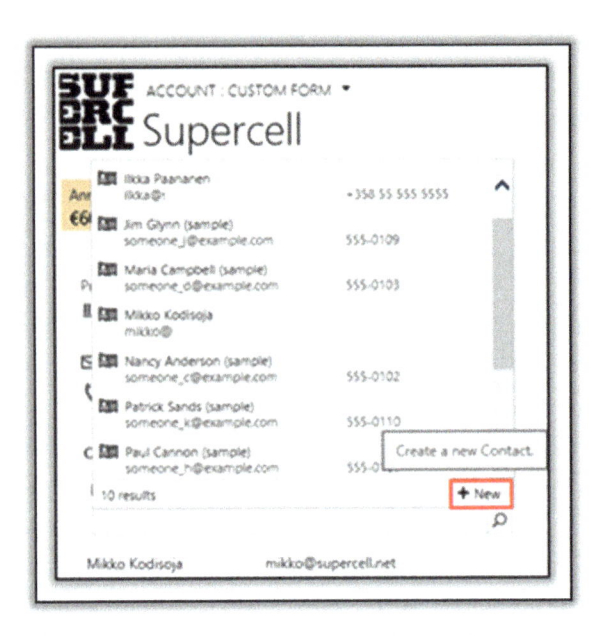

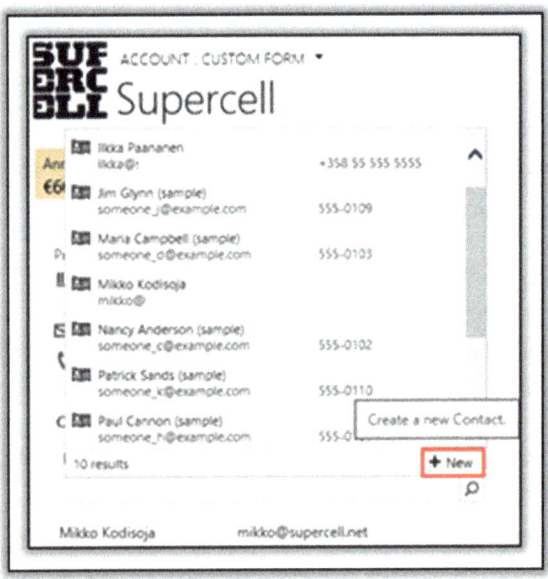

What drives the behavior of the subgrid "+" button is what some of you CRM 2011 veterans may recall from the Ribbon: the action of "add existing record". Since CRM 2013 now only shows a single button for adding related records, the choice of new vs. existing is no longer something that the end user can make. To provide the ability of linking an existing record to the current one, this experience is presented as the default option, which the user can then skip by navigating through it with the two additional clicks previously described.

Luckily this behavior can be configured. If the option for adding an existing record is removed, the Quick Create form will be opened on the first click. There are two ways you can achieve this:

- Set the child record's lookup field to the parent record as a business required field. In the account/contact scenario, this would mean setting the parent account relationship (Company Name field in CRM 2013) to be compulsory for the contact. In a B2B scenario this might well be a desired option anyway, to stop the creation of orphan contacts without parent accounts.
- Manipulate the Ribbon XML and hide the Add Existing button from the entity's subgrid Command Bar. You can find the required steps from this blog post by Gareth Tucker: http://garethtuckercrm.com/2013/11/19/fixing-the-sub-grid-user-experience-in-crm-2013/

After completing either one of the customizations, you'll now see Quick Create form launch immediately after clicking on the "+" button on a form subgrid.

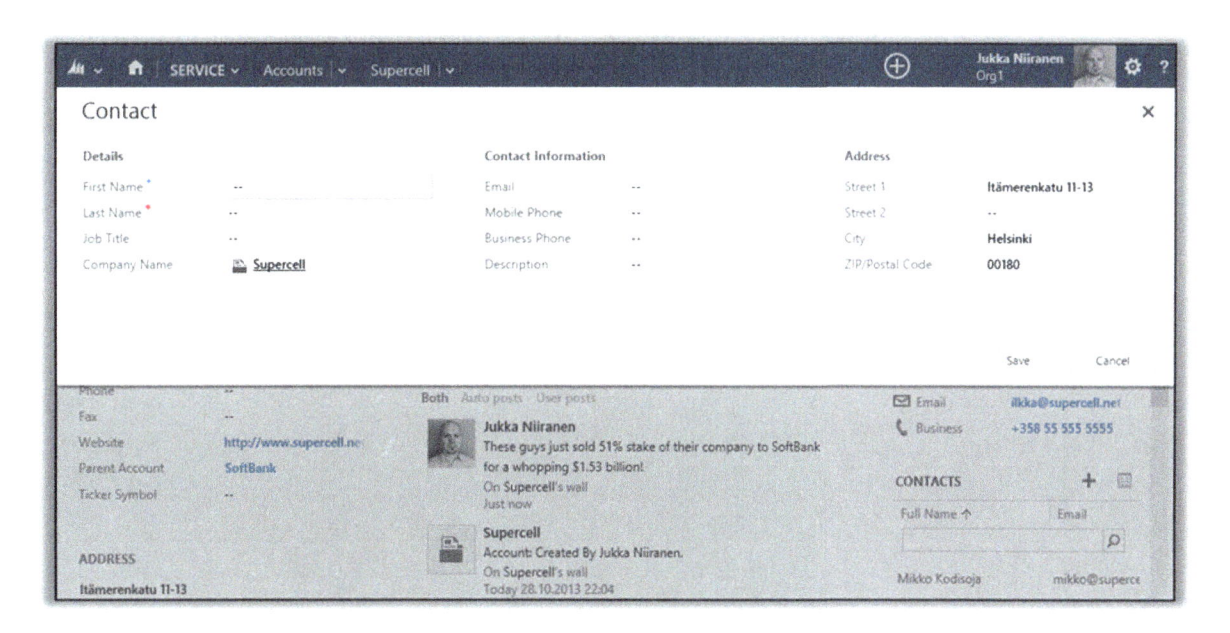

Of course the scenario of actually linking an existing child record to the parent record from the subgrid will now be blocked as a result of this change. However, as the users are able to associate existing records from the child record's form by changing the lookup field value, in many scenarios it will be advisable to design the user experience for the most common actions to be as streamlined as possible by imposing this new limitation as a trade-off to the reduced amount of friction in the process of adding new child records.

Forms

Entity forms are perhaps the one area in which a Dynamics CRM customizer with experience from the previous versions of the application will need to "un-learn" many of the past design principles that used to be valid up until CRM 2011. While CRM remains a platform that allows the customizer to choose from a wide variety of presentation options when putting together the forms representing data stored in the system, there are a number of reasons why it makes sense to challenge the previous design choices when crafting a solution for the CRM 2013 version.

Layout changes

Viewing the CRM 2011 and CRM 2013 account forms side by side clearly illustrates the differences in the UI design of these two product versions. Whereas CRM 2011 forms were a combination of data and menu options, CRM 2013 maximizes the screen real estate available for presenting the content and minimizes the amount of UI "chrome". Another way in which the ratio of visible content vs. commands has increased is the use of a single browser window to display individual records instead of the previous versions' popup windows. It is now much more likely that the record will be viewed in a maximized browser window that utilizes all the available pixels on the client device's screen.

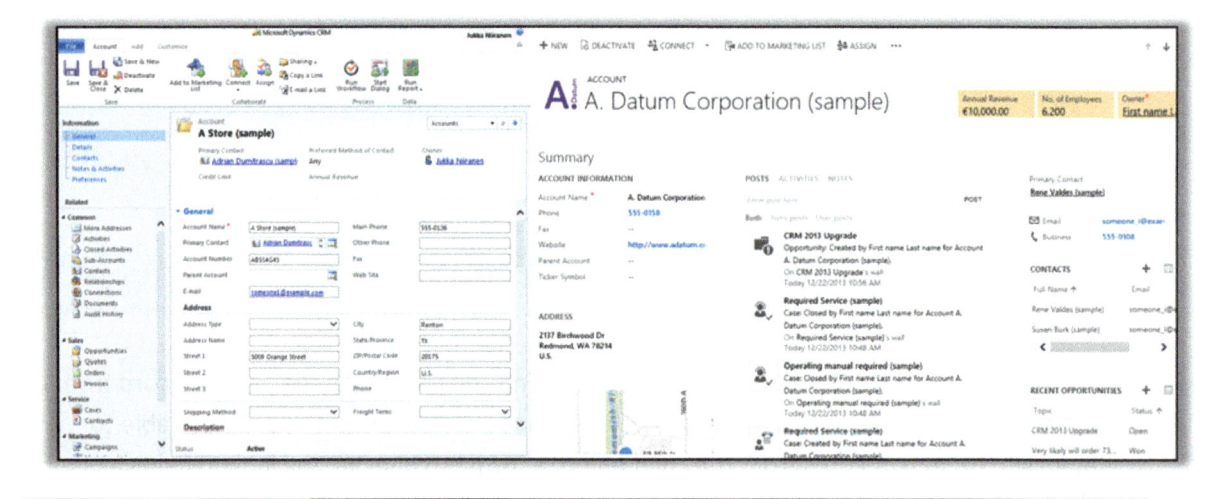

When working in this brave new single window world that no longer actively promotes the hierarchical nature of the CRM application's logical structure (list of records -> individual record -> child record and so on), the lines between a dashboard and an entity form start to get blurred. The end users will most likely no longer pay too much attention on maintaining a mental map of where they have navigated to in the application's hierarchy, since the new global Navigation Bar will always offer them the option of getting to any other part of the application.

With the added space available on the forms, you really should consider them more as "mini dashboards" rather than the traditional containers of facts about a single database row. After all, when a user opens a CRM record like an account, the expectation shouldn't be that the information they are looking for would necessarily be an attribute on the account itself. It may rather be something *regarding* the account that is of interest to them, such as:

- What are the latest sales opportunities that we are working on with this account? (subgrid)
- Who is the primary contact person for this account and how can I get in touch with him or her? (Quick View Form)
- What are our own organization's most recent actions regarding this account? (Activity Feeds)

This is the kind of information that CRM has already in its previous versions been very effective in tracking, by offering a structured storage location for the relational data surrounding the account. What it hasn't always been so good at is providing a quick answer to the person looking for this information – especially someone who may not know whether the data exists in the system or not. The big shift in the design of entity forms in CRM 2013 is that their primary purpose is no longer to describe the record itself; rather they are the key component for describing the world around that record. Be it a child or a parent record to the object we are looking at, that isn't a reason anymore to exclude the information from being shown on the form if the user can be expected to benefit from seeing it there.

If you're upgrading an existing CRM organization to 2013, one of the first things you'll want to do is reconfigure your entity forms to resemble those that come with an out-of-the-box CRM 2013 instance. Rather than just adding components onto existing forms, it may well be easier to take the new default forms as the baseline and start adding and removing fields to match the customized business processes and data model of your existing CRM solution. This approach will allow you to more freely experiment with the new presentation and UI style, whereas taking the old CRM 2011 forms as the starting point might make it more difficult to challenge the structure that was originally built for a completely different looking CRM application.

The users will expect a similar layout to be persistently used across the application. Therefore only upgrading the common account and opportunity forms and leaving everything else as it is should be avoided. Following a consistent structure like "subgrids on the right, activities in the middle" enables the users to quickly orient themselves on the contents of the screen, no matter which record they land on while following links within the CRM user interface.

Related records

Up until CRM 2011 there was a UI behavior that made it easy to quickly expand the data model by creating new entities, link them underneath their parent records with a N:1 relationship and have these entities automatically appear as menu items in the parent form's left side navigation. The system customizer didn't really need to pay much attention to the UI side of things when configuring the underlying data model to meet the requirements of the various business processes.

This convenience of customization imposed a toll on the end user, as the list of related entities presented on the form of a top level entity such as the account could far too easily grow out of control. What might have been crystal clear to the person designing the relationships between the entities in the CRM organization's data model was not necessarily as easy for the average CRM user to comprehend. While there was of course the option for the customizer to organize the menu items and determine the visibility of each entity on a granular level, there wasn't really anything forcing him or her to go through the process of designing the navigation and data visibility. It was optional, because you could basically do without it and assume the users would adjust.

CRM 2013 is reorganizing the entity form user interface by making the record content front & center while minimizing the majority of menu options visible to the user by default. The obvious change from CRM 2011 is the conversion of the Ribbon into a Command Bar with maximum of seven menu items visible by default. The more impactful change, however, is the fact that there isn't a single related entity menu visible on any record form once you navigate to it. Yes, you can expose the list of child records by clicking on an arrow on the navigation bar, right after the record's name, but there's a world of difference between an ever persistent list of all related entities and a tiny option hidden at the end of a breadcrumb trail.

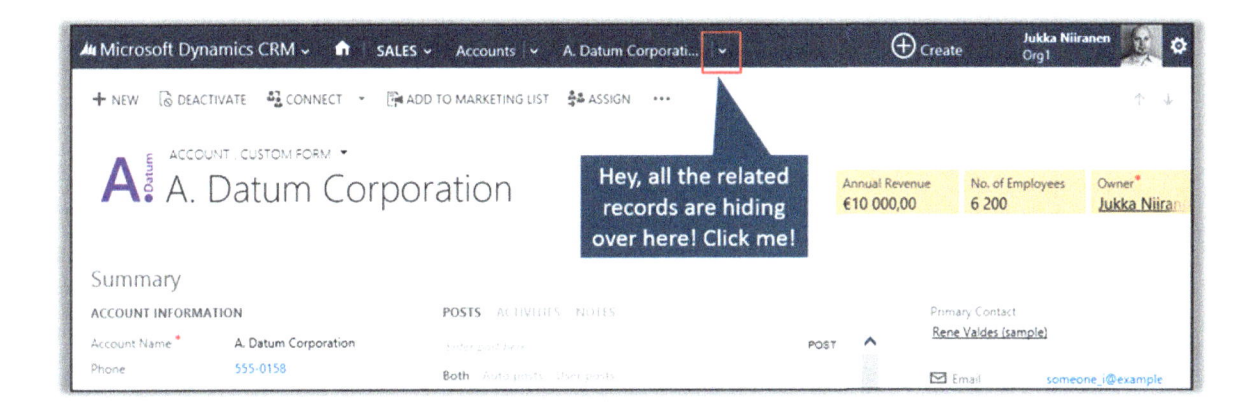

What does this mean in terms of user experience design then? If we can't show the users the wonderful network of connected entities existing in the database, won't CRM turn into a flat, single entity data management system that loses one of its most important features? Fear not, as instead of using the traditional associated entity views from the left side navigation we have the option of showing this data through a form subgrid. Yes, this option was introduced already in CRM 2011, only now it's no longer an option but rather the default approach you should apply in configuring the UI.

All the child entities that a user should actively be examining/creating/updating basically need to be brought up to the parent entity form in CRM 2013. Otherwise the risk of the average user not understanding where to go next to work with the right related records would just be too high. What the real priority of each entity is should determine the inclusion on the form and also the relative position on it in terms of vertical scrolling required to reach the subgrid. Although the new CRM 2013 forms are loaded in multiple stages and the main layout together with current record fields are processed in the browser before moving on to loading the subgrid contents from the server, there will inevitably be a performance impact based on how many subgrids are included on the form.

Some of you might ask "won't this make it more difficult to present all the tens of entities that can be linked to an account record?" The answer is: yes, it will force you, the system customizer, to make choices about what is the most relevant content to be shown on forms. At the end of the day, that is what user experience design is all about: making choices. What's there and, more importantly, *what isn't there*.

If you're having a hard time finding a working compromise of what items to show in the UI to meet the needs of different user groups, don't forget to explore the options that role-based forms can give you for targeting specific form designs to specific users. For example, you could create variations of the form for different user groups and place the fields and subgrids that are likely to be less relevant to them inside collapsed form tabs. This way everyone can still access all of the information if needed, but the most important content will be given the top space.

The power users of CRM can still access each of the related record menus that are available on the form's left side navigation menu as shown on the form designer window. They'll just need to learn the new method for accessing these menus from the top navigation bar. In fact, since many of the child entities will now have a subgrid on the parent entity form, you might even want to remove these from the form's related records menu altogether. This could help in tidying up the menu and having less items to scroll through, with no redundancy of the same related entity being presented in two separate locations on the parent entity form. Remember that the full related view of any child entity can be opened up from the view icon available on all form subgrids, so you don't necessarily need to use the navigation bar for reaching this view.

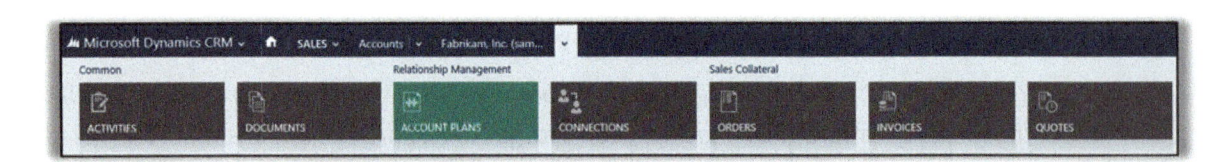

Record properties

One thing that's no longer available in the new entity forms is the record properties menu. This has traditionally been the place you could go to in order to check who had created or last updated the record and when. Not a big loss really, as most users would not have known how to venture here to access the information. But that doesn't mean the information itself wouldn't be valuable. Quite the contrary, any user who's interested in securing the validity of the data he or she is looking at will typically be searching for an answer to three questions:

- How old is it this database entry?
- Has it ever been updated?
- Who's the user I can ask for more information?

Due to the frequent need to have access to this information, it's generally a good idea to include it on the forms of each entity you are actively using. Although every CRM entity has the fields, none of the default forms are showing them. To provide a consistent user experience and teach the users to leverage these built-in timestamps as quick data validity indicators, you could add a "Timestamps" section to each form with these four fields.

An even better way to make the information accessible would be to include the fields in the form footer. With the new widescreen form layout, thanks to the missing left side navigation menus, you can quite comfortably fit these fields side by side at the bottom of each page. After all, it's not easy to think of much better information that the footer should hold. All the important fields to be highlighted should naturally be included in the header of the form, so the footer would be a natural place to store these timestamps and user references.

> **NOTE**
> CRM 2013 only refreshes the form footer fields when opening the record for the first time, not after create or save events. Therefore the timestamp fields will initially remain blank after you've created a record. But at least you should be well aware of who was in charge of that particular entry...

Fields

The most granular level of CRM customization components are the actual fields of an entity that hold the data of your CRM organization. Even though the contents of the database will of course be largely driven by the real life business processes that CRM is used for managing, there are a number of design choices that you can also make on this level to ensure that the user experience of working with the data is as pleasant and intuitive as possible.

Naming convention

Adding fields into the Dynamics CRM data model is super easy. This doesn't mean you should proceed with the creation of new fields without some upfront planning, because it's too easy to cause confusion for the end user while doing so. When designing the required extensions to the data model, you'll inevitably need to define the data type of a field to allow it to store the information in the right format. What's always not so obvious is the impact of the choice of names you give to the fields, however.

CRM does not enforce uniqueness on the display names of fields. This means in a worst case scenario you could end up with a field called "Email" that represents an email address, email contact permission, channel preference, lead source etc. Generic terminology like "Status" may conflict with built-in fields, resulting in the users not being sure which one to leverage when configuring their personal views. Always be specific enough in the naming of the field and invest a few extra characters if there's any possibility of confusion.

While customizing the data model you sometimes end up with entities that start to resemble a long questionnaire, even if you initially tried to keep it simple. That's OK, since CRM can be a great tool for profiling accounts through a variety of questions on past purchase behavior and current needs, for example. When designing these type of data rich forms you often build them out through the Form Designer, where you add new sections on the form and then create the required fields for a particular group of questions. What looks neat & tidy on the form may be something quite different behind the scenes, though. You can arrange a hundred fields into logical groups visually, but how do they look like when operating without any visual guidance?

This will be the experience that a user who's building a view or querying for campaign target group members will encounter when looking at the alphabetically sorted list of field names in the Advanced Find UI. It can be a pain even for the system customizer to remember what was the name of the field when scrolling through such a list, let alone for an end user who doesn't have a mental map of the CRM data model in his head. To ease off the pain of locating fields related to the same logical group, consider prefixing the field display names with a category title. Instead of creating fields called "Past Year", "Year to Date", "Next Year's Estimate" and spreading them all over the alphabetic list, group them with the labels "Purchases: Past year", "Purchases: Year to Date", "Purchases: Next Year's Estimate".

Repeating all of the grouping terminology in field display names on the form may not be necessary. In fact, given the way how longer labels may fade out in CRM 2013 forms, any additional text will now have a higher cost in the form's usability. While a general best practice is to ensure that the fields' display names and form labels are identical (again, to allow the users to locate them from the list), unnecessary redundancy of labels on the forms should be avoided. Instead of using the display names of the aforementioned example fields on the form, just create a form section with the header "Purchases" and drop the prefix from the individual fields' labels.

Another area that may force you to compromise on the information quality of your field display names is the view column headers. To improve information density, you should strive to cut away unnecessary whitespace from the views by adjusting the column width to match the expected average length of the field contents. Spreading a bit field with Yes/No values onto a 200 pixel wide column just doesn't look sensible. While adding field display name prefixes to group fields together you should consider whether there will be a requirement to show them on entity views, because you won't want to have several columns with "Purchases...", "Purchases..." and "Purchases...".

Searchable fields

Default entities like the account come with a lot of default fields (100+) that will most likely never be used in your organization. Not all of them are even present on the default entity forms, but they still exist in the data model. Although you may think than cleaning up the forms of all the unnecessary fields would mean you don't need to worry about them anymore, that's not exactly the case.

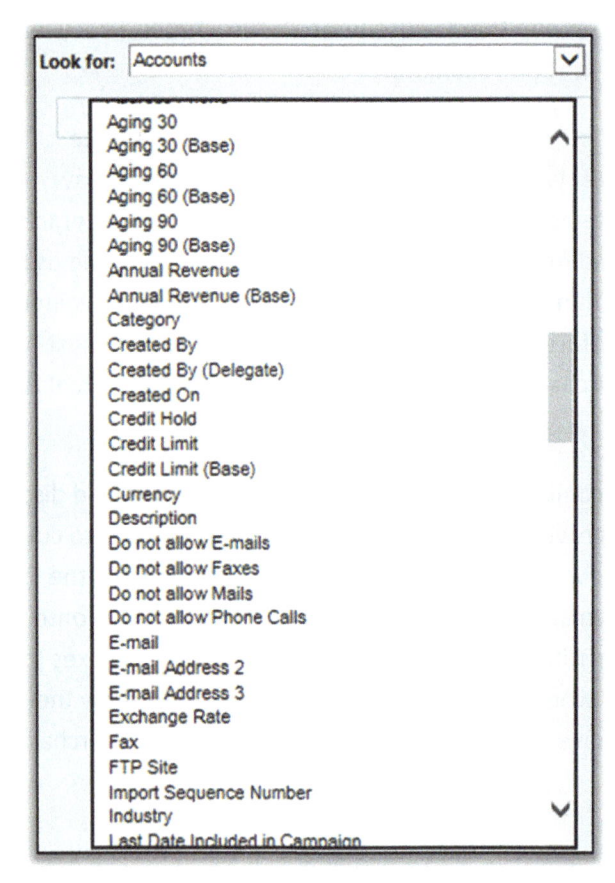

```
Look for: Accounts

Aging 30
Aging 30 (Base)
Aging 60
Aging 60 (Base)
Aging 90
Aging 90 (Base)
Annual Revenue
Annual Revenue (Base)
Category
Created By
Created By (Delegate)
Created On
Credit Hold
Credit Limit
Credit Limit (Base)
Currency
Description
Do not allow E-mails
Do not allow Faxes
Do not allow Mails
Do not allow Phone Calls
E-mail
E-mail Address 2
E-mail Address 3
Exchange Rate
Fax
FTP Site
Import Sequence Number
Industry
Last Date Included in Campaign
```

Whenever a user opens up Advanced Find to build a new view or change the query in an existing view, he or she will be presented with the full list of fields for the particular entity being searched (or any related entity, depending on the query criteria). Even if the user just wants to add a custom filter on the view, the long list of fields with bizarre or overlapping names is likely not going to make the experience of ad-hoc data analysis inside CRM very streamlined.

While you definitely don't want to go and delete any standard attributes that the system expects to be found from the CRM database, there's something you can do to improve the usability of your CRM application. You can set the Searchable property of the existing fields to "No", which will hide away the fields from Advanced Find. The fields will therefore remain available for anyone or anything accessing the system through an API, but the end user will never have to encounter them.

> **Attribute Bulk Updater**
> *Instead of going through the fields one by one and setting their properties, download the XrmToolBox application developed by CRM MVP Tanguy Touzard and leverage the included Attribute Bulk Updater to streamline this process considerably: http://xrmtoolbox.codeplex.com/*

Regarding the default fields, you should note that not all of the fields are set as searchable in the out of the box configuration of Dynamics CRM. In fact, there are some fields that you'll very likely want to use in Advanced Find query criteria but which are not available there. An example of this is the "Do not allow bulk emails" (donotbulkemail) field, which should be a part of every target group query criteria for your email direct marketing campaigns. While you are editing the Searchable properties, turn this on for leads, accounts and contacts, so that your marketing users don't have to contact the CRM administrator the first time they want to send out email campaigns.

Primary fields

Not all fields of an entity are created equal. For every default and custom entity there is a single field that is nominated the primary field. This is the value that will be shown in lookup fields when you link child records into a parent entity. For example, the name of the parent account record that a contact record has been associated with will be shown in the Company lookup field on the contact's form because this is the primary field of the account entity. On the parent entity itself the value of the primary field will be displayed at the top of the entity form and also in the title of the browser window.

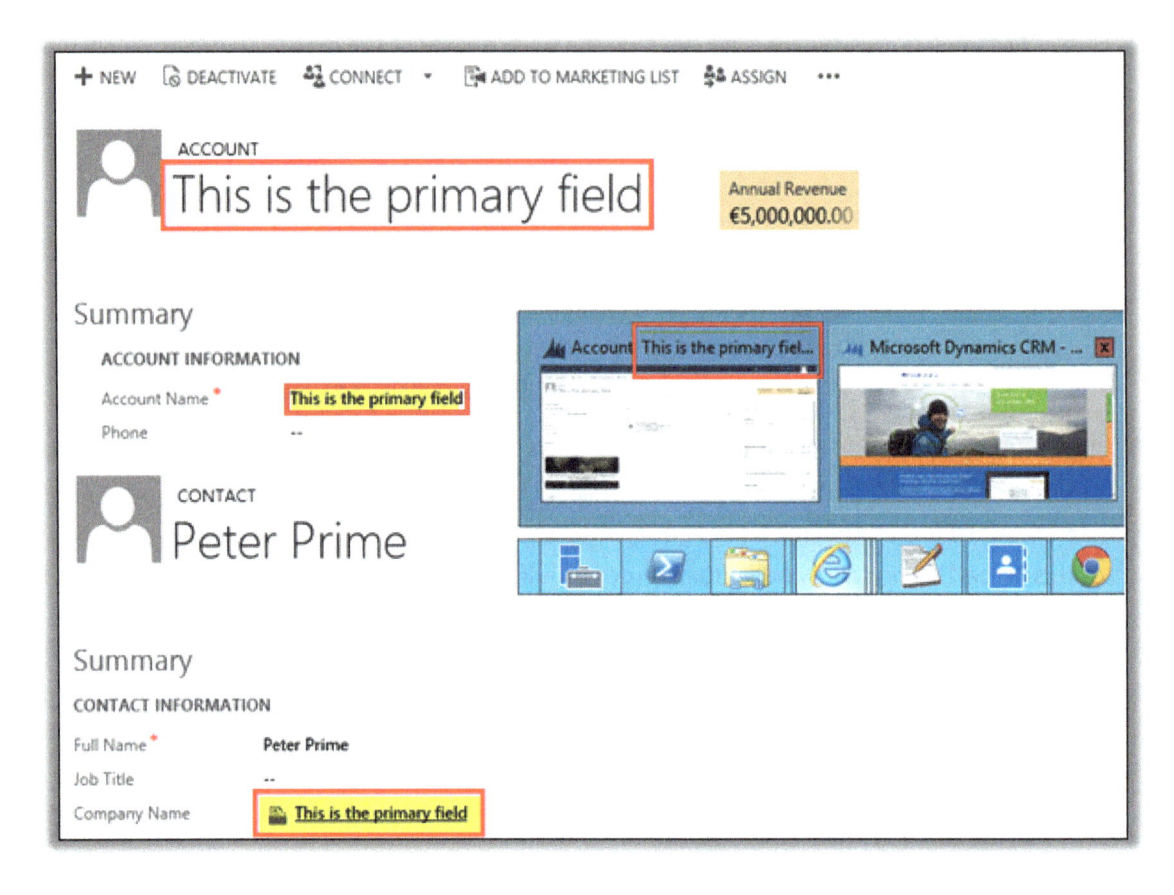

For custom entities the primary field is automatically added by CRM when you create the entity. What's common to both default and custom entities is that you can never change which field is the primary one. What you can do, though, is make the field optional by removing the default setting of "business required". This is a tempting option in many cases where the record being created does not have a proper name in the real world. Contacts and companies have obvious names that most people can agree on (well, even company names can have interesting variations), but many types of business transaction records you deal with in CRM don't really have an unambiguous name property. Think about the names for line items of a custom contract entity, for example: they usually exist in the context of the surrounding records and may have a free text description, but how would you give names to such objects?

Forcing the users to come up with arbitrary values for a default name field isn't a good practice and should be avoid. On the other hand, leaving primary fields blank is not a recommended practice either. If the entity has any child entities, a blank value in the lookup field on those entities' forms would look very odd and cause confusion. Even with entities that don't have any children the entity form would be missing the title values.

Whenever the name of a record is not a natural requirement for the user to define, you should automate the population of the primary field. Use a combination of fields to construct the value from the most important required field of the entity and input these into the field with CRM's process automation tools like Business Rules or workflows. For example, instead of relying on your sales people to follow a specific pattern on naming their opportunity records and ending up with a set of very unpredictable data in your CRM, why not just ask them to select the customer and product category (or whatever you use for segmenting your sales funnel), then automatically construct the name field value for the opportunity record.

Field mappings

Any entity that has relationships to parental entities, meaning it's on the N side of the 1:N relationship, can benefit from the automatic inheritance of field values from the parent record. A typical example would be the copying of the address of a parent account to the child contacts that are added underneath it. You can greatly reduce the need for repetitive data entry by automatically inheriting the values for identical fields on both entities via the Mappings settings on the entity relationship's configuration screen.

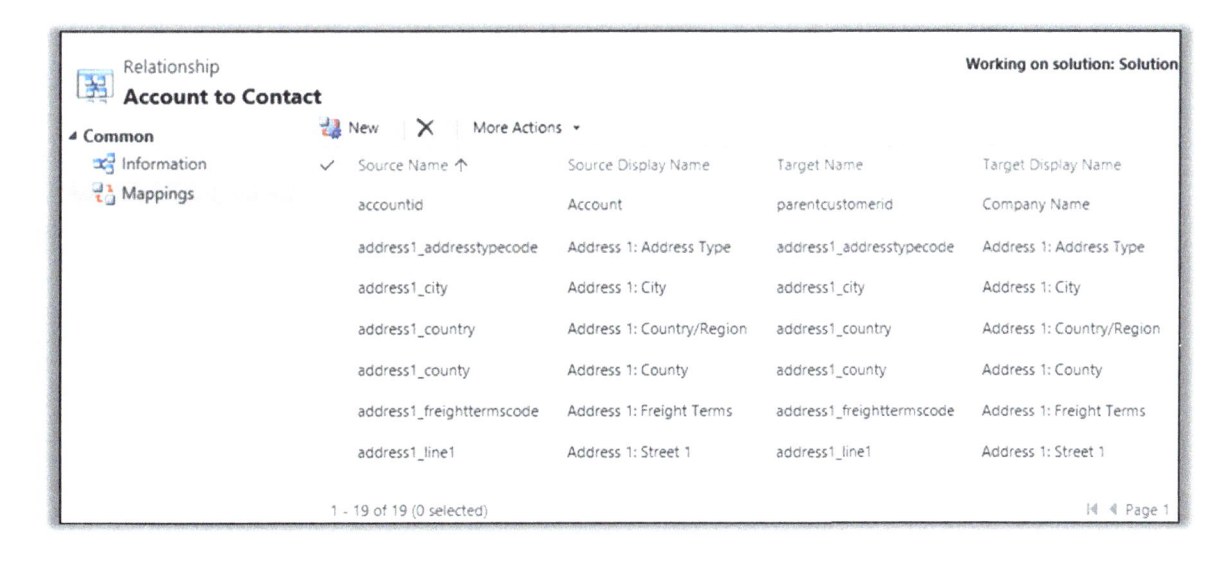

Source Name ↑	Source Display Name	Target Name	Target Display Name
accountid	Account	parentcustomerid	Company Name
address1_addresstypecode	Address 1: Address Type	address1_addresstypecode	Address 1: Address Type
address1_city	Address 1: City	address1_city	Address 1: City
address1_country	Address 1: Country/Region	address1_country	Address 1: Country/Region
address1_county	Address 1: County	address1_county	Address 1: County
address1_freighttermscode	Address 1: Freight Terms	address1_freighttermscode	Address 1: Freight Terms
address1_line1	Address 1: Street 1	address1_line1	Address 1: Street 1

Some of the mappings already come preconfigured with CRM, but you should still always review them to ensure that everything a user would expect to be mapped from the parent to the child record has been added to the mappings. For example, only selected Address 1 fields get inherited from accounts to contacts by default, so if you've surfaced the Address 2 fields on the entity forms don't forget to add them into the relationship mappings, too.

Obviously with custom entities or custom fields on a standard entity it is squarely the responsibility of the system customizer to configure the mappings. This is especially important with lookup fields in a data model consisting of several levels of related entities that each should be linked to one another consistently to make sure reporting on the data gives expected results. Another common custom mapping need would be inheriting the record owner lookup field value from the top level entity onto each child record.

Since this relationship mappings inheritance only works when the new record creation has been started from the parent entity, the feature may not always seem very consistent to the user. "Why does the system behave differently on this record compared to the one I created earlier? I could have sworn that..." Particularly with the new user interface design of CRM 2013 that reduces the visible hierarchies between records and makes the application appear more "flat" to the user, it will be increasingly difficult to try and enforce rules about always creating the child record starting from the parent record form (even though it would still be a preferred practice).

This is one place where the new real-time workflows can be used to fill the gaps of user expectations and the platform default functionality. Let's consider a scenario where the user clicks on the Global Create button on the Navigation Bar to create a new contact record while being on the account form, instead of using the contact subgrid "+" button visible further down on the form. As the global button is not contextual, none of the address or telephone fields will be copied over from the parent account to the child contact.

All we need to have in place to fix the issue is a workflow process that runs on the create event of a contact record. If the parent account field (Company Name) contains data but the address fields do not, we can fire up a "Copy Address from Parent Account" real-time workflow to populate the missing data from the account's fields.

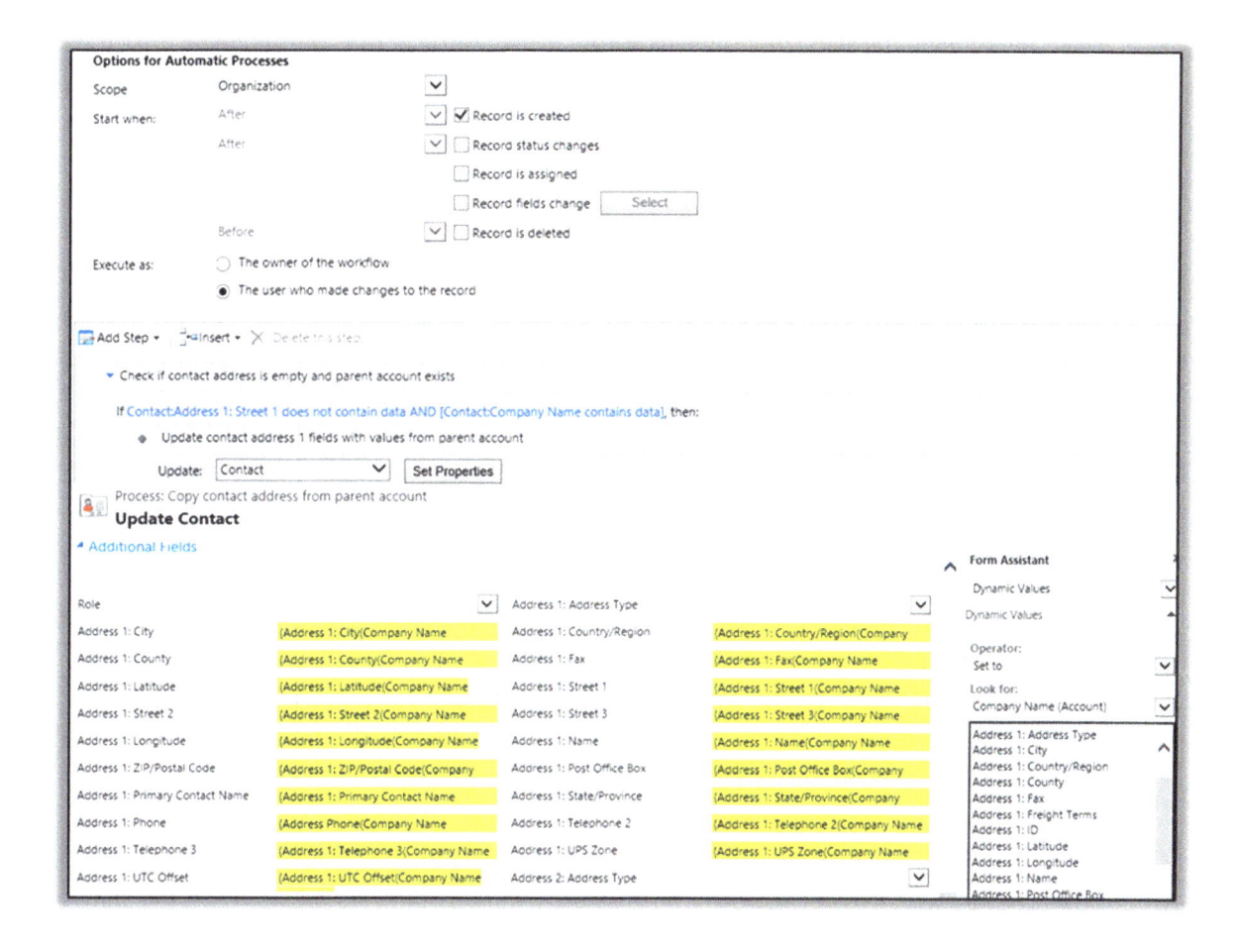

Since this real-time workflow will run synchronously at the very moment the contact record is added into the database, the address fields on the contact form will also be updated immediately. The CRM user will never even know he or she did something "wrong" in this process, which is the sign of a well-designed system that adapts to whatever path the user chooses to take to achieve the goal.

Although the redundancy of having the same field values copied onto several different records in the CRM database isn't exactly optimal from a database normalization perspective, sometimes there are solid business reasons for designing a bit of redundant data storage into the processes, to improve overall system usability and information value. To ensure that the relationship mappings and other field inheritance methods don't lead to a reduction in data quality, it's a good idea to leverage these types of workflows also for monitoring updates that take place after the initial record creation. If the parent account of a contact record changes later on, for example, running the same workflow to automatically retrieve the address fields from the new account onto the contact record might be in order.

Guiding the user

After we have designed our CRM system's functionality and UI to be as intuitive as possible, it is quite likely that there will still be areas left where presenting the users a text based instruction message would be an effective way to ensure that they remain on the right path. There are four new features in CRM 2013 that make it easier to provide "inline" instructions to the end user. Let's explore the capabilities and potential use cases for each of these, to determine what is the best approach to take for guiding the users through the different actions expected from them.

Tooltips

CRM 2013 has introduced tooltips that can be used for presenting instructions to the user on what the field is for. Rather than a new setting in the UI, this feature simply leverages the existing Description attribute of an entity field.

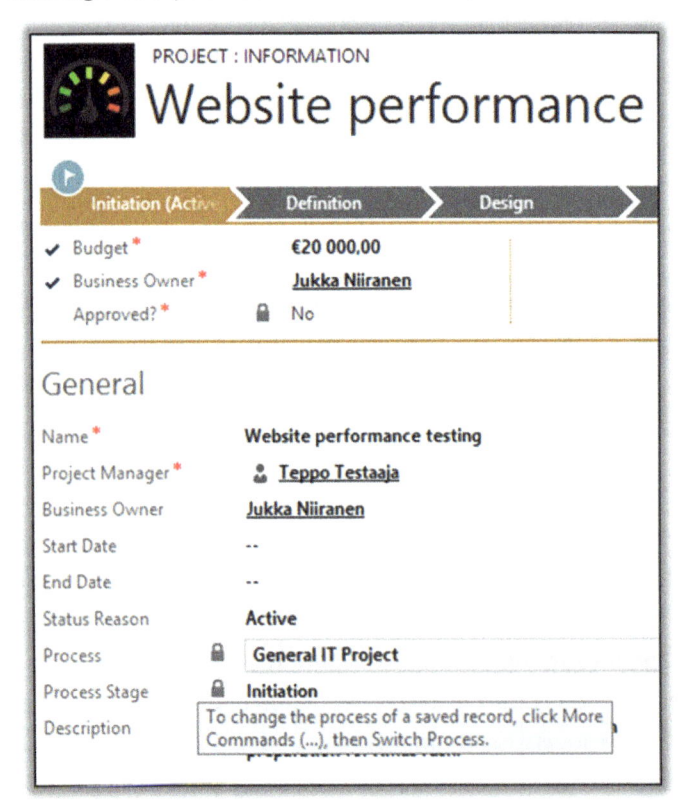

Tooltips are a great addition, but if you were a long-time Dynamics CRM user and you didn't know that proper tooltips had been introduced in the latest version, would you know to look for them? Probably not. Also, unless the system customizer has taken the effort of adjusting each field's description value to something more tooltip-ish, the chances are the user may hover over a field a few times, see a non-informative message and then continue to ignore them as a source of information.

This doesn't mean you should ignore investing in tooltips. Just keep in mind that of all the user guidance capabilities in CRM, these are the least prominent ones. Convenient for the user who wishes to explore the UI and understand the purpose of each field; invisible to those who are less keen on spending time with the system and just want to get their data entry tasks over & done with.

Business Rules

Business Rules allow you to display an error message next to a specific field if the rule condition is met. A typical example of a rule you could build with this feature is verifying that a combination of fields is filled in a certain stage of a process. Unlike the field requirement level setting, not only can you control the existence of data in a field but also check that the values entered are within the allowed limits. For example, when the value of a sales opportunity goes beyond a certain threshold, an automated approval process associated to it may need more input to send out the necessary approval request email. With Business Rules in place the CRM UI can immediately give feedback to the user on additional steps required based on a previous data entry action.

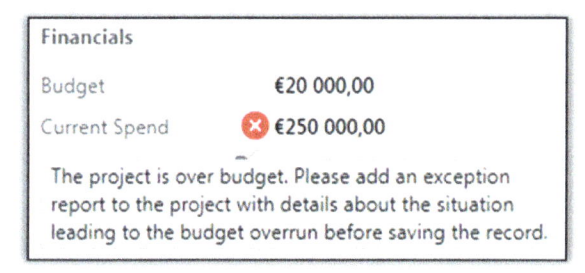

```
Financials

Budget              €20 000,00
Current Spend     ❌ €250 000,00

The project is over budget. Please add an exception
report to the project with details about the situation
leading to the budget overrun before saving the record.
```

Error messages, as the term suggests, should only be applied in situations where the information entered does not comply with the business logic of the system and requires immediate actions from the user. As long as the field value meets the error message criteria of the Business Rule, the record cannot be saved, which effectively halts the process on the CRM side.

In CRM 2013, Business Rules do not support a non-error type of notification that we could use to alert the user but allow the related business process to continue for now. In order to simply capture the attention of the user while not requiring immediate corrective actions from him or her you'll need to look for alternative guidance methods.

Form notifications

There is one new feature that falls outside of the "no code" scope of this chapter, but which should be noted in the context of discussing messages presented to the user by the system. CRM 2013 SDK now contains an officially supported way of showing notifications on the top of the form, by calling the setFormNotification function under the Xrm.Page.ui namespace in your form's JavaScript. This allows presenting a more "global" message on the form compared to the field level messages supported by the Business Rules. The notifications are a very prominent component of the record's form that the user is unlikely to ignore, compared to an error message displayed next to one of the tens or potentially hundreds (hopefully not!) fields placed somewhere down the sections of the entity form.

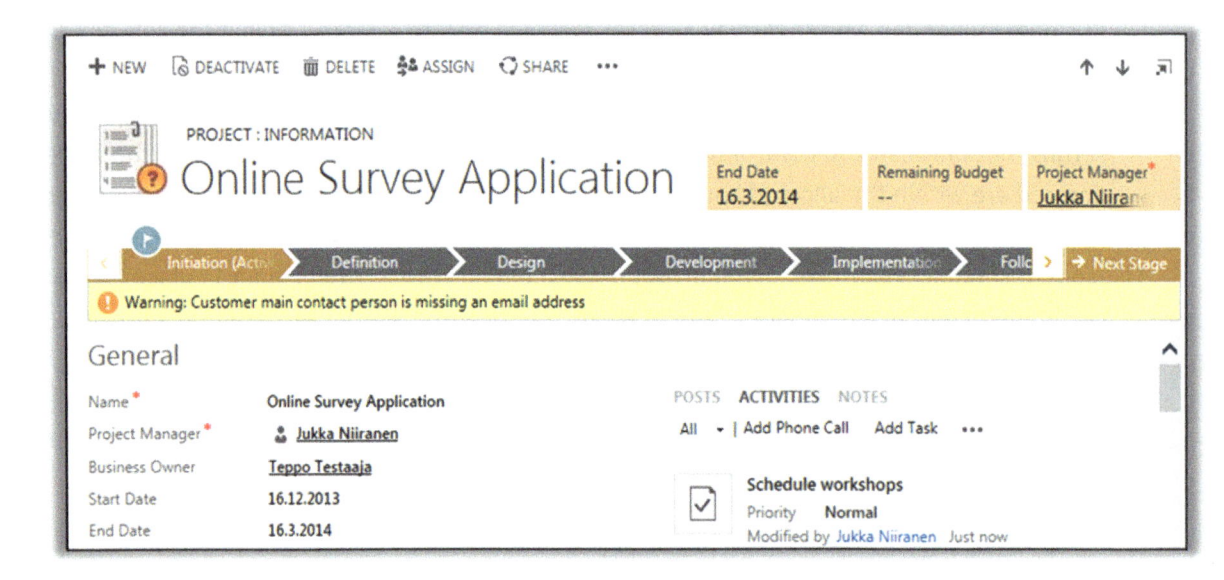

In addition to the red X icon error messages supported by Business Rules, the form notifications can also be mere warnings (yellow exclamation icon) or purely informational messages (blue "i" icon). This type of notifications are a great fit for situations where the attention of the user should be drawn to a potential issue that either exists on a record related to the currently viewed one, or problems that may lie ahead further down the process stages unless the user fixes the field values.

Business Process Flows

Business Process Flows (BPF) are a highly visual method for presenting the status of a record in a given process. They act as the main guiding tool for the actions expected from the user in the particular stage that the record is in. You can also promote different fields to be filled during each stage of the process. This is a great way to reduce the amount of fields visible to the user on the record form at any given time, since any information that's not immediately required when a new record is created can be surfaced at a later stage by only including it in the BPF control and not the actual form itself.

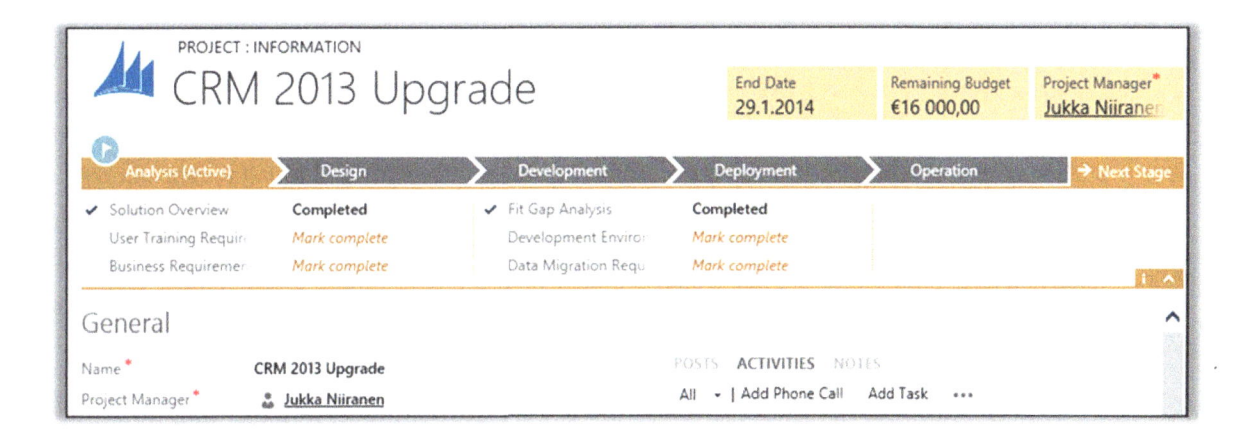

If you look at some of the default Business Process Flows that come bundled in with CRM 2013, you'll notice that they also contain a variety of two option fields that are used for indicating whether a particular step in the process stage has been completed or not. This is a somewhat different approach to the traditional activity driven method of tracking the completion of tasks related to sales opportunities and other transactional records. Instead of generating individual task records for every action required via background workflow processes, the BPF control provides a checklist type of presentation to the same work items.

While individual task activities remain the way to assign specific work with a deadline, deliver a reminder to the owning user's Outlook and provide other data input fields related to the task, the checklist approach of Business Process Flows is much better in providing a big picture view to what's been done and what remains to be done. The nature of individual task records traditionally hasn't always been that helpful in allowing the user to focus on the right actions at the right time. This is because tasks can easily get scattered into long lists and interrupting reminders that are often encountered outside of the context of the main record. BPF on the other hand is all about showing the work items in the context of the process, next to the record details, which means they are not merely a tracking tool but also a guidance tool for showing the road ahead.

As tempting as it might be to offer the users all of the information related to the process via the BPF control, this may not be the best strategy in practice. The presentation of fields on the BPF section of the form is constrained by a fixed layout that cannot easily accommodate very long texts. Field labels in CRM have physical limitations in the allowed length, so you should not try to incorporate an instructional text into the label but rather just keep it as the name of the variable for which the actual input field provides data. In short, don't name the fields based on the "how", but instead use them for communicating the "what".

Custom instruction fields

If the Business Process Flow feature can't fit in all the information we'd like to provide to the CRM end user working with the records, what are our options for delivering it? Should we just keep those details outside of CRM and created traditional training materials with Word and PowerPoint, to be handed out to new users while providing them training on how to use the system?

It is certainly advisable to ensure that sufficient training materials exists to support new employee onboarding, but quite often it's not only the first time that a user accesses the system when instructions would be needed. Business processes managed with the help of CRM tend to grow in complexity over time and also change shape as the surrounding world or the technical platform evolves. The best support system should be both easy for any users to access and easy for system administrators and key users to maintain.

Like most software, CRM contains an Online Help feature that allows users to click open the instruction materials provided by Microsoft. Earlier versions of Dynamics CRM allowed administrators to customize the contents and adapt the Online Help file to the specific business processes and system customizations of the organization. However, the sad truth is that people are not very likely to access the Online Help content. It is often perceived as a software manual and as several studies in the field point out, most manuals are never read, some not even taken out of the shrink wrap (back in the days when printed manuals still existed).

The CRM 2011 version removed the support for customizing Online Help and instead introduced a new feature intended for user guidance, called the Getting Started Pane. This was effectively a built-in method for showing content sensitive help to users who were browsing a grid of records, with links to help articles presumed to be of interest to users based on the entity they were accessing. Although the pane did provide customization capabilities, updating the content still remained a too cumbersome task for most organizations to really leverage in their user guidance. The additional pane with its default content ended up cluttering the already busy UI of CRM 2011 and users preferred to simply switch it off. As a result, this feature was also dropped and is no longer included in CRM 2013.

Some of the problems with both the previous methods for user guidance were:

- Context: either the information was not in an obvious enough place for users to discover it (Online Help) or it was forced onto them at moments it was not needed (Getting Started Panes).
- Content: the process for updating the information was too complex to support active maintenance

They say that *"content is king, but context is kingdom"*. With this in mind, how could we implement a user guidance system for CRM that is able to provide up-to-date content to the users in exactly the right context that it's required in?

Although it is not a specific built-in feature for instruction delivery, the new Quick View Forms of CRM 2013 could easily be leveraged for bringing in information stored on another entity and showing it on the form to the user who's working on the actual business record. Here we have an example of a process stage specific instruction section embedded on the opportunity form:

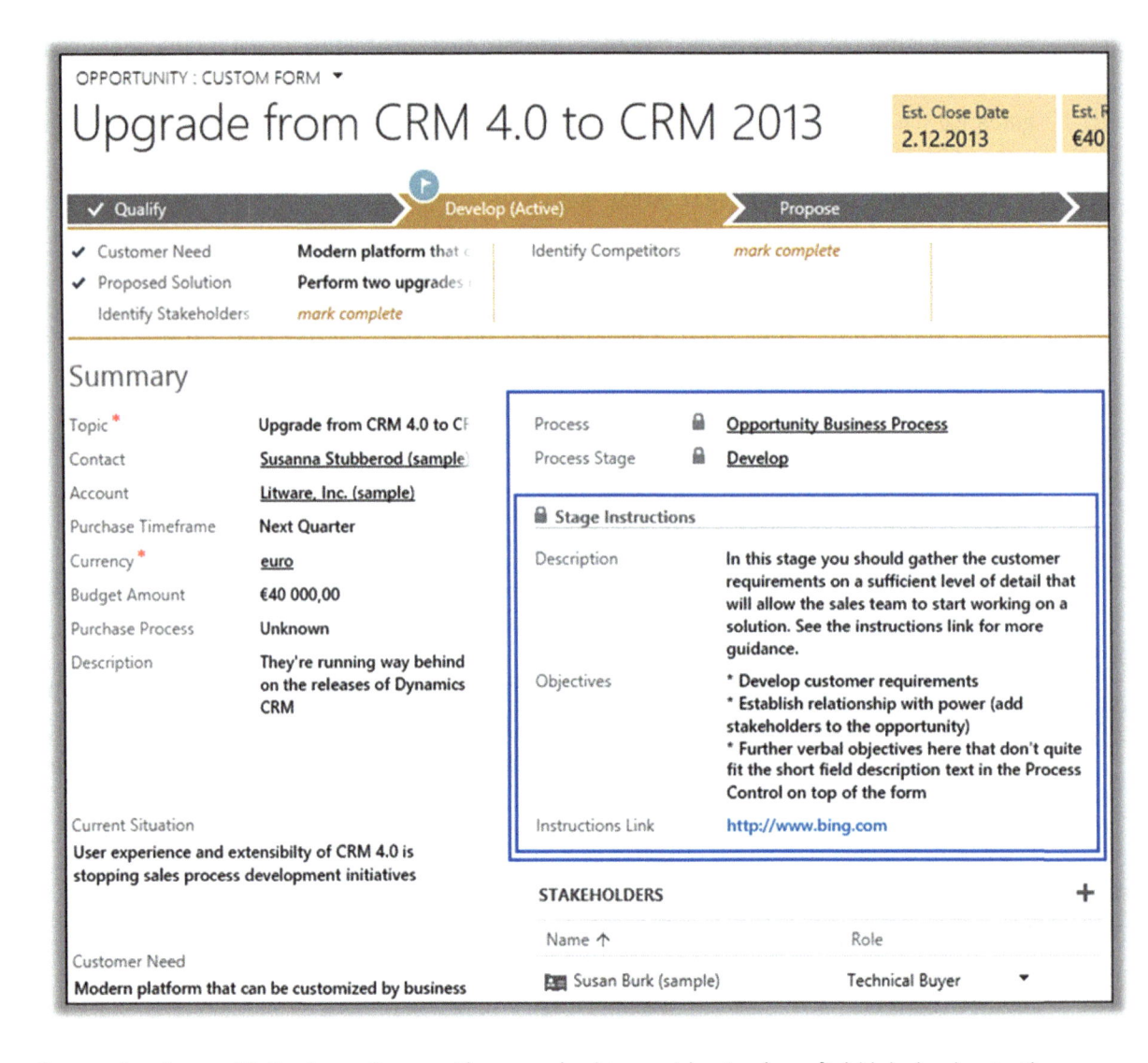

Remember how with Business Process Flows we had to avoid using long field labels, due to the attribute limitations and the fact that only some of the labels would be rendered visible in the BPF control? Well, when using Quick View Forms none of those limitations are a concern to us, since we can show the actual field *data*, not just the label.

In our example there are two multi-line text fields included on a custom entity called "Business Process Stage" and a URL field for pointing the user towards a page that offers additional information. All of the content can be easily accessed and updated by any CRM users given editing rights to the entity. Just like the end user can click the URL on the target entity form to read the in-depth documentation, the process owner or system administrator can just as easily navigate to the Business Process Stage record and update the instruction text to reflect the frequently asked questions received from users or to highlight recent changes to the process. The barrier for content maintenance could hardly be any lower than this.

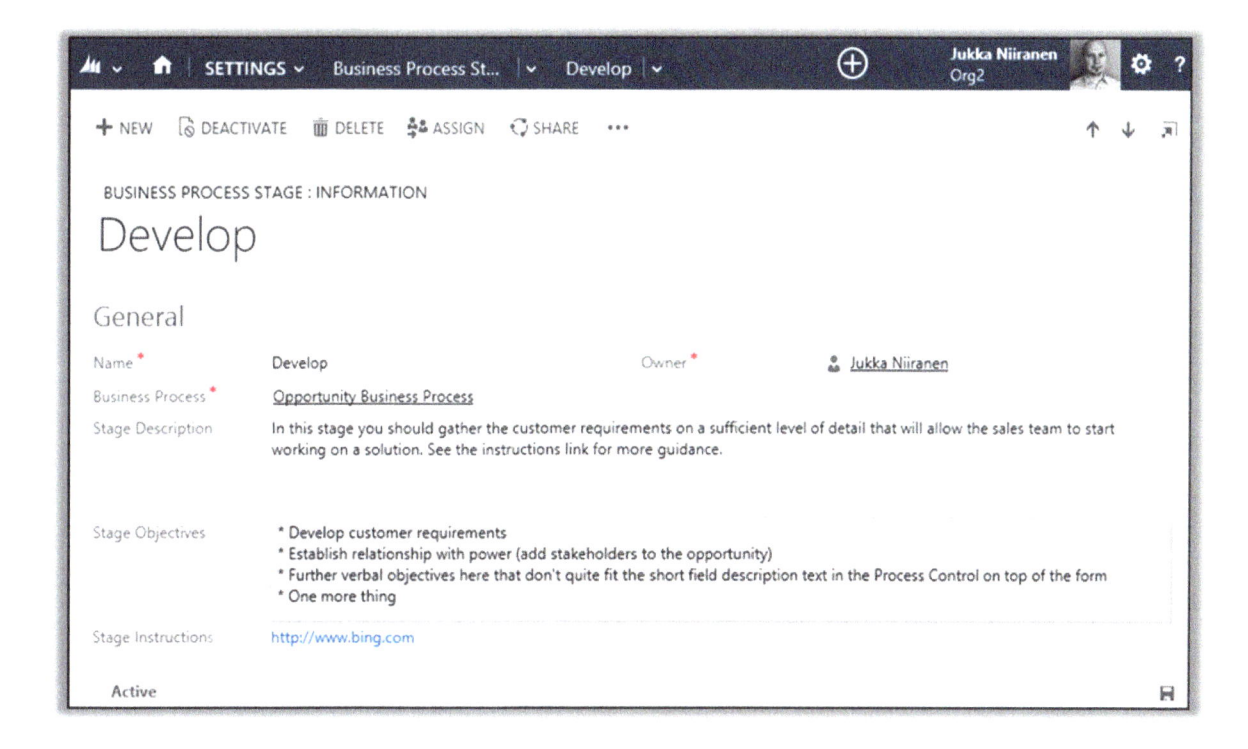

How about the contextual part then? How do we display the instruction fields to the end user at the right time, on the right record? To achieve this, we'll need to have a few relationships between the instructional records and the business records, as well as a workflow rule to update the references to these instructions once a user moves through the different stages of a business process.

In the data model the Business Process and Business Process Stage entities will need to be parents to the opportunity entity via a 1:N relationship. This will allow showing fields from them via the Quick View Form.

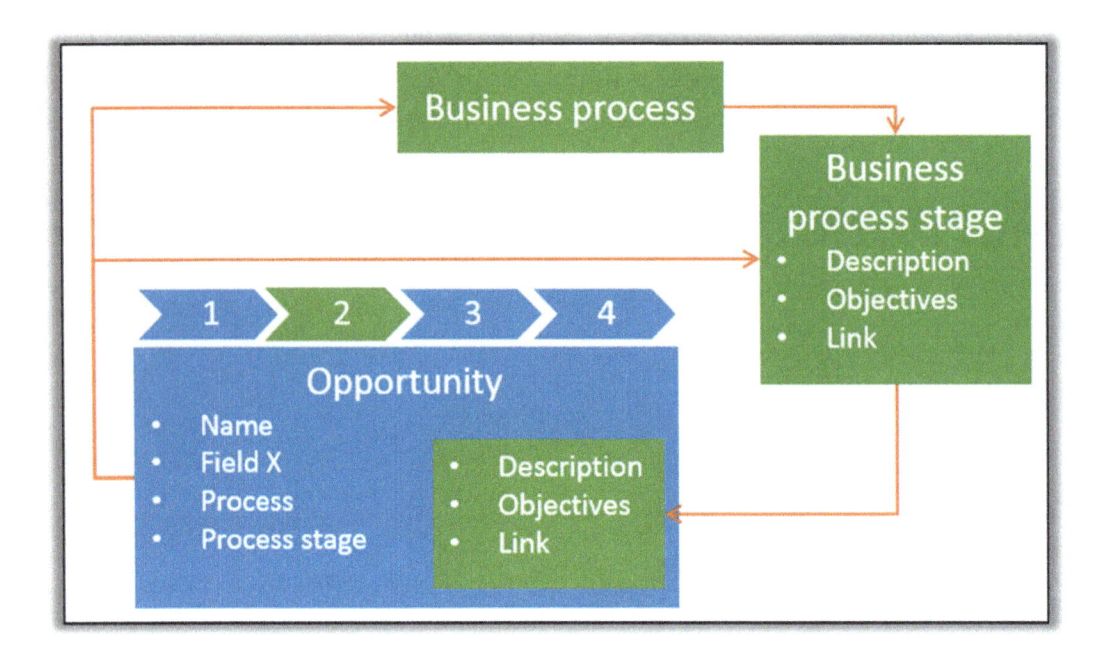

Since each stage of the sales process should have a different set of instructions shown on the opportunity form, we'll need to create a workflow rule that will set the field value of the Process and Process Stage lookup fields on the opportunity to the correct records. While the Business Process Flow control's forward & backward buttons can be used to drive the changes in the associated BPF process, the related custom lookups for Business Process and Business Process Stage entities should be updated based on these change events in the stage. To capture these and update the instruction fields on the opportunity immediately after the user proceeds from one stage to another, there should be a real-time workflow process added for the opportunity entity, to monitor any changes in the default field Process Stage (stageid).

As a summary, in order to create a user guidance system as described above, here are the steps you should follow:

- Plan the process variations and each of the stages required in them
- Identify the type of instructions the users may require during the process execution
- Create your custom process and/or process stage entities to hold the instructions
- Create the Quick View Form for presenting this information in the context of the main entity's form
- Decide whether the process is a good fit for being driven by the Business Process Flow control (you can also use other process status indicators, like option sets)

- Design the business logic that will update the lookup fields to the custom entities, which in turn will change the instructions presented via the Quick View Form

If your needs for showing instructional messages in a process are more limited and don't warrant the creation of custom entities to manage the content, it is also possible to implement a more light weight variation of the method described above. Instead of Quick View Forms you could leverage just normal fields on the entity form. Just put them into read-only mode and update the field contents directly via a workflow process.

Putting it all together

Considering all the options we have covered on how to guide users through a business process, these methods can be ranked by their relative prominence in the following order:

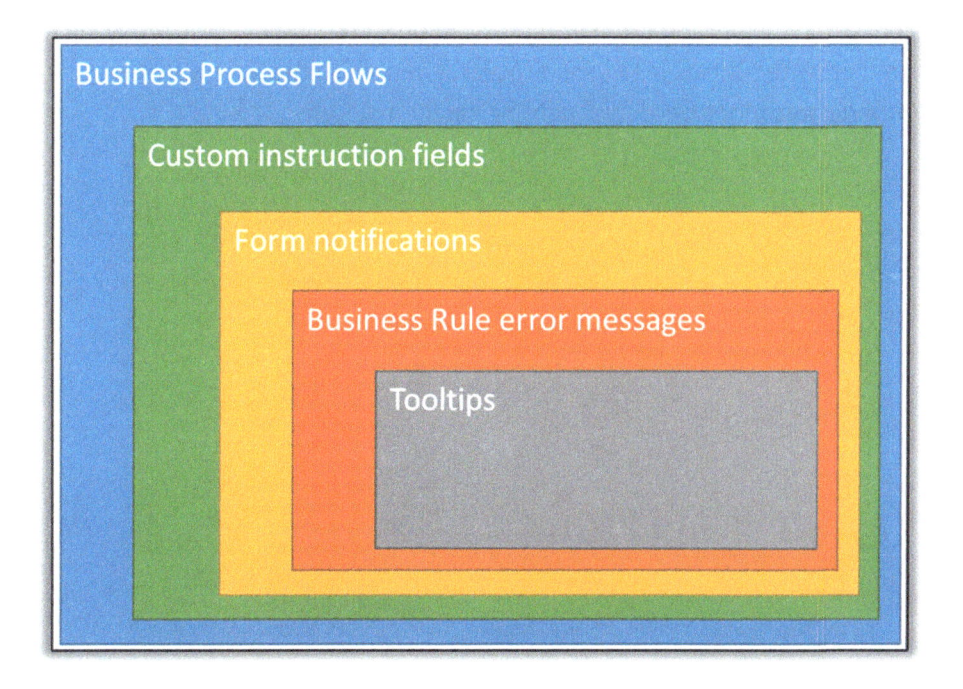

Business Process Flows
Custom instruction fields
Form notifications
Business Rule error messages
Tooltips

Business Process Flows are the most visually notable component of the CRM forms, whereas field tooltips may easily go unnoticed. Form notifications and Business Rule error messages are present in the UI only when something has gone or is about to go wrong, while custom instruction fields can deliver a more persistent information area for the user to view in their time of need.

Depending on the complexity of the business process you need to manage through CRM (specifically from the eyes of the end user and not just the technical platform), you may choose to utilize only a few road signs to warn the users about the wrong turns they should not take. On the other end of the spectrum you may need to provide a detailed map of the paths the users should follow and provide guidance on several different levels, to ensure that all the decision points along the way are equipped with sufficient information to keep the process flowing smoothly.

Going beyond the user guidance tools listed here, you should also remember that CRM offers the Dialogs feature that you can use for building a highly controlled data entry process. While this method limits the user's ability to control the order or the pace in which specific fields are filled and what related information is viewed, dialogs can be applied in many scenarios as a form of a gateway to steer the user through a more narrow part of the process path. Also the steps for creating a record with complex data requirements can often be simplified by replacing it with a wizard style UI implemented through a dialog process, after which the user will continue working on the CRM records more freely through the traditional forms.

3

Customizing Entities and Forms

One of the top items sited by users of Microsoft Dynamics CRM for their choice over a different CRM product is the ease of extending the platform. CRM includes fantastic, rich standard functionality, but customizing the user interface makes the application "your own," and every CRM implementation is unique.

CRM 2013 adds to the already extensive customization options. In this chapter we will discuss how to effectively use these options and best practices for customization in CRM 2013.

New Entity Definition Options

When you go to Settings→Customization→Customize the system, you can select an entity that you wish to customize or create a new entity. You will notice that the entity definition in Dynamics CRM 2013 includes some new options.

CRM 2013 Quick Start

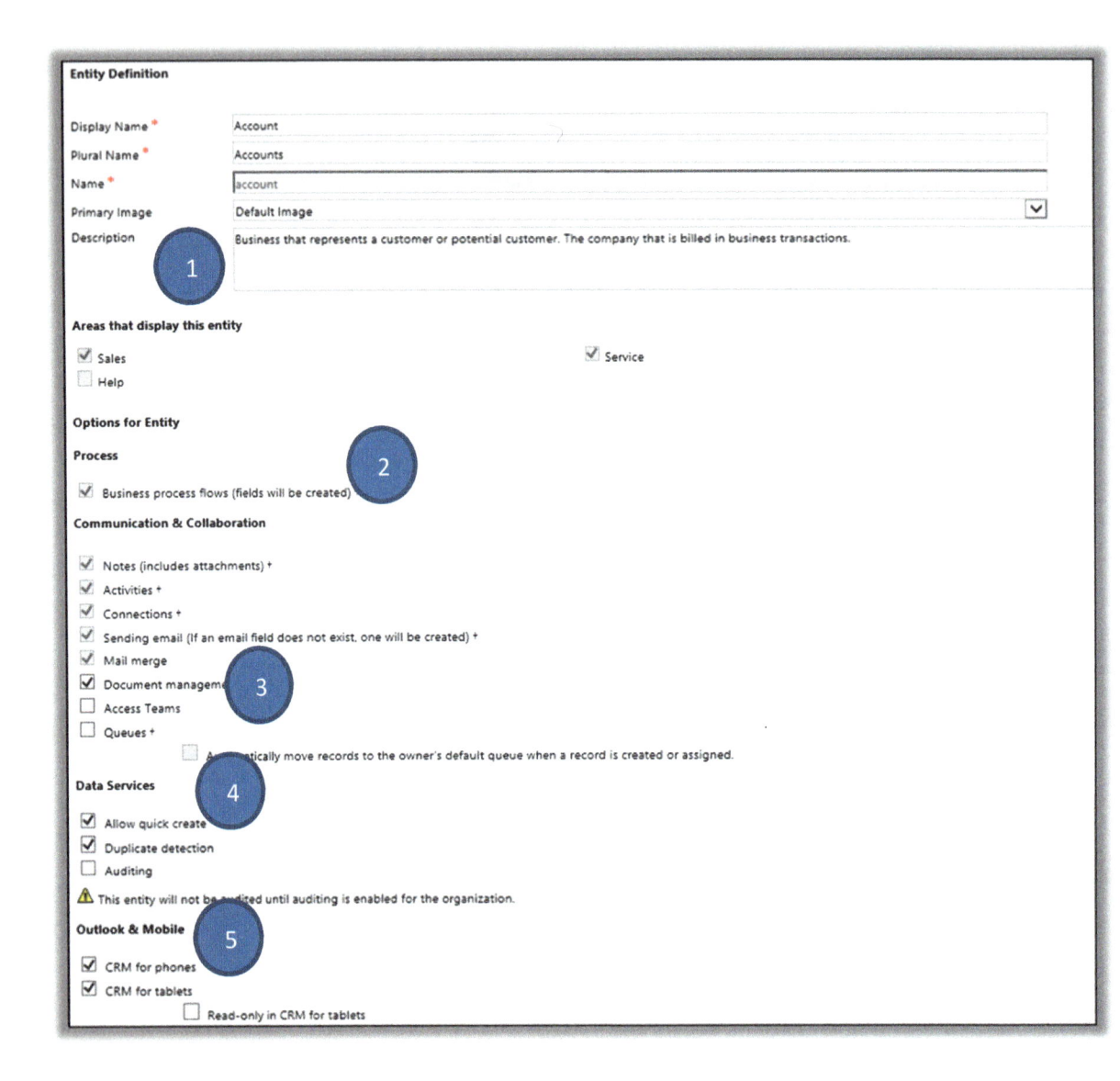

Microsoft Dynamics CRM

1. Primary Image field: This determines if the form will display the new entity image. The image field is covered later in this chapter. This option can be changed after the entity is created. Options include "none" and "entity image." If "entity image" is selected, it will display the image for the record in the form header.

2. Business process flow: This enables the new business process flow functionality for the entity. Note that the entity options that have '+' by them cannot be disabled once they are enabled. This is because these options create fields on the entity when enabled.

   Note that most system entities have this box checked. Some, like activity entities, do not have this box checked, but it can be checked if you wish to enable it. There are a few system entities that business process flow cannot be enabled, such as background entities and service entities.

   After enabling business process flow on an entity, the business process flow bar will be visible on entity forms, as long as at least one Business Process Flow type process record is published.

3. Access teams: Access teams are covered in the Security Model chapter. This option enables the entity for Access Teams.

   Once you enable access teams here and create an access team template, when a member is added to the access team sub-grid on the form, the members will be automatically added to the access team, and whatever permission granted to the team via the access team template will be granted to the user.

   Access teams are a major advance in security functionality from version 2011. Consider these scenarios:

   - A team selling scenario where the members of the team are different for each account. Using traditional owner teams is very cumbersome, because you must manually build the team, then assign or share the record with the team
   - Record specific tiered access, such as where a user should have full access to opportunities in one market and read access to opportunities in another market. You can add two access teams to the opportunity entity, one with read and write privileges, and another with read access, then add users that should have full access to the read write team and users who should only have read access to the read only access team.

   Once enabled, this option can be disabled later.

4. Quick Create: Quick create forms are covered in the new form type section later in this chapter. This entity option must be enabled before you can use quick create for an entity. For example, if you have a subgrid of custom entity records on your account form, and you want someone who clicks the '+' on the sub-grid to see the quick create form rather than the full create form, you must enable quick create on the custom entity. This option can be disabled after it has been enabled.

5. CRM for phones/CRM for tablets: If you want an entity available from the new phone and tablet apps for Microsoft Dynamics CRM 2013, these options must be enabled. This option can be disabled once it is enabled. The new mobile apps are covered in the "CRM on the road" chapter of this book.

New Form Types

Dynamics CRM 2013 introduces two new types of forms: Quick View Forms and Quick Create Forms. Both of these forms reinforce the goal of CRM 2013 to give users the functionality and data that they need where they are, without having to navigate somewhere else.

Quick View Forms

Consider this scenario: You are on a case for Acme Corp, and you need to know the phone number for the client. In CRM 2011, you would have to click the link in the "Customer" field, pop up the form for the account, and look up the phone number on that form. This scenario meant that users would often have multiple windows open, which contributed to a sometimes confusing user experience.

Some system administrators solved this issue by creating customer phone number fields on the case form, then using a process like workflow or JavaScript to copy the phone number from the customer to the case. While this solved the first issue, it create a second, worse issue. By copying the same data to multiple records, you violate good data practices. Any data should only have one home. When the contact changes her phone number, the cases that contain that phone number are not updated, so someone who opened that case and called the client would not reach her.

Quick view forms allow you to embed a miniature copy of a record into the form of a related record. The quick view form is tied to a lookup field, so when a value is selected in the lookup field, the related record quick view form is displayed in line on the form. This is seen below in the Account Card quick view.

The following figure shows the Account Quick View form open in the form designer.

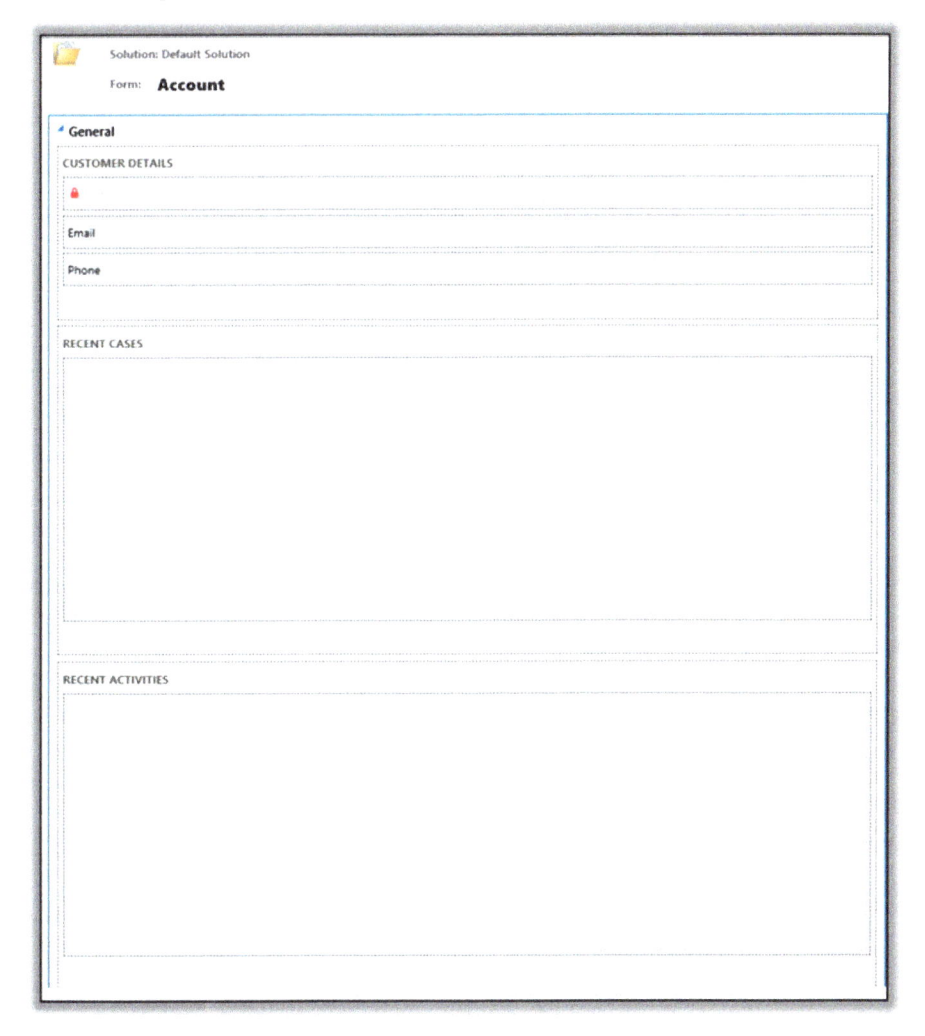

The following figure shows how the quick view form – highlighted in this example at the right side of the case form -- appears to the user.

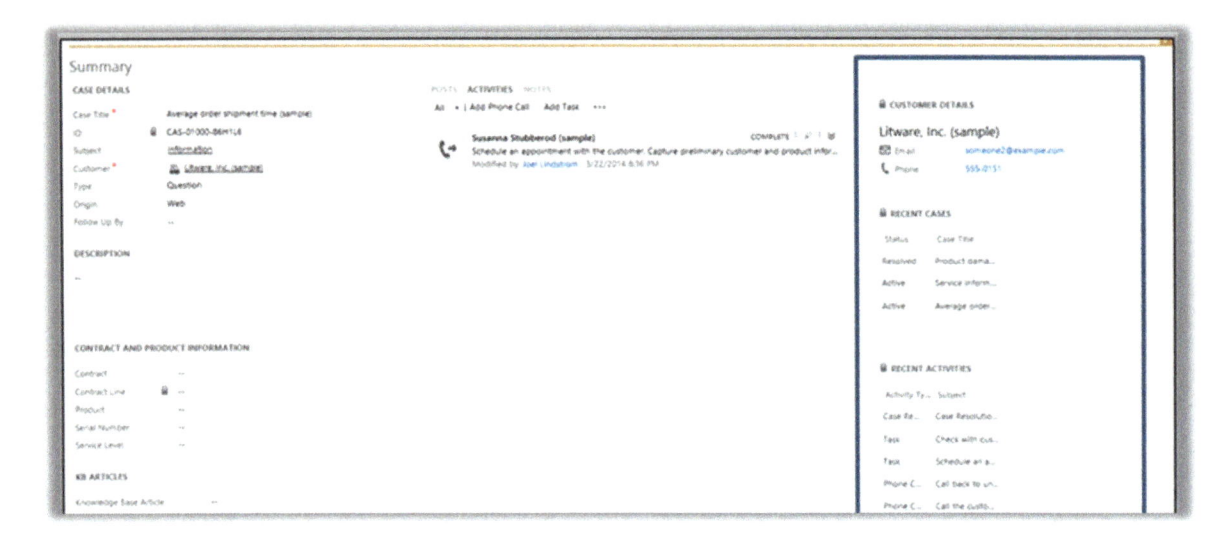

Important things to know about Quick View forms

- Quick View forms can contain sub-grids. Records displayed in the sub-grid can be opened, just like sub-grids on the main form.
- Email and phone format field hyperlinks work, just like on the main form.
- Quick view forms are read only.

Quick view forms eliminate most requirements to copy related entity data. They also have several unexpected and useful applications.

For example, want to have a filtered sub-grid of activities related to the parent customer on an opportunity? This can be very useful, so an account manager working on an opportunity can see the other sales activities related to the customer. But what if you have some opportunities linked to accounts and others linked to contacts?

Simply create a quick view form in both the contact and account entities. In these forms, only insert a sub-grid of related activities. Insert both quick view forms into the opportunity form. Now when you link the opportunity to a contact or you link the opportunity to an account, the appropriate list of related activities will appear. Since the quick view form only contains a sub-grid of activities, it will appear to users just like any other sub-grid.

Creating Quick View Forms

1. Go to Customization
2. Click to expand the "Entity" node
3. Click to expand the desired entity to customize
4. Click "Forms"

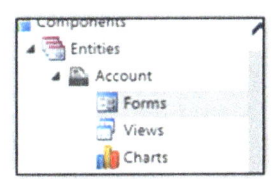

5. Click "New" and select "Quick View Form"

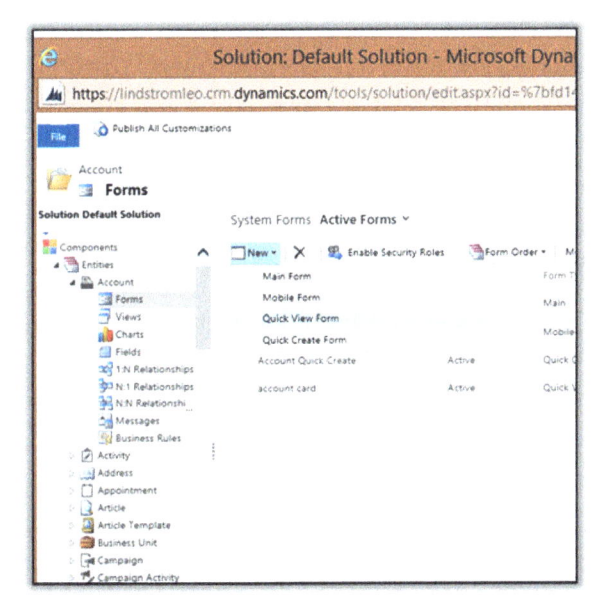

6. Add desired fields and sub-grid to the Quick View Form, then save and publish.

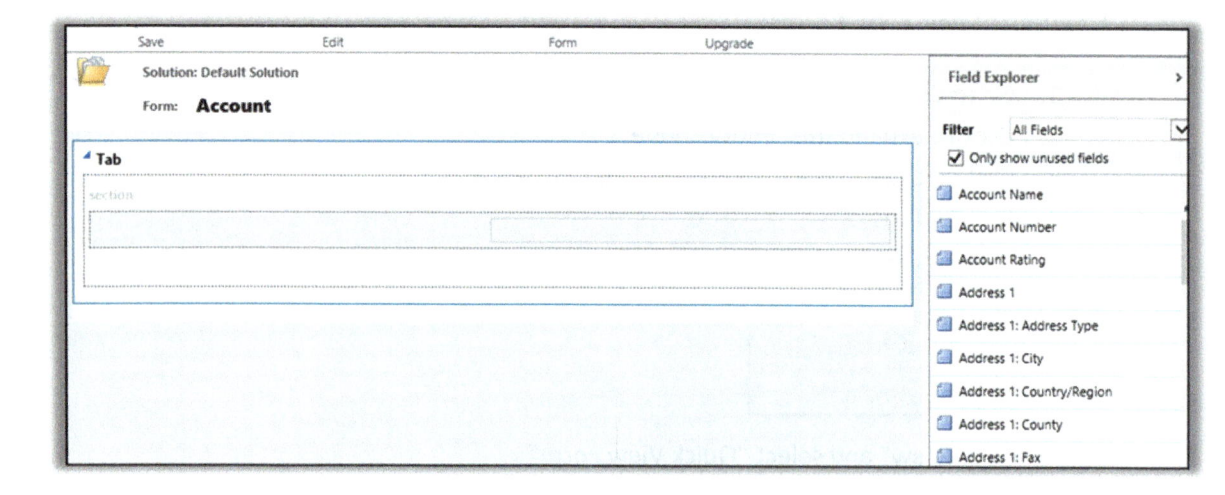

Once you have published your new Quick View form, navigate to the form customization for the entity form that you want to embed your new Quick View form into. Remember, this form must contain a lookup field for the entity for which the Quick View form was created.

In this example, we are going to add the Account Quick View form to the contact entity. The Contact has the Parent Customer field, which looks up to Accounts.

Navigate to the Contact entity customization and select the "Contact" form customization.

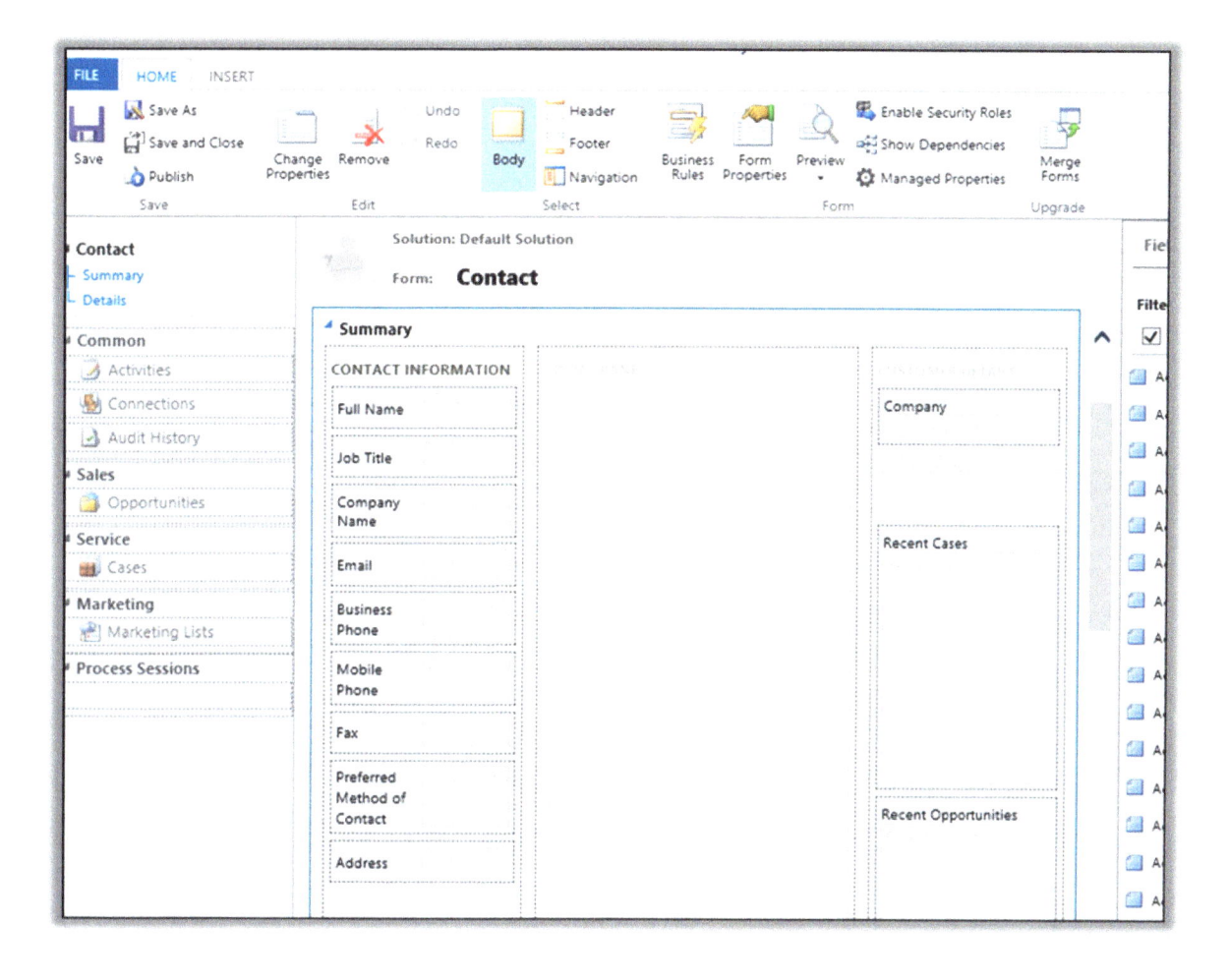

Select the section of the form where you wish to add your Account Quick Create form and click the "Insert" tab of the form ribbon on the top.

CRM 2013 Quick Start

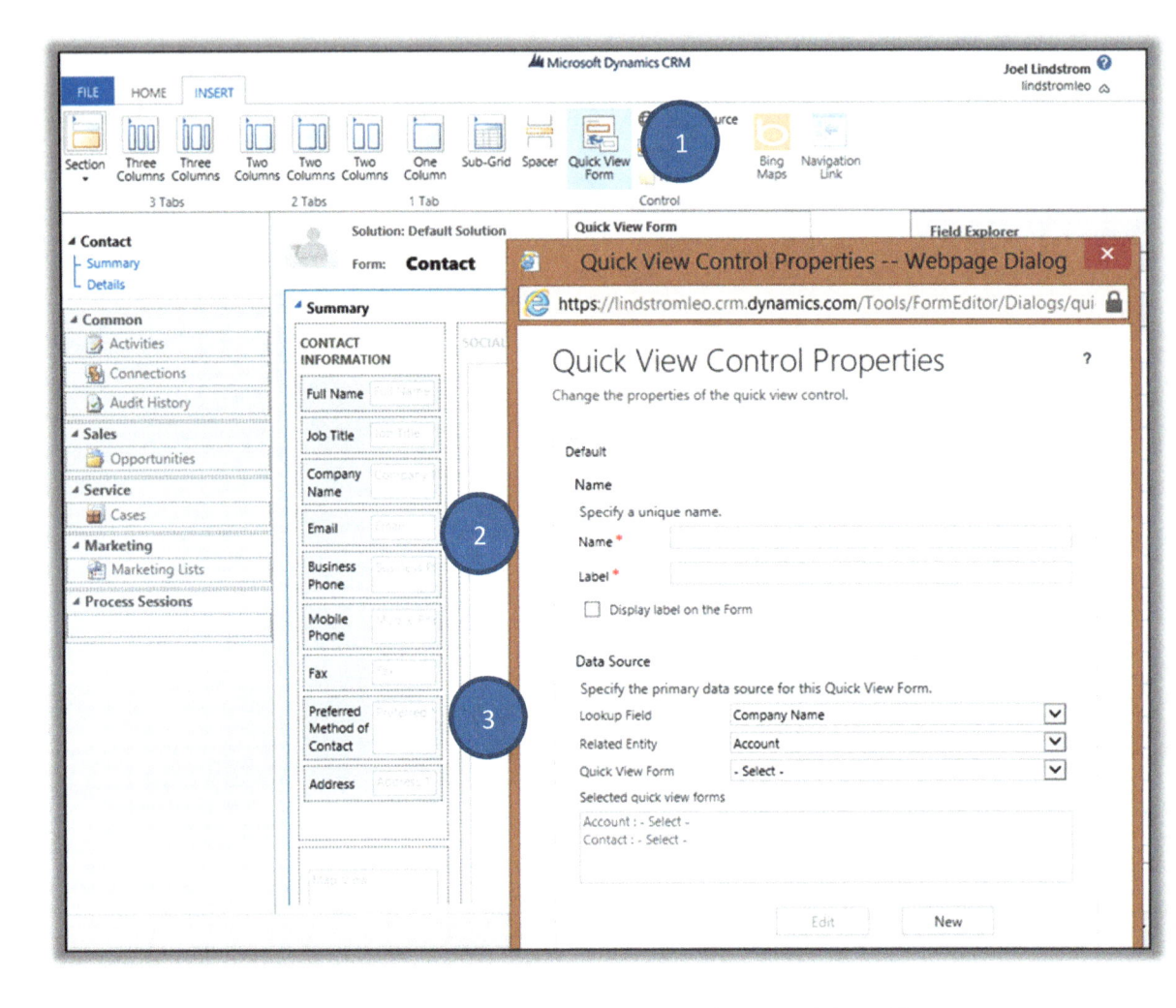

1. Click the "Quick View Form" button from the "Insert" menu of the ribbon.
2. Give the embedded quick view form a name and label. This is the name of the section on the form. The name cannot contain spaces
3. Select the lookup field to link to the Quick View form, and select the related entity and the quick view form for that entity that you wish to display on the form.

Quick Create Forms

Quick Create Forms are a new form type that allow you to quickly create a related record in-line in the form you are on. This allows for quick data entry without losing context of where you are in CRM. For example, if you are on an account, and you wish to add a related opportunity, you can click the '+' on the opportunity sub-grid and create a related opportunity without leaving the

Account form. Note that the behavior of the '+' button on sub-grids may behave differently based on certain settings. See the "working with sub-grids" section of this chapter for more details.

You can also click the "Create" button on top CRM web client user interface to launch a quick create form. Note—when you create a record from the create button on the top, it will not be automatically related to the record you are viewing—this only happens when you create the record from a sub-grid or record navigation bar.

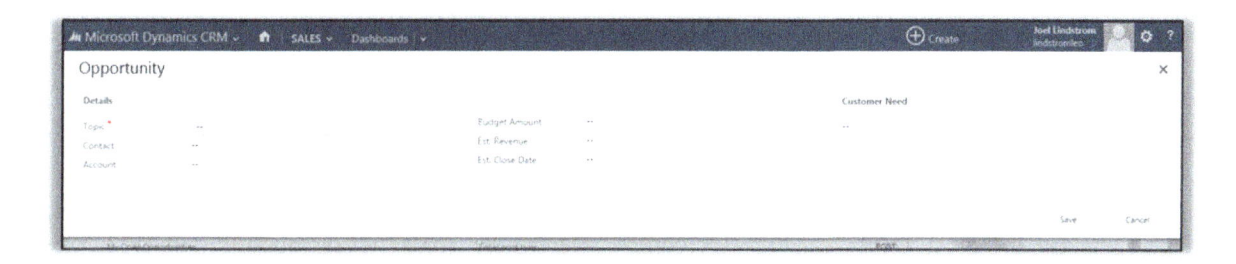

Important things to know about Quick Create forms

- Quick Create Forms are role based, just like any other form. Users will see the highest quick create form for which their security role has been given permission.
- Quick create forms are limited to one three column section
- Quick create forms cannot contain sub-grids, iframes, or embedded web resources.
- Quick create forms can have javascript web resources and form javascript events
- Records created with quick create forms will trigger workflows.
- Quick create forms do not include the button to associate business rules with Quick Create forms, but business rules can apply to Quick Create forms. If the Business Rule has a scope of "All Forms" and the Quick Create form includes all of the fields referenced in the Business Rule, the Business rule will apply to the Quick Create Form.
- Remember that Quick Create must be enabled at the entity level (by selecting the Allow quick create option discussed in the New Entity Definition Options section above). It is not enabled by default for custom entities.

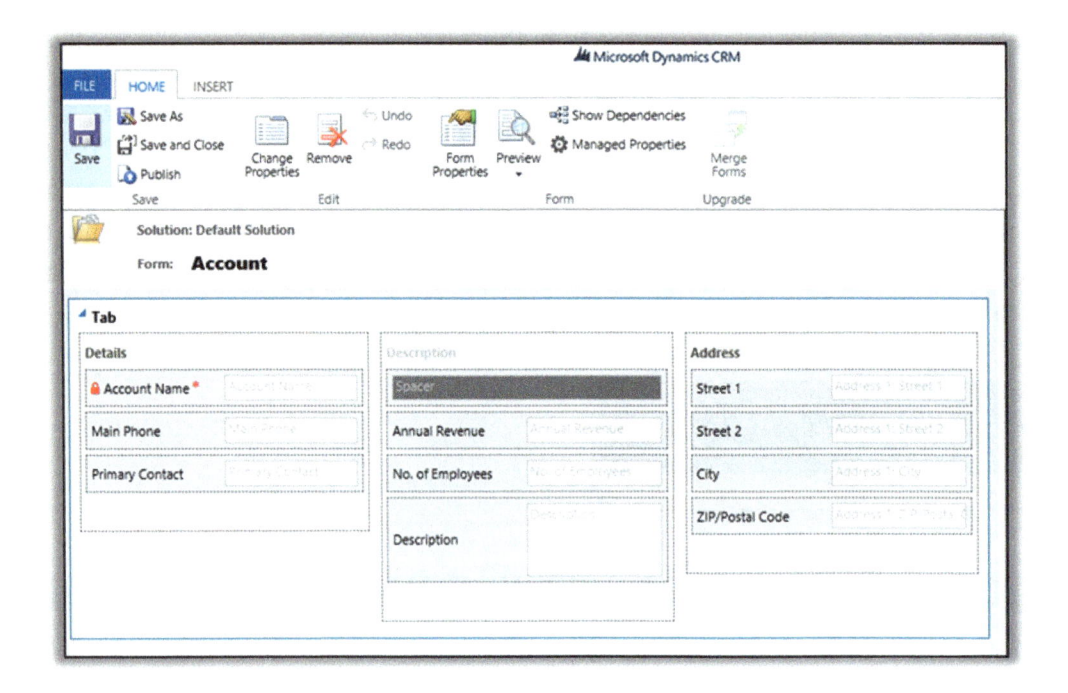

Activity Quick Forms

There are another type of Quick form in Dynamics CRM 2013 that is only found in the Phone Call and Task entities. This form is called the "Quick Form."

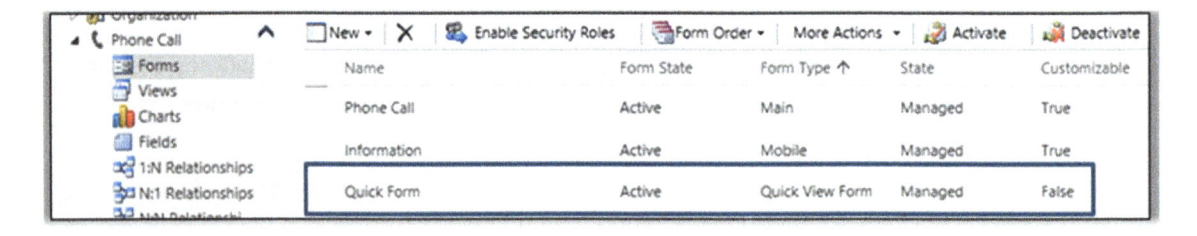

This form has confused some users because it is listed as a Quick View Form, but it does not work like a typical Quick View Form. It is not configurable. No fields can be added or removed from it.

This form is the form used by the new activity/notes pane control on CRM 2013 forms. When you click the "Add phone call" or "Add task" link on the activity pane, this form opens in line with the activity pane, making it very easy to enter a basic activity.

CRM 2013 Quick Start

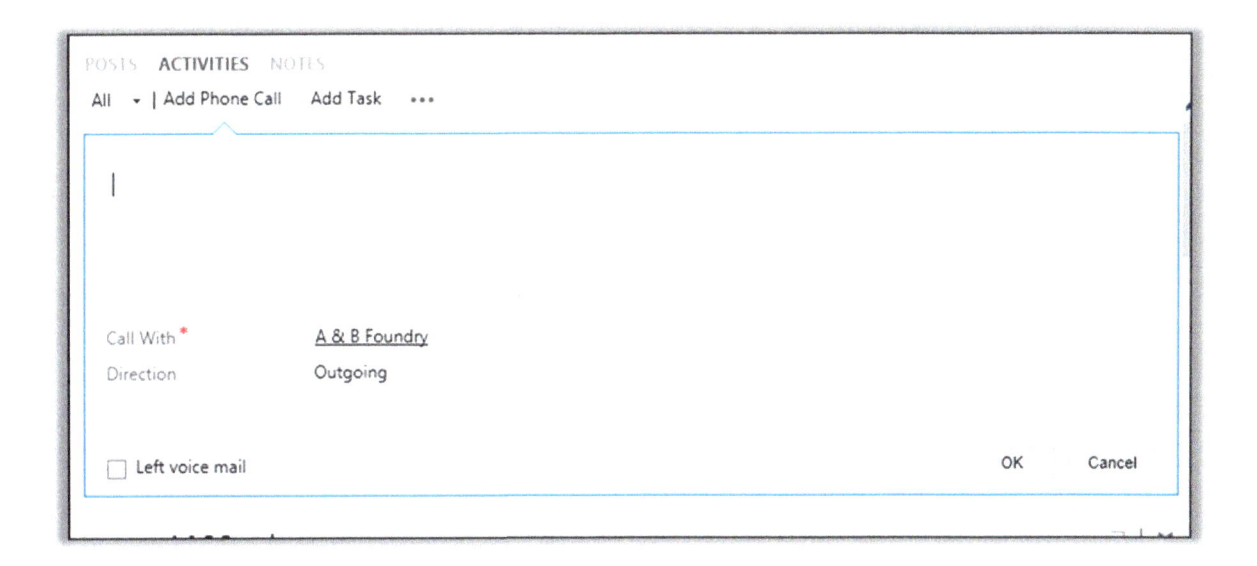

[Screenshot of an activity quick create form showing POSTS, ACTIVITIES, NOTES tabs with Add Phone Call and Add Task options. Fields shown: Call With* "A & B Foundry", Direction "Outgoing", checkbox "Left voice mail", with OK and Cancel buttons.]

So while this form is listed as a Quick View form in customization, it works like a Quick Create form, but it really is neither. If you click the phone call button under the Quick Create button on the top of the web user interface, you will get the full phone call form, not the quick create form.

Activity entities in Dynamics CRM 2013 cannot have Quick Create Forms. From customization, the application will allow you to create Quick Create forms for activity entities, but the checkbox to enable Quick Create is unavailable to be selected from the General tab of an activity entity. So you can create a Quick Create form, but you cannot enable it.

What's New With Fields

When you add custom fields, you will notice that Microsoft Dynamics CRM 2013 includes some new field data types, such as Telephone Format, and Image Data Type.

Telephone format

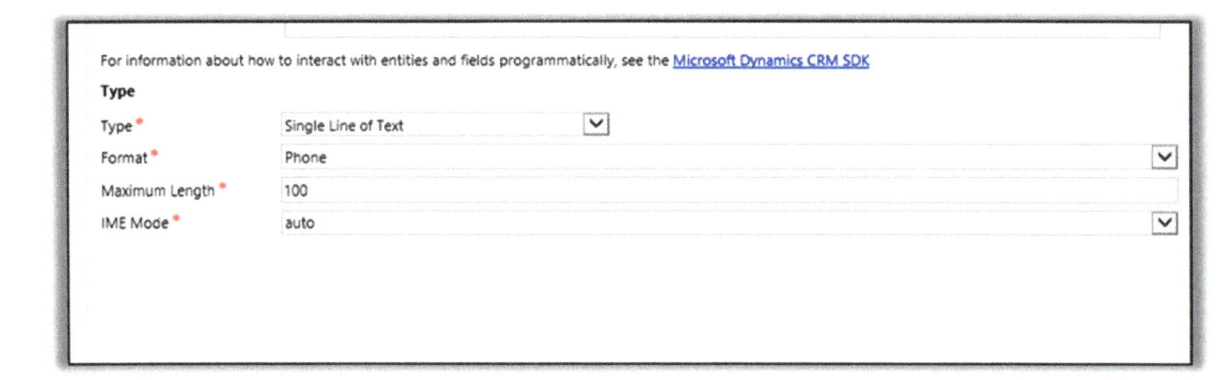

You can now designate a text field as "phone" format. Note, this does not mean that it will format the number and insert dashes or parenthesis. This means that the field will be enabled for click to dial.

When clicked, phone fields can dial the number using either Skype or Lync, as long as the client is installed on the computer. Some third party telephony integrations can also override this to have the call go through the third party telephone system.

Field format and data type cannot be changed after the phone is created. If you have an existing field that you wish to make phone format, create a new field and move the existing field data to the new field.

To specify whether to use Lync or Skype when a phone field is clicked, go to Settings→Administration→System Settings.

On the General tab, specify Lync or Skype under "Set the Telephony Provider."

When you click on a phone field in a grid or a form, a dialog will appear confirming that you wish to call the number with Skype or Lync. By hitting allow, your selected telephone provider will dial the number.

Image Data Type

Another new type of field is image.

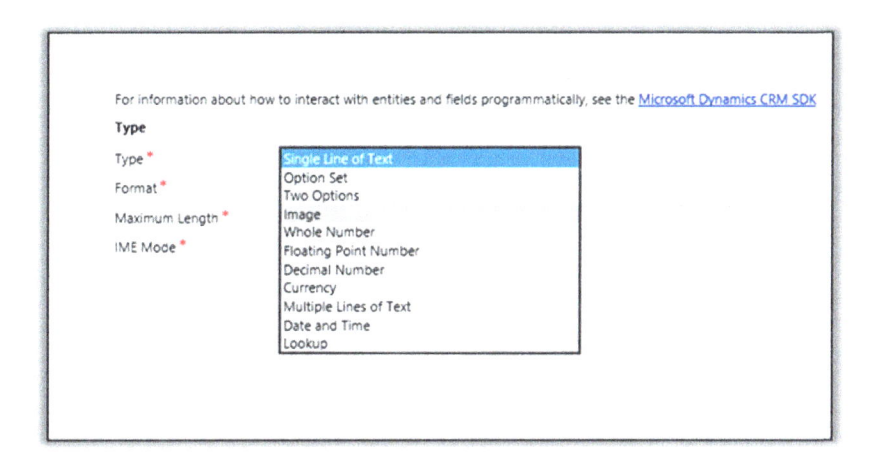

Important things to know about using image data type

- The image field type is designed to provide a single image per record.
- You cannot add more than one image field to an entity. This is not the solution for a collection of images tied to a record.
- The schema name of the attribute is hard coded to "entityimage." This cannot be changed.
- Image type fields can be added to any custom entity.
- Image type fields are only available from the following system entities:
    - Account

- Competitor
- Contact
- Lead
- Product
- Publisher
- Resource
- User
- The image data can be retrieved via the SDK, so you can use the images for other application uses, such as SSRS reports.

Enabling Image Type Fields on an entity

Once you have added your image type field to your custom entity, the next thing to do is enable it on the entity.

Go to the General tab of the Entity definition in System Customization

Set the "Primary Image" field to the name of the image field you defined for the entity.

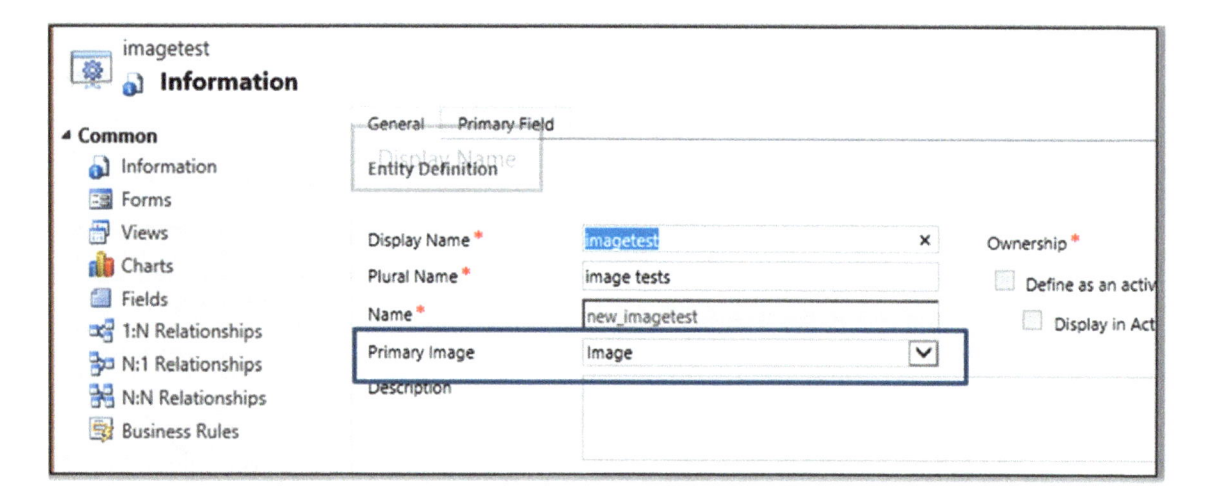

Adding images to records

Now that you have enabled the entity for images, you can now add images to records. The entity for the image will be displayed by the record name.

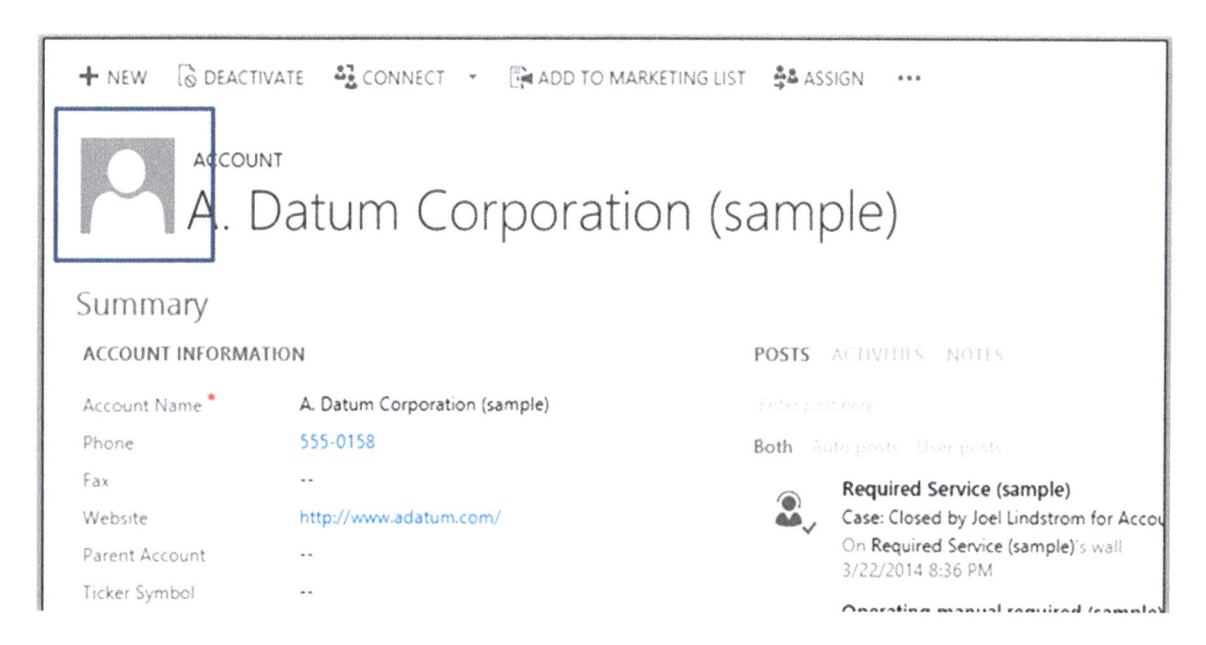

To change the record image, click on the image field to launch the "Edit image" dialog.

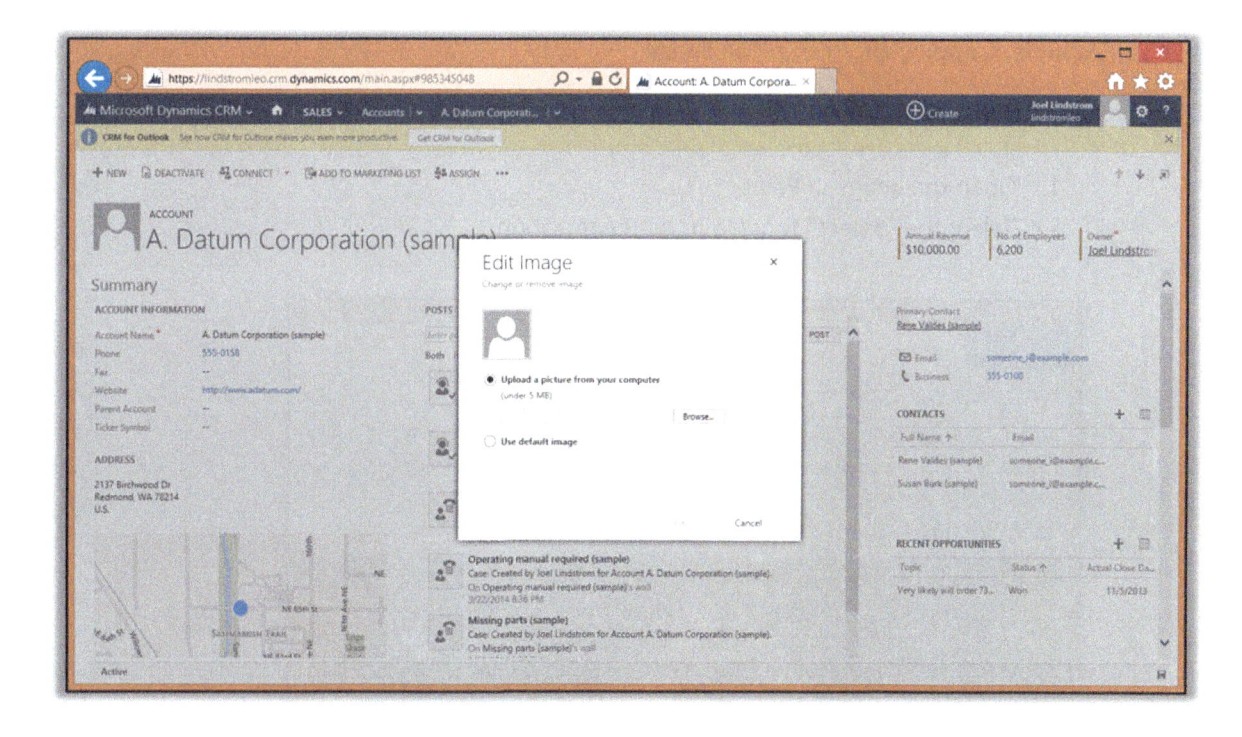

Browse to upload a file, then click OK.

Image sizing recommendations

Images must be in one of the following formats:

bmp

jpg/jpeg

gif

tif

tiff

png

Images will be reformatted to jpg format and resized to 144 px X 144 px when you upload them. It is a best practice to resize the images manually before uploading them, to verify that they will look good after they are uploaded.

Example: cropping and resizing an image

Using the Paint program on any Windows PC, you can resize any image to the appropriate size.

1. Open the image in Paint
2. Select the "Select" tool from the Paint ribbon

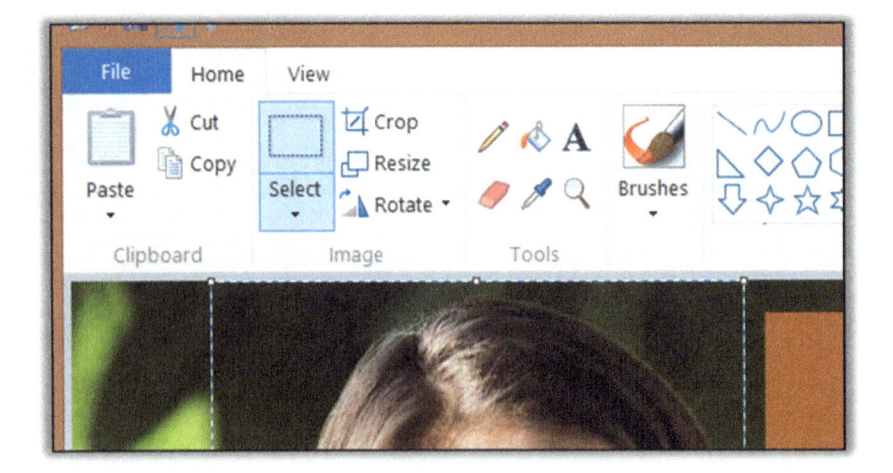

3. Click the upper left hand corner of the section of the image you wish to make your record image. Drag the mouse down and to the left to select the image.

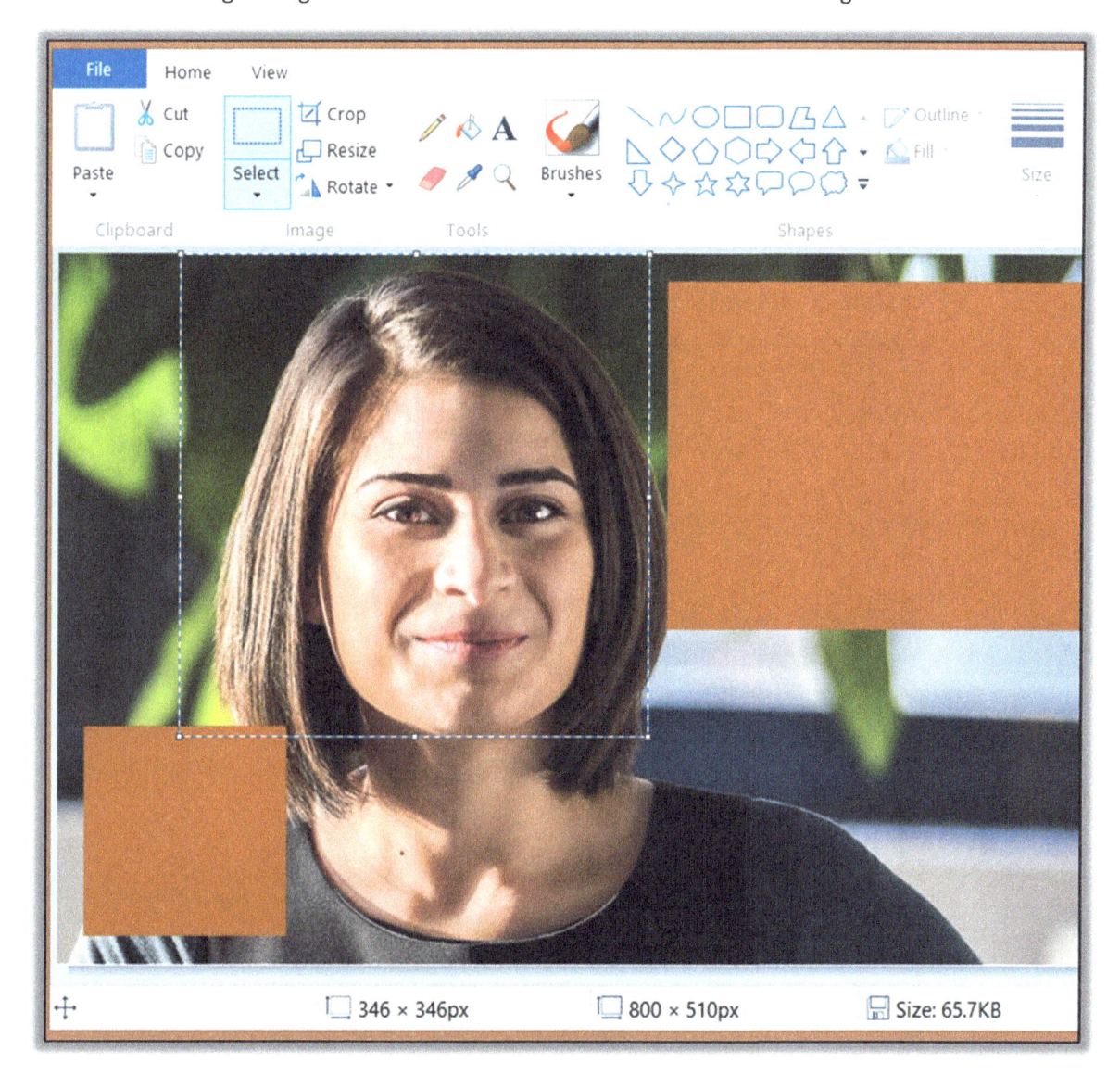

4. Underneath the image you will see the dimensions of the selection. Select an area that has the same number of pixels horizontally and vertically.
5. Click the "crop" button in the paint ribbon.

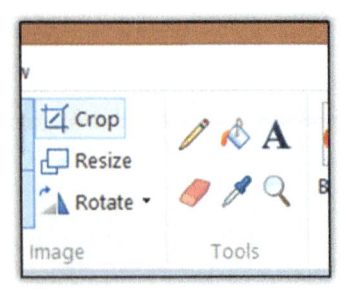

6. Click "Resize"
7. In the Resize and Skew dialog, change "Resize by" to "pixels," and enter 144 for horizontal and vertical, then click OK.

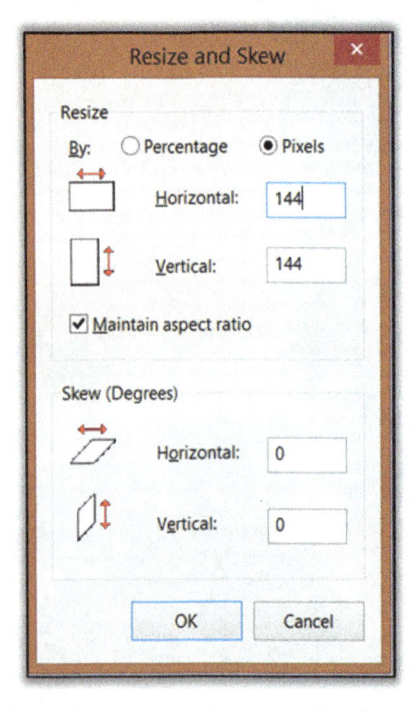

8. Save the cropped image as jpg format, then upload to the appropriate CRM record.

Adding Help Text to Fields

Dynamics CRM has always included a "Description" field on the field definition, but that description has traditionally only been visible in customization area.

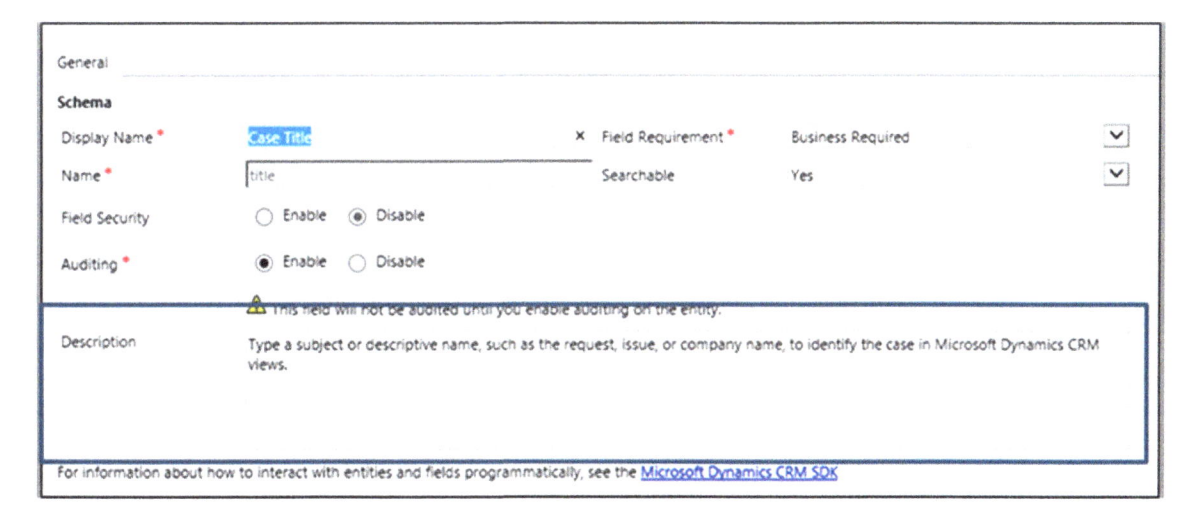

In Dynamics CRM 2013, these field descriptions become much more valuable, as they now are surfaced as tool tip help for fields on forms.

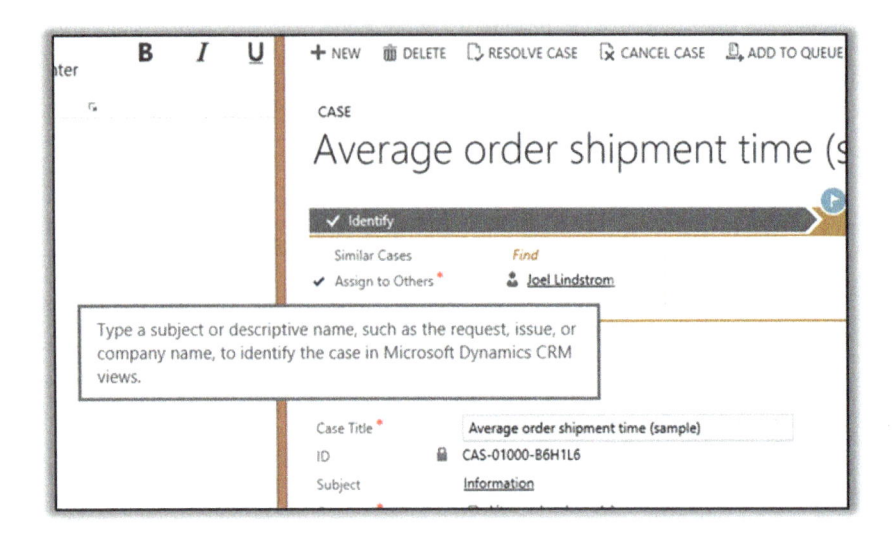

Tool tip help text is displayed to users when they hover their mouse over the field label, or tap on the label when using tablet browser or CRM for Tablets.

To change the tooltip help text, simply edit the description of the field in customization and publish.

Want to update tool tip help text in bulk? MVP Jerry Weinstock from CRM Innovation has written a great tool that allows you to easily modify multiple field tool tips without having to navigate to each field individually.

You can request this free solution here: http://www.crminnovation.com/blog/crm-2013-tool-tip-manager/.

Form customization in Dynamics CRM 2013

The form has seen some major changes in Dynamics CRM 2013. Traditionally, CRM forms have had a two column design, split into sections and tabs. Navigation bar and ribbon were displayed at all times.

Dynamics CRM 2013 shakes things up by minimizing the navigation bar and ribbon. This frees up much additional real estate, and the system forms take advantage of this additional space by defaulting to 3 columns wide, with multiple tabs and sections horizontally.

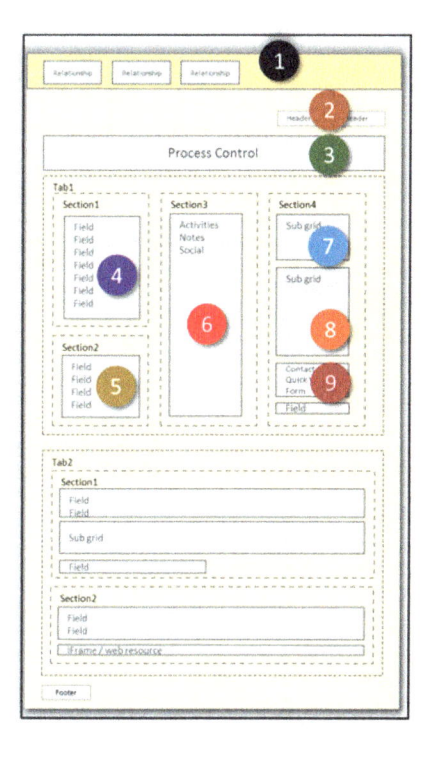

1. Navigation bar moves to a drop-down menu on the top of the form. This frees up space on the form while making the navigation to related entities available when needed. Note—when customizing a form, the navigation bar is still displayed on the left side like it was in 2011; however, keep in mind that users won't see the navigation bar unless they click the drop-down arrow.
2. Form header displays fields at the top of the form, like it did in CRM 2011; however, now the header is editable, as long as there are no more than four fields in the header.
3. The business process flow (if enabled for this entity) is displayed on the top of the form.
4. The most important information (like name, account number) are displayed on the upper left section of the form.
5. Supplemental information, such as address and phone number are displayed in the second section of the form.
6. The Activity/note pane is displayed in the middle section. This makes activities, notes, and social posts readily available to users. For more details on the notes/activity pane, see the "new form component" section later in this chapter.

7-9. The right side of the form displays related entity sub-grids and less important fields.

Responsive User Interface

Dynamics CRM 2013 user interface is a responsive UI. This means that the form will resize based on the dimensions of your screen. If viewed on a computer with a large monitor, you will see 3 columns wide. If viewed on an iPad in Safari in portrait mode, the sections will reposition themselves to fit the screen.

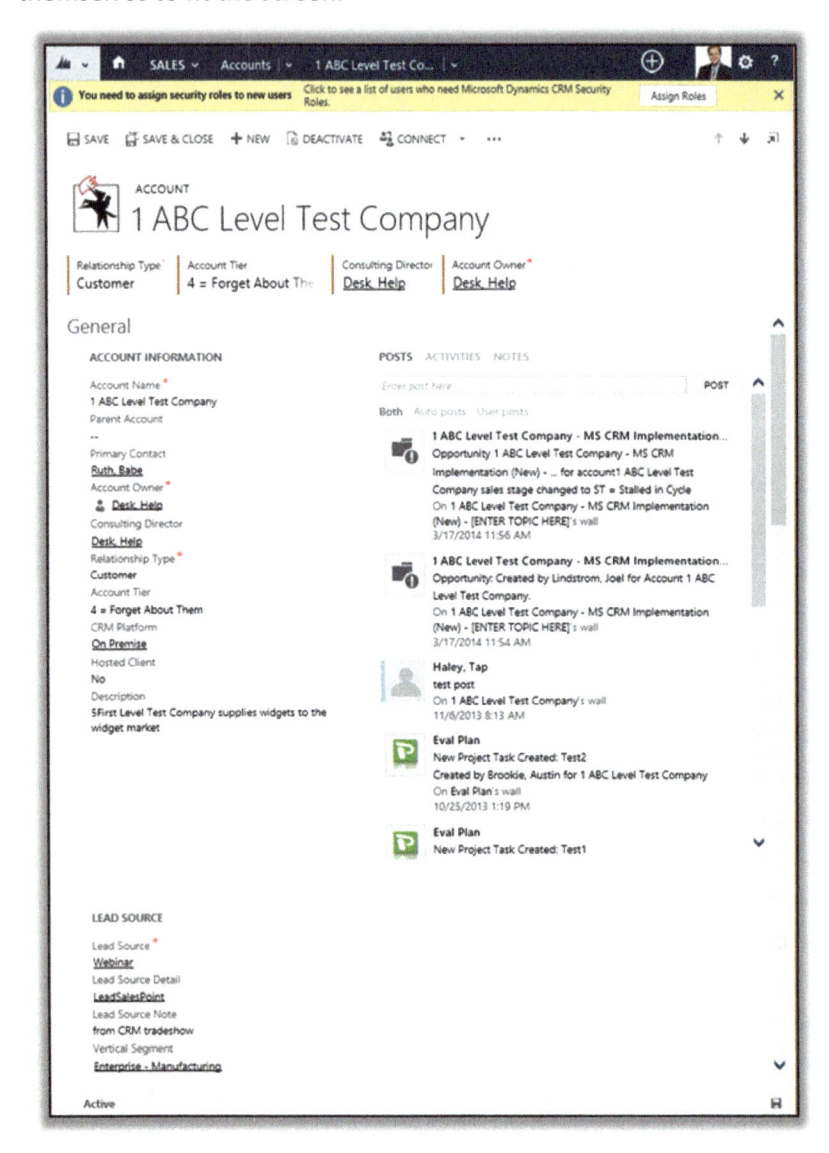

When the window is smaller, the sections on the right side move down under the left columns. This makes Dynamics CRM 2013 usable on virtually any size screen. However, it also means that you will want to take this into consideration as you configure your forms and verify that the sections are arranged as desired based on the screen resolution that your users will be using to access CRM.

Form Configuration Best Practices

The form customizer has more flexibility than ever before with the new Dynamics CRM 2013 user interface. It is more important than ever that you follow best practices when configuring forms to deliver optimal usability to your users.

- Try to keep your form layouts consistent. Don't like having the notes/activity pane in the center of the form? That's ok, just make sure that it is in the same area on all of the main forms that your users use regularly. Having dramatically different form layouts will hinder user adoption.
- Configuring sections to place field labels above the field is generally preferable to having field labels on the left side of the field. Studies have shown that placement of labels on top of text fields makes the form more readable, as users do not have to move their eyes as much to read the form.
In Dynamics CRM 2013, since the standard layout displays 3 columns wide, each column has slightly less horizontal space, so if columns are displayed to the left of the field, if the label text is lengthy, it may be truncated.

To set the field label orientation, in Form Customization, select the section and click "Change Properties" in the ribbon.

On the "Section Properties" dialog, select the formatting tab. At the bottom of the dialog, you will see the "Field Label Properties" section. Select "Top" then click "OK" to change the field labels to appear above the fields in the section.

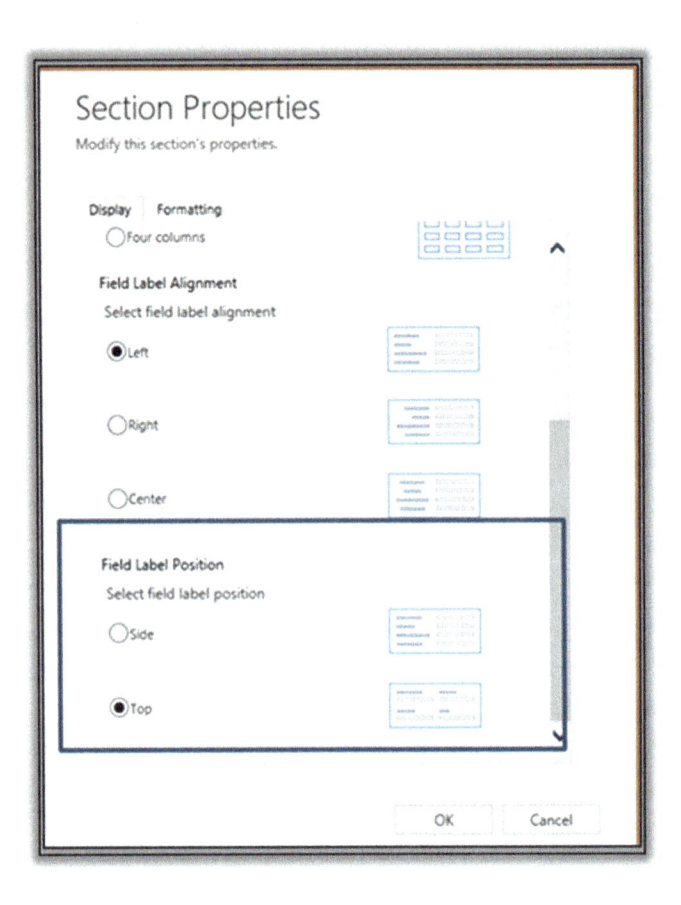

Whether you use top or side position labels, it is important to use the same position for all fields on a form to maintain a consistent user experience.

- Since the navigation bar is hidden, and the tab navigation links are not displayed, navigating long forms can require users to scroll. If the form is very long, a good way to make the form easier to navigate for users is to collapse all tabs other than the main tab. This will make the most important visible to all users when the form opens, and they can then easily click the tab that they want to go to (making it similar to the user experience of CRM 2011 navigation links).

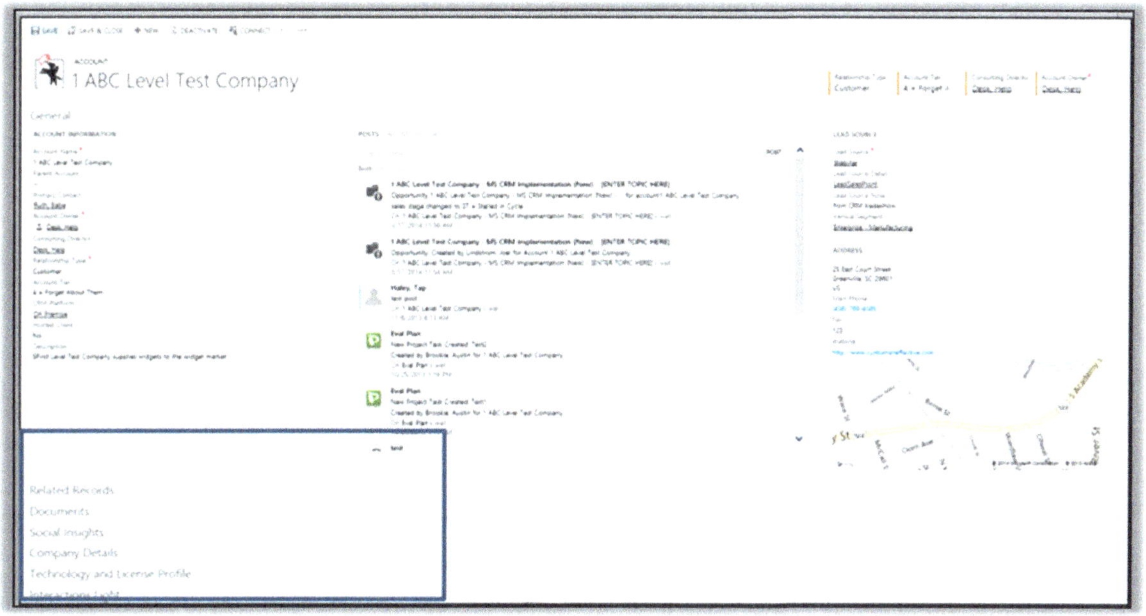

- If you use many sub-grids or embedded web resources, placing them inside of collapsed tabs will make the form open faster, as contents of collapsed tabs are not rendered until the tab is expanded.

Working with Sub-grids in CRM 2013

CRM 2011 introduced sub-grids in forms as a convenient way to work with related records.

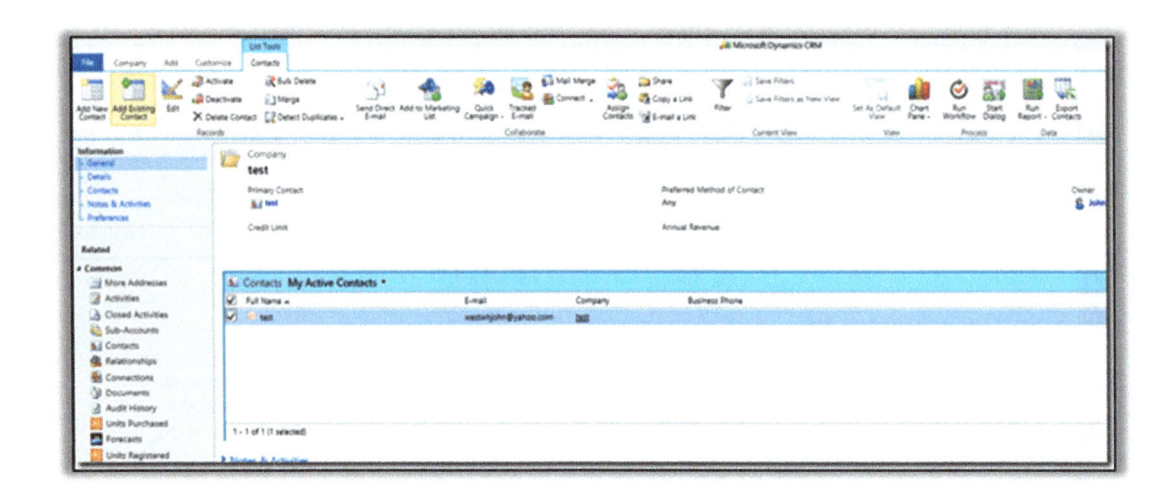

When a user clicked on the sub-grid the ribbon menu would change to the ribbon for the entity in the sub-grid. This provided the full menu for the related entity in context of the parent entity form, which was great for power users when they needed those options.

However, it also meant that there were many buttons on the ribbon, and depending on where you clicked, the ribbon would change. Some users were confused by the changing ribbon and clicked buttons for a sub-grid ribbon when they meant to select the button on the form ribbon.

In Microsoft Dynamics CRM 2013, the sub-grid evolves following the simplified design themes you see elsewhere in the application. Like command bars and sitemaps, the sub-grid menus are designed to be there when you need them but get out of the way when you don't.

ACCOUNT
1 ABC Level Test Company
Related Records
Related Contacts
Active Contacts Subgrid View
Full Name
Business Phone...
Mobile Phone
Email
Aaron, Ha...
(864) 250-2170
(864) 414-4665
scott_millwood@yahoo...
Cheese, C...
(555) 123-6543
lindstrom@live.com
Contact 3, Test
(888) 888-8000
DiMaggio, Joe
Garr, Ralph
(888) 888-8000
Johnson, Barn...
Johnson, Dena

In CRM 2013, the sub-grid menu is minimized, with only the "add new" button displayed, along with a button that looks like a spreadsheet. This provides a simple interface for users that just need to view the records in the sub-grid.

For power users, all of the options that you are used to are still there. Simply click the second button to open the full grid.

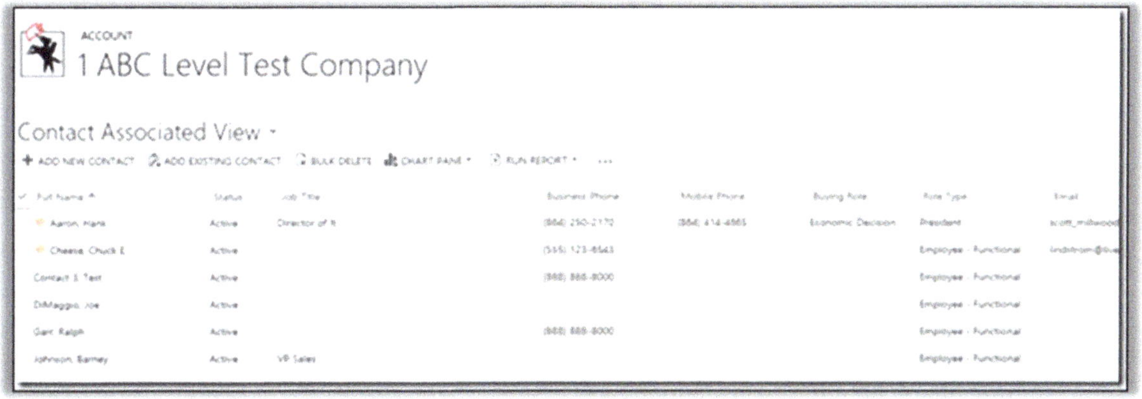
ACCOUNT
1 ABC Level Test Company
Contact Associated View

You now have the options to export the grid to Excel, view a chart, or run a report. In the same amount of clicks as clicking on the sub-grid and then clicking the ribbon button in CRM 2011 you can pop the grid out and select the button from the command bar in CRM 2013. You can then click the "back" button (or your keyboard backspace key) to go back to the form.

This design simplifies your forms while still providing power users what they need for managing related records. So if someone asks you "where did my (insert name of button) button go?" The answer is, "It is still there."

Controlling the behavior of sub-grid '+' button

In Dynamics CRM 2013 you can add a record to a sub-grid on a form by clicking the + button in the upper right hand corner. You will notice that for some sub-grids you will get a lookup field, while others will give you a new record form.

The reason for this different behavior is that the new button (+) can either function as "add new" or "add existing." For example, when you are adding an opportunity, you probably will want to have the new button create a new opportunity, while when adding a contact to an account, you may want to have the user select from an existing list of contacts (or search existing first, then add a new one).

To control the behavior of the new record button on sub-grids, look at the child entity being selected in the sub-grid. If the lookup field for the parent is required, the user will get a "new record" form when clicking the + button (or "Quick Create" if the entity is enabled for Quick Create). If the lookup field for the parent entity is not required on the child entity, the user will get the lookup field to "add existing."

If you don't want to make the lookup field required, you can still force the '+' button to "add new" behavior by editing the child entity sub-grid command bar and hiding the "add existing" button. This can be done using the Develop1 Ribbon Workbench for Dynamics CRM, available here: http://www.develop1.net/public/page/Ribbon-Workbench-for-Dynamics-CRM-2011.aspx.

Mobile considerations

Dynamics CRM 2013 mobile options are covered in detail in the "CRM on the Road" chapter of this book. There are a few items that you need to keep in mind as you configure your forms if users will be accessing Dynamics CRM via the CRM for Tablets app.

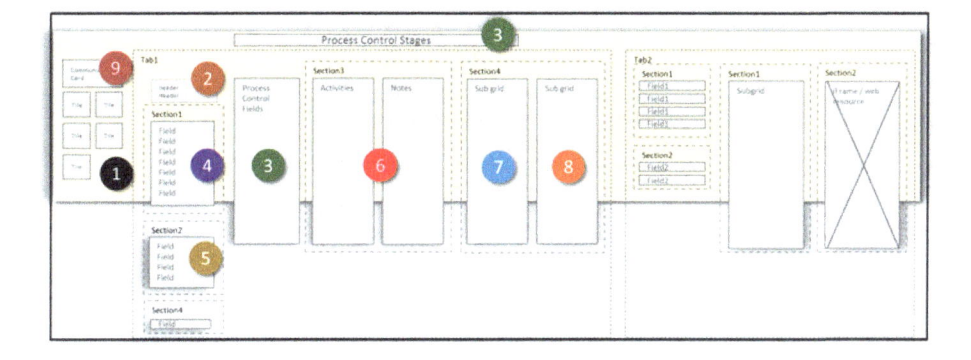

- CRM for tablets does not display the full form. It will display the first 75 fields or first five tabs. Anything beyond that will not be rendered by the tablet app.
- JavaScript events, Form Business Rules, and Workflows all work with CRM for tablets
- Embedded web resources and iframes are not rendered
- Forms are rendered in HTML 5. Several hundred records are cached, and can be viewed in read only mode when disconnected.
- Apps are currently available for Windows 8.1 and IOS (iPad). Android tablet support is expected mid 2014.

When configuring CRM for Tablets, it is important to know if users will be accessing the entity via the tablet app (and a safe assumption is that at some point, the answer will be yes).

Place the most important fields in the top five tabs. If you have any on load JavaScript that needs to function correctly on the tablet app, be sure that any tabs or fields referenced in the script fall within the top 75 fields or five tabs.

Alternatively, if you wish to make a script only run when not viewed in the tablet app, you can use Xrm.Page.context.client.getClient() in your script to get the client type. If Xrm.Page.context.client.getClient() = "Mobile," it is the tablet app.

New Form Components

Dynamics CRM 2013 includes some new form components. In this section, we describe how to use them.

Bing Maps

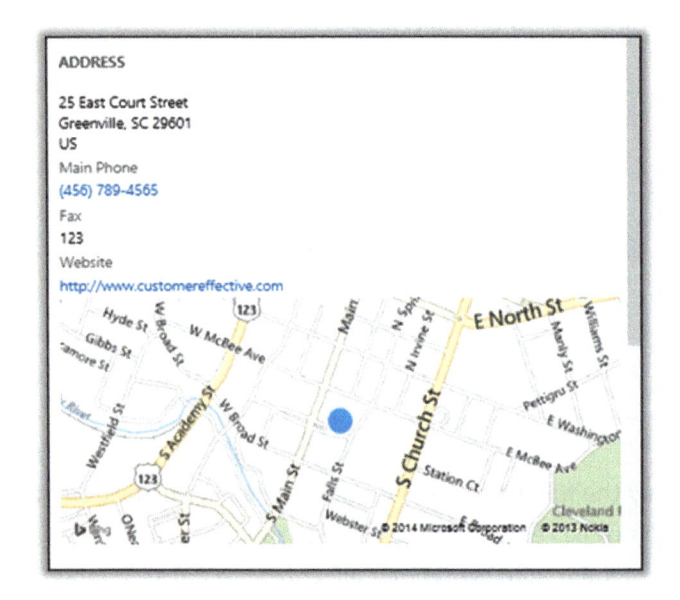

Bing Maps integration is available from a limited number of system entities, including Accounts, Contacts, and Leads. The standard Bing Maps integration cannot be added to custom entities, but it can be removed from the system entity forms if you wish to disable it.

Bing Maps can be added to custom entities via JavaScript using the SDK, or through a third party add on, such as Power Objects PowerMaps. http://www.powerobjects.com/add-on-subscriptions/powerpack/powermap/

Notes/Activity Pane

As mentioned earlier, Microsoft Dynamics CRM includes a consolidated Notes/Activity pane that displays activities (both open and closed), Notes, and Activity Feed posts.

CRM 2013 Quick Start

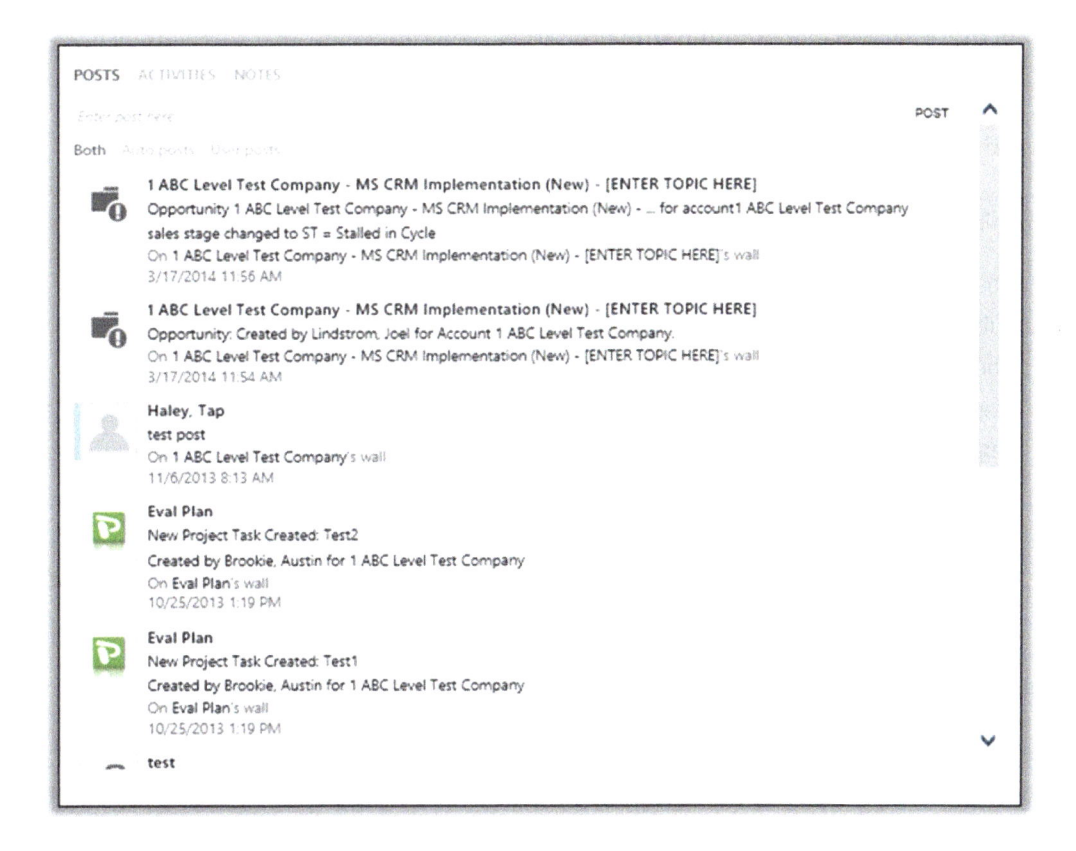

[Screenshot of Posts/Activities/Notes pane showing multiple posts including "1 ABC Level Test Company - MS CRM Implementation (New)" entries, "Haley, Tap" test post, and "Eval Plan" project task entries.]

Important things to know about the activity pane

- The posts/Activites/Notes section will only show up if these items are enabled for the entity. For example, if an entity is not enabled for Activity Feeds, you will not see the "Posts" link.
- The Activities section shows both open and closed activities and displays related regarding record activities as well.
- Quick Activity forms for phone calls and tasks make entry of activities very quick without navigation to a new form.
- The Activity Pane is enabled by default on most system entities. For custom entities, it can be added manually. In the form customization ribbon it is called "Notes Control."

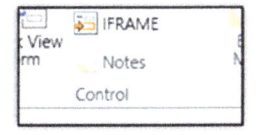

[Screenshot of ribbon showing IFRAME and Notes Control options.]

~ 113 ~

- In the Activity pane/Notes Control properties, you can define which pane is displayed by default when the form opens (Posts, Activities, or Notes).

Why use the Activity pane

There are some very compelling reasons to use the activity pane:

- The activity pane saves significant space on the form when compared to having separate sub-grids for notes, activities, and social wall.
- The activity pane displays activities related to the record and rolls up the related regarding record activities. The CRM 2011 activity sub-grid could not display the related regarding record activities—you had to navigate to the closed activities navigation bar link.
- The activity pane activity icons are very easily selected from touch interfaces.
- Phone Call and Task Quick Forms make creating standard tasks and phone call records very quick

Why not use the Activity pane

For some scenarios, the activity pane may not provide the best user experience, and the traditional activity grids or navigation bar link may be most convenient way to manage related activities.

- You require custom fields when creating tasks or phone calls. The Activity Pane Quick Forms for Phone Call and Task cannot be customized.
- You have a high volume of activities and wish to display a higher quantity of activities on the form than can realistically be displayed with the Activity Pane.
- You wish to separate open and closed activities into separate sub-grids for organizational purposes. Some companies with activity centric sales processes have closed activity goals (like calls completed) and need to easily distinguish which activities have been completed.

Consolidated Address Field

Dynamics CRM 2013 still includes the standard address fields for entities like Accounts, Contacts, and Leads, but it also now includes a consolidated address field for Address 1 and Address 2 in each of these entities.

Behind the scenes, this field still contains the standard address fields, but it displays the address to the user in a single field, just like in Microsoft Outlook contact records.

When a user clicks on the field to edit it, they are presented with the individual address fields.

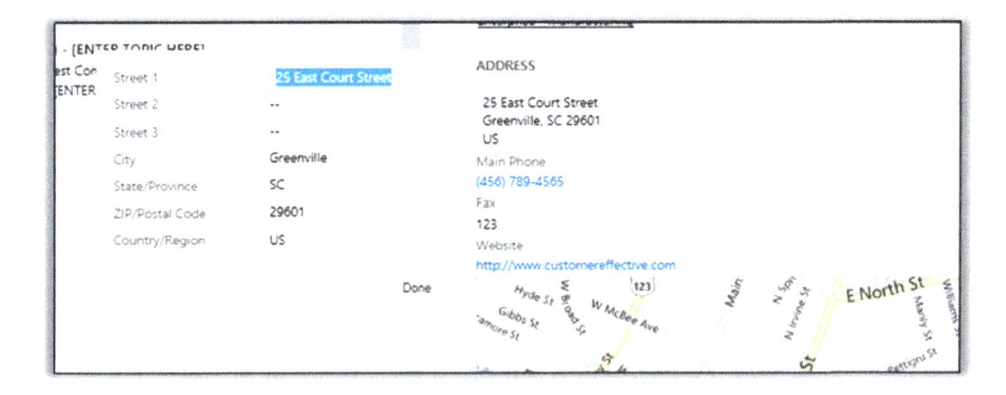

When customizing a form, the consolidated address control is presented like any other field. For each address, you will see a corresponding combined address field.

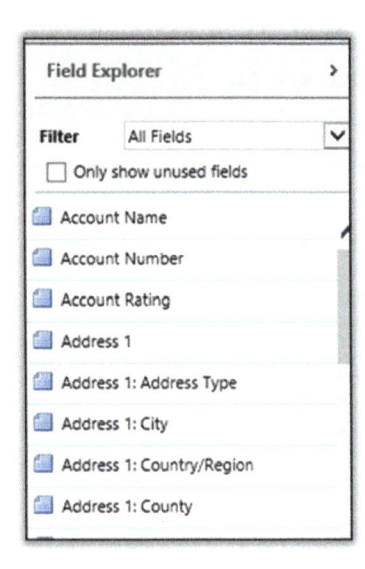

Important things to know about the combined address control

- The combined address is only available from system entities with addresses. This includes Accounts, Leads, Contacts, Competitor, and User
- The combined address cannot be added to custom entities
- You can have OnChange JavaScript or business rules on the combined address. The easiest way to do this is to add the individual address fields to the form and set them not to be visible. Then add the desired OnChange events to the individual address fields. When one of the fields is updated in the combined address, the event will fire.

Why to use the combined address fields

- The combined address fields take up significantly less space than separate individual address fields
- The combined address fields are consistent with other modern systems, such as Outlook 2013.
- The combined address fields are easier to read than separate individual address fields.

Why not to use the combined address fields

- If users like to navigate strictly by tabbing through the form when creating records, separate address fields may work more smoothly.

- If you replace the standard address fields with custom fields (such as if you make the state field a custom lookup field), the custom fields cannot be added to the combined address field, so you will most likely want to stick with separate address fields.

Upgrading forms to Dynamics CRM 2013

The process of upgrading from Dynamics CRM 2011 to Dynamics CRM 2013 is covered in detail in the upgrading chapter of this book. In this section we cover important considerations for upgrading your forms to CRM 2013.

The CRM 2013 upgrade process was designed to be non-destructive to your CRM 2011 forms. When you upgrade, most system entities will include a new form with a layout similar to the layout described earlier in this chapter. They will also still contain your legacy forms, the "Information" form.

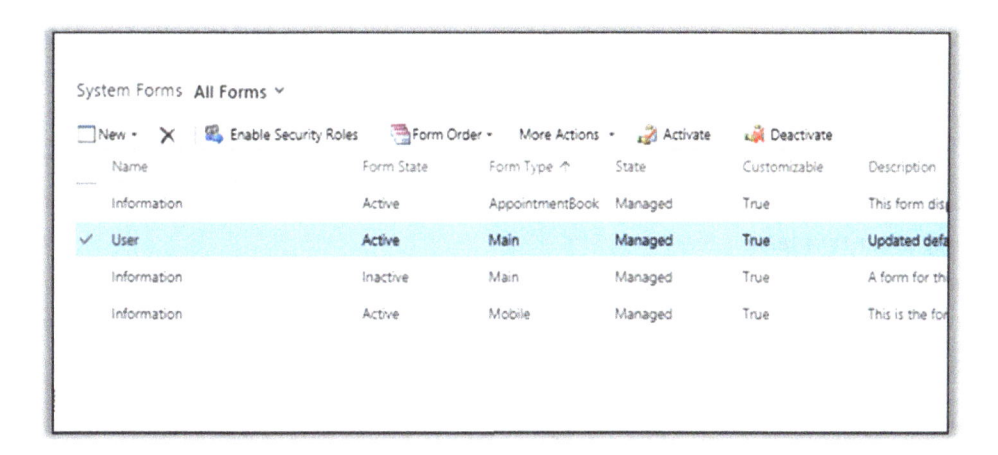

You will not be forced to switch to the new forms, but it is strongly recommended to upgrade your forms to take advantage of the new user interface. Your two-column "information" form will not make optimal usage available space.

Form upgrade and merge process

1. Save a copy of the new form. This allows you to undo the process if you mess up. Open the new form customization and click the "save as" button to save a copy.
2. From the new form customization form, click the "Merge Forms" button on the ribbon and select the "Information" form when prompted.

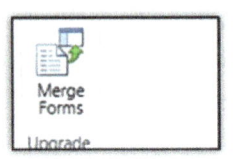

3. This will merge the contents of the legacy form in with the new form. The information form sections and header will appear below the new form sections. This process also adds and form web resource and JavaScript events to the form.
4. Remove any redundant components, such as the legacy header and any fields or sections that appear on both the legacy Information form and the new form. For example, you may have two summary sections on the form. In cases where there are two sections or tabs with the same name, remove the old information section and leave the new one. Remove redundant note and activity sections.
5. Reposition remaining tabs and sections to fit optimally in the new layout.
6. Verify web resources and javascript events are correctly associated with the form. If you have the 2011 Activity Feed web resource associated with the form OnLoad event, you can remove it (since it is now included in the Activity Pane).
7. Save and close the form.
8. Set the form to fall first in form order and verify that the form is associated with the correct security roles.
9. Once you have tested and verified that the new form works, deactivate your copy of the new form, move it to the bottom of the form order list, and remove all security roles from the form.
10. Deactivate the legacy "Information" form, move it to the bottom of the form order list, and remove all security roles from the form.

The reason I recommend not only deactivating the legacy forms but also stripping them of all security roles is because it is possible that the form may get inadvertently reactivated again. For example, if you import a managed solution from a third party that has the information form active, it can make the legacy form become active again in your environment. This could make users start to see the legacy form rather than your new form.

By removing the security roles from the form, it provides an additional layer of security against someone seeing that form again. There is no supported way to delete the legacy Information form post upgrade.

Bringing it all together

Microsoft Dynamics CRM represents a significant advancement in the Dynamics CRM user interface. We now have a modern, responsive, touch friendly UI, and an even greater number of tools in our customization bag.

To effectively use these tools we must follow best practices. Look at the layout of the system entity forms. They are configured to optimally display data that users need when they need it.

Be sure you use consistent layouts across all entities. Don't position common components in different places on different entities.

Positioning field labels on the top of fields may make your forms more readable, and the new controls for activity pane, Bing Maps, and consolidated address fields provide greater amount of information in a smaller amount of space.

Quick View form and Quick Create forms give users quick access to what they need without having to go someplace else in the application.

New field data types allow users to quickly place phone calls, personalize records with images, and display helpful tool tip text.

4

Security Model Changes

Today's global business challenges the traditional organization structure as people form dynamic teams to work on individual opportunities or other data in CRM. Securing data is a key requirement in virtually all CRM projects. Data security requirements often cover a broad spectrum of needs from just keep non-users from seeing it, all the way to complex rules that are challenging to implement in a non-dynamic security model. Architecting a security model is all about trading off and ensuring the right level of protection with the least amount of friction that slows down the user from doing their job. And of course ensuring the security design implemented doesn't slow down the system any more than necessary.

At its heart, CRM is a role based system that grants users access to data within a defined scope. Scope can be defined as large as Organization and as small as just things that a single user owns. Organizations are broken down into Business Units that have Teams, with both providing collections of users. CRM 2011 introduced the concept of team ownership of data. This new feature helped projects resolve challenges of single user ownership as well as when access needed to cross Business Unit boundaries. For purposes of this chapter we will refer to these type of teams as Owning Teams. In moderation, Team ownership of records works well, however when taken to extremes of one team per record it falls over faster than ideal.

CRM 2013 addresses that challenges with a new concept of Access Teams. Access Teams are a new feature of CRM 2013 that are in addition to the Owning Team support. Unlike Owning Teams, new Access Teams are designed simply to give users access to a record based on a template for the role they are working in. Behind the scenes CRM creates and manages a team that can dynamically have its members added and removed. In fact, the team itself is created when the first member is added and removed after the last, optimizing the number of teams in the system.

In this chapter, we will explore how Access Teams work. In addition, the rest of the chapter will look at how to decide what security concept should be part of your full security model. This includes when to use Owning Teams vs. Access Teams.

Owning Teams vs. Access Teams

The two types of teams are Owning Teams and Access Teams. Access Teams are the new light-weight type of team added in CRM 2013. While creating either creates an entity record of type "Team" each have their own features that are available. The following table highlights some of the differences.

Feature	Owning Teams	Access Teams
Can contain members from same or different business units	X	X
Can have Security Roles assigned and users that are members of team inherit privileges	X	
Ability to Own Records	X	
Team dynamically created as needed for a record		X
Manual Sharing	X	X
Automatic Sharing when first member is added to record team – access granted using an Access Template		X

Manual Creation of an Access Team

Access teams can be created manually or automatically when a record is created. Manual creation of Access Teams make sense when you have static teams that don't need to own a record or have security roles assigned to them. Creating an Access Team manually is done via Settings ->Administration -> Teams. When you create the team choose the Access Team option as shown in the following image.

CRM 2013 Quick Start

TEAM
New Team

General

Team Name *	Emergency Response
Business Unit *	North America
Administrator *	Jill Frank
Team Type *	Access ←

Once saved, you can add team members to the new team just like you would an Owning Team. One thing to be aware of the default view for teams don't show Access teams (or owning teams for that matter). If you select the All User Access Teams views you will see them at that point.

All User Access Teams ←

✓ Team Name ↑	Business Unit
Emergency Response	North America

Next, you can share access to individual records with the Access Team. You would do this just like any other sharing from the record.

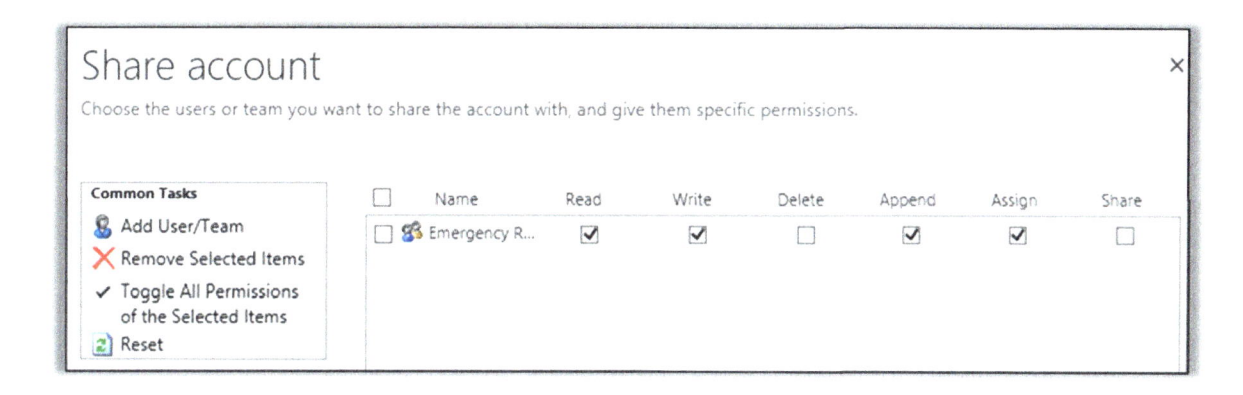

You don't need to enable the Access Team entity definition option in order to share a record with an Access Team. Enabling that option is only required for automatic creation of the Access Teams and support for Access Team templates.

Just in case you were wondering, you can try to assign a record owner to an Access Team but it won't work and you will get a message similar to the following

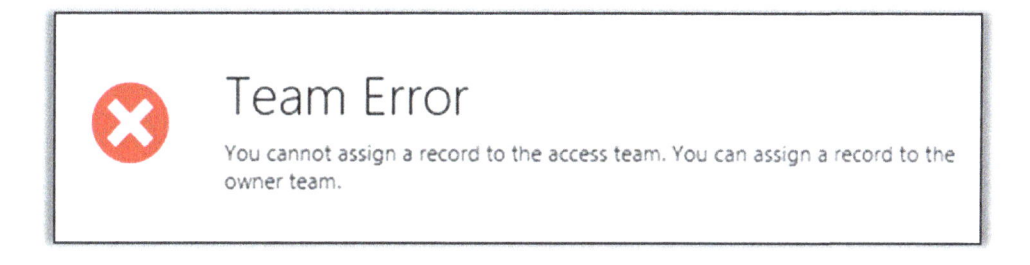

This is because Access teams are not able to own records only Owner Teams are.

Automatic Creation of Access Teams

Automatic Access Team creation happens on a record by record basis. Each record gets its own unique access team created behind the scenes by CRM when the first time a user is added to the record team.

Enabling Access Teams for the Entity

The first step in using automatic creation is to enable Access Teams for the entity on the entity definition page as you can see below

Remember this is only required for automatic creation and the ability to create a template. If all you want to do is manual access teams leave this unchecked as there is a limit in the number of entities you can have enabled for Access Teams.

By default, five entities can be enabled for access teams. This is configured by a deployment level setting **MaxEntitiesEnabledForAutoCreatedAccessTeams**. So for on-premise this can be increased but in CRM Online it is not changeable. You will know right away if you exceed this when you see the following error:

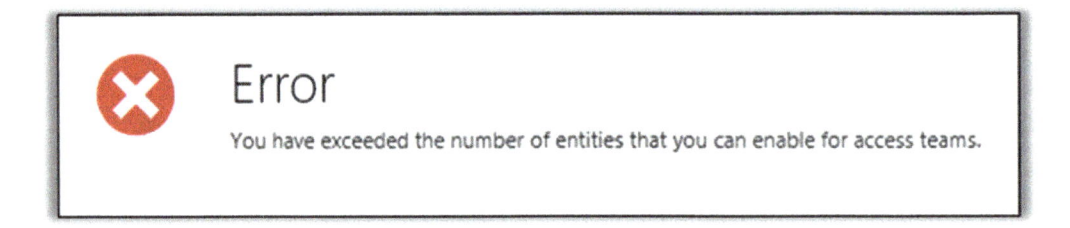

Creating Access Templates

Access Templates provide the pattern for what access should be granted to a user via the Access Team when they are added to the team on the record. Templates can be created for any of the entities that are Access Team enabled via Settings - > Administration - > Access Templates. As you can tell from the following image the template offers similar access that you would find on the Share dialog.

CRM 2013 Quick Start

Team template				Team templates	
New Team template					

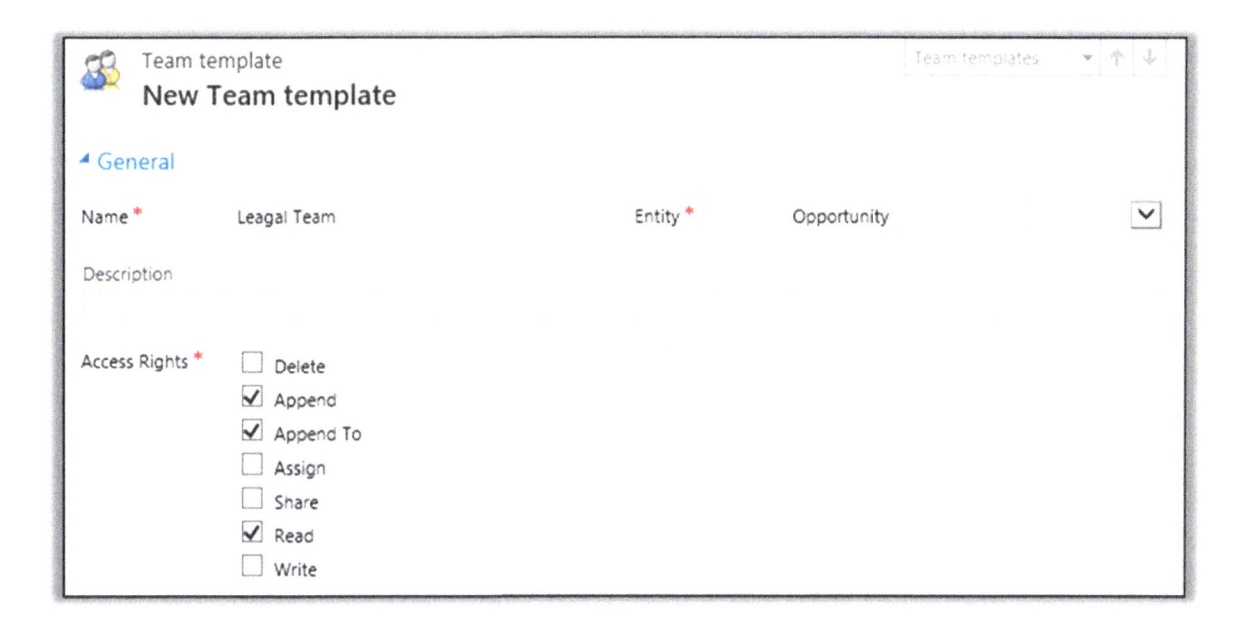

▲ General

Name *   Leagal Team   Entity *   Opportunity

Description

Access Rights *
- ☐ Delete
- ☑ Append
- ☑ Append To
- ☐ Assign
- ☐ Share
- ☑ Read
- ☐ Write

By default you can only create two Access Templates for an enabled entity. So you could have "Sales Staff" and "Service Staff" each having a template that defines their access that will be provisioned on the auto share. If you need more than that and you are on-premise you can increase the value of the deployment setting **MaxAutoCreatedAccessTeamsPerEntity**.

Managing Teams on the Form

This is where the magic happens. By adding a grid to the form for the entity users can manage the list of users that are part of the team for that record. When the first user is added to the team behind the scenes CRM automatically creates an Access Team and Shares the record with that team using the Access Template to determine the access granted. The following image shows inserting a sub-grid on the form and setting it to work with the Access Team.

Set Properties

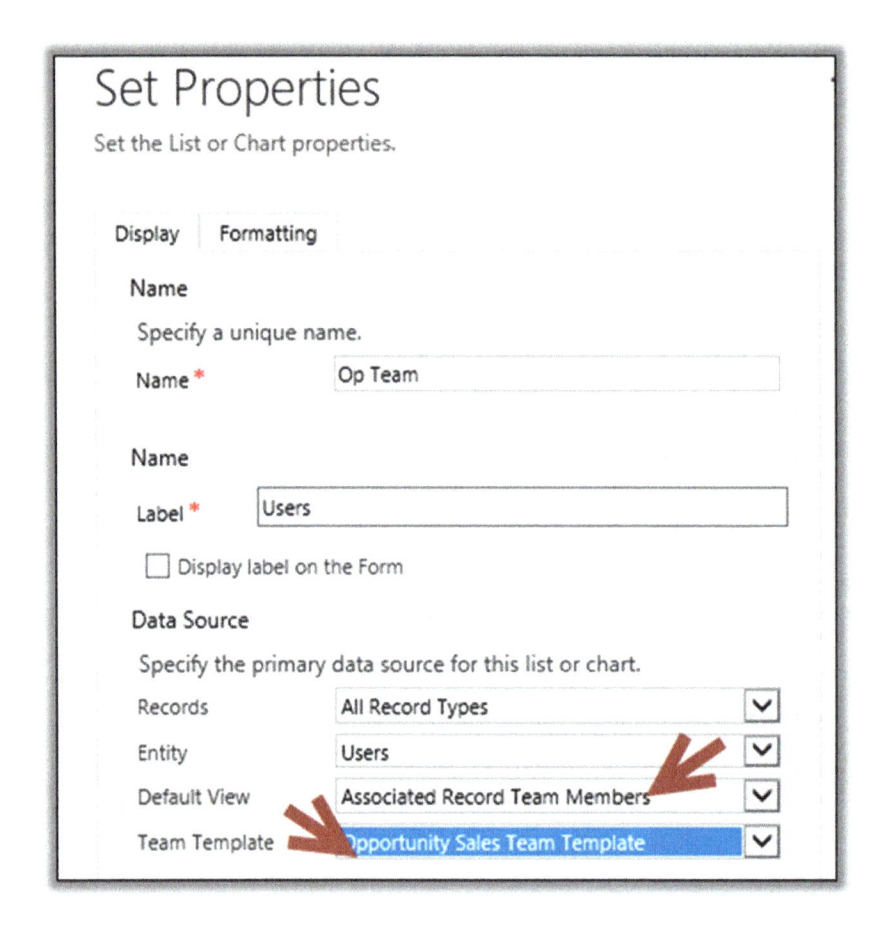

Set the List or Chart properties.

Display | Formatting

Name

Specify a unique name.

Name * | Op Team

Name

Label * | Users

☐ Display label on the Form

Data Source

Specify the primary data source for this list or chart.

Records	All Record Types
Entity	Users
Default View	Associated Record Team Members
Team Template	Opportunity Sales Team Template

Notice the following key settings that are required to configure the sub-grid for Access Teams:

- Records is set to All Record Types and not Related Records
- Entity is set to Users
- Default View – this is important, it must be set to Associated Record Team Members in order to see the next drop down for Team Template
- Team Template allows to you configure which Access Template is used when a user is associated with this sub-grid

It's important to understand that if you don't choose All Record Types you will not have the option to specify the Team Template. Since Related Records is the default, it is easy to overlook changing this option and becoming confused why the Team Template dropdown doesn't show.

Once you've added the sub-grid and look at the form on a new record you will see the grid showing the following message:

Opportunity Team

Full Name ↑   Title

To enable this content, create the record. ⬅

Create the record and then it will allow you to select users to add to the record team. The following shows the grid with a single user added.

Opportunity Team

Full Name ↑   Title

Adam Barr

It's important to understand that whoever is adding members to the dynamic team must have Share and at least the same access rights the Access Template would grant to the user being added.

Further, the user being added must have at least User level rights to the entity. If this is not true you will see a message like the following:

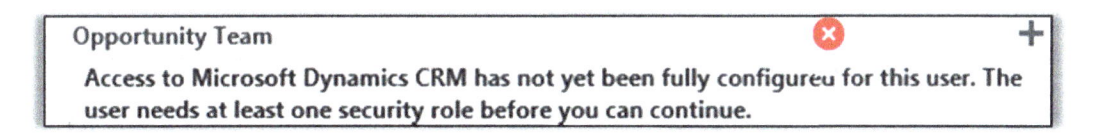

Opportunity Team ❌ ➕
Access to Microsoft Dynamics CRM has not yet been fully configured for this user. The user needs at least one security role before you can continue.

Once you have successfully added a user the team will be created with a GUID for the Team Name as you can see in the following example.

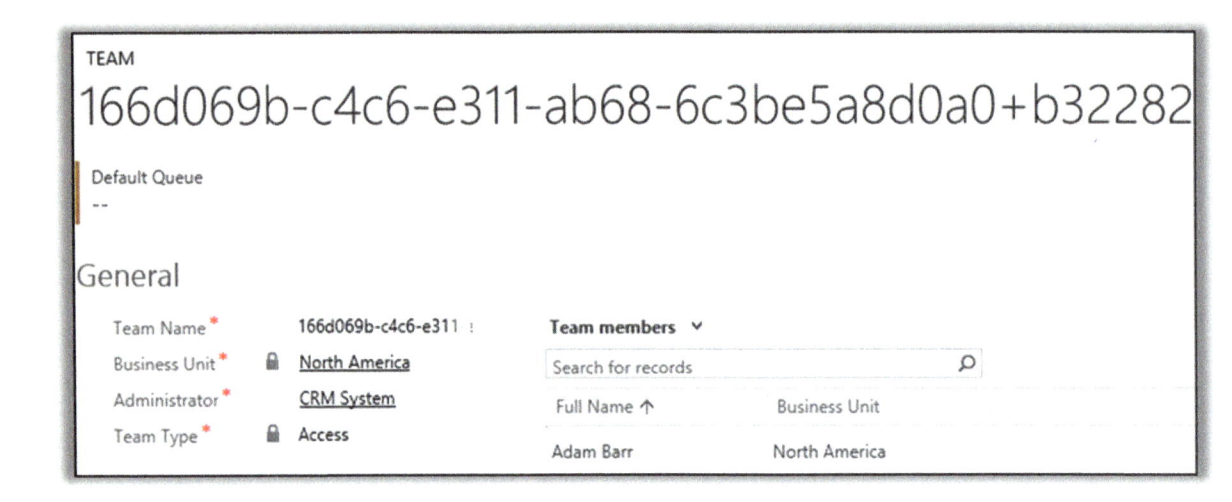

> **TEAM**
> # 166d069b-c4c6-e311-ab68-6c3be5a8d0a0+b32282
>
> Default Queue
> --
>
> General
>
> | Team Name* | 166d069b-c4c6-e311 | Team members ▾ |
> | Business Unit* | 🔒 North America | Search for records |
> | Administrator* | CRM System | Full Name ↑ | Business Unit |
> | Team Type* | 🔒 Access | Adam Barr | North America |

NOTE: *You won't see this in the Teams lists unless you do a personal view and remove most of the criteria. These are hidden on purpose, imagine one per record how many you could have.*

That is all it takes to setup and use the dynamic Access Team feature.

Automating Access Teams with Code

For Manual Access Teams and Owner Teams developers can use AddMembersTeamRequest and RemoveMembersTeamRequest to manage members of a team programmatically. Dynamic Access Teams can also be managed via the API using AddUserToRecordTeamRequest and RemoveUserFromRecordTeamRequest. The big difference when you call the dynamic option is you are simply specifying the template and the record ID and CRM manages the Team ID. Behind the scenes CRM will create the team on the fly if this is the first member being added and also perform the sharing action between the record and the newly created Access Team.

Automating via the API allows for powerful scenarios where people get or lose access automatically based on some other event in CRM.

It is also possible to convert an Owner Team to an Access Team in a onetime process. This is very helpful if prior to CRM 2013 you were creating one Owning Team per record you can now convert to the lighter weight Access Team.

When to use Access Teams?

First of all, it's important to understand it's not all or nothing. Access teams are just another component to help build the overall security model.

Use Owning teams when you have a small number of teams e.g. National Accounts Team, Emergency Response Team etc. that need access to records and you want them to have ownership of the records.

Use Manual Access teams when you need to give a team access to a record but they don't need to own it.

Use Dynamic Access Teams when you need different team members for different records. This strategy can co-exist with other strategies for giving access to the record for handling exceptions. For example, most Opportunities you could give access by the owner of the record being the Sales Person, but for complex deals additional staff could be added to a Dynamic Access Team allowing each record to have extended sales staff collaborating.

Don't go to Access Teams as your default way of handling access. You should first look to Business Units and Security Roles to isolate collections of users and collections of records. Next, add normal teams because they can own records which is more efficient than sharing when there are a small number of teams. Teams can also cross business unit boundaries matching closer to today's cross business line collaboration. Use Access Teams, either manual or dynamic, to fill gaps that you can't handle with other options. Access Teams, even though they share under the covers, are a better approach than sharing with individual users if you occasionally have more than a single user getting access.

Wrapping Up

A good security model is a simple one that is understandable and will protect the data while at the same time enables the users to be productive. There isn't a single part of a CRM project that is worth having lengthy discussions and pushing for simplicity. Access Teams are a great feature but they are not a silver bullet to fix all your problems. Good security models come from using all the tools you have available and balancing secure with productive.

5

Building Business Process Flows

Dynamics CRM Processes, and Business Process Flows

Dynamics CRM provides several ways to model your real-world business processes and implement them as part of an overall solution. Specifically, four different types of processes are available, and while this chapter focuses on one of them – **Business Process Flows** -- it is important to have a high-level understanding of all of them, and of how process flows fit into the overall context of modeling your organization's processes. The following table summarizes the four different types of processes available in Dynamics CRM 2013.

Process Type	What it's Used For
Workflow	Model real-world business processes. Can be run in the background or in real time; can be triggered by events or run manually by a user.
Dialog	Interactive, step-by-step "wizard" style processes. Requires user input from start to finish.
Custom Action	Create a new operation not available in CRM, such as combining several discrete steps into a single operation.
Business Process Flow	Create visual, staged processes for sales, service, or other business areas.

When you create a new process, you must specify the category. The following figure shows the **Create Process** dialog, with the **Category** option set selected, and highlights the fact that business process flows are one of the four categories of processes you can create in Dynamics

CRM 2013.

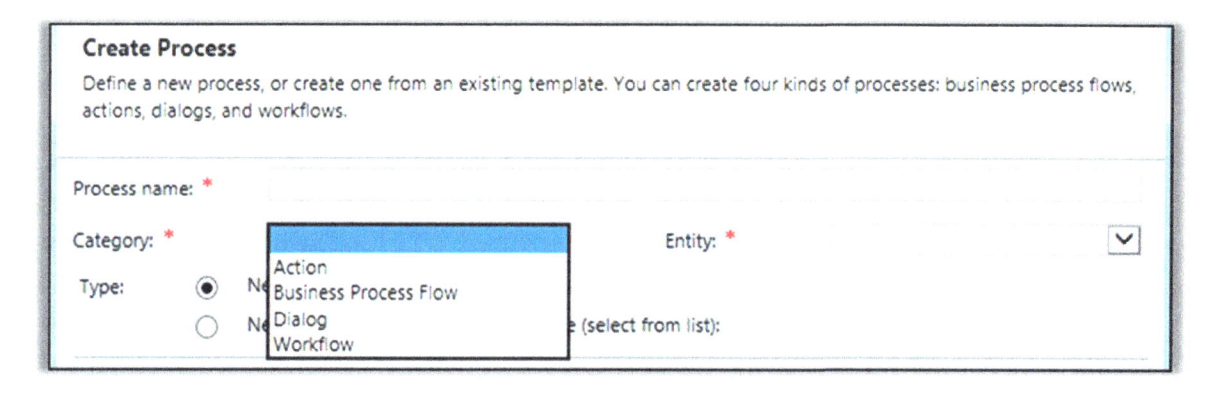

```
Create Process
Define a new process, or create one from an existing template. You can create four kinds of processes: business process flows,
actions, dialogs, and workflows.

Process name: *

Category: *        [                    ]          Entity: *                    [v]
                    Action
Type:      (•) Ne  Business Process Flow
           ( ) Ne  Dialog              (select from list):
                    Workflow
```

While this chapter is specifically about business process flows, we should probably start with some context.

First, it's important to understand that business processes shouldn't be siloed off by themselves. Everything we refer to as a *business process* is really part of a broader category of techniques you can use to customize Dynamics CRM. In a general sense, we can think of a continuum of customization techniques along a "degree of complexity" scale as in the following figure:

Dynamics CRM Customization Techniques, from Least to Most Complex

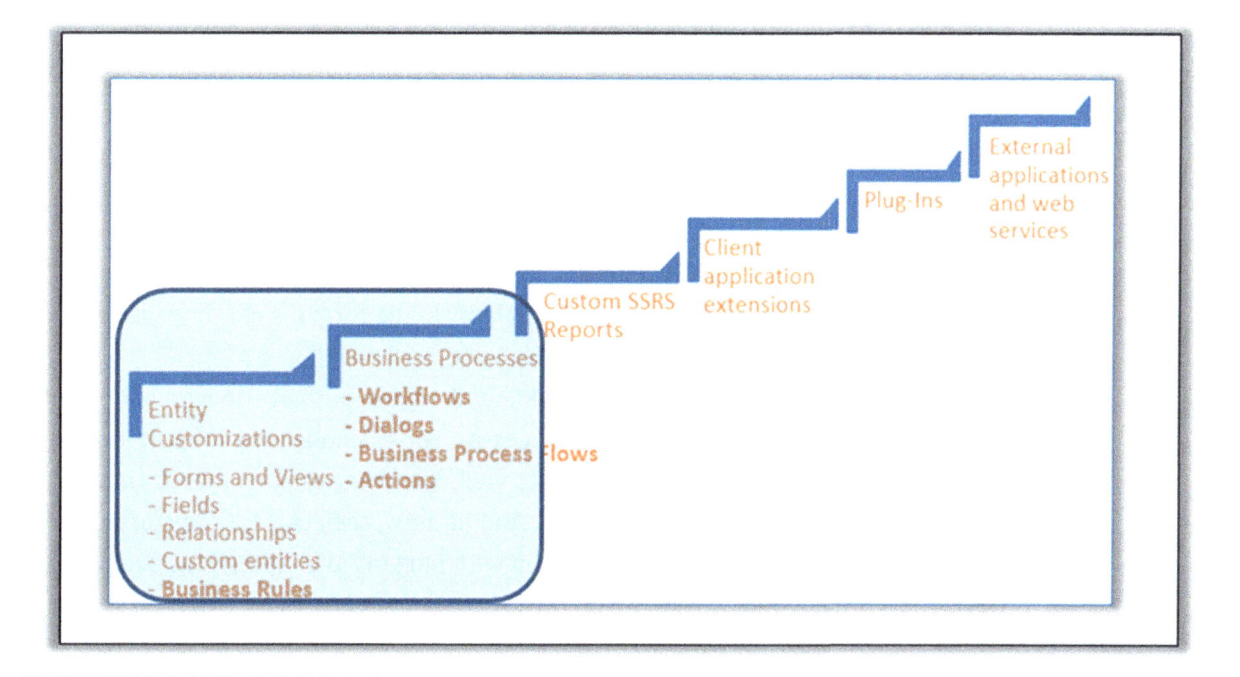

```
                                                                    External
                                                                    applications
                                                         Plug-Ins   and web
                                                                    services
                                              Client
                                              application
                                 Custom SSRS  extensions
                                 Reports
                  Business Processes
                  - Workflows
    Entity        - Dialogs
    Customizations - Business Process Flows
    - Forms and Views - Actions
    - Fields
    - Relationships
    - Custom entities
    - Business Rules
```

With reference to the figure, here are some of the points we should emphasize:

- In a strict sense, the *business process* category includes four things: workflow processes, dialog processes, business process flows, and actions. You saw that in the figure in the previous section.
- Strictly speaking, *business rules* are not considered business processes; they're actually an entity customization. But regardless of how we categorize them, they are super-important and are also intended to be used by the same people who will work with business processes. Also, they're often used in combination with other techniques (including business processes) as part of a comprehensive solution.
- The highlighted techniques – entity customizations and business processes – can all be thought of as "no-code" customization techniques. In our view one of the most remarkable aspects of the Dynamics CRM platform is the broad scope of customizations that can be accomplished without code. And the new version – with its profusion of new features in the no-code customization category – broadens this scope more than ever. The beauty of "no-code" customization techniques is that they can be accomplished by an administrator versus requiring a developer.

With that, here's a quick guide to the most important new business process and related features in Dynamics CRM 2013 and where they're covered in the book.

- **Business process flows**. This chapter (I thought I'd start with an easy one!)
- **Business rules, or "portable business logic".** These allow you to create, using declarative logic rather than code, dynamic forms experiences that in previous versions would have required Jscript. Business rules allow you to conditionally perform form actions such as showing/hiding fields, changing field requirement settings, set the value of fields, or making fields read-only. These are covered in Chapter 6.
- **Real-time workflows**. In previous versions workflow processes came in one flavor: asynchronous. Dynamics CRM 2013 still has these (now referred to as "background" processes) and adds an important new capability in the form of real-time workflow processes. These are covered in Chapter 7.
- **Custom actions** are created with the workflow designer, but have several important differences from traditional workflow processes. For example, they support input arguments and can return output values as well. Also, they can be created globally, rather than being tied to a specific entity. And for now, they can only be started from custom code. Custom actions are discussed with plug-ins in Chapter 11, Developers, Developers, Developers.

Introduction to Business Process Flows

Business process flows provide a visualization of your business processes by placing special controls at the top of entity forms. Users are guided through successive stages of sales, marketing or service process. Process flows support multiple stages and multiple steps within each stage. They are easy to customize, and provide a code-free process design experience to add or remove steps, change the order of stages or steps, or add new entities to the business process flow.

Here are just a few of the most important features of and reasons to use process flows:

- Provide users with a visual guide to sales, service and marketing processes.
- Enforce business requirements that must be satisfied at stages of processes.
- Create processes that span multiple entities.
- Allow non-technical business users to create and modify processes.

The Business Process Flow User Experience

Working with Stages

Business process flows are presented to the user in a special area at the top of an entity form. This is illustrated in the following figure, which shows a sample opportunity form with the business process flow area highlighted.

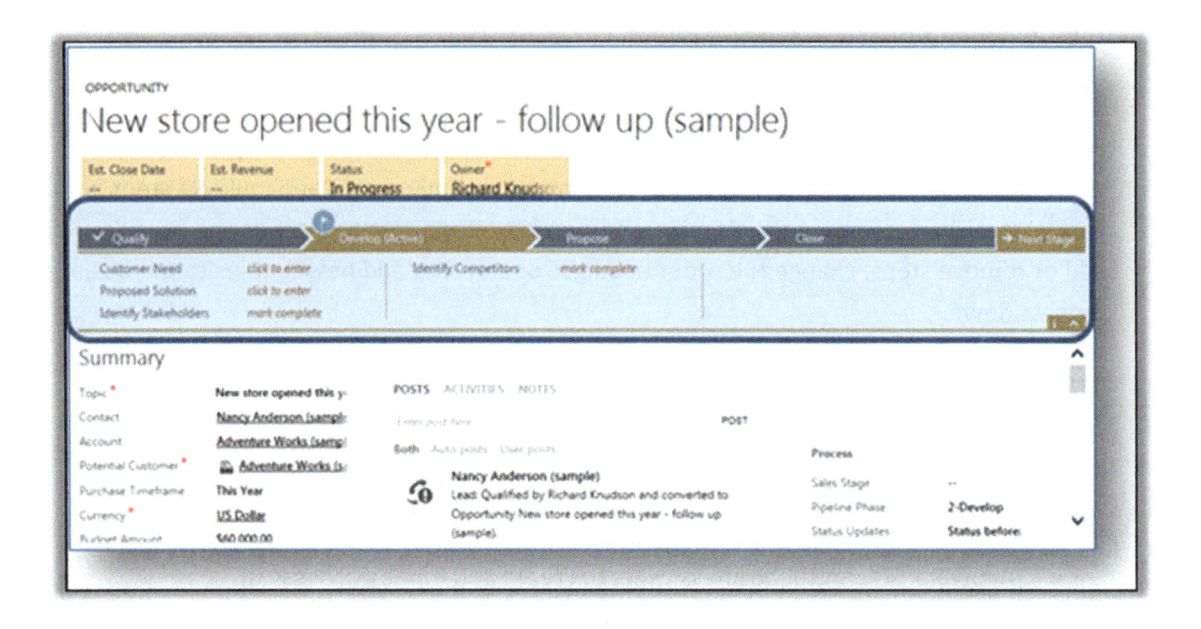

To understand how to work with business process flows, refer to the following figure:

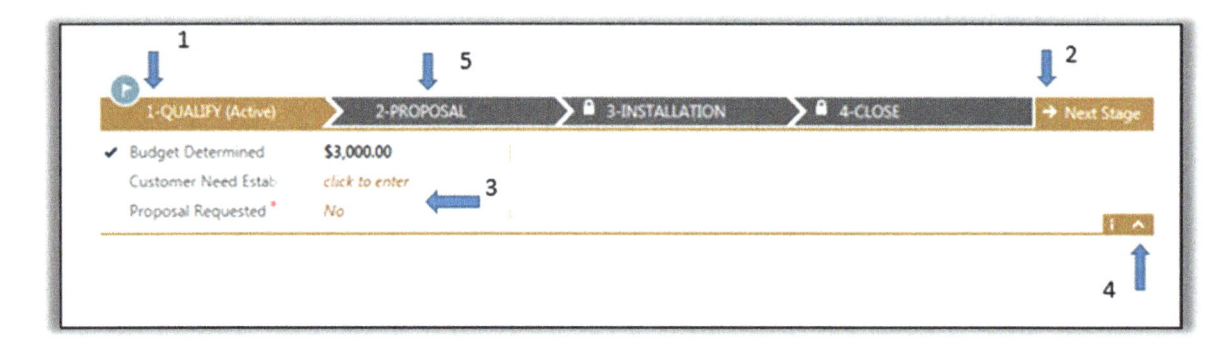

Referring to the figure, here's a brief guide to how you can interact with the various business process flow controls:

1. **Current Stage.** The flag icon always identifies the currently active stage.

2. **Advance to next Stage.** Click [→ Next Stage] to advance to the next stage.

3. **Stage Steps.** These correspond to fields for the current record type, and appear in the area beneath the stage names. Some may be required, as the **Proposal Requested** field is in this example.

4. **Hide controls.** To free up screen real estate, click the Hide Steps icon at the lower right.
5. **View a stage without changing active stage.** If you want to see the steps in a different stage without changing the stage, just click the stage name. You can't always do that, however, and if you can't view a stage yet it will be flagged with the lock icon as the INSTALLATION and CLOSE steps are in this example.

Switching Between Processes

Multiple business process flows can be defined for a record type such as opportunity. For example, you might have one process for opportunities below a certain revenue threshold and another for larger opportunities. Or one department might have a different process than another. If you have multiple processes, a user can switch between them by clicking the **Switch Process** command on the **More Commands** menu. In the following figure you can see **Switch Process** available on the **More Commands** menu.

And after selecting that command, a user might have access to several different business process flows to choose from:

[Screenshot: Select Business Process Flow dialog showing options: Opportunity Sales Process (selected), Collaborative selling, Opportunity to Invoice (B2B), Mortgage Banking Process]

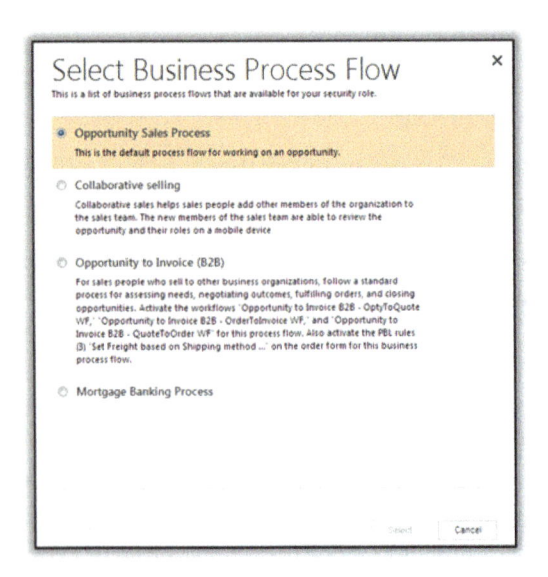

A little later in the chapter we will discuss security considerations regarding business process flows, and how you can determine which users can run them.

Using Multi-Entity Process Flows

One of the most distinctive characteristics of business process flows is their ability to span several entities. This is an important new feature, with the potential to fundamentally change the CRM user experience, from a records and forms model to one more focused on the process itself. Several business process flows are included out of the box in Dynamics CRM 2013, and at least one of them – the **Lead to Opportunity Sales Process** – spans multiple entities. To appreciate the importance of this new paradigm, let's examine how this business process flow works.

Let's start by examining a new lead record, illustrated in the following figure.

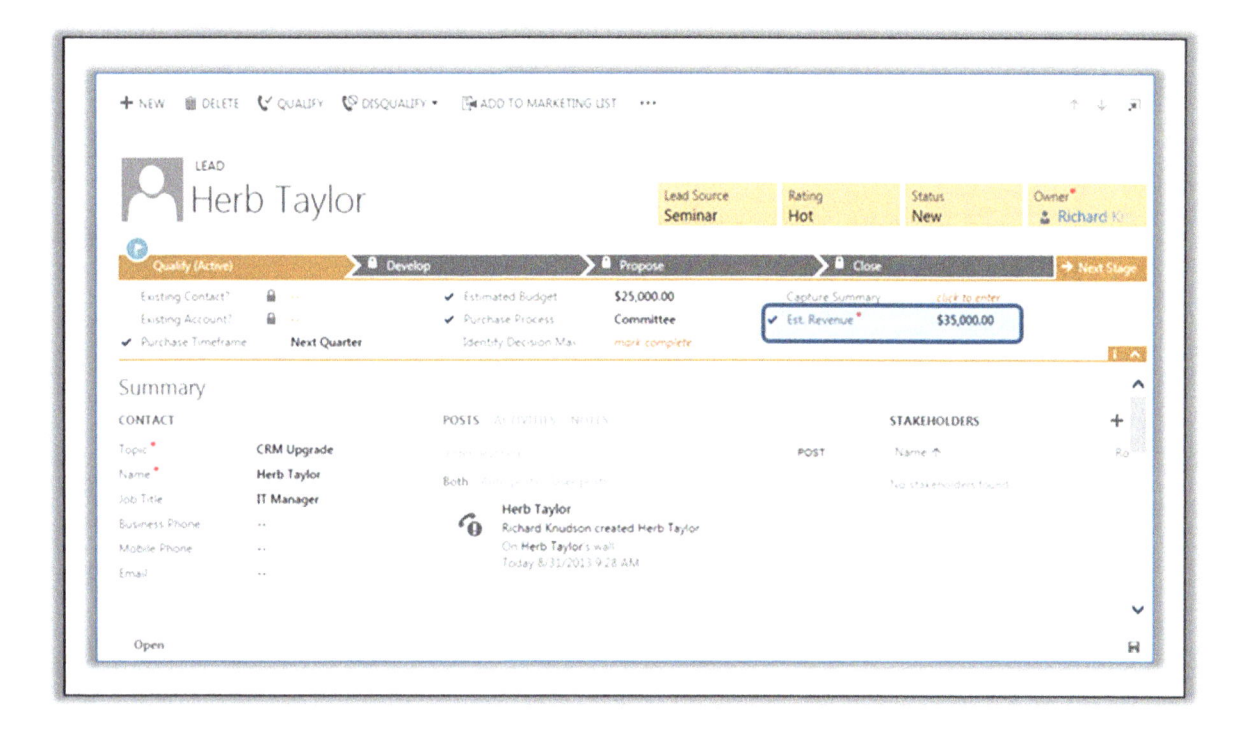

[Screenshot of a Lead record form for Herb Taylor in CRM 2013, showing the Qualify stage active with Est. Revenue of $35,000.00 highlighted.]

Here are the most important things to note in the figure:

- The form is for the **Lead** record type.
- The status (shown on the status bar at the bottom of the window) is **Open**. (The Status field referred to in the form Header with the value of New is actually Status Reason.)
- The currently active stage of the process is **Qualify**.
- The **Est. Revenue** field, highlighted in the figure, is not on the lead form by default, but the field is available on the lead entity. For this example, it has been added as a custom step on the process, to illustrate a point we will discuss below.

Now, suppose you're ready to qualify the lead. If you clicked the **QUALIFY** button on the ribbon, the next thing you'd see is something like the following figure:

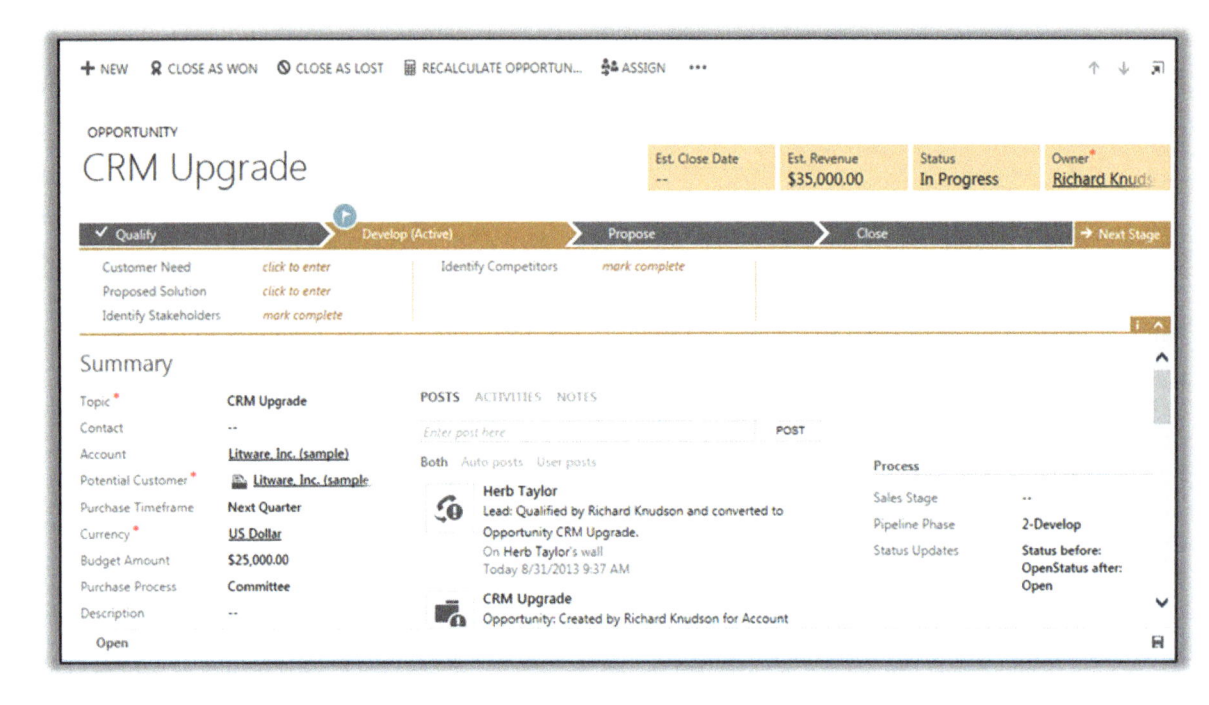

In comparing these two figures, and how we got from one to the next, the things to focus on are these:

- The form is now for the **Opportunity** record type.
- The status (of the opportunity record) is **Open**. (Again: the Status value is actually shown on the status bar at the bottom of the window; the In Progress value referred to in the header is Status Reason.)
- The active stage of the process is now **Develop**.
- The **Est. Revenue** field on the opportunity record has been auto-filled with the value provided on the lead.

From the user's perspective the lead qualification process really *is* seamless: no windows appeared or disappeared, no pop-up blocker alerts. But behind the scenes important things happened:

- The lead was qualified. (You can click the **Qualify** stage in the process flow area and verify that for yourself by viewing the qualified lead record on its now read-only form.)
- The new opportunity record was created, with all of the default mappings from lead to opportunity enforced. If you look carefully, you'll notice that the **Estimated Budget** field from lead carried over to the **Budget Amount** field on opportunity.

- Any custom mappings created from lead to opportunity will also be enforced. That's why I previously mentioned the **Est. Revenue** field I'd added to the lead form. In addition to adding it to the form, I also created a custom mapping from that field to the Est. Revenue field on the opportunity entity. This illustrates an important point: **when working with multiple-entity process flows you are not limited by Dynamics CRM's default behavior**. In fact, there are plenty of important business requirements that can be satisfied with business process flows…but that require some basic customizations. We will revisit this topic shortly.

There's one more important point to emphasize, which might be confusing at first. Note that we advanced the process from the **Qualify** to the **Develop** stage by using the built-in lead qualification process – that is, by clicking the **QUALIFY** button on the lead form. That's different from the approach reviewed previously for advancing a process by clicking **Next Stage** in the process flow area. The reason it's different is that this is an example of a special process flow, created by Microsoft, that has some built-in secret mojo, that, while good and useful, cannot be created with the out of the box process flow designer.

Since this is an important point, let's review how a multiple-entity process flow works when *you* build it: that is, *without* the built-in secret mojo Microsoft used to create the Lead to Opportunity Sales Process. As an example, let's walk through a process flow that starts on a phone call form and allows a user to create a case record as part of the process. This is a pretty common real-world scenario and does a good job of illustrating the standard business process flow user experience. I'll refer to it as the **Phone to Case Process**. Here we'll assume it's already been created and focus on the user experience. A little further along in the chapter we'll walk through how to build it.

Start with the following figure, which shows the business process flow area on a Phone Call form.

[Screenshot of a Phone Call form titled "Another question about derivatives" showing the business process flow stages: Intake (Active), Consulting, Diagnostics, Limitation, Next Stage. Form fields include Client (custom): Magenium Test Client, Client Person(s): Richard Knudson; Rod Carew, Product, Phone Number, Regarding, Subject: Another question about derivatives.]

Notice that the current stage is **Intake**. Let's play the role of a service rep on the phone with a client, and we don't yet know what's going to happen next. We're gathering information, and may simply mark the call as complete and be done with it...or we might need to create a case, associate the call with an existing case, or something else.

Suppose we don't need to create a case: we're on the phone call form and after taking the information and politely answering the client's question, we can simply click **MARK COMPLETE** on the ribbon and we're done.

But suppose we do want to create a case. Since we have some experience with these business process flows, we know that clicking **Next Stage** will advance us through the process, and the figure below shows what happens when we do: since the next stage involves the case entity, we need a case record to which we can transfer control. So, a little section drops down below the **Next Stage** control, allowing us to either select an existing case or create a new one. This is the standard user experience. As you can see in the figure, our only option is to create a new one, so that's what we do.

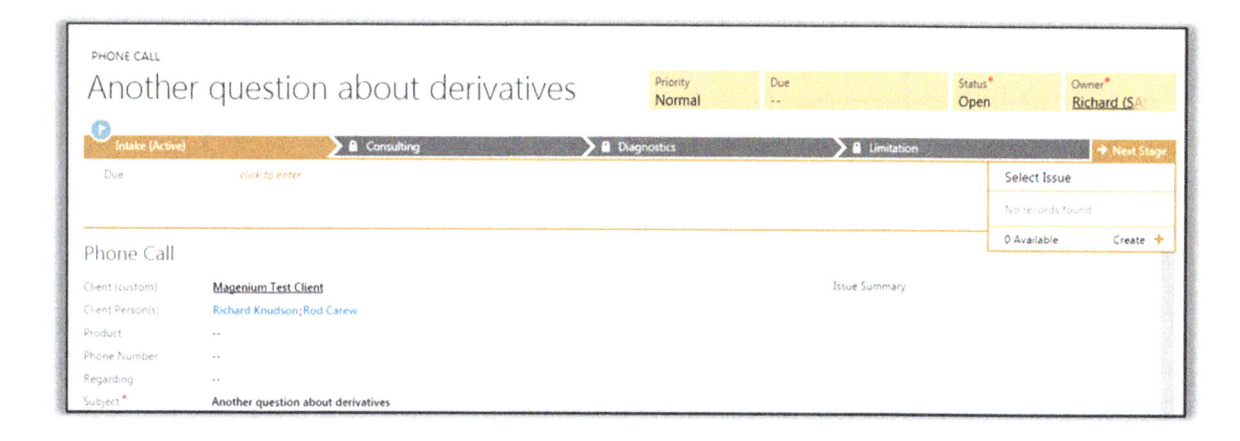

After clicking Create, we see the New Case form:

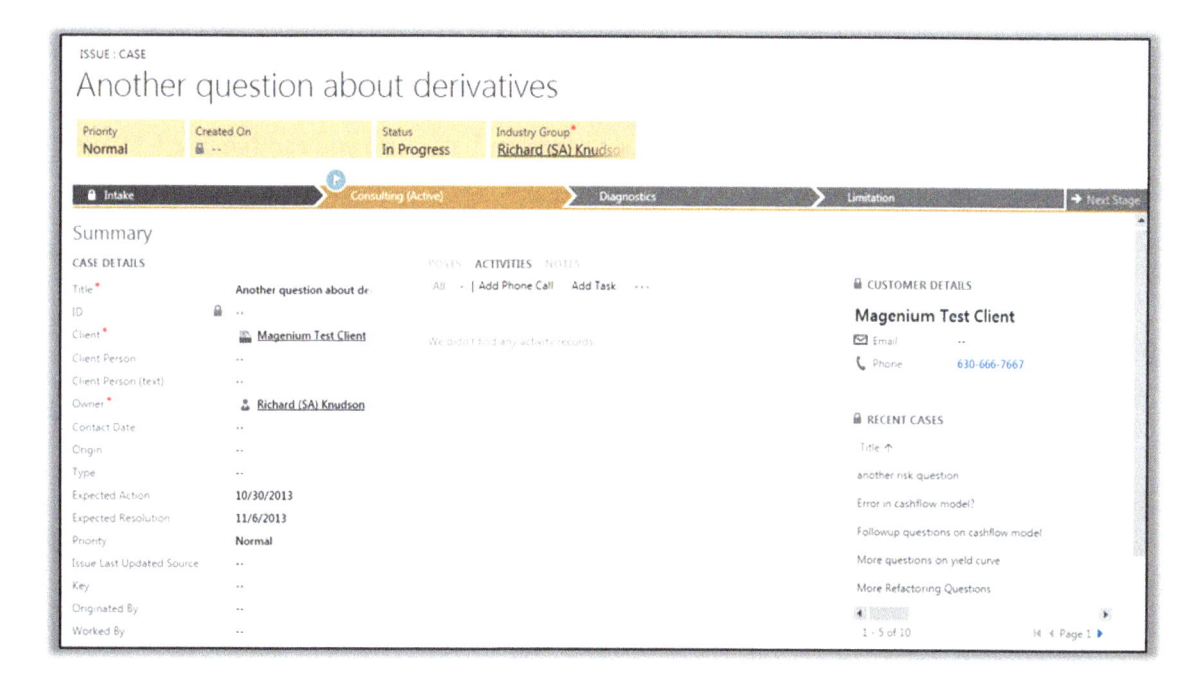

If you look carefully, you'll notice that several fields on the new case form are auto-filled. Behind the scenes, we're taking advantage of an important customization technique -- field mapping – which allows us to define how fields from the parent record type (in this case, phone call) map to fields on the child record type (here, case). But as users, we don't need to get caught up in the details, so let's return to those when we learn how to build these.

Also, note in the previous figure that the new case record has not been saved yet – it won't actually be created until the user clicks **Save** on the ribbon. This is the standard experience for multi-entity business process flows.

Customizing Business Process Flows

Security Required to Create, Run and Activate Business Process Flows

CRM users' ability to create or modify CRM business process flows is determined by the security roles assigned to them. Specifically, two privileges on users' security role determines whether they can create, modify, or activate process flows:

- Privileges on the **Process** entity
- Privilege to **Activate Business Process Flows**

To understand how this works, let's examine the **Sales Manager** security role. On the Customization tab, notice that this role has **Create** and **Write** privileges on the **Process** entity at the Business Unit level. This is indicated by the yellow half-circle you can see in the following figure:

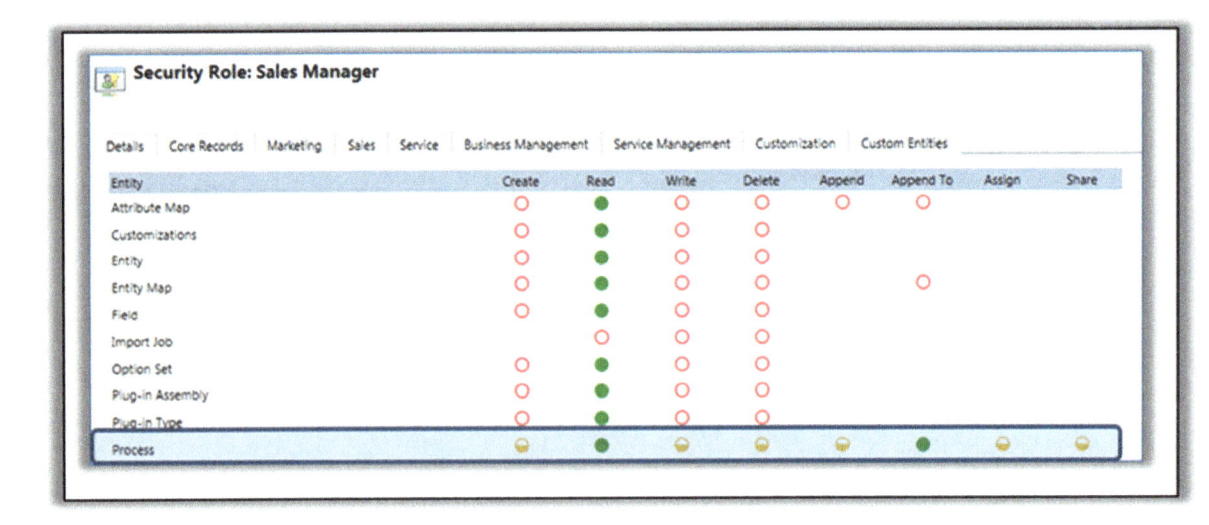

Next, in the Miscellaneous Privileges section of the Customization tab, notice that the **Activate Business Process Flows** privilege is set to Organization (the full green circle):

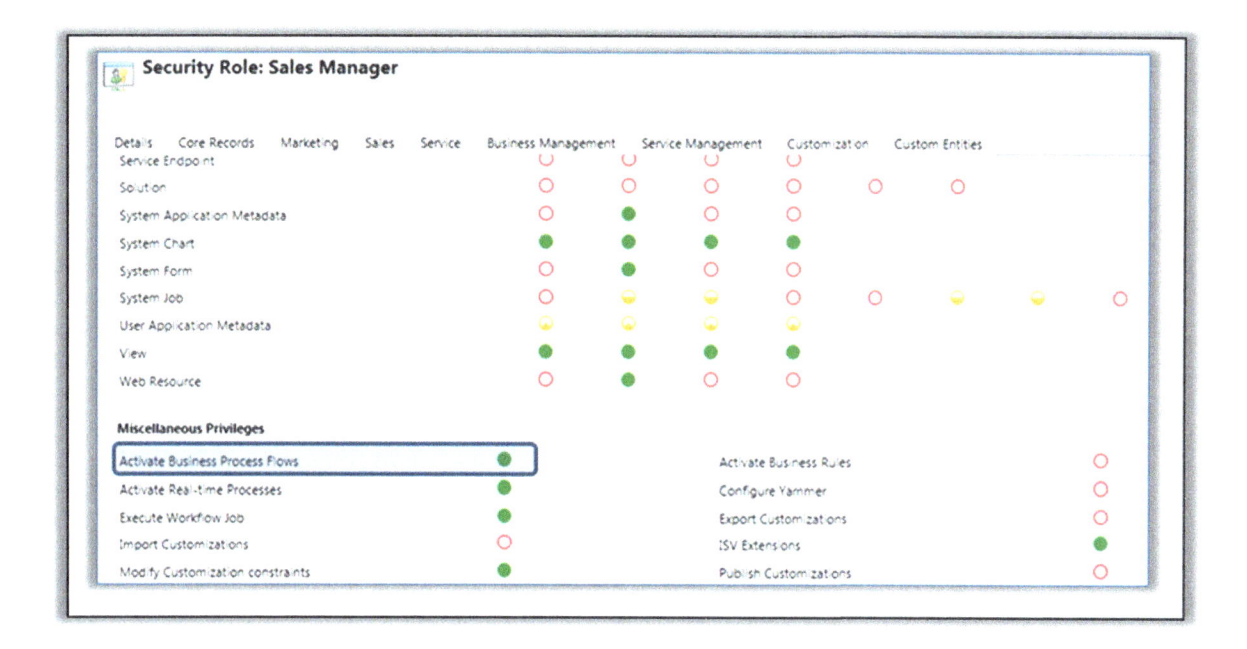

[Figure: Security Role: Sales Manager screen showing privilege settings]

Together, these privileges mean that users with the Sales Manager security role can create a save processes, and can activate any processes they create. The Business Unit level on the Create and Write privileges mean that the processes will be accessible to other users in the same business unit.

Let's compare the Sales Manager security role with the Salesperson role. The following two figures show just the relevant sections of the Sales Person role:

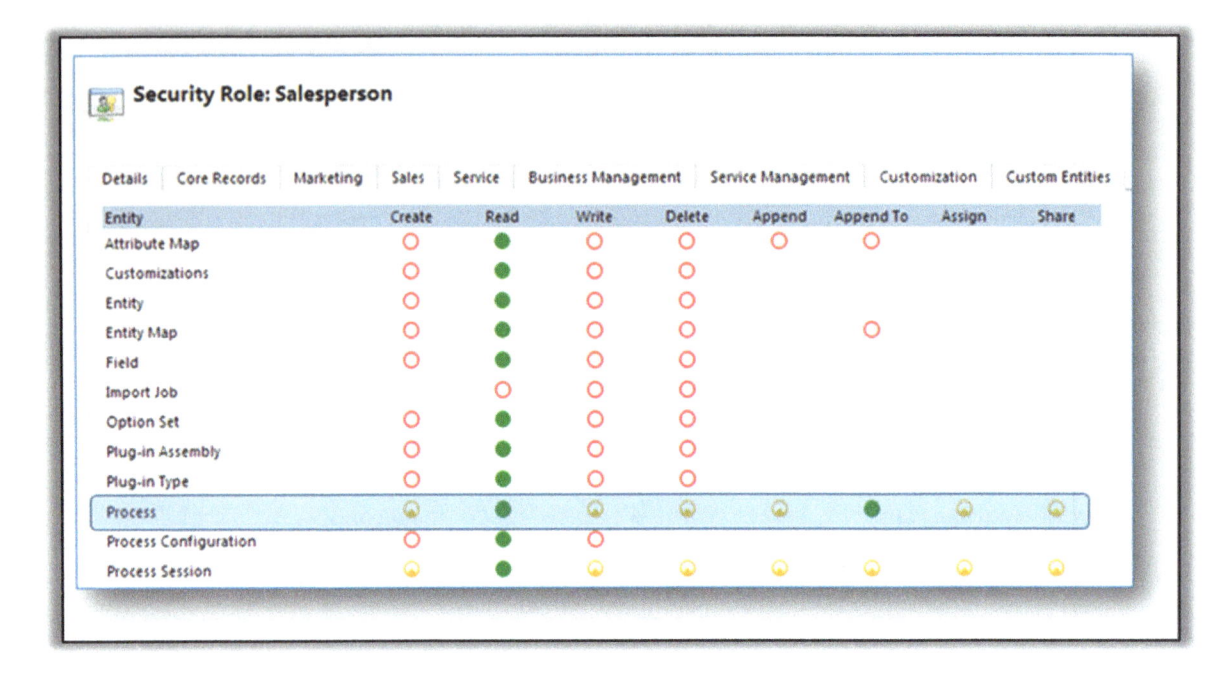

The full green circle in the **Read** column means users with this role will be able to *see all* process created by any user in the organization. But the quarter yellow circle ("User level") means that they cannot assign a process to any other users, and they cannot update any other users' processes.

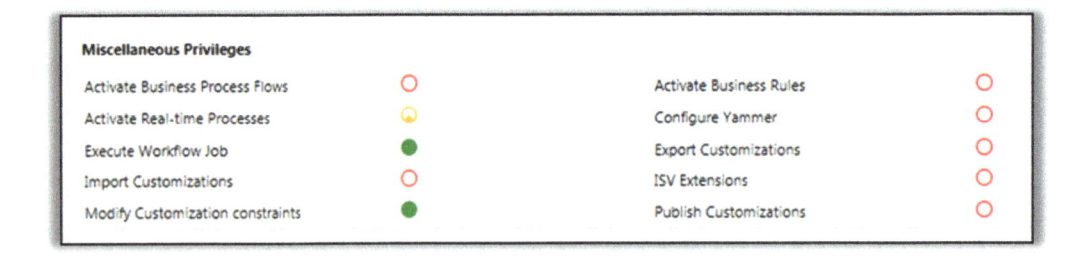

In the **Miscellaneous Privileges** section, you can see that users with this role cannot activate business process flows at all. So the fact that they can create one doesn't have much disruption potential, since they can't activate it anyway. This might be considered a poor design process: what's the point of allowing users to create a process they cannot activate? On the other hand, some organizations might want to allow a user to create a draft process, effectively submitting it to another user, such as the sales manager, for approval and activation. (An analogy can be found in the Dynamics CRM Knowledge Base, where some security roles have privileges to create a Draft article, but cannot promote an article to Published status.)

Targeting Business Process Flows

The discussion in the previous section has to do with users' access to business processes and business process flows granted by the privileges in their security roles. With business process flows, however, there's an extra level of granularity that allows you to target them to specific users. The basic idea is to assign a security role to a business process flow (similar to how you can assign a security role to forms). Any users assigned to that role will have access to the process; remember, the user experience is that they will be able to manually select that process by using the **Switch Process** command from a form's **More Actions** menu. If you do not want users to run an inappropriate process, you simply need to make sure that they aren't assigned any security roles to which the process has been targeted.

For example, suppose you're the sales manager for a bank, and you create a special process appropriate for mortgage bankers. After you save the process, you can click the **Enable Security Roles** button on the process designer ribbon:

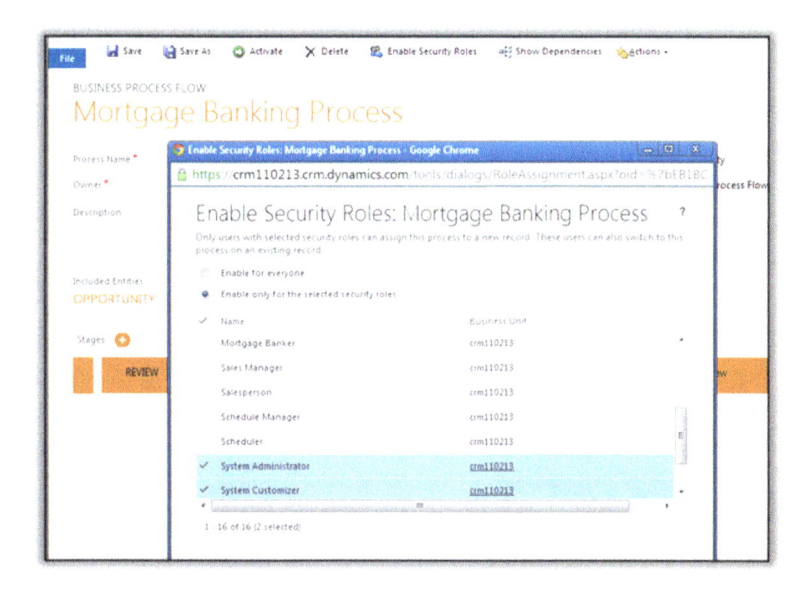

Notice by default that only two security roles are enabled for a new process, the **System Administrator** and **System Customizer** roles. You can target this process by de-selecting any roles you don't want to use it, and selecting those you do. For example, being the sales manager you may want access to it, and for this example we've created a custom security role that the process is designed for:

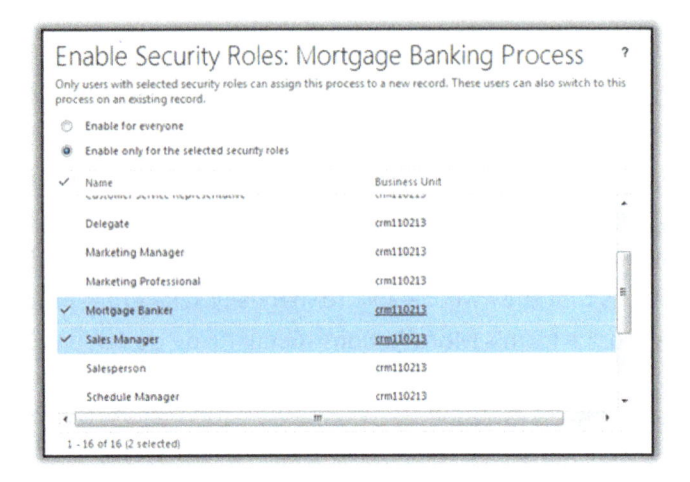

[Screenshot: Enable Security Roles: Mortgage Banking Process dialog, with Mortgage Banker and Sales Manager selected]

So to determine if a user will be able to run a specific business process flow, you need to know two things:

1. Do they have sufficient privileges from their security roles to run business process flows at all?
2. Do they have a specific security role that has been targeted for that business process flow?

To take this discussion full cycle, consider this from the perspective of a user. In our example, suppose a user has these security roles:

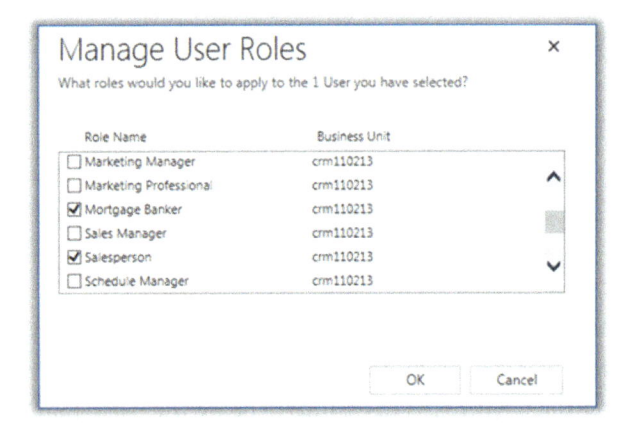

[Screenshot: Manage User Roles dialog, with Mortgage Banker and Salesperson checked]

Somebody with this role would be able to run the Mortgage Banker business process flow: their salesperson role gives them privilege to run business process flows generally, and they've been assigned the role to which the business process flow in question has been targeted.

But if you de-selected the Mortgage Banker role for this user, they wouldn't have access to the Mortgage Banking Process, although they might have access to other business process flows.

Creating Business Process Flows

There are several ways to create a business process flow:

You can navigate to Processes and simply create a new process (Settings->Processes->New), and select **Business Process Flow** in the new process dialog:

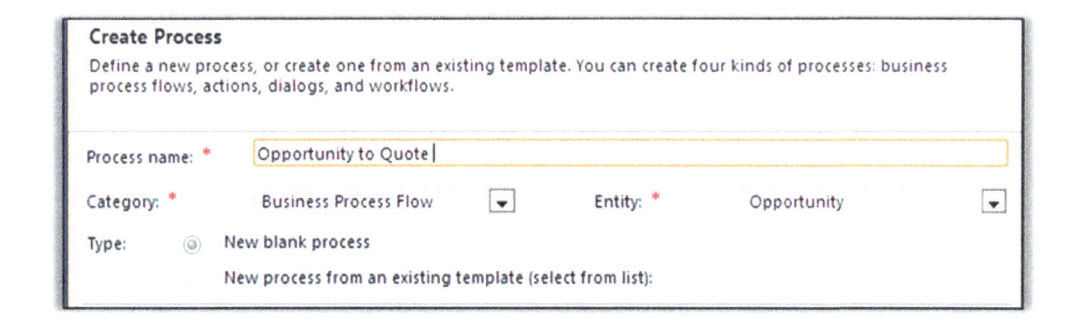

Or you can start from an existing one, and either edit it according to your requirements, or use the convenient **Save As** command to create a new one based on the existing functionality. A quick way to access an existing business process flow, you can start on a form with an activated business process flow selected, and click the **More Commands** menu and then click **Edit Process**:

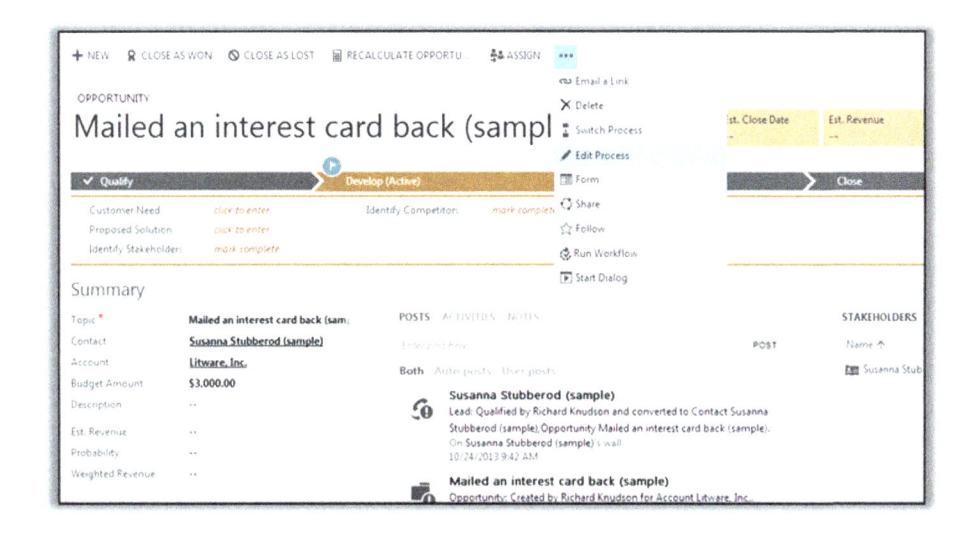

And keep in mind that business process flows are solution components, similarly to workflow and dialog processes, so you can open a solution and access them there. (Whether you can modify them within a solution is a different matter – more on that in the Tips & Tricks section.)

To gain a full appreciation of building a business process flow, let's create a new one for cases. This one will be similar to the Phone Call to Case process we reviewed previously, but since it starts on the case entity, it won't have the Intake stage for the phone call.

Follow these steps to create a 3-stage business process flow for cases.

1. Navigate to Processes and click **New**.
2. In the New Process dialog, do the following:
    a. Type Case Process in the **Name** field.
    b. Select **Business Process Flow** in the **Type** field.
    c. Select **Case** in the Entity field.
    d. Click **OK**. The Business Process Flow Designer opens, and should look like the following figure:

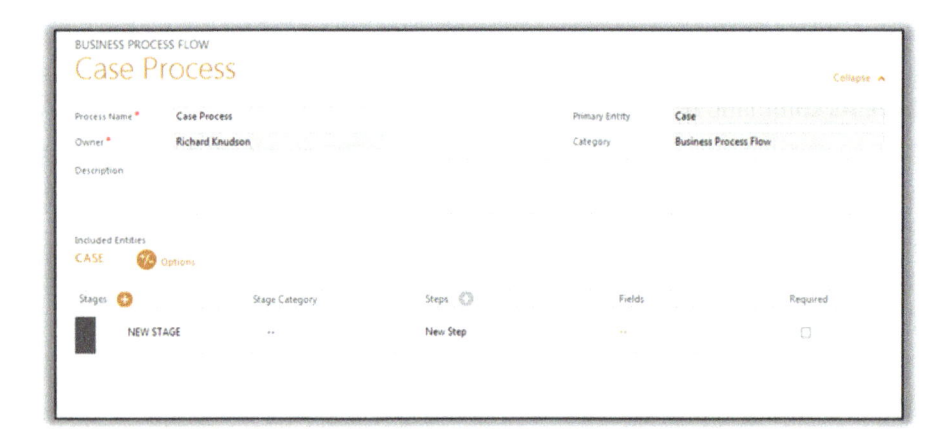

3. Click where it says **NEW STAGE** and enter the name of the first stage. Then click the **Add Stage** button to add a second and then a third stage. For the Route, Research and Resolve stages in this example, it should now look like this:

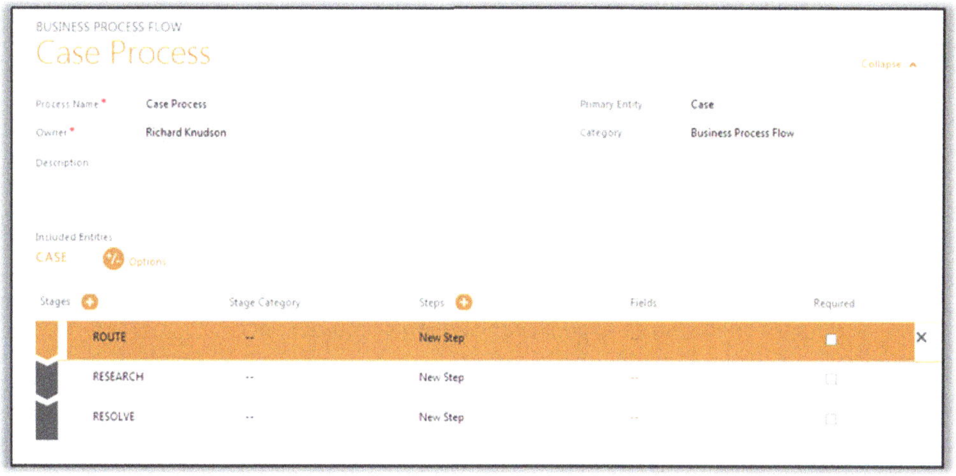
BUSINESS PROCESS FLOW
Case Process
Collapse
Process Name
Case Process
Primary Entity
Case
Owner
Richard Knudson
Category
Business Process Flow
Description
Included Entities
CASE
Options
Stages
Stage Category
Steps
Fields
Required
ROUTE
New Step
RESEARCH
New Step
RESOLVE
New Step

4. Although stage categories are optional, I recommend you use them. You select the **Stage Category** from an option set, which means you can only select from existing values. This may provide an additional level of validation, compared to the text values that can be manually entered at any time into **Stage Name**. Stage Category is a global option set, and you can see in the following figure I've selected Route as the category for the first stage, and am currently selecting the category for the second stage:

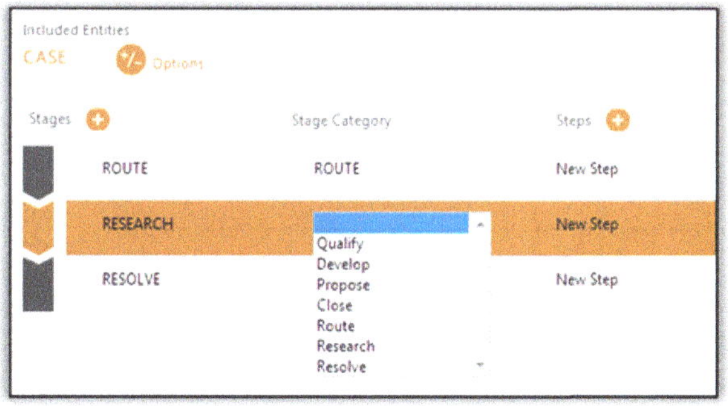
Included Entities
CASE
Options
Stages
Stage Category
Steps
ROUTE
ROUTE
New Step
RESEARCH
New Step
RESOLVE
New Step
Qualify
Develop
Propose
Close
Route
Research
Resolve

> **NOTE**
>
> ***Stage Category***
>
> *In this example I've customized the values in the Stage Category global option set, so you will likely see different values for the last three options. It's worth pointing out that this single option set will provide the possible values for ALL your business process flows, whether for sales, service or any other kind of processes. Notice that the first four values have a salesy flavor to them, and the last three are decidedly service-ish. Effectively, Microsoft has provided us with some sample values; you can either use the existing ones or customize to your organization's requirements.*

5. After specifying the categories for all three stages, we next need to add some steps. (As you may discover, you can't save a process if it contains any stages without steps.) You can add a step using the plus sign next to the step column. Remember, a step is really just a field – in this example from the Case record type – and you select them in the Fields column. In the following figure you can see the **Owner** field has been selected, but a more descriptive term, **Assign to**, has been entered as the Step name:

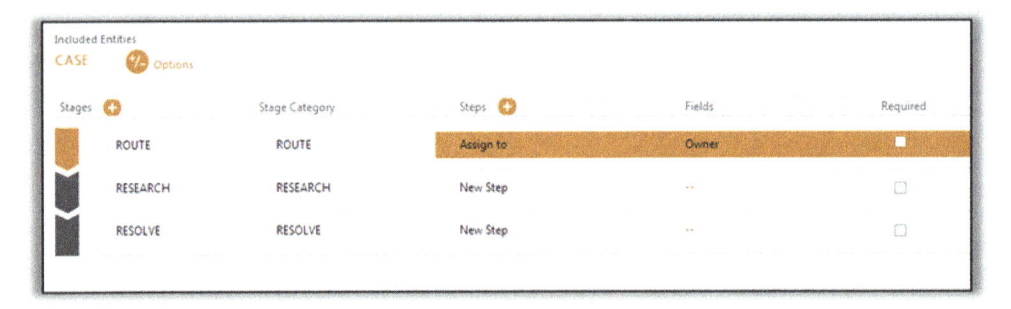

Stages	Stage Category	Steps	Fields	Required
ROUTE	ROUTE	Assign to	Owner	■
RESEARCH	RESEARCH	New Step	--	☐
RESOLVE	RESOLVE	New Step	--	☐

Included Entities: CASE

6. Let's build out the rest of this process by adding two more steps to the **Route** stage, two steps to the **Research** stage, and one to the **Resolve** stage:

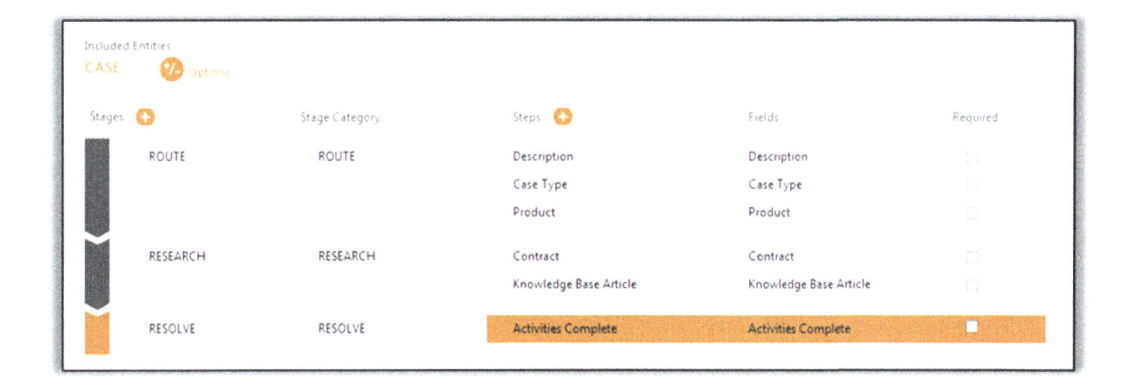

Included Entities				
CASE Options				
Stages	Stage Category	Steps	Fields	Required
ROUTE	ROUTE	Description	Description	
		Case Type	Case Type	
		Product	Product	
RESEARCH	RESEARCH	Contract	Contract	
		Knowledge Base Article	Knowledge Base Article	
RESOLVE	RESOLVE	**Activities Complete**	**Activities Complete**	

7. Now we're done. Make sure to save your work, and then click Activate so you can start using it.

A word on Fields and Steps: If you're used to workflow and dialog processes from previous versions, it might be confusing at first knowing which fields to select for the steps within your process flow stages. Apart from pointing out the obvious – that you should expose the most important fields a user should supply at each stage – we can provide a little more guidance. Therefore, here are a few points we've found helpful to consider:

• Note that we've included Case Type and Product in the Routing stage. Data like these are often used to automatically route cases to the appropriate support engineer, and below we'll see an example of how you can use workflows in conjunction with business process flows to accomplish that.

• Once you start thinking about triggering a background (workflow) process by a change in the stage, it becomes natural to think about the fields exposed at each step as inputs that can be used by the background process.

Note the use of the Activities Complete field in the Resolve stage. If you know you want a stage in your process, but you aren't yet sure what steps it should require...that's a good place to plop down the **Activities Complete** field. This is because a stage must have at least one step, and as you're prototyping or performing initial design on a process you may know that *something* has to take place at the Resolve stage, but you aren't yet sure what. In this context, a field such as Activities Complete can function as a "placeholder", allowing you to save and test the process, and reminding you to come back later and provide the details when you figure them out.

Creating a Multi-Entity Business Process Flow

When building a process flow that spans multiple entities, the first thing to note is that the entities must be related to each other. Specifically, in order to add an entity to a process flow it must be a child of the current entity. For example, if you start a process flow on the opportunity entity you can add a next stage on the quote entity because it's a child record of opportunity. (That's equivalent to saying that opportunity is the parent of quote; and for short we may say that opportunity has a 1:N relationship to quote.)

Here, we want to start on Phone Call and proceed to Case. But that's a problem, because Phone Call does *not* have a 1:N relationship to Case. If you start building the process flow on Phone Call and try to add a stage for Case, it's easy to see the problem: when you click the Options control and examine the **ADD ENTITY** list, the only thing you see is **Campaign Response**, as you can see in the following figure.

This is a good illustration of how CRM processes and customizations work together. For this example, since our business process needs to start on a phone call and proceed to a case, we've discovered a customization requirement: we need to create a custom 1:N relationship from phone call to case. Since this chapter is on business process flows, we won't go through a detailed step-by-step presentation on creating the custom relationship between these two entities, but the following figure shows you the Custom Relationship dialog, which we've accessed by opening the solution explorer, expanding the **Phone Call** entity node, clicking 1:N Relationships, and then clicking the **New 1-to-Many Relationship** button:

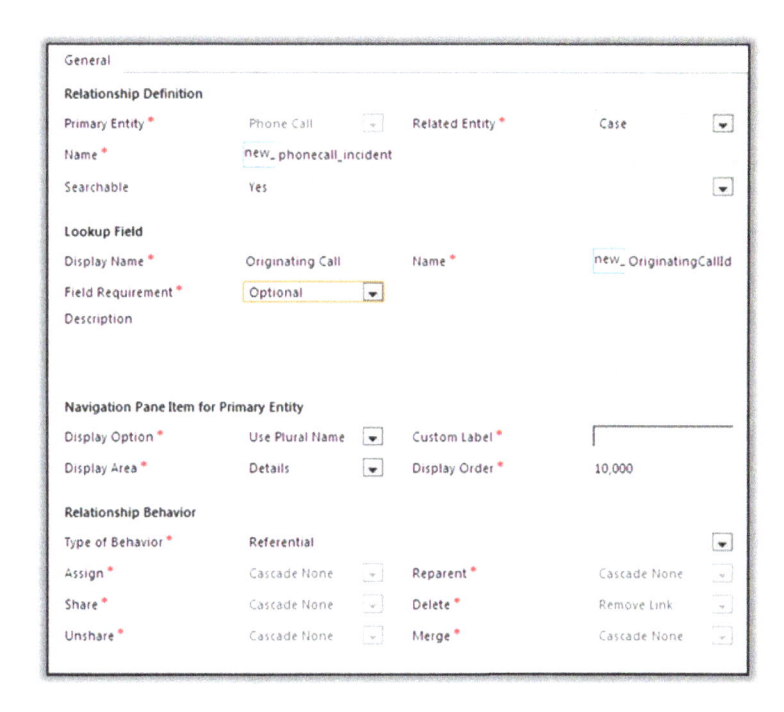

In this example we've used most of the default settings, and entered **Originating Call** in the **Display Name** field. Taking the approach we did here, this will be the name of the lookup field that will be created on the Case entity as part of this customization. If we did want to place the field on the case form we could optionally do that, but it would probably be best to make it read-only.

After adding the custom relationship and publishing, we're ready to resume our business process flow creation activity. Follow these steps to create a 4-stage process starting on a phone call and proceeding to a case:

1. Navigate to Processes and click **New**.
2. In the New Process dialog, provide the following information:
    a. **Process name**: "Phone Call to Case"
    b. **Category**: Business Process Flow
    c. **Entity**: Phone Call
    d. **Type**: New blank process
3. Then click **OK**, and the Business Process Flow designer opens. Collapse the properties section at the top of the designer to give more room to the stage editor.
4. For the first stage, provide the following information:
    a. **Stage**: Intake

b. **Stage Category**: Qualify
c. Add three Steps for the Intake stage, selecting in order **Description**, **Regarding**, and **Priority** in the Fields column, and modifying the Step names as you like in the Steps column:

5. After the Intake stage we want to proceed to a case, so click the Options control and this time, because of the custom relationship we created, Case is available in the **ADD ENTITY** list:

6. Select it, and then you can add stages and steps for the Case entity. In this example, let's use the same stages and steps for the multi-entity **Phone Call to Case Process** that we used for the single-entity **Case Process**:

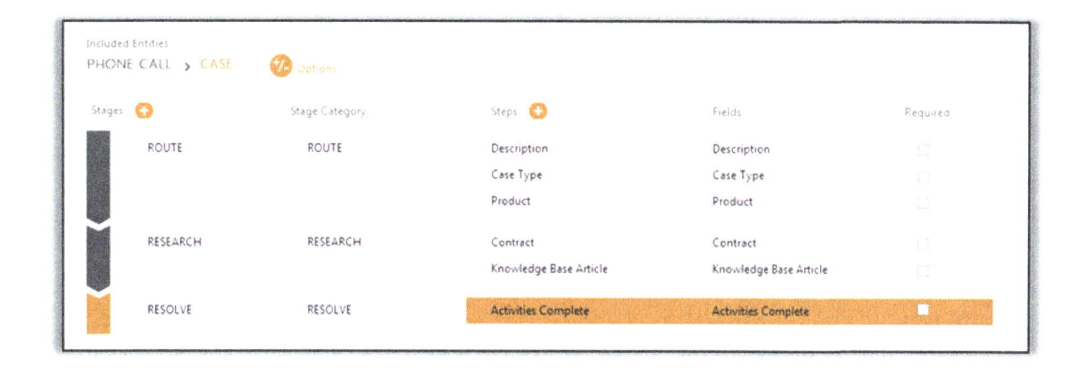

Stages	Stage Category	Steps	Fields	Required
ROUTE	ROUTE	Description	Description	
		Case Type	Case Type	
		Product	Product	
RESEARCH	RESEARCH	Contract	Contract	
		Knowledge Base Article	Knowledge Base Article	
RESOLVE	RESOLVE	Activities Complete	Activities Complete	

Included Entities: PHONE CALL > CASE

Now click **Activate** and your multi-entity process is ready to use.

Business Process Flows and Workflow Processes

Process Flows and Workflow Processes: Better Together

To appreciate why you will often need to combine functionality available from both *business process flows* and from traditional *workflow* processes, consider the following actions that business process flows by themselves cannot perform:

- Create or update records
- Change the status of records
- Assign tasks, send emails
- Apply conditional logic

It's almost correct to say that – apart from presenting a visualization of your processes and being able to create child records -- business process flows don't really *do* anything. Suppose that in the case process examples we've been working with, we want something to happen when a case is advanced from the Route to the Research stage. Referring back to the previous section, you can see we will have gathered enough useful information during the Route stage to … well… route the case when we get to the next stage. Let's suppose based on the case type (problem, question, etc.) and the product associated with the case, we want to apply conditional logic and assign the case, or route it to the appropriate queue. This sounds like a job for a workflow, so let's see how it's done, focusing specifically on how business process flows and workflow processes work *together*.

Trigger a Workflow Process from a Process Flow

For the purposes of this chapter, we'll assume you have some experience with workflow processes. We'll create a real-time workflow process (new to CRM 2013), so we can see immediately on the case form the impact of changing stages. And since this is effectively going to be a companion process to our Case Process business process flow, we'll give it the same name as well.

Since we want our automatic workflow process to be triggered when the business process flow changes, we will need to use the **Record fields change** trigger, as you can see in the following figure:

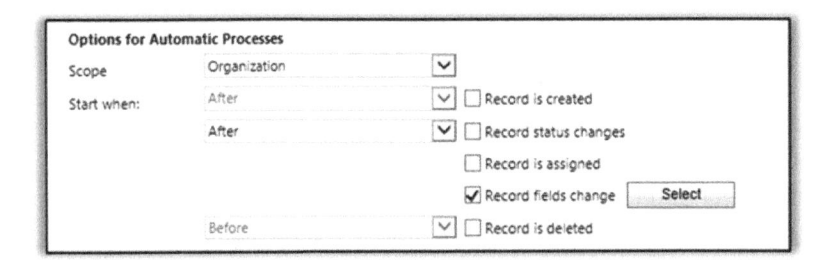

Then of course the question becomes, which field to use? That's often an easy question to answer, but it turns out in this scenario it's not. The problem is that the business process fields available directly on the case entity (and other entities enabled for business process flows) *do not change when the stage of a business process flow changes*. (Bear with me – I know this seems odd the first time you learn it!)

The two fields I'm talking about here are **Service Stage** and **Case Stage** – these are both available on the case entity, and you'd think that they would change when a user advances a business process flow, but they don't. Customize the case form and place these fields on the form to prove this to yourself.

Fortunately, there is a field that changes when the stage changes; it's the **Process Stage** field, so this is what we should use to trigger our workflow process. You can see this in the Select Fields dialog for this workflow, shown in the following figure:

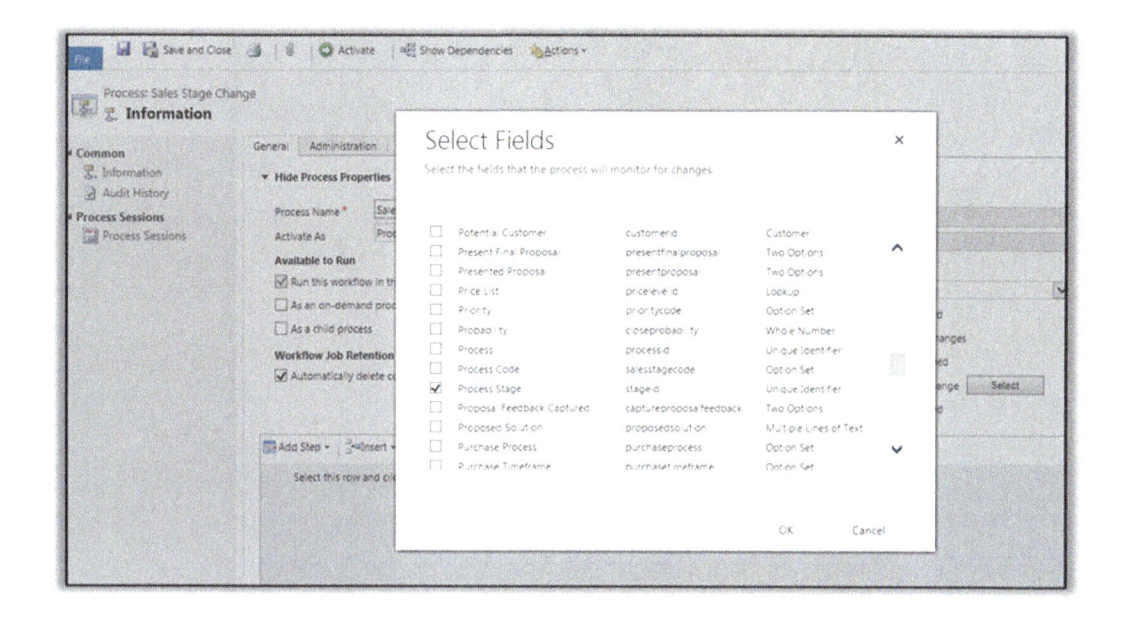

Since the Process Stage field is what's changing, you might think you can use conditional logic to test its value and take the appropriate action (remember, in our process we want to assign the case to the appropriate user or product team when the case advances to the Research stage). So here's the next problem: the **Process Stage** field is a GUID, as you can see if you look carefully at the previous figure, so it's not appropriate for conditional logic.

It turns out that any entity involved in a business process flow is a child record of another record type – the **Process Stage** entity – and that the Process Stage field is actually a lookup to the specific record in the Process Stage entity that corresponds to the current stage of the process.

This means that the conditional logic in workflows triggered by a change in the stage of a business process flow must be done slightly differently than you might be used to. Unless you want to perform conditional checks against the value of a GUID field, you need to check the value of one of the fields from the Process Stage entity. The following figure shows how you might test for the current value of the stage category field:

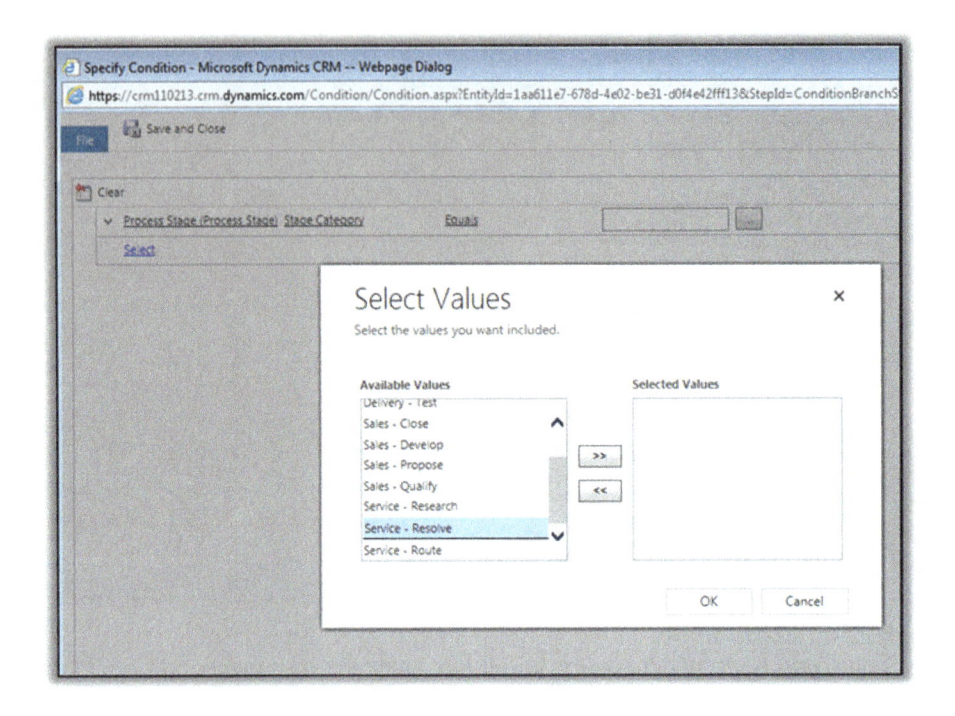

![Specify Condition dialog with Select Values popup showing Available Values including Delivery - Test, Sales - Close, Sales - Develop, Sales - Propose, Sales - Qualify, Service - Research, Service - Resolve, Service - Route]

Here's what a workflow might look like, with three different sets of actions that could be done, depending on the stage category:

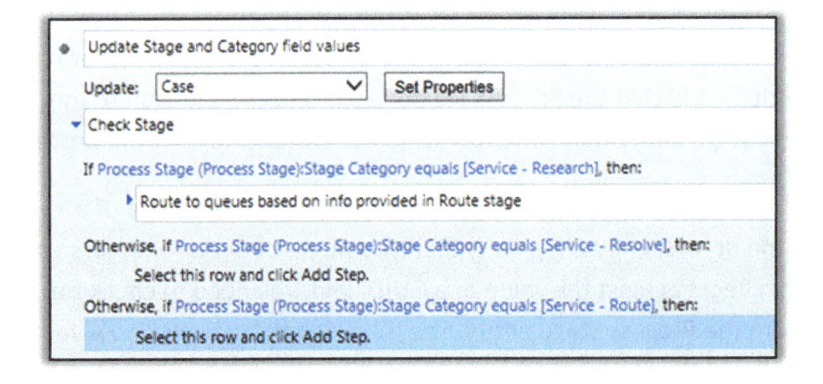

![Workflow showing Update Stage and Category field values, with Check Stage conditions for Service - Research, Service - Resolve, and Service - Route]

Again, since you can't use the GUID field on the case record to check for the stage you're in, you need to drill up through the Process Stage field and test against one of its values. Notice here that I'm checking against the stage category field rather than the stage name. You could really use either, but I like the stage category field for a couple of reasons we'll discuss at the end of the chapter.

So after this preliminary work, we now have what we need to implement conditional business logic in our companion workflow process. Here's an example:

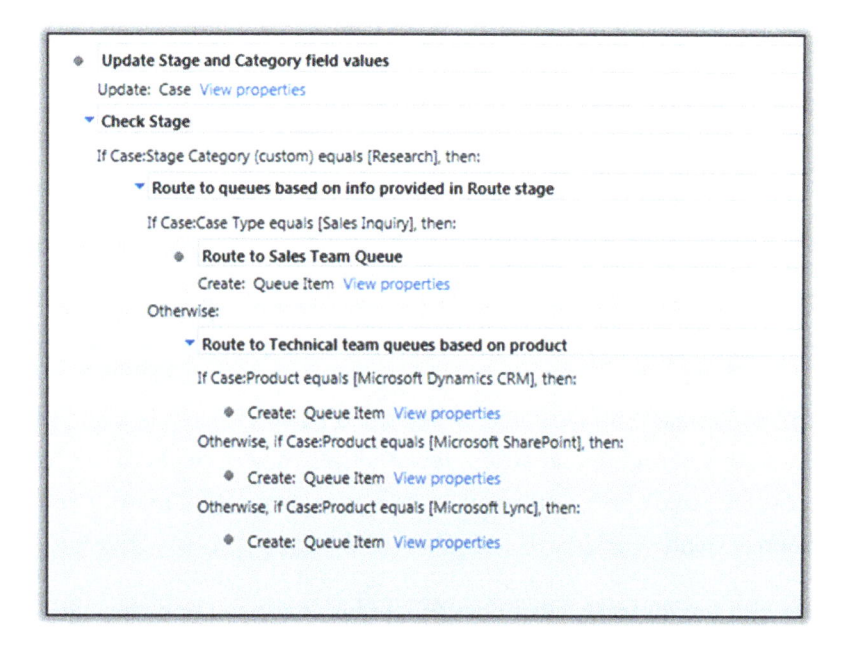

```
● Update Stage and Category field values
   Update: Case  View properties
▼ Check Stage
   If Case:Stage Category (custom) equals [Research], then:
      ▼ Route to queues based on info provided in Route stage
         If Case:Case Type equals [Sales Inquiry], then:
            ● Route to Sales Team Queue
               Create: Queue Item  View properties
         Otherwise:
            ▼ Route to Technical team queues based on product
               If Case:Product equals [Microsoft Dynamics CRM], then:
                  ● Create: Queue Item  View properties
               Otherwise, if Case:Product equals [Microsoft SharePoint], then:
                  ● Create: Queue Item  View properties
               Otherwise, if Case:Product equals [Microsoft Lync], then:
                  ● Create: Queue Item  View properties
```

The first action in the workflow process is on the **Update: Case** step, which was illustrated above. Once the stage fields contain the value of the current stage, we can apply conditional logic, which in the previous figure is done in the **Check Stage** conditional block. The specific scenario here uses the selection of the Case Type and Product fields to route a case to one of several queues. (To keep the workflow simple and focus on the essentials, we've left out conditional checks you'd probably want in a production process, such as what happens if a product isn't selected, etc..)

Tips, Tricks and Traps

Using the Ready-to-Use Business Processes

Business process flows are not as well documented as they could be, which of course makes learning how to use them more challenging than it should be. One of the best early learning resources I've found is the collection of **Ready-to-Use Business Processes** available on the **Data Management** page in Dynamics CRM 2013.

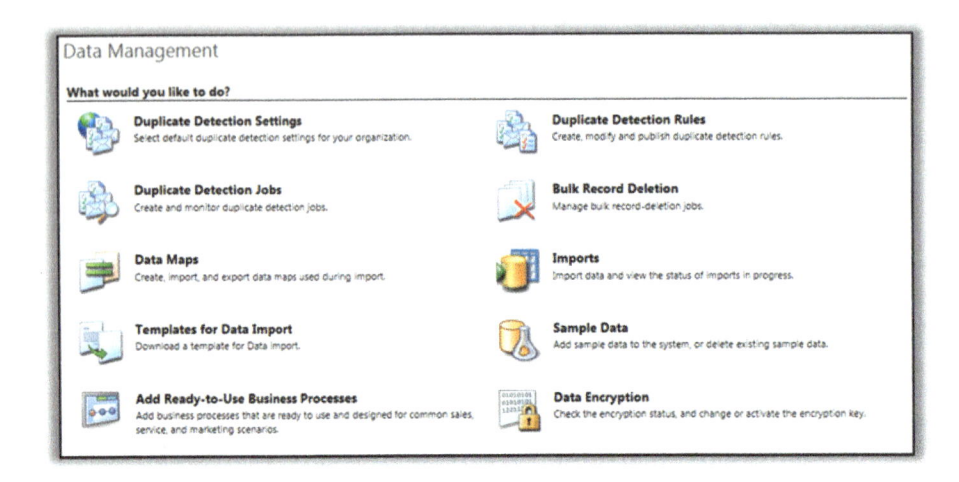

These function similarly to the Sample Data available on the same page: click the link and you can install the processes in the background, and after a few minutes they're ready to use. These are an excellent learning resource and I encourage you to take advantage of them. As you do, here are a few things to keep in mind:

- When you click the **Add Ready-to-Use Business Processes** link, a solution package containing the business processes is imported into your Dynamics CRM organization. It's a managed solution, and one of the features this managed solution has is that *the processes it contains cannot be customized*. You can see this if you open the Business Process solution after importing it. The default view of customizable processes contained in the solution looks like the following figure:

    You might do a double-take the first time you see that, but changing the view from **Customizable** to **All** sheds light on the structure of the solution:

The solution doesn't contain any *customizable* processes because the **Customizable** property has been set to **False** for all of them. This is a common practice for a managed solution: because one of the advantages of a managed solution is one-click uninstall, solution publishers generally don't want to allow customizations to solution components. If they did, you might be tempted to customize them…and then lose your customizations when uninstalling the solution!

Fortunately, you can still use these processes as a starting point and make changes from there. The business process flows designer comes with a handy new Save As command, so just open the business process flow you want to make changes to, click **Save As**, and you will see something like the following:

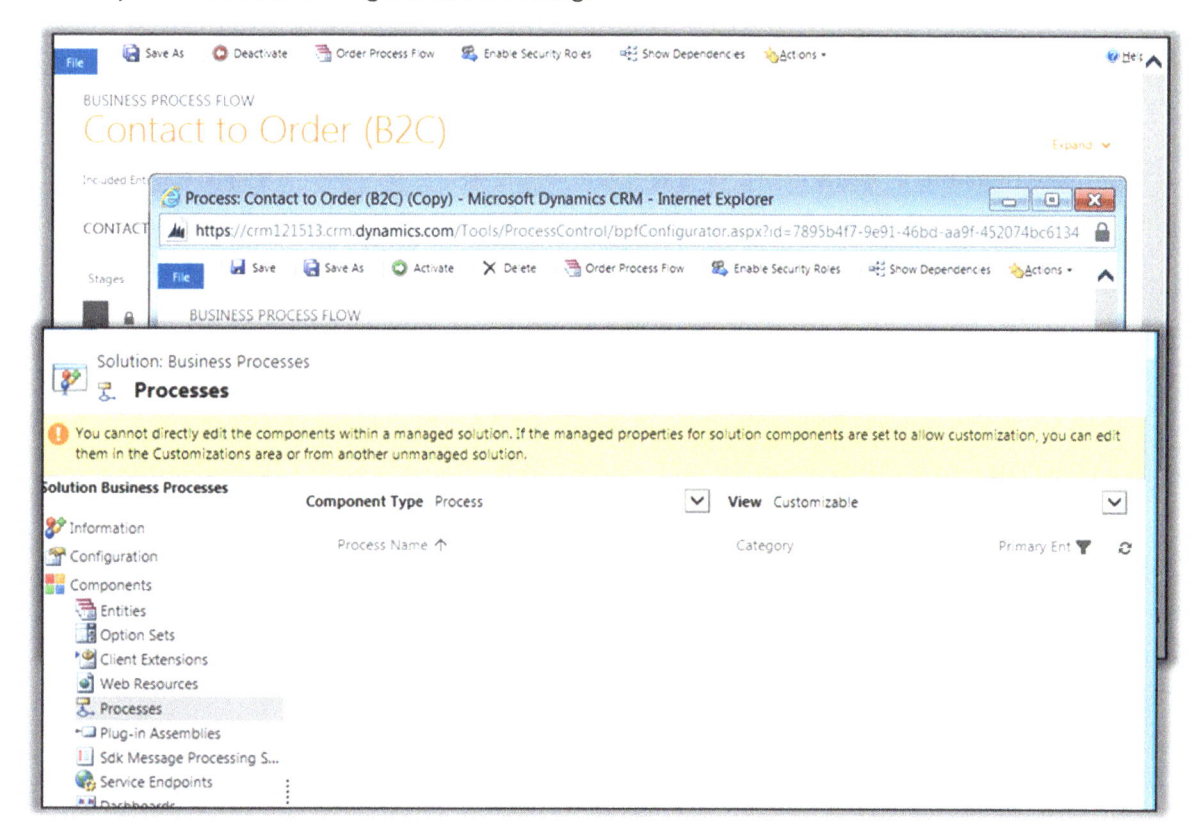

The copy is available in the default solution and is customizable.
- When you import the solution, you may notice that some of the processes are activated and some are not. Look a little closer and you will notice that all of the business process

flows are activated; their companion workflow processes are not. In order to use them effectively, review and activate as needed.

Which Entities Support Create Business Process Flows?

You can create process flows for any custom entity, after you've enabled the **Business process flows** option in the entity definition. You can also create them for any of the system entities which use the updated "flow" forms:

Account	Appointment	Campaign	Campaign Activity	Campaign Response
Competitor	Contact	Email	Fax	Case
Invoice	Lead	Letter	Marketing List	Opportunity
Phone Call	Product	Price List Item	Quote	Recurring Appointment
Sales Literature	Order	User	Task	Team

Business Process Flows and Custom Entities

Custom entities can support business process flows, but you need to enable them by selecting the **Business process flows** checkbox on the General tab of the entity's Information form, as the following figure shows:

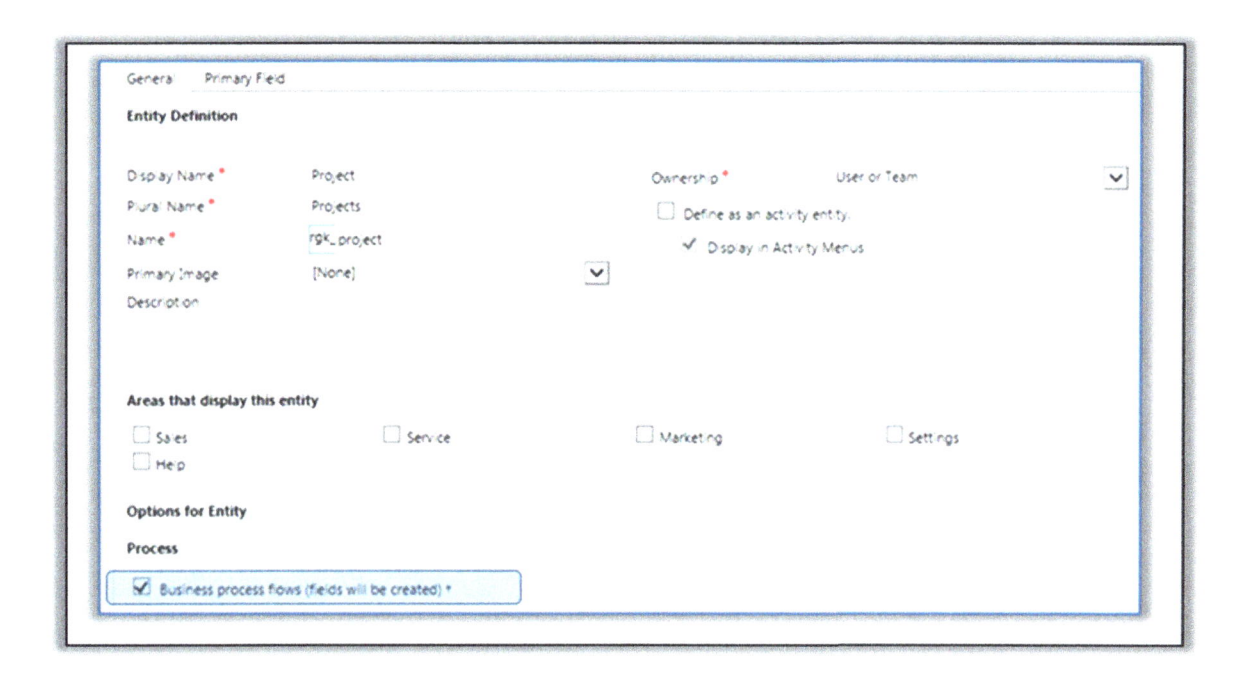

After enabling business process flows for a custom entity, you will notice that two additional fields – **Process ID** and **Stage ID** – are created on the entity. You can see these in the following figure, after we've turned on process flows for a custom entity Project:

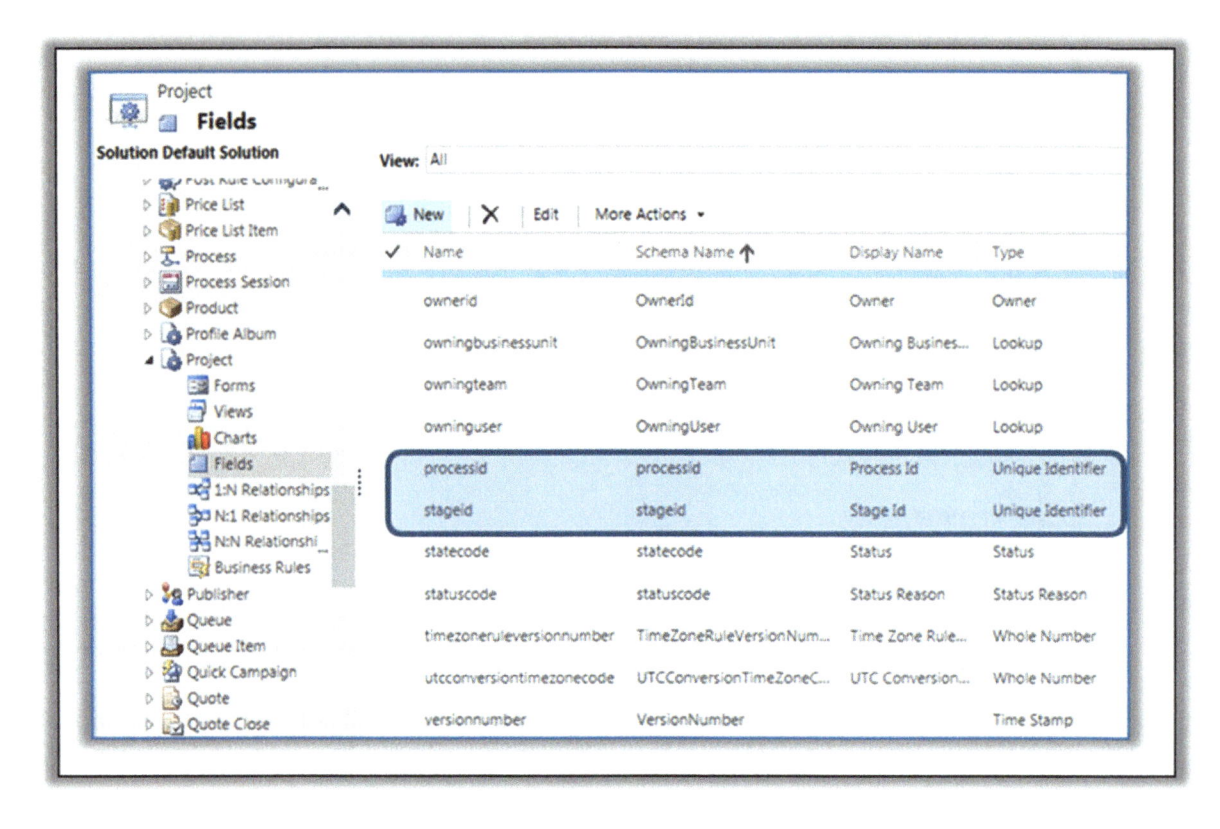

However, if you add those two fields to an Advanced Find view of Project and examine their contents, you'll have a better appreciation for the previous long discussion of why we needed to fill in custom fields on the case entity. For example, here's an Advanced Find view on the custom Project entity, with those fields added to the view:

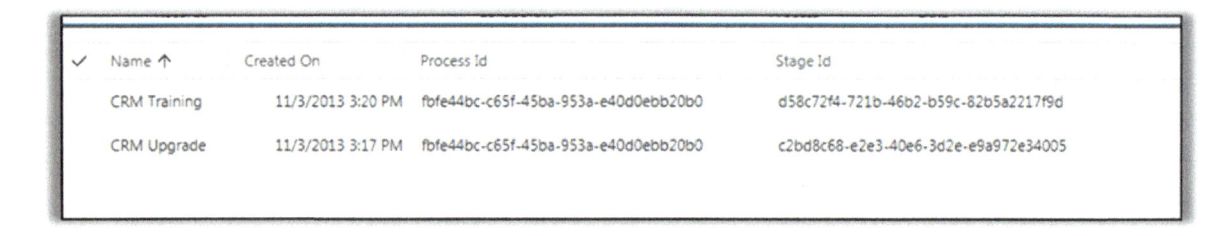

Here's a more interesting view, after adding fields from the Parent entity, drilling through the Stage ID lookup field in Advanced Find:

Name ↑	Created On	Process Id	Stage Id	Primary Entity (Stage Id)	Process Stage Name (Stage...	Stage Category (Stage Id)
CRM Training	11/3/2013 3:20 PM	fbfe44bc-c65...	d58c72f4-72...	Project	Develop	Develop
CRM Upgrade	11/3/2013 3:17 PM	fbfe44bc-c65...	c2bd8c68-e...	Project	Resolve	Resolve

Again, a workflow process can be triggered by the stage change of a business process flow, but when you check for the value of the current stage, remember to use the fields from the parent Process Stage entity and not Process Id or Stage Id.

If you can run a Process, will it Work?

Previously we discussed the security requirements regarding creating, running and activating business process flows. That discussion had to do with the access users' security roles give them to *processes*. Here's a related but different issue: if a user has access to run a process, will it work?

And here's an example to illustrate the potential problem: suppose you've created a multi-entity business process flow that starts on a lead, proceeds to an opportunity and then to a quote. And suppose a user's security role allows him/her full access to leads and opportunities, but only read privileges on quotes. If users have organization-level read privilege on the Process entity (as the standard security roles, provide; refer back to the security section if necessary) they'll be able to run the process. But when they get to the part of the process flow where a quote record is created, they'll get an error message, because they do not have privileges to create quotes.

Even if you are *not* a (Dynamics CRM) security expert, it's easy enough to understand that a user would need create privileges on any of the record types that a business process flow tries to create. But it's slightly more complex than that, because records created within a business process flow are child records of the previous record in the process. (So in the example, the lead record would be the parent of the created opportunity record, which in turn would be the parent of the quote record.)

And to understand why this matters, it helps if you *are* a (Dynamics CRM) security expert: not only do you need privileges to create quotes, but you also need privileges to associate them with parent opportunity records. In terms of Dynamics CRM security concepts, here are the privileges your security roles would require in order to run the process without errors:

- **Create** privilege on the quote entity
- **Append to** privilege on opportunity

- **Append** privilege on quote

Targeting Business Process Flows and Switching Processes

Previously we discussed using security roles to target business process flows. In this context, it's important to be a little more precise in how we use the word *target*, since it might not work the way you expect it to. Let's walk through a scenario to illustrate, with this starting point:

- User A has a single security role, Security Role A.
- User B has the single role Security Role B.
- You have created two business process flows for opportunities: Process A is targeted to Security Role A; Process B to Security Role B.
- Both security roles have organization level privilege to read and modify opportunities.

With that as background, consider the following scenario:

1. User A creates a new opportunity, Opportunity A. Process A is automatically applied. At this point, User A cannot see any other business process flows.
2. User A saves and closes the opportunity.
3. User B opens the form for Opportunity A.

Q: What process flow does User B sees on Opportunity A?

A: User B sees Process A, just the way User A saved the record.

Even though that process flow is not targeted to him, User B can work the opportunity, advance through the stages of the process and so forth. Also, User B can switch to Process B. And after switching to Process B, User B cannot switch back to Process A, since it's not targeted to him.

The problem is that even though users cannot *switch* to a process not targeted to their security roles, they are *not* prevented from accessing and interacting with a process already applied to a record they can access. So "targeting" really only prevents users from switching to a business process flow, not from messing around with a process they aren't supposed to use! Whether or not this is a big problem depends on several factors: how you intend to use process flows, how many CRM users you have, and the like.

About the only real solution is to rely on security roles to restrict record access. Suppose we modified the previous scenario so that User A and B were in different business units, and their security roles only gave them business unit level access on the Write privilege for opportunities.

With that modification each would be able to open the other's opportunity records and see the process flow, but not be able to interact with it.

Maxima, Minima and So Forth

Here are three of the most important constraints to keep in mind when designing business process flows:

- The maximum number of activated processes per entity is 10.
- The maximum number of stages in each process is 30.
- The maximum number of steps in each stage is 30.
- The maximum number of entities that can participate in a process is 5.

Customizing the Stage Category Global Option Set

Previously, in the discussion of how workflows and process flows work together, I mentioned that I prefer using the stage category field for conditional testing rather than the stage name. The main reason I say that is that it's an option set field: so when you're designing a process you select it from a list of available options, rather than typing it. To review, you can see that in the business process flow designer:

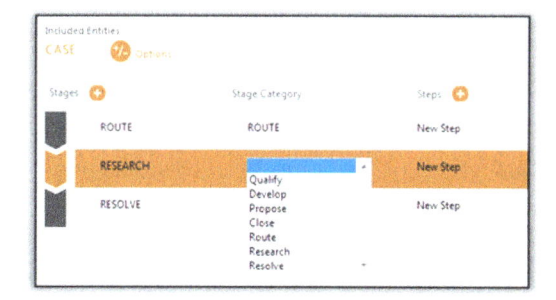

The values in the Stages column – ROUTE, RESEARCH AND RESOLVE, in this example – are text that you type; the values in the Stage Category column are selected from the option set values.

Which is one of the reasons I prefer doing my conditional logic against the stage category field rather than the stage name: I can select it from a list, rather than having to remember it and type it exactly as I entered it in the process flow designer.

But that leads us to another potential issue that it's probably too early to have developed best practices for, but that should be on your radar, and that has to do with the fundamental design of business process flows. The Stage Category option set is the single field we have to reliably categorize all of our business process flows, whether for service or sales processes, or processes against custom entities, you name it. It's in danger of becoming one of the most over-used global option sets in the history of Dynamics CRM, so be careful how you use it!

To provide guidance on which categories should be used for which kinds of business process flows, you might consider customizing it along the lines shown in the following figure:

But whatever practices you implement around this, make sure you *have* some. By default, only system administrators can modify the **Stage Category** global option set. But since it's intended to be used by business users as they build their business process flows, you should have a strategy for how it will be customized, and how it should be used.

My Take on Business Process Flows

In previous versions of Dynamics CRM, the out of the box forms for opportunities and cases have been essentially process-free, with nothing in the UI that even hints at processes, stages or the like. Traditionally, this has been a notable contrast to other CRM software, many of which come pre-configured with sales or service processes. For example, salesforce.com has an out of the box 7-stage sales process, in the form of a customizable pick-list on the opportunity form.

In Dynamics CRM 2013, Microsoft has gone from a process agnostic to a true believer. And to me it appears to have been an inspired leap of faith, as opposed to say, a carefully calculated response to user requests for "something at the top of forms where you can see your process stages and the fields that should be provided before proceeding to the next stage". Microsoft isn't simply "checking the box" by adding this functionality but instead adding a robust configurable solution that can be used to build complex solutions.

But I don't mean to sound negative: I think it's refreshing that the Dynamics CRM product team re-designed the user experience as dramatically as they have, and I think that with subject to a couple of caveats, we can use the new tools to build productive process-centric user experiences that our users will even...enjoy!

Start Slowly

So here are my caveats:

- **Go slow on multiple-entity processes.** If you need any examples of how confusing they can be, examine the Ready-to-Use Business Processes we discussed previously. The processes contained in that managed solution are intended as examples only, of course, but for me the initial user experience, especially for the sample 5-user process flows, was a lesson in how to confuse users.
- **Go slow on multiple processes per entity**. As we've seen, until we have a way of really targeting processes – as in, preventing users from having visibility to or being able to interact with a process -- the only solution is through security. And for most organizations, it would probably take a pretty compelling requirement for process-switching to justify locking down security roles enough to make it feasible.

Data Architecture, and Potential Extensions

I really like the data design underlying the new business process flow architecture. Effectively, what we have are the entity relationships illustrated in the following Visio diagram, with a 1:N relationship from the Process to the Process Stage entity, and in turn a 1:N from Process Stage to every entity that supports process flows:

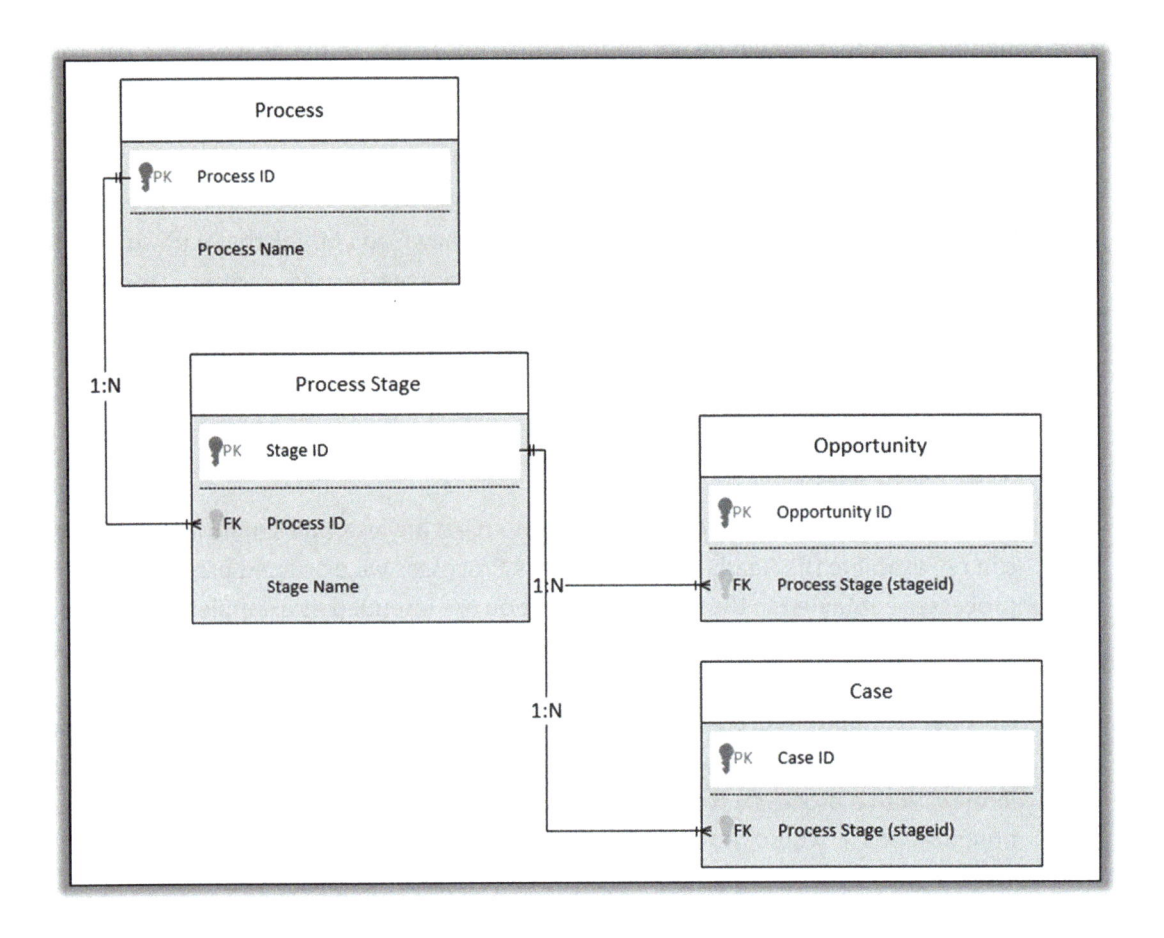

One of the reasons I like this data design is that it validates an essentially identical pattern I've used on several engagements and wrote about in this article, http://www.magenium.com/Techblog/2013/August/Flexible-Sales-Processes-Part-1.aspx. (This is an example of independent discovery, by the way: I've used the technique for several years, and you can see in the article that that screenshots are all CRM 2011. And the article was published too late for anybody from Microsoft to have been inspired enough to impact the design of Dynamics CRM 2013!)

But the key point of the article – captured in the **Flexible Sales Processes** title – is that this architecture has important business benefits. The following figure (from the article) draws attention to the potential benefits of the approach discussed in the article:

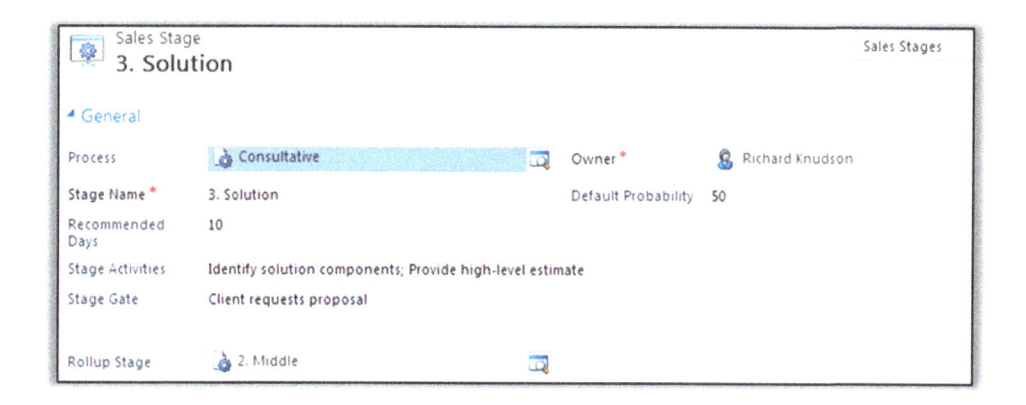

![Sales Stage 3. Solution form screenshot showing Process: Consultative, Stage Name: 3. Solution, Recommended Days: 10, Stage Activities: Identify solution components; Provide high-level estimate, Stage Gate: Client requests proposal, Rollup Stage: 2. Middle, Owner: Richard Knudson, Default Probability: 50]

The key point is that stages can have important metadata; for example, **default probability** and **recommended days in stage** as shown in the figure. The ability to store custom data (e.g., CRM fields) on process stages would provide significant advantages. And it would be an important extension to the current Dynamics CRM 2013 implementation of business process flows, because the **Process Stage** and **Process** entities are both not customizable.

Summing Up

Business process flows, along with several other new features in Dynamics CRM 2013 -- especially business rules and real-time workflows -- continue to increase the scope for non-technical business users to customize CRM. This is appropriate for an application typically driven by business users, and it's one of the great advantages of the Dynamics CRM platform. But it also raises important issues which may be new ones for many organizations. For example, business teams may not have experience with formal application design and development practices that are taken for granted by IT. On the other hand, IT may not appreciate the rapid pace of change faced by business users, and the importance that places on a flexible, responsive application design. Whether your role is IT, business, or some combination, make sure you take these into account as you explore how cool new functionality like business process flows can be put to use for your organization.

6

No Code Business Rules

At the heart of every CRM implementation is a boat load of business requirements, many of which are implemented by one or more business rules. Generically, a business rule is often one or more simple conditions that must be true and when they are one or more actions occur. CRM comes out of the box with a number of business rules implemented that are expected to meet a large number of business needs. Many of these can be customized so they are tailored to fit more specific project needs. Beyond that, developers can use code to implement client side rules with JavaScript or server side rules with CRM extensions like plug-ins.

In a perfect world, CRM would have simple switches that you could magically toggle to do everything needed. That is simply not realistic, and having developers create code for every possible rule is also usually cost prohibitive for most projects. So more typically what happens on projects is business rules are prioritized and many of the less important ones that would result in custom code simply don't get implemented. For many of these they become part of the procedures for use of the system and users are trained and expected to handle them. You can imagine how that turns out, often times with them being forgotten after the first couple weeks the system is live.

Microsoft Dynamics CRM 2013 tries to improve this situation with a new feature called CRM Business Rules. CRM Business Rules are a customization oriented feature that allows declarative definition of business rules without requiring custom developer code. CRM Business Rules allow you to specify one or more conditions and one or more actions that execute when the condition is true. Rules can be created by functional consultants or developers expanding the pool of resources that can help implement a projects requirements. These rules are packaged in CRM Solutions and delivered with the other project assets. Developers using code will still be essential to implement business rules of any level of complexity. In the rest of this chapter we are going to dive deeper into how CRM Business Rules work.

Introducing CRM Business Rules

New features must be envisioned by their architect in their mature state, but are often implemented with only a small amount of what they expect it to mature to in the future. CRM Business Rules is no exception. In CRM 2013, CRM Business Rules (Let's call them CBRs for short) should be used for simple conditions that need to execute one of the provided actions on client side only. Client side only is a great example of CBRs start small but have a big potential for the future. In the future, CBRs are architected so they could execute on both the client and server side. Why is server side execution important? Server side execution ensures a business rule is implemented regardless of how the action occurs. For example, if there is a rule that Account Credit Limits can't be over $50,000 and its implemented only client side, then if data is imported using the CRM Import feature it could completely bypass that rule. A server rule on the other hand would have caught it. Today, developers implement server rules using plug-ins or other code extensions that will continue until CBRs have server side support.

So what do I mean by client side? Let's be a little more specific. By client side we are talking about rules that are implemented on CRM forms and if the interaction with the data or service isn't via the forms the rules don't have any impact. Today, developers build client script that uses the client API (Application Programing Interface) provided by CRM from custom JavaScript to implement business rules. This custom code is then hooked up to each form for an entity to determine when it executes. The code executes On Load, On Save or after change of one of the field controls on the form. If you have 3 forms for an entity these events must be hooked up to the custom code for each different form that is created.

CBRs on the other hand are created once and can specify that they should execute either for one specific form or for all forms for that entity. The CBR under the covers uses the same CRM Client API to implement the rule, however it is expressed by the implementer using a web editor similar to building Advanced Find criteria. The rule is then stored in CRM as part of a CRM Solution and when a form is rendered CRM uses that definition to build the same type of script that a developer would have built.

One nice thing to keep in mind is CBRs and custom developer code are designed to co-exist on the same form. It's also important to understand the goal of CBRs is not to get rid of the custom developer script. Sure over time the amount that requires custom code may reduce, CBRs are really targeted at this point to the simple rules that are tedious to do in code. Stay tuned for more details on how these two styles of implementing business rules co-exist within the form event lifecycle later in the chapter.

Creating and Managing Rules

CRM Business Rules (CBRs) are created in the context of an entity such as Contact or Account. CBRs can be viewed created and modified in multiple places within the administration pages of the CRM web client. There is no single right answer to when to use each of the options as they are there for your convenience. The following explains where you can find the starting point for managing CBRs.

> **NOTE** *Developers can also create CBRs via the CRM API, however, the API calls are not well documented to do this.*

From Solution Explorer

As you expand an Entity in Solution Explorer you will now see a new navigation option for business rules. This is the most direct path to get to rules for an entity. Here you will see and be able to create rules that are associated with any form for that entity.

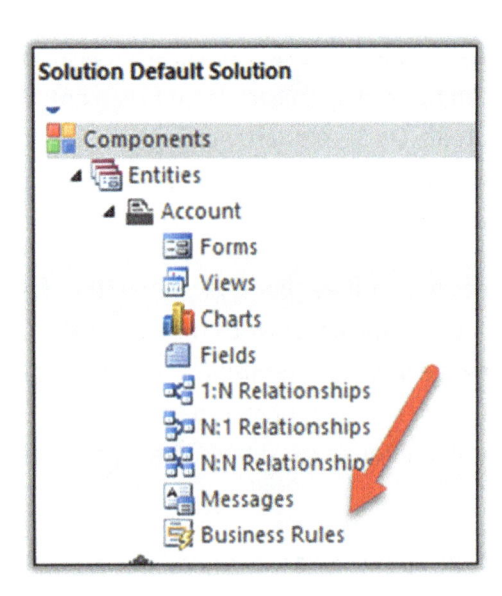

This is probably the easiest place to create a rule and if I was tasked with creating 10 or 20 of them this is where I would start.

You can also click on Business Rules when you are working with a specific field to quickly manage the rules that are associated with that field.

This is a great place to work when you have a set of rules for a specific field you are trying to quickly create or manage.

From the Form Editor

It's very common to be looking at a CRM Form and have an "Ah Ha!" moment when you realize that you should have a rule that happens on the form. This is probably going to happen more often in less formal projects where a list of business rules isn't necessarily provided but more developed on the fly as the customizations evolve. From the CRM Form Editor you can quickly see the CBRs that apply to that form by clicking on the Business Rules button in the Ribbon. When you click the button the Field Explorer is replaced with a Business Rules Explorer.

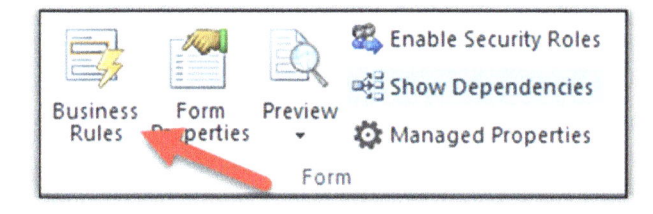

> **NOTE**
> *CBRs created from here default to only execute on the form being edited. Make sure you read the discussion on Scope later in this chapter.*

You can also get to rules for a specific field by opening Field Properties and clicking on the Business Rules tab.

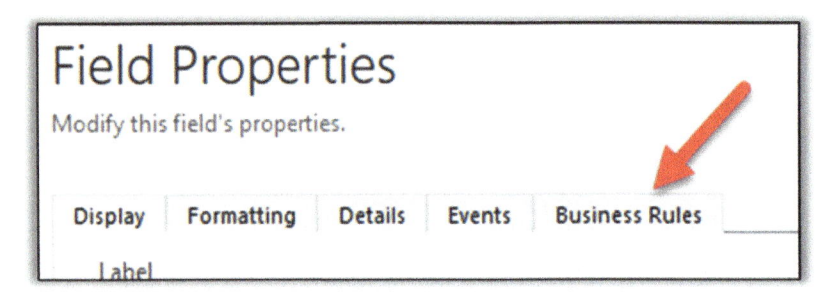

Field Properties
Modify this field's properties.

Display | Formatting | Details | Events | **Business Rules**

Label

This is a great way to quickly see only the rules for that field when you are working on changing a form.

> **NOTE** *CBRs will still execute while a user is offline or using the CRM for Tablets but they must be created while on-line.*

Naming and Describing Business Rules

When you create a new CBR, there are two fields you should consider providing as a best practice. The Name and Description fields are not required, but can be very helpful during system maintenance and enhancement. The Name field is pre filled with "Enter Rule Name". Guess what is saved if you don't provide a Name value? You got it, "Enter Rule Name". Imagine looking at a list of rules all having "Enter Rule Name" in the Name field. It wouldn't make it easy to find the rule that enforced Maximum Value for example.

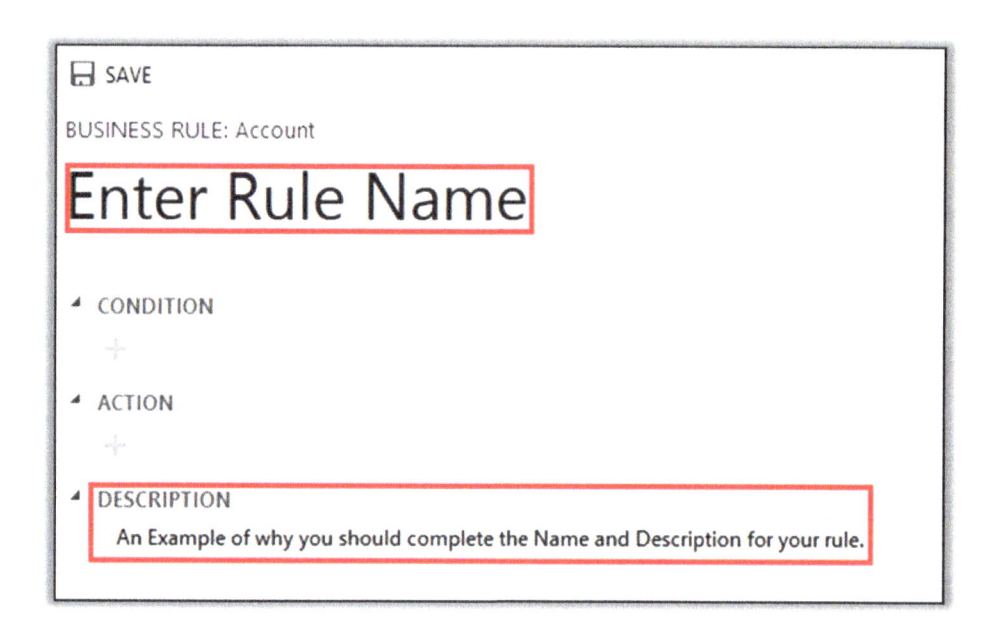

```
SAVE
BUSINESS RULE: Account
Enter Rule Name

▲ CONDITION
  +

▲ ACTION
  +

▲ DESCRIPTION
  An Example of why you should complete the Name and Description for your rule.
```

You might be tempted to put in the primary field name in the Name value. That falls apart as soon as you have 5 rules for the same field.

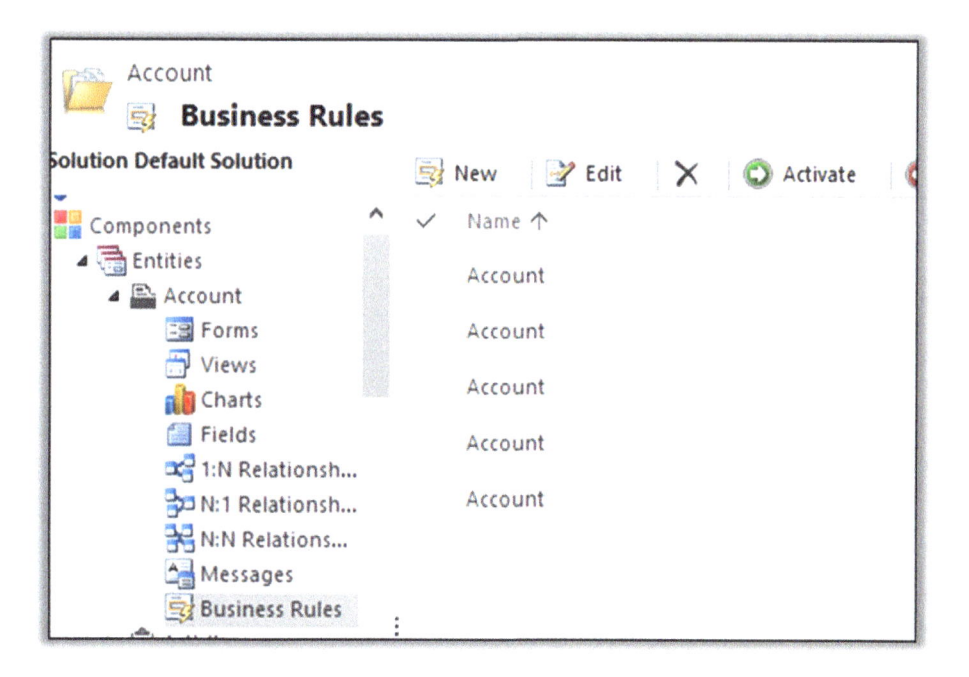

```
Account
  Business Rules
Solution Default Solution          New    Edit   X   Activate
Components                    ✓   Name ↑
  ▲ Entities
    ▲ Account                     Account
        Forms                     Account
        Views
        Charts                    Account
        Fields                    Account
        1:N Relationsh...
        N:1 Relationsh...         Account
        N:N Relations...
        Messages
        Business Rules
```

It's also tempting and easy to just use something relating to the condition or action being taking. Imagine if you were making Credit Limit Required for Colorado Accounts. You might be tempted to name the rule "Required" if you were creating it from the Field Properties thinking only about rules for that Field. The problem is when you look at all the rules for that entity you now could have many rules all saying "Required" without any idea what they are requiring.

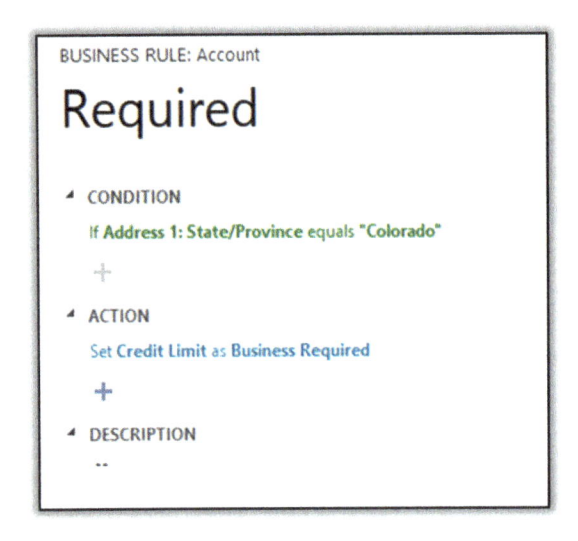

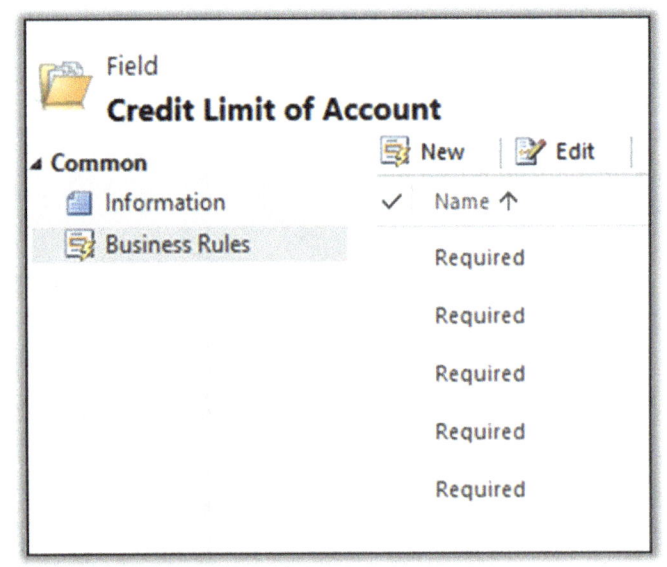

BUSINESS RULE: Account

Required

⊿ CONDITION

If **Address 1: State/Province** equals "Colorado"

+

⊿ ACTION

Set **Credit Limit** as Business Required

+

⊿ DESCRIPTION

--

Field
Credit Limit of Account

⊿ Common
- Information
- Business Rules

	New	Edit
✓	Name ↑	
	Required	
	Required	
	Required	
	Required	
	Required	

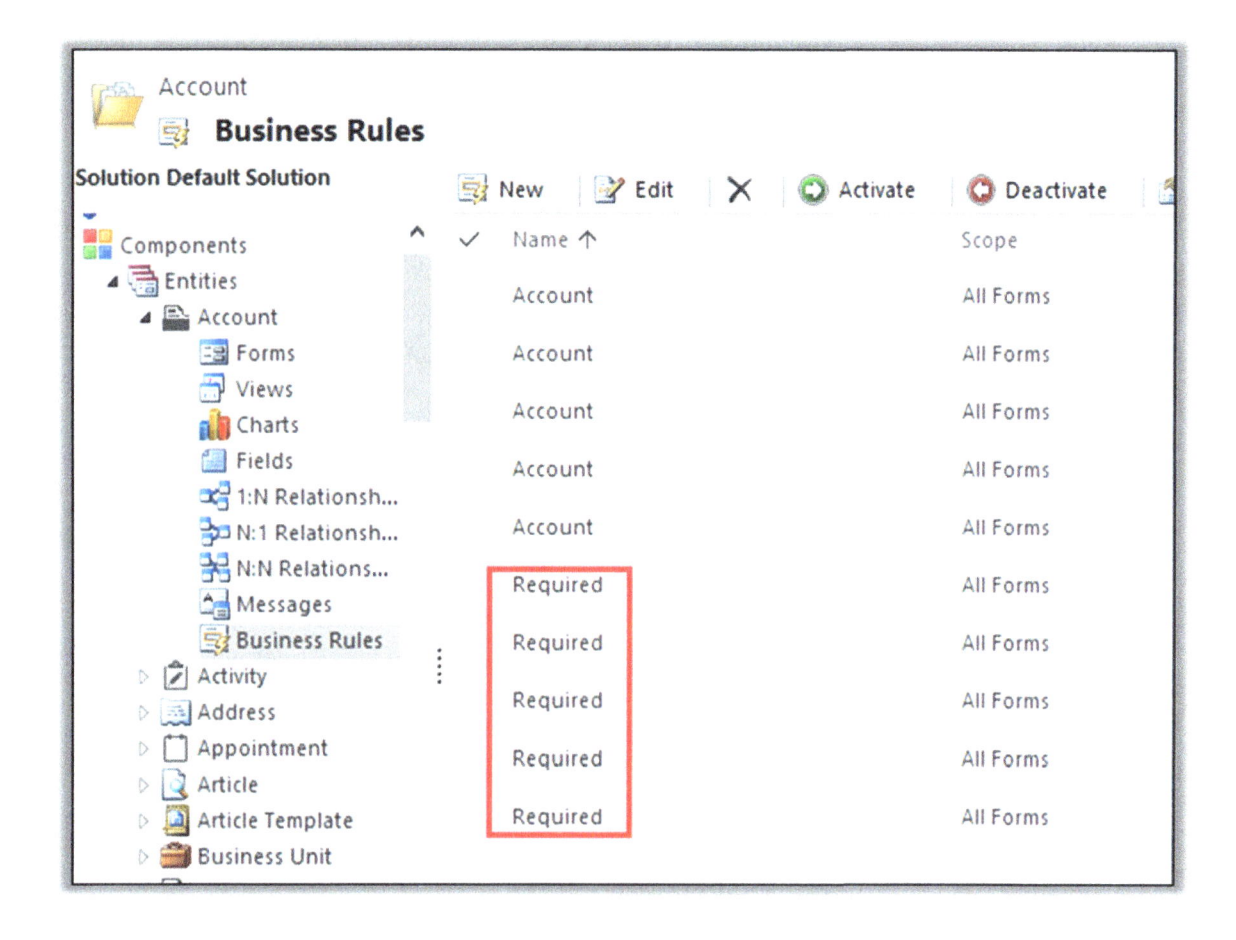

So perhaps pairing the primary Field name with some type of action or condition might be a good place to start. For example "Credit Limit – Required". While not perfect, it does quickly tell you what the rule is all about. You might even further qualify it to "Credit Limit – Required – Colorado" to make it clearer.

> **TIP** *Name should convey the elevator pitch of why the rule exists and should be as unique as possible for other rules for that same entity.*

Rules are often created in pairs, one that checks for a condition and performs a positive action and one that checks for the reverse condition and performs the reverse action. For example, if

State is Colorado Require Credit Limit. The pair might be If NOT Colorado, do not require Credit Limit. Testing our prior naming of "Credit Limit – Required – Colorado" could also then be "Credit Limit – Not Required – Colorado" for the pairing.

Description is another place you can provide a more detailed version of why this rule was created. When naming and describing rules imagine if you were coming back to look at a rule one year later - what would you want to know by simply looking at the Name and Description field. Even worse, it's not you looking at it, but some stranger that inherited the great system you created - what would they need to know to maintain that rule and know why it exists.

Rule Traceability

Projects that have formal requirements often have requirement numbers that can be used to help traceability. One possible idea of how to improve traceability of CBRs is to include that requirement # either in the Name or the Description. That would allow someone later to look back at what business requirement caused the rule to be implemented. This would also be helpful if later a business requirement was dropped, by looking for all rules with that number the impact assessment of the change is a lot easier to perform.

Simple obvious rules don't cause much impact if not traceable, but any with substance can cause project team in maintenance to spend unnecessary time researching why a rule was added. It also can cause rules that should be left alone to be removed because someone coming along later didn't understand why the rule was necessary.

Lifecycle of a Rule

CBRs follow a Create, Save, Activate model. New rules do not execute until they are activated. If you want to change a rule you must first de-activate it make the change, save it and then re-activate it.

Rule Scope

By default rules created from the Entity editors are created scoped for All Forms and rules created from the Form Editor are scoped to that Form. Generally speaking, it is best to create rules that are scoped to All Forms unless the rule implements something that would break other forms. The reason for that is if you were to specify only a single form because there is only one form in the system at the time, what happens later when someone creates a second form? Simple, that new form doesn't run the rules scoped to the first form leaving the business requirements not implemented. It's easy to overlook so try to keep rules scoped to all forms.

But what if my fields aren't on a form won't the rule break? Good question but no rules are designed to handle the fact that all forms won't have all fields. A form that doesn't have the field won't execute the rule. This could also cause problems with inconsistent business rule implementation. One way to work around this is to still add the necessary fields to the form and make them hidden. This does require the customizer to recognize that this problem exists.

When else would it be a good idea to scope to a single form? The most obvious is you have a rule that only needs to be checked on a specific form. This might be to enforce a rule that is role specific. For example, imagine if we didn't want Sales People to set Credit Limits but only when the Account State is Colorado, but Sales Managers can. In this example, you could consider creating two forms one for Sales People and one for Sales Managers. You can't just remove the field from the Sales People because for every other state they are able to provide a credit limit. On the Sales People form you could have a rule that only ran on that form to hide the Credit Limit field if the state is Colorado, and show it when it is another state.

Another place it gets tricky is if you need to not have a rule run for a specific form. Imagine if you had 5 forms for Account. There is no "All Forms Except Form X" option. A rule runs on all forms or a single form. So in this example you would have to change it to single and clone it for all the forms that needed it to run. This should be avoided whenever possible as it is a maintenance nightmare.

Business Rule Conditions

CBRs can be simply thought of as When X is true, Do Y. X is the Condition(s) that must all be true in order for Y to happen. Each CBR can specify one or more Condition that is evaluated during two events in the form/field life cycle. First, when the form is loaded this allows for doing things like show or hide a value based on another value. Second is when a field changes values that is part of a condition the rules are compared. This allows on the fly reaction to things that the user is doing on the form. Conditions are NOT checked though when the form is Saved. There is also no way to force a rule conditions to be evaluated on demand or by a developer invoking them from custom client side script.

Conditions are simple IF X, Then Y and don't support the ability to have complex branching logic you might find in developer created custom script. Even something as basic as IF Condition A, Else If Condition B, Otherwise Action C is not supported in the current release of CBRs.

Editing Conditions

When building a condition you can use either the drop down list of field names or simply type in the text box and it will attempt to show you matching fields. For entities with a lot of fields it is a lot easier to use the search feature and let the editor locate the right field.

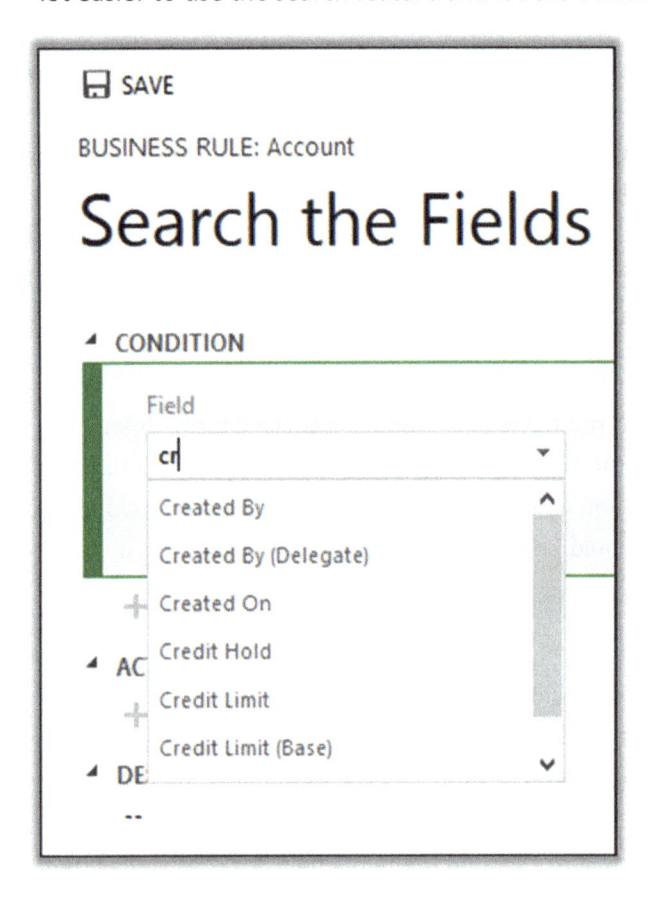

```
SAVE
BUSINESS RULE: Account
```

Search the Fields

▲ CONDITION

Field

cr|

- Created By
- Created By (Delegate)
- Created On
- Credit Hold
- Credit Limit
- Credit Limit (Base)

TIP — *When creating similar rules it is a lot easier to use the Save As and edit an existing Condition to make it negative, for example, than it is to create a new rule from ground zero.*

~ 182 ~

Types of Conditions

CBRs Conditions start with the specification of a field you want to compare against something else. You can compare that field to the following:

- Another Field on the entity
- Static (hard coded) value
- Formula (a calculated value, more on this later)

Formulas are only available for Dates and Numbers.

Conditions are not required for a rule to be activated. When not provided the actions are executed when the form is loaded without regard to any condition.

Don't forget that CRM has the ability to do some rules for you. For example, on numbers you can specify the minimum and maximum values on the attribute properties. No rule is necessary to enforce that when a user is editing a record. This is a better way than creating a Min/Max value rule for example.

Operators Supported

- Equals
- Does Not Equal
- Contains
- Does Not Contain
- Begins With
- Does Not Begin With
- Ends With
- Does Not End With
- Contains Data
- Does Not Contain Data
- Is Greater Than
- Is Greater than or Equal To
- Is Less Than
- Is Less Than or Equal To

Using Formulas in Conditions

Formulas fill a critical need of allowing a condition to compare against a calculated value for Dates and Numbers. Using Formulas you can calculate basic values using add, subtract, multiple and divide. Therefore Formulas can be used for simple calculated values not complex calculations. Anything involving more complexity would be best done via script or server side via a plug-in.

To use a formula simply choose Formula in the type for the right side of the condition. Once selected, the Condition edit area will expand to allow you to choose a Field, Operator and a Type (again). In this case type can be either another field or a static value. The following is an example of implementing a calculation to check if the Account 90 Day Past Due Amount is greater than 25% of their Credit Limit

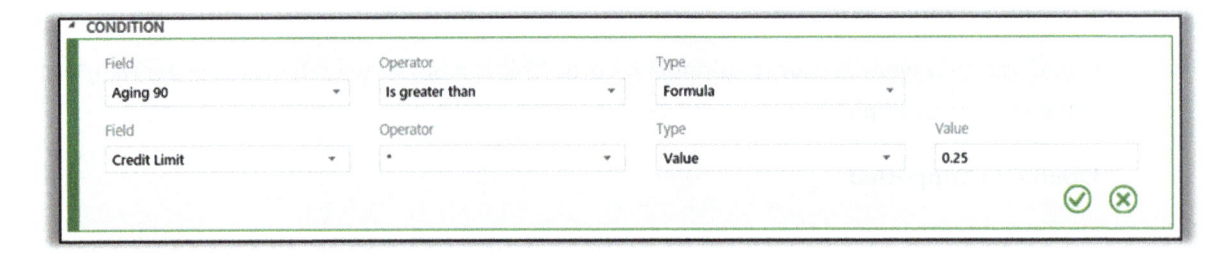

Field	Operator	Type	
Aging 90	Is greater than	Formula	
Field	Operator	Type	Value
Credit Limit	*	Value	0.25

So with formulas at best you can use either a field plus a static value or a field plus another field. If you had a more complex calculation such as Field 1 + Field 2 + Field 3 that wouldn't be possible using formulas and you should do it via script.

Multiple Conditions

You can create multiple conditions for each rule. This allows for rules such as State is Colorado and Credit Limit is less than 10,000. When you create multiple conditions though they must all be true. So perhaps you had a requirement that says When State is Colorado or California and Credit Limit is less than 10,000 do X. So using this multiple condition feature you created a rule with the following conditions

- State is Colorado
- State is California
- Credit Limit less than 10,000

While it looks good on paper, it will never cause the action to execute because State can only have one value at a time and therefore the first two conditions would never be both true. When doing multiple conditions, ALL conditions must evaluate to true and there is no "or" support.

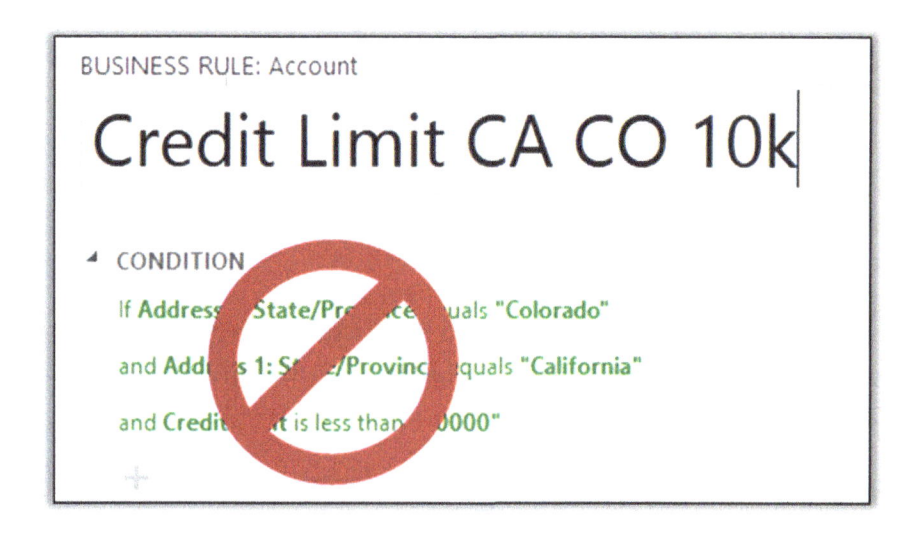

BUSINESS RULE: Account

Credit Limit CA CO 10k

▲ CONDITION

If Address State/Province equals "Colorado"

and Address 1: State/Province equals "California"

and Credit Limit is less than "10000"

Your options to work around this is to either create multiple rules one for Colorado and one for California in this case or simply have a developer do it in script like you would have in prior versions. Remember there is nothing wrong with still using script to solve problems that CBRs can't easily solve. For 2 or 3 different conditions creating separate rules is probably ok, if you find yourself creating rules for each state, you should probably be using code instead.

Business Rule Actions

Actions are why we create rules, to do something when a condition is true. Each CBR can have one or more actions that are executed in order. In this initial debut of CBRs there is a limited set of actions available to use. If the action you want to perform isn't one of them using script would be the way to go. The following are the Actions available currently in CRM:

- Show an Error Message
- Set a Field Value
- Set Business Required/Recommended
- Set Visibility
- Lock or Unlock a Field

There are things you should know about each of these so let's take a minute to look at each type of action in more detail.

> **TIP**: *Creating one rule with multiple actions is better than creating multiple rules with the same condition on each rule.*

Show an Error Message

This action is perfect for custom validation scenarios on a field. Using this action you can show a message next to the field like the following example: if the State is Colorado and Credit Limit is greater than 10,000.

When using the Show Error Message action realize it blocks saving of that field's value.

Keep in mind that developers can show two types of messages. Field Control level messages which is the same as CBRs error messages as well as Form Messages. The main difference is the form message is a notification shown at the top of the form that can easily get the users attention. The form level message is also a non-blocking message.

Set a Field Value

Setting a value of a field is a common way to do things like simple calculated fields or setting default values. Take the following simple example that sets the Credit Limit to 500 if it doesn't contain data.

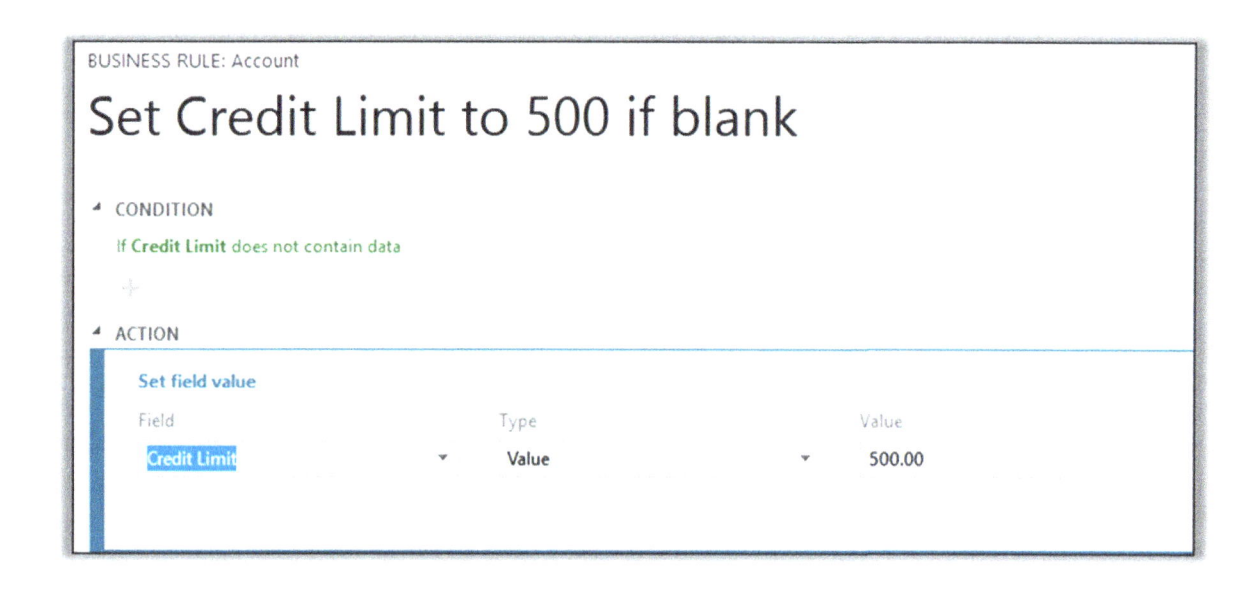

```
BUSINESS RULE: Account
Set Credit Limit to 500 if blank

▲ CONDITION
  If Credit Limit does not contain data

▲ ACTION
  Set field value
  Field                    Type              Value
  Credit Limit       ▼     Value        ▼    500.00
```

Notice you can set the value to another field, a static value or a formula like we described earlier. This allows for basic computations to be done but it does have its limits. If you need to involve multiple fields in the calculation for example, one work around would be to use multiple actions. For example, if you wanted to have a Total Fee field that was calculated by adding Item Fee + Item Tax + Item Royalty it wouldn't be possible to do this in a single action

- Set Total Fee = Item Fee
- Set Total Fee = formula of Total Fee plus Item Tax
- Set Total Fee = formula of Total Fee plus Item Royalty

While setting the value via a business rule is simple and easy to do consideration should be given if the calculation should be done on server side instead or in addition to via the CBR. The reason is simple, CBRs only execute on the client side and the value will only be set if the record is modified via the form. Any data imported or records created or changed by a developer will not have the values set. Client side setting of values should be done when immediate response is needed without saving the record. The first alternative to look at is to use the new Real Time Workflow feature which would run server side and populate the value after the record is saved. The next alternative would be to have a developer do it in code which would also be how to handle setting values that required more complex calculations.

Another important consideration if you are mixing CBRs with developer created scripts is what happens when the CBR Set Value action runs. Currently, the value will change but the On

Change event will not fire which means any script dependent on receiving an On Change event will not execute.

Set Business Requirement Level

Dynamically setting the requirement level can come in handy when a field is only required based on specific conditions. In the initial implementation of CBRs you can only set the requirement level to Business Required or Not Required. There is not currently a way via CBRs to set the requirement level to Business Recommended. If that is required you should client script to implement the rule.

Don't forget that on the Attribute properties you can set the requirement level for the field. You should only use a rule to override this value when it depends on another value and use the attribute properties option when possible.

Set Visibility

This action allows hiding or showing a field. This is good to use when you have a few fields to hide. If you to change the visibility on a lot of fields at once this can be a little tedious. There is no direct support for hiding Form Sections or Form Tabs so if you need to do that you would need to either hide all fields in a section or have a developer do it via client script which might be cleaner.

If you plan on showing a field only some of the time a good thing to do is set the initial visibility on the control on the form to be hidden rather than hiding it with CBR on load. This will be less intrusive to the user so that when the form loads it won't start flashing changes on the form.

Lock or Unlock Fields

The Lock/Unlock action is a good way to make a field read-only or editable based on conditions.

If you plan on locking fields, consider locking them as the default option on the form control and then unlocking. This avoids the user possibly seeing the field as available for edit, then having it set to read-only.

Ordering Actions

When using multiple actions you can control and change the order in which they execute.

When Do Business Rules Run?

CRM Business Rules execute during the On Load event of the form. They also execute anytime one of the referenced fields in a condition changes. CBRs do not execute during the Save or Auto Save form events.

Order of Execution

CBRs co-exist with system scripts that CRM comes with out of the box as well as custom script that developers implement. CBRs execute after these types of client scripts.

Most of the time the order that CBRs execute won't matter. It is important though to understand though that there is a defined order in which they run and it isn't the most intuitive. When there are multiple CBRs they execute based on the activation timestamp on the rule. The oldest is executed first then the more recently activated rules are executed. This is tough; if you need a rule to run in a specific order you will need to de-activate and activate in the right order. This can be very fragile if someone else makes a change not knowing about the ordering needs of your rules. Best practice is to do your best to have rules not be dependent on execution order. The following illustration shows the order that CBRs and client script is executed.

CRM System Scripts → Developer Custom Scripts → CBR Activated 11/16/2013 → CBR Activated 11/17/2013

Turn it on, Turn it off

An important concept to understand with CBRs is that if you build a rule to turn something on, in most cases you need the opposite rule to turn it off. For example, if you set a field to be required and don't provide a rule for when it is not required the only time it will reset is when the form is reloaded. Typically the best user experience is when this happens right away as the user changes values.

The Show Error Message Action is special in that you don't need to build a rule to turn off the error message. When the condition that caused the message to be turned on evaluates to false the error message is turned off automatically. For example, if you Show an error when Credit Limit is over $10,000, once the user changes it to $9,999 or less the error message is hidden automatically.

Business Rule or Client Script?

A common decision when implementing rules is deciding if you can do it with a CBR or if developer created client script is required. The following explains some of the things that should influence your decision:

Use CBR When...	Use Client Script When...
• Rule does not require "Or" logic • Rule does not involve multiple entities • Simple actions like setting default values • Simple calculations to compare or set value • Raising errors to users based on data input	• You need to work with tabs, sections etc. • You don't know all the fields or there are a lot of them • You need to call other JavaScript functions • You are working with a field not available via rules

Example Scenarios

In the following examples let's take a look at a couple of scenarios and explore if we would use CRM Business Rules, Client Script or some other form of customization.

Scenario 1 – Required Fields

The requirements for this are straight forward. If the Account is located in the United States then set the Credit Limit field on the Account entity as required.

To implement this requirement a new CBR is created with a condition to check the country and then an action to set the Credit Limit field to Required.

BUSINESS RULE: Account

Credit Limit required in US

- **CONDITION**
    If **Address 1: Country/Region** equals "United States"

- **ACTION**
    Set **Credit Limit** as **Business Required**

Once the rule is created, Save As is used to create the rule for when the Account is not located in the United States and to set the Credit Limit to be Not Required.

BUSINESS RULE: Account

Credit Limit Not Required Outside of US

- **CONDITION**
    If **Address 1: Country/Region** does not equal "United States"

- **ACTION**
    Set **Credit Limit** as **Not Business Required**

Scenario 2 – Validate Data

The requirements for this are as follows:

- Require at least 4 characters to be input in the Account Name
- Show an Error Message to the user that at least 4 characters are required

Currently it's not possible to implement this using CBRs and you would need a developer to write a simple client script. The reason is there is no way to evaluate the length of a single line of text field using a CBR Condition.

A developer using client script could create a simple client script that ran On Change of Account Name. The script would check the length and then use the CRM Client API setNotification method on the control to set an error message.

Scenario 3 – Multi Entity

As part of the project requirements sales people must not be able to approve an order for fulfillment if it is over their personal limit. A custom field has been added to the User entity to specify the maximum order that the user can approve without having their manager approve the order. The requirements stated that the sales person should be informed real time during the editing of the order if further approval is required.

It's tempting to try to see if CBRs could do this but there is no support for working with multiple entities. In order to determine the max limit for the sales person you would need to access the custom field on the user record associated as the owner of the order. CBRs strictly work with the primary entity unlike workflows that have the ability to interact with fields on N:1 related entities.

NOTE
This also means that rule Actions cannot impact fields on related entities either. So it's not possible to calculate a value and store it on a related entity field for example.

To solve this, it would probably be best to try to use a Real Time Workflow or Plug-in. If the real time notification was still a requirement, that would probably require additional developer client side script that would retrieve the user limit and notify the sales person if they are over it.

Deploying Business Rules

CRM Business Rules are associated with and deployed with an entity the same way Forms and Views are included. Once an entity is added to a CRM Solution when it is exported so is the CBRs associated with that entity.

Inside Business Rules Architecture

In this section we want to take a minute and dive deeper into the architecture of how CBRs are implemented. If this gets too technical feel free to skip over the rest of this section.

Early on we mentioned that CBRs were architected for now and the future. Now CBRs are simply client side rules, but we wanted to explain how the architecture is setup to allow them to do more than that in the future. Under the covers when you create a CBR it is creating a record in the Process entity. You might recall that "Process" is simply the display name for the workflow entity because that is what the Process entity used to be called. Processes took on an expanded role in CRM 2011 when Dialogs were introduced. The entity use is further expanded in CRM 2013 as Business Rules and Business Process Flow definitions are now also stored in the Process entity. If you go to Solution Explorer or Settings-> Processes however you will not see any CBRs listed because they are hidden from that view. If you export a solution however, you will see inside the Workflow folder a file is created for each CBR just like one is created for each Workflow and Dialog.

CBRs are stored as XAML when saved. The XAML is then converted to client script when it is rendered on the target form. The following is an example of the XAML that is stored for a simple CBR.

```
</mxswa:GetEntityProperty>
<mxswa:GetEntityProperty Attribute="creditlimit" Entity="[InputEntities(&quot;primaryEntity&quot;)]" EntityName="account" Value="[ConditionBranchStep2_4]">
    <mxswa:GetEntityProperty.TargetType>
        <InArgument x:TypeArguments="s:Type">
            <mxswa:ReferenceLiteral x:TypeArguments="s:Type">
                <x:Null />
            </mxswa:ReferenceLiteral>
        </InArgument>
    </mxswa:GetEntityProperty.TargetType>
</mxswa:GetEntityProperty>
<mxswa:ActivityReference AssemblyQualifiedName="Microsoft.Crm.Workflow.Activities.EvaluateExpression, Microsoft.Crm.Workflow, Version=6.0.0.0, Culture=neutral,
    <mxswa:ActivityReference.Arguments>
        <InArgument x:TypeArguments="x:String" x:Key="ExpressionOperator">SelectFirstNonNull</InArgument>
        <InArgument x:TypeArguments="s:Object[]" x:Key="Parameters">[New Object() { ConditionBranchStep2_4 }]</InArgument>
        <InArgument x:TypeArguments="s:Type" x:Key="TargetType">
            <mxswa:ReferenceLiteral x:TypeArguments="s:Type">
                <x:Null />
            </mxswa:ReferenceLiteral>
        </InArgument>
        <OutArgument x:TypeArguments="x:Object" x:Key="Result">[ConditionBranchStep2_3]</OutArgument>
    </mxswa:ActivityReference.Arguments>
</mxswa:ActivityReference>
<mxswa:ActivityReference AssemblyQualifiedName="Microsoft.Crm.Workflow.Activities.EvaluateExpression, Microsoft.Crm.Workflow, Version=6.0.0.0, Culture=neutral,
    <mxswa:ActivityReference.Arguments>
        <InArgument x:TypeArguments="x:String" x:Key="ExpressionOperator">CreateCrmType</InArgument>
        <InArgument x:TypeArguments="s:Object[]" x:Key="Parameters">[New Object() { Microsoft.Xrm.Sdk.Workflow.WorkflowPropertyType.Money, "0.25" }]</InArgument>
        <InArgument x:TypeArguments="s:Type" x:Key="TargetType">
            <mxswa:ReferenceLiteral x:TypeArguments="s:Type" Value="mxs:Money" />
        </InArgument>
        <OutArgument x:TypeArguments="x:Object" x:Key="Result">[ConditionBranchStep2_6]</OutArgument>
    </mxswa:ActivityReference.Arguments>
</mxswa:ActivityReference>
<mxswa:ActivityReference AssemblyQualifiedName="Microsoft.Crm.Workflow.Activities.EvaluateExpression, Microsoft.Crm.Workflow, Version=6.0.0.0, Culture=neutral,
    <mxswa:ActivityReference.Arguments>
        <InArgument x:TypeArguments="x:String" x:Key="ExpressionOperator">SelectFirstNonNull</InArgument>
        <InArgument x:TypeArguments="s:Object[]" x:Key="Parameters">[New Object() { ConditionBranchStep2_6 }]</InArgument>
        <InArgument x:TypeArguments="s:Type" x:Key="TargetType">
            <mxswa:ReferenceLiteral x:TypeArguments="s:Type">
                <x:Null />
            </mxswa:ReferenceLiteral>
        </InArgument>
        <OutArgument x:TypeArguments="x:Object" x:Key="Result">[ConditionBranchStep2_5]</OutArgument>
    </mxswa:ActivityReference.Arguments>
</mxswa:ActivityReference>
```

CBRs don't use special client side calls to support their operation they use the same APIs that developers use when creating client side script. The following is an example of a CBR that sets the value of Name to be Dave if the field didn't contain data.

```
function pbl_cec7b6235a14e311940400155d502683()
{
    try {
            var v0 = Xrm.Page.data.entity.attributes.get('name');
            if ((v0 == undefined || v0 == null))
            { return; }

            if (true)
            { v0.setValue('Dave'); }
    } catch (e)
    {
        Mscrm.BusinessRules.ErrorHandlerFactory.getHandler(e, arguments.callee).handleError();
    }
}
```

It's pretty simple to see that with a little effort, and possibly a flag that indicates it should be executed on the server also, CBRs could be executed server side as well.

Wrapping Up

CRM Business Rules are a positive step towards improving how business rules are implemented in a CRM project. CBRs can be created by functional consultants as well as developers. CBRs are defined in a way that CRM can handle upgrading and maintenance easier than custom developer created client script doing the same thing. CBRs are also architected in a way that server side execution could also be in the future creating a consistent way to implement business rules. Developer custom script is still essential however for implementing more complex client side business rules that can't be implemented in the constructs provided by CBRs.

7

Real Time Workflows

Workflows in CRM have for a while been a powerful way to automate tasks that would otherwise be tedious for users or to ensure consistency in processes. Workflows however were limited to being able to run in the background. While this works great and makes sense for long running processes that could take months, it is not ideal when you desire the user to see results immediately. For these needs CRM projects turned to developers to create plug-ins that had the ability to run real time. While plug-ins are powerful, and still have a place for many small tasks using a workflow to define the steps would be adequate if workflow simply could run immediately.

As of CRM 2013, workflows can now be configured to be Background (like they previously ran, asynchronously) or Real Time (synchronous like plug-ins). This opens the door for many simple project requirements to be able to be implemented using Workflows that can be created by a broader set of customizers. Using the declarative approach (defining via Configuration instead of Code) for defining workflows is a much more upgradeable approach than using code that often requires developer resources to upgrade form one version to the next. To be clear however, don't think for a minute that you should replace every plug-in with a workflow, as we will explore in this chapter there are considerations for when to use each approach.

In the rest of this chapter we will introduce how Real Time Workflows work and things you should consider when using them to meet requirements.

Getting Started

Workflows can be configured to be real time any time when they are in draft status. By default all new workflows start out configured to run in the background. You can change that at creation time by simply unchecking the "Run this workflow in background" option.

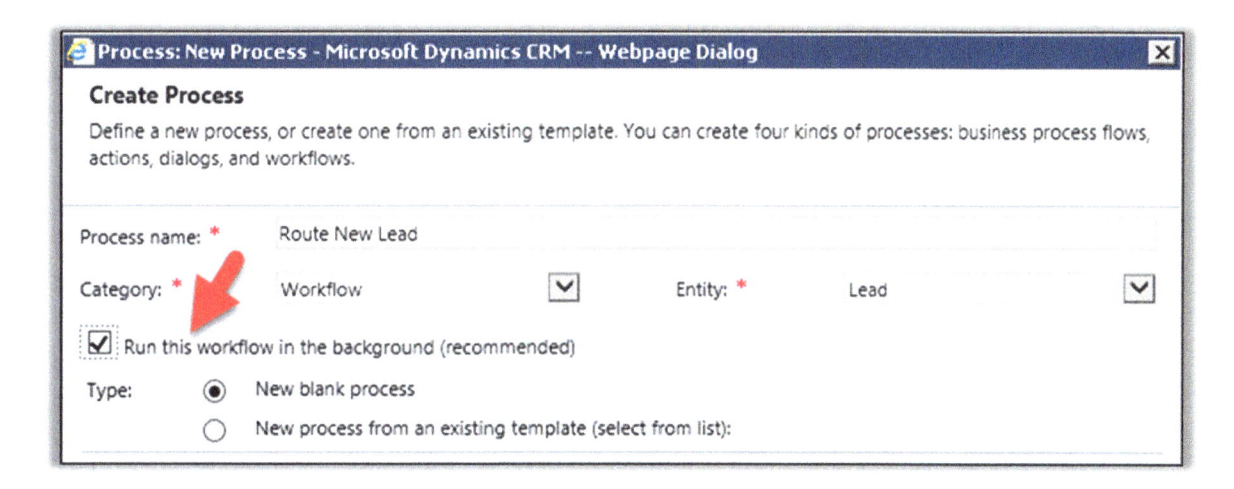

Once the workflow is created you can switch between background and real time by "converting". You can find the Convert option in the Command Bar once you have opened the workflow for editing.

You can tell if a workflow is Background or Real Time by looking at the "Available To Run" options.

Don't be confused though if you try to change it here this checkbox is just there to be pretty and tell you the current status, you must still use the Command Bar button to actually change the state.

Option to Run Differences

One of the more significant areas that is changed to support Real Time workflows are the options for running the process. Scope is still available and has the same implementation for both styles of workflows. "Start when" has changed to allow specification if you want to trigger before or after the CRM Operation (e.g. the Create, Delete, Change etc.) executes if your workflow is real time.

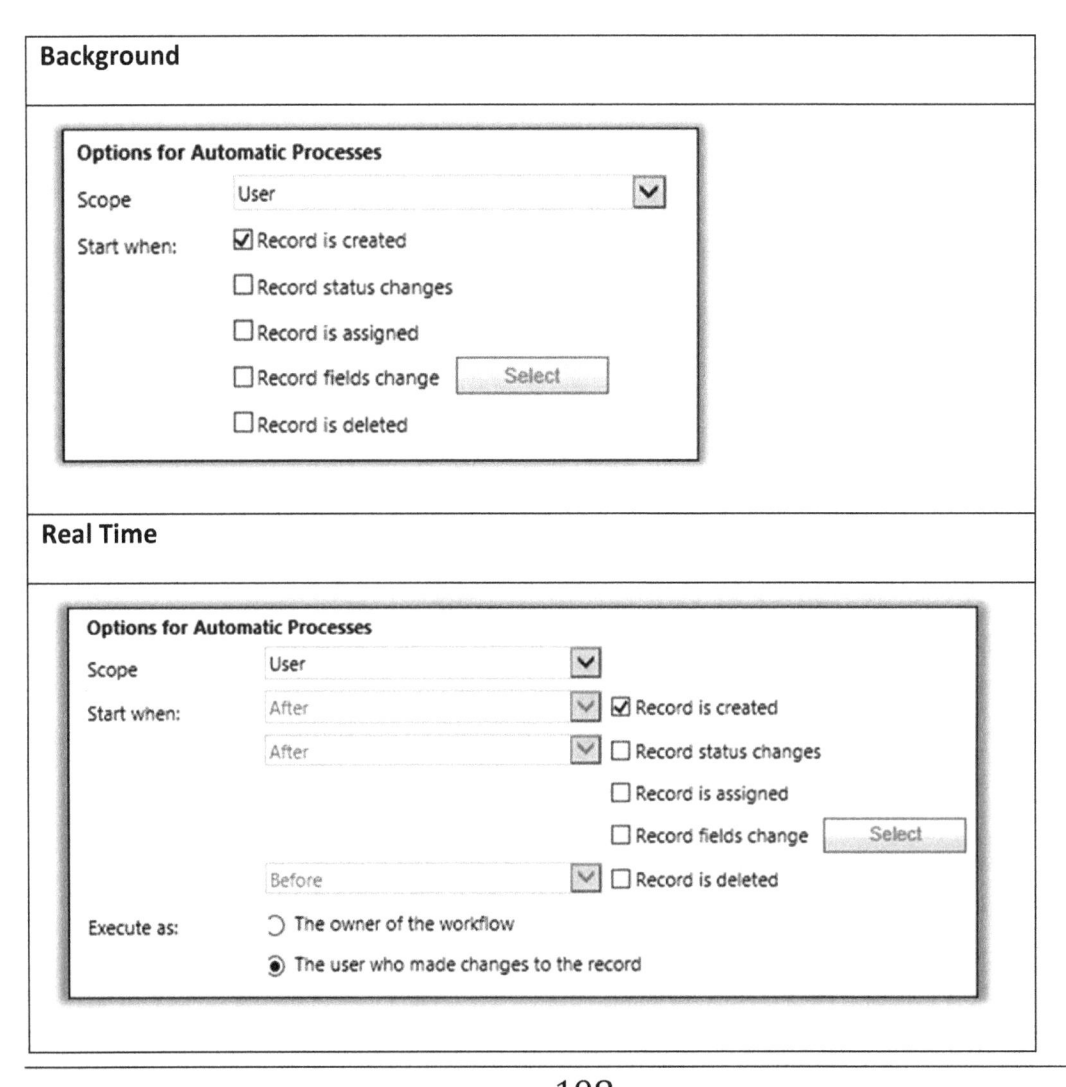

Background

Options for Automatic Processes	
Scope	User
Start when:	☑ Record is created
	☐ Record status changes
	☐ Record is assigned
	☐ Record fields change [Select]
	☐ Record is deleted

Real Time

Options for Automatic Processes		
Scope	User	
Start when:	After	☑ Record is created
	After	☐ Record status changes
		☐ Record is assigned
		☐ Record fields change [Select]
	Before	☐ Record is deleted
Execute as:	○ The owner of the workflow	
	● The user who made changes to the record	

~ 198 ~

There are some limitations in the current implementation for Create and Delete. Create can only run After the record has been created. This is different than how a plug-in works where it is possible to have custom code execute against the in memory version of the record before CRM creates it on the database. Often times this is used to do validation or set default values. Both of these can still be done. In the case of validation you would simply do a Stop Workflow with an error and CRM would roll back the record that was already created in the database. For setting default values use same thing but you would be required to do an additional Update in your workflow that would in turn result in a second update being performed against the record. We will discuss more on the impact of this later in the chapter. Delete is also restricted to only executing before the record is removed from CRM.

For the other triggers you can choose to run Before or After. In either case the work you do in the workflow is part of the CRM transaction and either it all works or all fails. Additionally, anything you do either before or after will be completed and persisted before the user regains control.

So why would you choose before? Before gives you the ability to have your workflow steps execute and access the before values of the records. Again to contrast this to how plug-ins work it is a little different. In a plug-in you can have access to both the before values and the about to be changed values. This allows comparing or validating differences in values. In workflows, you only have access to the before value of the record and related N:1 records without the about to be changed data being provided. In some cases this difference might result in a plug-in being a better implementation choice.

Security Execution Context

You might have noticed a new section in the options for Execute as.

Execute as:
○ The owner of the workflow
● The user who made changes to the record

Background workflows always run in the security context of the workflow owner. The Execute as Owner provides a powerful way to escalate security to allow a workflow to do more than a user is allowed. Execute as the running user allows you to maintain the security and keep the workflow from doing anything that the user isn't supposed to do. Both remain valid options but with Real Time workflows you can choose what is appropriate.

Step Differences

There aren't a lot of differences between the Out of the box (OOB) steps for a Background workflow compared to a Real Time workflow.

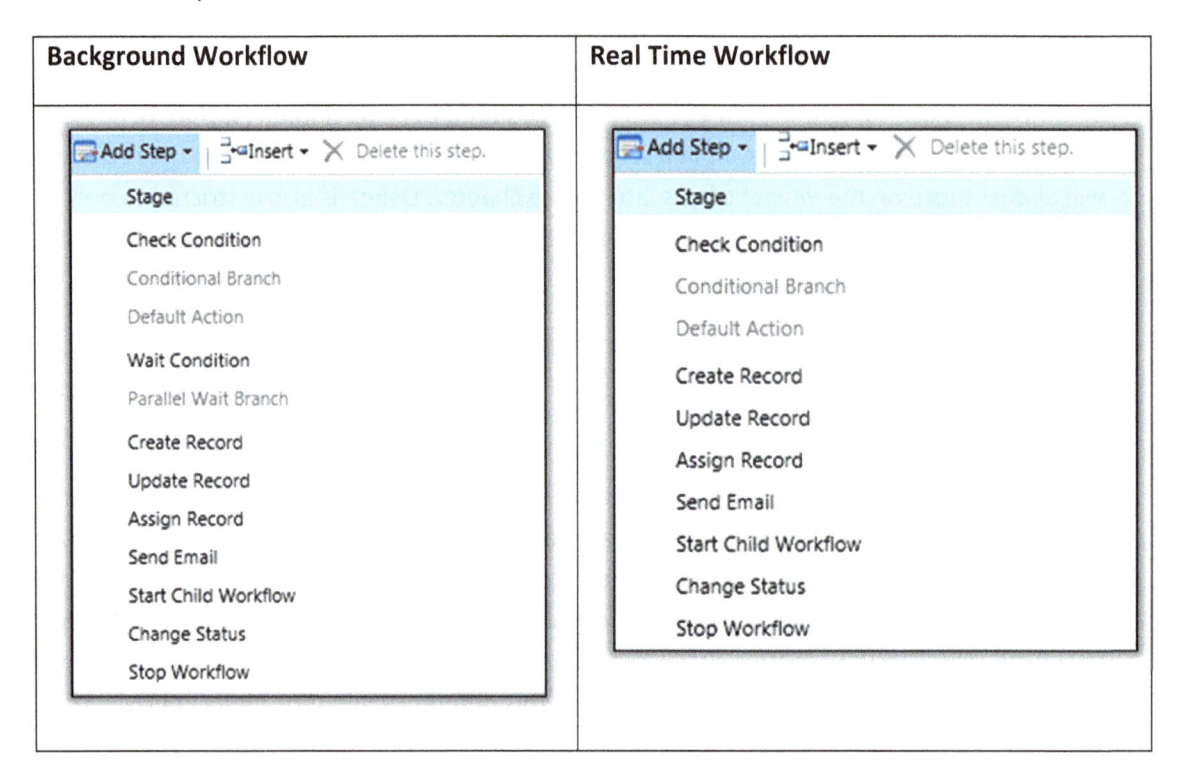

Background Workflow	Real Time Workflow
Add Step ▾ Insert ▾ ✕ Delete this step. Stage Check Condition Conditional Branch Default Action Wait Condition Parallel Wait Branch Create Record Update Record Assign Record Send Email Start Child Workflow Change Status Stop Workflow	Add Step ▾ Insert ▾ ✕ Delete this step. Stage Check Condition Conditional Branch Default Action Create Record Update Record Assign Record Send Email Start Child Workflow Change Status Stop Workflow

As you can see the big difference is the lack of Wait conditions in Real Time workflows for the obvious reasons. If you have any custom steps that have been created by developers there is not currently an option to have the show only for one type of workflow, they will show for both Real Time and Background. Most the time this won't cause a problem but imagine if you had a custom step that did integration with another remote system that took multiple seconds to process – putting that step in a Real Time workflow would impact the users' perception of response time.

New Security Privileges

CRM 2013 also introduced a new security privilege specifically to control activation of real time workflows. This is important because even though an organization might want to empower users to create workflows they might not want them to create Real Time ones that could impact user performance.

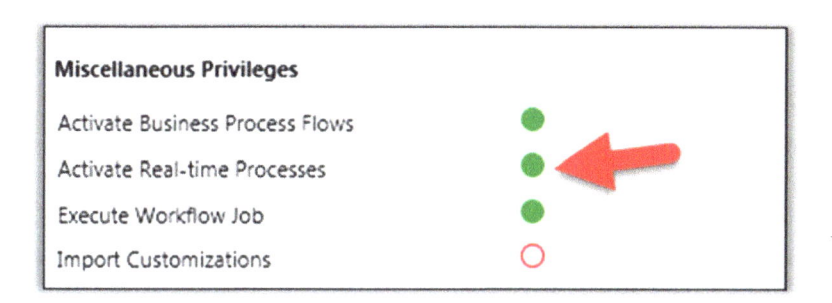

Miscellaneous Privileges

- Activate Business Process Flows 🟢
- Activate Real-time Processes 🟢 ⬅
- Execute Workflow Job 🟢
- Import Customizations ⭕

In most organizations this option should probably not be enabled for normal users and should be reserved for system accounts and special circumstances. Having this separate from activating a background workflow however allows you to still allow power users to activate background workflows without the temptation of setting to real time. After all who could resist the temptation of making something run REAL TIME!

Monitoring Workflow Execution

You are probably used to seeing the following to determine if the Background workflow job information is retained after it completes.

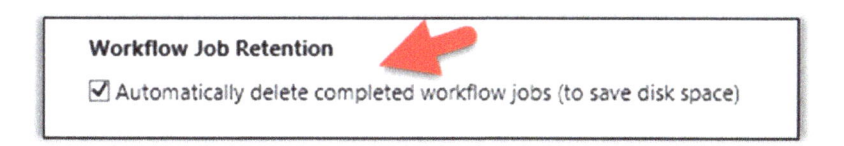

Workflow Job Retention
☑ Automatically delete completed workflow jobs (to save disk space)

If the option is unchecked or an error occurs with the workflow you can find the information via Settings ->System Jobs, the Background related link or the Process Sessions from the Workflow definition that shows all instances of that particular workflow.

Real Time Workflows are a little different they don't run as jobs, so there is no job record to look at for any information about the workflow execution. Instead you have the option to enable Workflow Log Retention. With Real Time Workflows if everything goes ok, there is no log created. If this option is enabled and an error occurs a record will be created in a new entity called Process Session.

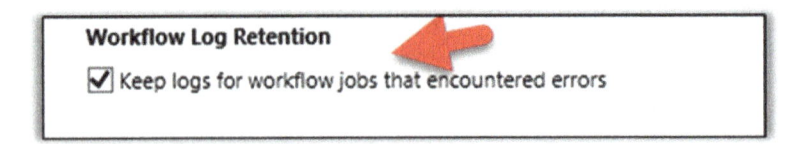

Workflow Log Retention
☑ Keep logs for workflow jobs that encountered errors

You won't find the records in the System Jobs link but you can find them still from the Workflow definition, in fact in the case of an error on a Create, this or advanced find are the only ways to see it since there isn't a record created you can look for.

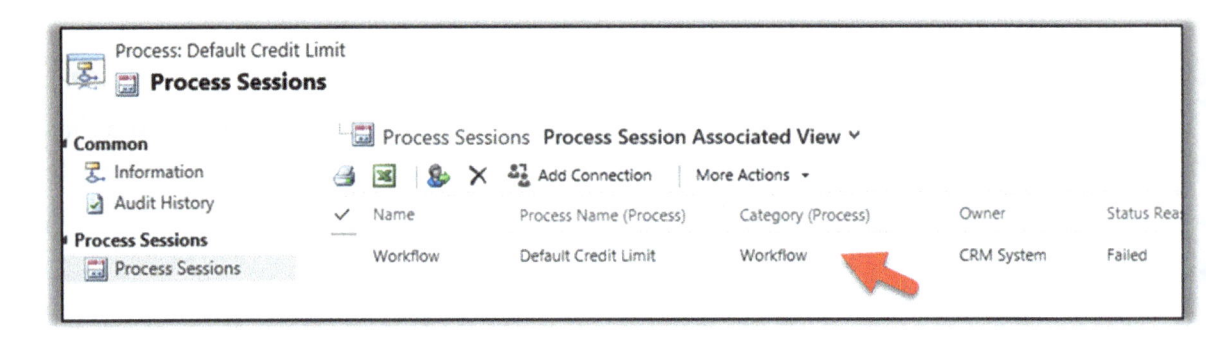

If you do leave this enabled plan on running a bulk delete to clean up old errors periodically just like you would with the workflow system jobs. This bulk delete would target old records in the Process Session. Keep in mind that using the Stop Workflow step is also treated as an error and will create a log record that must be cleaned up. So if you are using Stop Workflow as part of validation you might generate more records than expected if this option is enabled.

Real Time Workflows and AutoSave

The Auto Save feature of CRM can help and hurt you when working with Real Time Workflows. While it may be obvious, your Real Time Workflows will trigger for a regular Save or an Auto Save. For that matter, background workflows are handled the same way the only difference being that if multiple saves happen before execution you might end up with multiple workflows queued up to run, whereas with Real Time you would never have multiple queued for execution for the same record.

Since you can run multiple times, it is important to minimize the fields on an update that can trigger execution to the least amount possible. This reduces the false triggers, but does not eliminate them. Remember that CRM will still trigger a workflow or plug-in even if the value doesn't change but was provided on the call to the Update API call by the developer. In a plug-in you could avoid his by evaluating the before image and seeing the values didn't change. In a workflow there isn't a similar technique so if it's really important you might have to end up with a flag that is set when the action has already been completed so you don't do it multiple times.

Avoiding too many Updates

Real Time Workflows sound too good to be true? There must be some way to get in trouble right? One easy trap to fall into is performing too many updates to the record. How does that happen? Easy, using workflow to update a record is done by adding an update step and setting some values. What if "When" you should set those values is conditional? This isn't a problem, you simply add a Check Condition and include the Update step inside when the condition is true. If you have multiple fields to update if they don't already have values taking an easy example. You could easily on Account or Contact or Opportunity probably come up with ten different condition checks you would need to make to set ten field's default values. Each of those would have their own Update step. There are three natural consequences of this, first you get an audit record for each update step. Second, and more importantly, any other plug-ins or workflows triggering on change of that record could be fired. Third, and probably not the last, each update is more overhead than doing a single update to the CRM record.

Does this mean you shouldn't do it? No, it means pay attention and be aware of the consequences and if it starts to get to be too many or causes problems, it's time to reconsider using a plug-in. It's not a bad strategy early in a project to use workflows to prototype custom business logic and then later implement it as a plug-in once you have a better understanding of the real requirements. CRM projects tend to evolve, and this type of problem may not be apparent at first but can creep in as the requirements evolve so keep your eye out!

Mixing with Custom code

But I can't do that with the workflow steps provided...Not so fast! Custom Workflow Activities are a good way to introduce custom code into a workflow. Custom Workflow Activities can be used by both Background and Real Time workflows to invoke custom code. If you haven't seen them in use before they show up on the step list just like one of the out of the box steps.

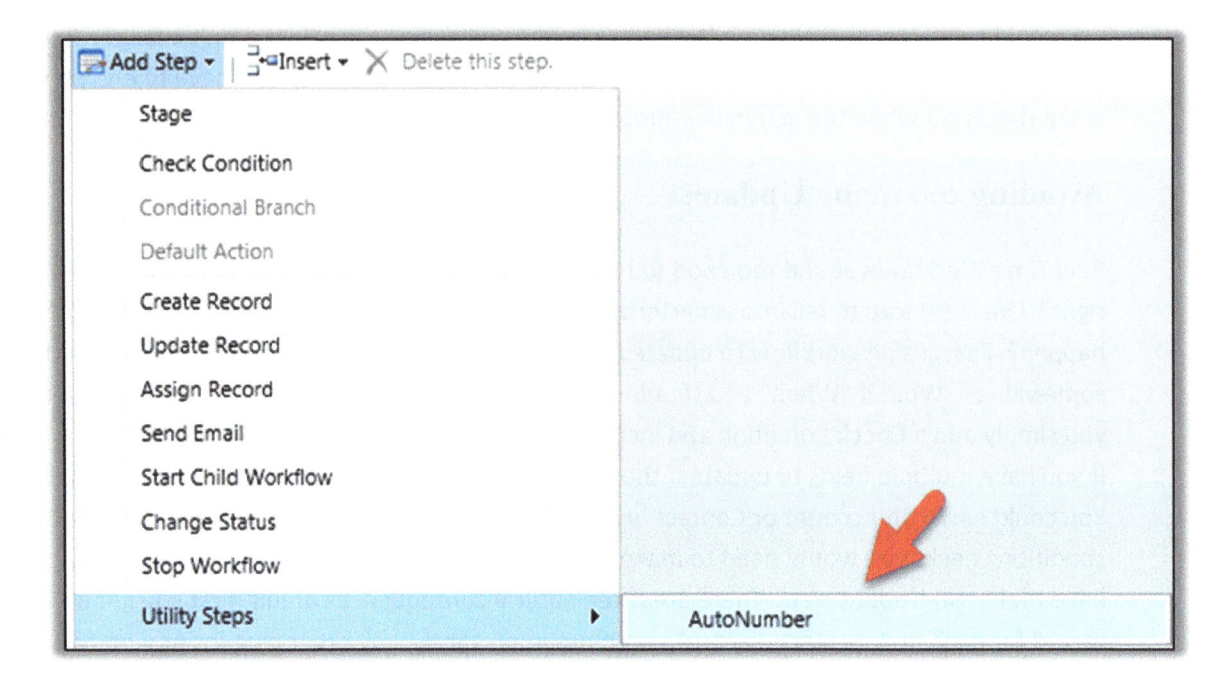

When developers create the Custom Workflow Activity they define input and output parameters that you populate when you invoke the step. For example, you might have a CalculateDiscount Custom Workflow Activity that takes percent of discount as input, a reference to the order item being processed and produces as output the new price.

While that's a very simple example, Custom Workflow Activities can do much of the same processing you would do from a plug-in with the added advantage that a non-developer can place it in one or more workflows, invoke it as many times as needed and as the business process changes for when it is to be called it can easily be moved around in the workflow flow. Later in the chapter check out the Auto Number scenario where we mix Real Time Workflows with a Custom Activity.

Real Time Workflows vs. JavaScript and Business Rules

Probably the most important thing to understand here is JavaScript and Business Rules today only execute client side. Workflows execute server side. Simply put, this means the only time JavaScript and Business rules execute is when a user is sitting in front of one of the standard CRM user interfaces that support them. Import of data or developer calls to the API will not run the custom logic. Workflows on the other hand consistently implement the logic regardless of how the interaction is done. JavaScript and Business Rules tend to allow giving a more responsive and constructive message to the user than you can with a workflow. It is possible and sometimes desirable to implement the same rule in both client side and server side to ensure both a good experience for the user and at the same time ensure the rule is always in force.

Another thing to consider if you have offline users both JavaScript and Business Rules are able to execute when the user is offline. Workflows only execute on the server and therefore they execute of a real time workflow would be deferred until the offline user synchronizes a triggering change back to the server when they go back on-line. In this scenario, JavaScript or Business Rules would give the user more immediate feedback

Real Time Workflows vs. Plug-ins

I hear the chants already, "plug-ins are dead…long live workflows". While maybe someday, however currently there are still some good advantages for using a plug-in. Let's explore a few of them.

Workflows register on a single entity and a single set of execution triggers. Plug-ins on the other hand, are created once, but can be registered against multiple entities and message triggers all pointing to a single set of code.

Workflows are limited in their ability to see the before and after image of the data. Plug-ins can register to receive a Pre and Post image of how the record looked allowing logic that requires both values to execute.

Plug-ins have access to a scratch pad allowing a plug-in to run "Before" and hand off values to an "After" plug-in. This can be used to pass processing information or data that is expensive to retrieve to a secondary plug-in.

Plug-ins can do conditional logic in code and only do a single update to a record avoiding the "Too Many Updates" topic we discussed earlier.

Plug-ins can access the in memory record that is about to be created or updated allowing setting of default values before the update happens to the CRM database. This results in a more optimal performance as it reduces the need for an additional update call that a workflow would require. This alone though would not be enough typically on its own to suggest the need of a plug-in except in high volume scenarios.

Using a Custom Workflow Activity is a good alternative to doing a plug-in since it allows it to be invoked one or more times on demand in a workflow that is maintained by a functional consultant. Keep in mind though due to limitations of passing in generic entity references to a Custom Workflow Activity often times you would need to create a new Custom Workflow Activity you needed the logic for.

Workflows can be more efficient than plug-ins because they are able to execute in the CRM application process in an environment that is using CRM sandbox capability. This is true only for the standard steps that come out of the box, any custom steps you add would still be dispatched to the sandbox host for processing having the same overhead associated with a plug-in.

Are Background Workflows Still Needed?

It's easy to walk away after reading about Real Time Workflows and think that you should configure every workflow to be Real Time. After all, if you ask a user when something needs to be done of course they will say "right away!" So how do you make the decision Real Time vs. Background? For starters, anything that needs to run for any measurable length of time should be background almost all the time. Second, anything that needs to "Wait" for a condition or time to occur should also be executed in the background. Any workflow that does work that can at times be unpredictable in length such as calling an external service are good candidates for background execution as well.

So what you are hearing now is everything should be background? No, not so fast. Background workflows do require more overhead to exist, they must be queued up for the Asynchronous service, Dispatched and processed. They execute the out of the box workflow steps on nodes configured to run the Asynchronous service. Whereas Real Time Workflows execute in the Front End role and do not require the overhead of queuing for execution. So for short tasks, go ahead and make them a Real Time Workflow but for anything that is longer running, use the background option as it was designed.

In case you were wondering, in either option, if a Custom Workflow Activity is involved, that execution is outsourced to the Sandbox host when the activity assembly is not registered in Isolation Mode. CRM Online always runs Custom Activities in Isolation Mode and On-Premise can as well based on the assembly configuration.

The following table summarizes when to use Real Time vs. Background

Use Real Time	Use Background
Any workflow that the user must see the results before the page re-loads after create or update	Any workflow that uses Wait on a condition or time
Short workflows that simply use the out of the box activity steps	Any workflow that makes calls to external services that might have unpredictable execution time
That does work that need to be included in the original requests transaction	Where the failure of the workflow does not need to impact the original triggering request

Scenarios for Using Real Time Workflows

Now that we've discussed how Real Time Workflows work, how to decide when and how to use them let's look at some scenarios for using them.

Updating fields on or from the parent record

Triggered on Create or Update on a child record you might want to reach up and update the parent record. For example, you might want to update an Account record to have a pointer to the last order placed by an Account. This is also a great way to set a default value based on a value contained already in the parent record. This is not an uncommon thing to do with a Background workflow. Real Time should only be used when you need the value to show up right away.

Smart Delete/Inactivate Blocking

Real Time Workflows are a great way to enforce business rules before a record can be deleted or inactivated. Using this approach, the workflow would trigger on Delete or Status Changes and the workflow would use the Stop Workflow step if conditions were not ok for the action to proceed. This is a scenario that used to be only possible with Plug-ins.

Smart Stage Blocking

Business Process Flows offer Stage Gating, keeping a user from advancing to the next stage if required fields are not completed. This gating though only supports blocking if the required value is not provided, not if the value is within a specific range or other criteria. Using a Real Time Workflow you can perform custom stage gating using any Check Conditions that are valid on a record in a workflow.

Ensuring Proper Record Ownership

When you have records owned by Users or Teams and you want to enforce one of the other you can use a Real Time Workflow to Set or enforce the business rule. For example, you might have a rule that child records have the same owner as the parent. Or perhaps, case records can only be owned by teams. You can choose to enforce by setting a specific value, or by stopping the workflow with an error when requirements are not met.

Auto Numbering

CRM provides auto numbering support for a small set of system entities like Cases but there isn't support for other entities beyond that limited set. A common ask for projects is to be able to have a human readable number associated with a record (Yes, I'm saying humans don't think GUID's 0000000-0000-0000-000 etc. are readable. But even more important than that in this example shows how we go about solving it with a mixture of No Code Real Time Workflows and a Custom Workflow Activity. The custom code is reusable, and can be used from multiple Workflows that could be configured by a functional consultant. There are certainly approaches to solving this without code. In fact Real Time Workflows enable at least a couple other patterns that could be used, but when you look at them they trade off the ideal for a less than ideal approach just to be able to say "We Didn't Use Code".

So enough of that, how are we going to solve the Auto Numbering problem? Our solution starts with a custom entity named Auto Number Sequence (ctccrm_autonumbersequence) and it has two key fields; Name which stores the name of the counter and Current Value which holds the current value of the counter. One of the things we wanted to do is avoid having to build a relationship between the records – let's use Account in this example and the Auto Number Sequence entity. Why you ask? It just adds overhead and unnecessary relationships. The approach we decided on is a Custom Workflow Activity which will show up as a step in the workflow designer.

The Auto Number Custom Workflow Activity takes the name of the Sequence as an input parameter and returns as an output parameter the next value. If you were to look at the code, it uses the name of the sequence to query the record from the Auto Number Sequence entity, retrieves the value of the Current Value, increments the value by one and updates the record. The new Current Value is returned as the Next Value for the workflow that invoked the Custom Workflow Activity.

We then will create a new Real Time Workflow that is triggered on Create of Account (our example, replace with your favorite entity). In that workflow we have two steps, the first step calls the Auto Number custom step (custom step is user speak for a Custom Workflow Activity aka "The Code"). The second step uses the value from the Auto Number and updates the Account Number field on the Account record. The following is an example of how we would setup the workflow to run.

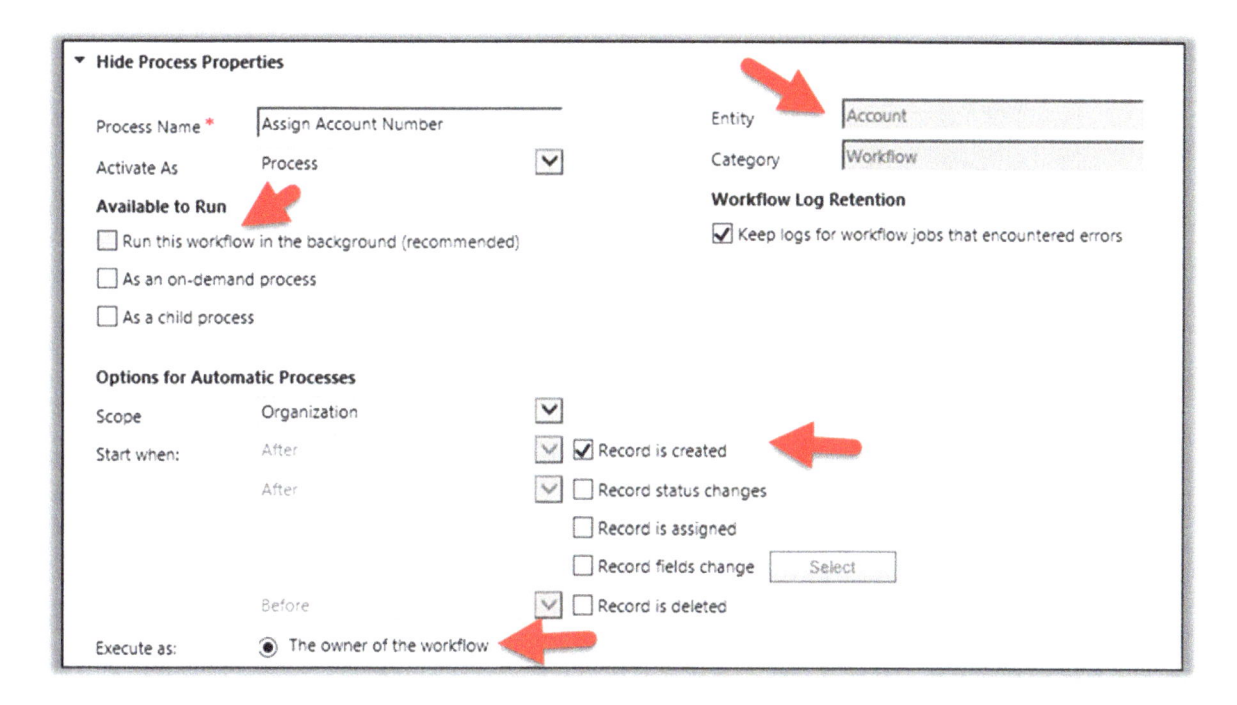

Notice it is set to run as Real Time against the Account entity. The workflow is triggered on Create. The workflow is set to run in the context of the owner because we don't want regular users to have access to update the Auto Number Sequence entity.

For the steps of the workflow, we insert the Auto Number from the step list via Utility Steps -> AutoNumber. This shows up when the developer registers the Custom Workflow Activity with CRM. The following shows where we would find this custom step.

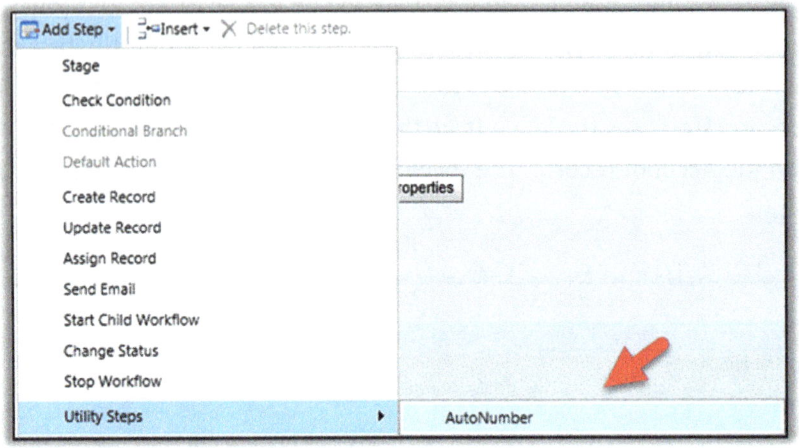
Add Step
Insert
Delete this step.
Stage
Check Condition
Conditional Branch
Default Action
Create Record
Update Record
Assign Record
Send Email
Start Child Workflow
Change Status
Stop Workflow
Utility Steps
AutoNumber

The actual steps once the workflow is created looks like the following. There are two steps, one to get the number, the other to update the Account record.

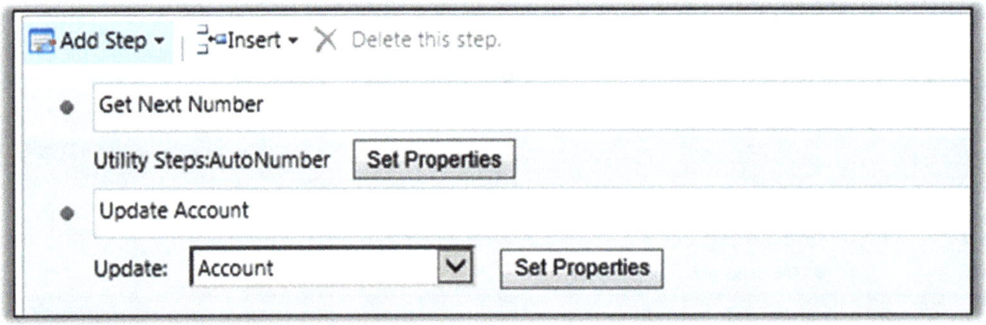
Add Step
Insert
Delete this step.
Get Next Number
Utility Steps:AutoNumber
Set Properties
Update Account
Update:
Account
Set Properties

To do this on any other entity, you would simply add a field to the entity to store the number, add a record to the Auto Number Sequence entity and build another real time workflow for that entity having similar steps, this would probably take less than 5 minutes to setup.

Just to dive a little deeper let's take a quick look at the Set Properties for those two steps. The first Step simply has us configure the name of the Auto Number Sequence record we want to use.

CRM 2013 Quick Start

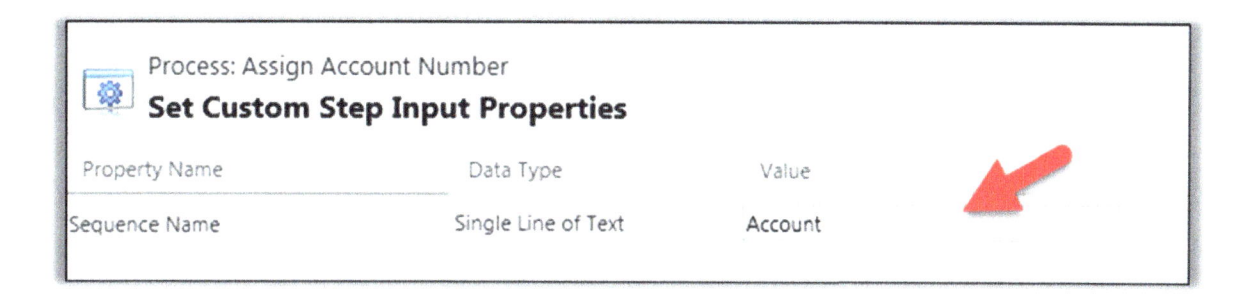

```
Process: Assign Account Number
Set Custom Step Input Properties

Property Name          Data Type              Value
Sequence Name          Single Line of Text    Account
```

The Update Step sets the Account Number field using a Dynamic Value that you look up using the Form Assistant. As you can see in the following image, the Auto Number from the prior step shows up in the list of Local Values allow us to choose that and then select the Next Value output parameter that contains the auto number.

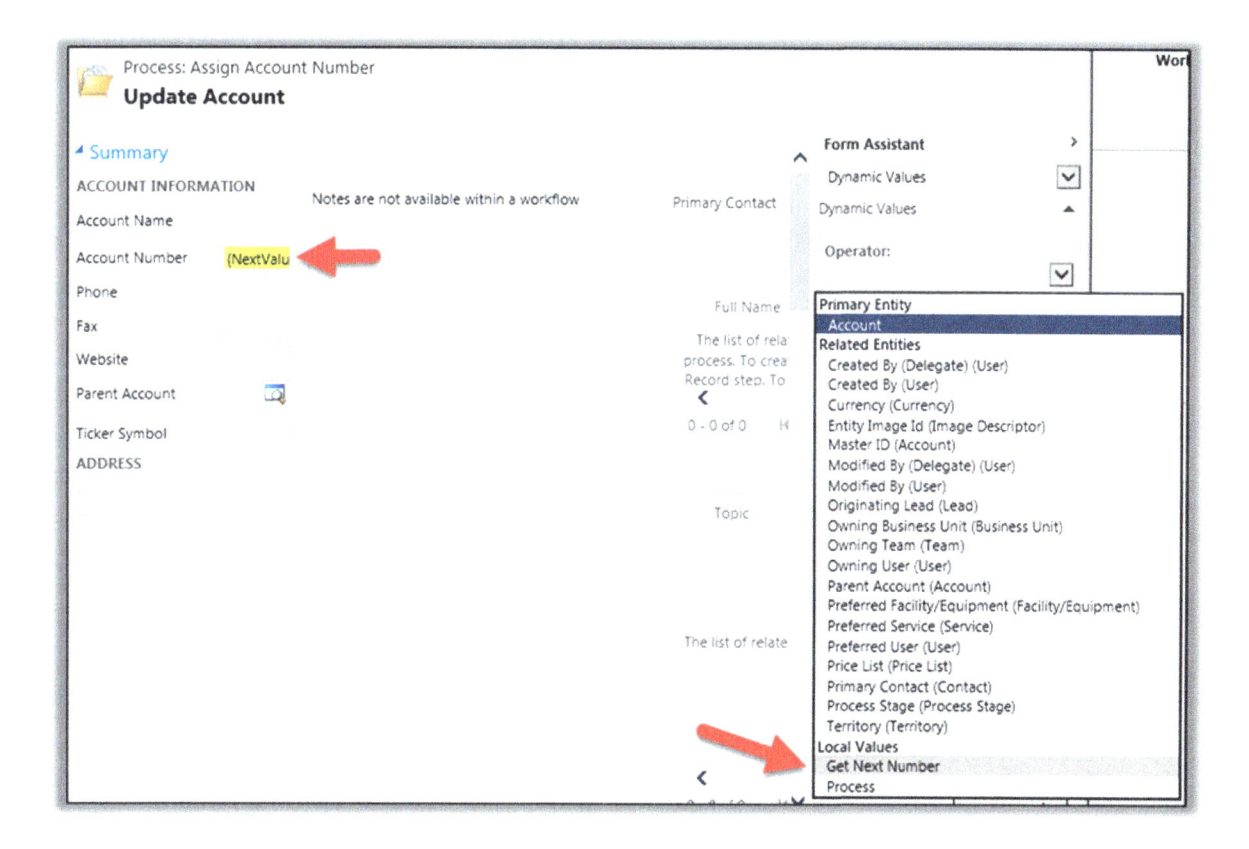

```
Process: Assign Account Number
Update Account

▲ Summary
ACCOUNT INFORMATION         Notes are not available within a workflow
Account Name
Account Number    (NextValu
Phone
Fax
Website
Parent Account
Ticker Symbol
ADDRESS

Form Assistant
Dynamic Values
Dynamic Values
Operator:

Primary Entity
  Account
Related Entities
  Created By (Delegate) (User)
  Created By (User)
  Currency (Currency)
  Entity Image Id (Image Descriptor)
  Master ID (Account)
  Modified By (Delegate) (User)
  Modified By (User)
  Originating Lead (Lead)
  Owning Business Unit (Business Unit)
  Owning Team (Team)
  Owning User (User)
  Parent Account (Account)
  Preferred Facility/Equipment (Facility/Equipment)
  Preferred Service (Service)
  Preferred User (User)
  Price List (Price List)
  Primary Contact (Contact)
  Process Stage (Process Stage)
  Territory (Territory)
Local Values
  Get Next Number
  Process
```

That's all there is to it, once activated and a new account created, the Account Number will have an incremented value. More important this pattern of mixing custom code and Real Time Workflows can be repeated for other similar challenges.

If you are interested in trying this out, there are pre-built CRM Solution files and step by step instructions for configuring the Auto Number utility located here https://github.com/davidyack/CRMAutoNumber. The source code is also open source if you need to make changes to adopt it to your own needs.

Basic Rollup Math

A very common thing to do is accumulate numbers and post them to a parent as summarized rollup data. Often times this is done with a plug-in but now with Real Time Workflows they become a candidate for doing this type of accumulation, **but probably still not the best tool for the job**. Doing rollups require capturing all the key events on the child records. Rollups that accumulate more than simple counts require access to the prior value to properly keep the parent record values in sync. For example, if you rolled up total order amounts and posted on the account entity you would need to do the following if the order amount changed after it was posted:

- Subtract old amount from Account
- Add new amount to Account

That sounds easy, but let's think through the mechanics of how it would work with Real time Workflows. For starters, unlike a plug-in Real Time Workflows can't simply ask for a pre-operation value you would need to run the workflow before. So in this case we would need a workflow registered Before – Update. This workflow would subtract the old value. Then you would need to have another workflow registered on After – Update that would add the new amount.

Also keep in mind the lesson we discussed with the Auto Numbering example when we are working with concurrent actions. Meaning, if multiple threads are updating the same order value there is no way a Real Time Workflow could ensure it won't get caught accessing values that were updated by another thread leading to inconsistent results. A plug-in or a Custom Workflow Activity however could do better by doing aggregate queries of all the values at that point in time. Again still probably a small window of opportunity for concurrent problems, but the window would be smaller and at least represent a snapshot at a point in time. Not all solutions will have this high value update risk, but do keep it in mind as you make trade offs in approaches you take.

Wrapping Up

Real Time Workflows are a great extension of the workflow capabilities of Dynamics CRM. Use Real Time Workflows to reduce the amount of code based plug-ins you create and to allow non-developers to be able to implement business logic that runs in real time. Don't overdo it, as we have discussed in several places in the chapter there are times that Real Time Workflows shouldn't be the tool of choice.

8

Upgrading to Microsoft Dynamics CRM 2013

Introduction

So you use Microsoft Dynamics CRM 2011, and are excited about all of the new capabilities in 2013. How do you make the move? In this chapter we will talk through the upgrade process, including how to prepare for the deployment, upgrade options, installation process, and post upgrade tasks.

A new version

It is important to note that Microsoft Dynamics CRM 2013 is a new version, not an update. Microsoft Dynamics CRM users are used to regular update rollups, which are cumulative patches and hotfixes. While several of these introduced new functionality to the CRM 2011 platform, these fixes were primarily break fixes. Microsoft Dynamics CRM 2013 is a major upgrade, making significant and deep changes to the application. In some ways, CRM 2013 is the biggest change to the CRM user experience since version 3.0.

Earlier versions of CRM added functionality and made slight changes to the form layouts, but CRM 2013 is the first version to totally change the way the sitemap navigation works and the way forms are rendered.

In other ways, CRM 2013 is not as big of an upgrade as 2011 was from an architecture standpoint. CRM 2011 introduced a new JavaScript SDK and endpoint, which was a major shift from CRM 4.0. During a typical CRM 4.0 to 2011 upgrade, there was a significant amount of work that had to be done to make customizations like plug-ins and form JavaScript supported in CRM 2011.

If you made the migration from CRM 4 to 2011, you should expect the technical customization upgrade to be easier with the move to 2013, but expect to spend some additional time on updating form and navigation layouts, taking advantage of the new client UI technologies like Form Business Rules, as well as training users on the new user interface.

How long can I stay on CRM 2011?

That's great, you say, but I'm not ready to move to CRM 2013. Perhaps you have just adopted CRM 2011, or maybe you have a very large user base or customization that is not supported in CRM 2013.

The answer of how long you can stay on 2011 depends on your deployment method.

CRM Online: if you are a customer of Microsoft's hosted CRM option, you will need to make the move during the early part of calendar year 2014.

CRM On Premise: if you run CRM 2011 installed on your own servers, you can continue to use CRM 2011 until you are ready to make the move. Microsoft will continue to provide support for 2011 until 2015, but no additional functionality will be added and new versions of SQL and Windows will not be supported.

Before you upgrade

Whether you are upgrading today or if you are preparing to upgrade in a few months, there are several steps that you should take now to get your CRM Environment ready for the move to CRM 2013.

Remove any CRM 4.0 custom code from your CRM environment.

If you moved your environment from CRM 4 to CRM 2011, there were some CRM 4.0 customizations that still worked in CRM 2011 without being upgraded. These included plug-ins, custom JavaScript code, and other custom developed components. If you have any of these items, you should upgrade them to use supported CRM 2011 methods now. Even if you are staying with CRM 2011 for the immediate future, upgrading these components will make your

CRM 2011 environment better, as it will allow you to use the latest 2011 functionality, such as the ability to use browsers other than Internet Explorer, and it will make your custom pieces work with CRM 2013 when you are ready to go there.

Items that should be replaced or upgraded:

- CRM 4.0 JavaScript form scripts (anything that begins with CRMForm.all)
- CRM 4.0 Plug-ins
- Custom web pages that reside in the ISV folder

Upgrade any third party ISV solutions to the latest version.

If you have any third-party add-ons in your CRM environment, upgrade these solutions to the latest version. Contact the vendor of your solution and verify that their solution has been tested with 2013 and will support it prior to upgrading.

Install CRM 2011 Update Rollup 12 or later.

UR 12 is required for upgrading your environment to 2013. If you are on a build earlier than Update Rollup 12, making the move to the latest Update Rollup will introduce the cross browser compatibility to your CRM 2011 environment, and in doing so, will help you identify any customizations that will not work with 2013. If your plug-ins and JavaScript work post Update Rollup 12 in browsers other than Internet Explorer, they probably will also work in CRM 2013.

Be aware of architecture components that will no longer be supported with 2013.

Got XP? Office 2003? These will no longer be supported for CRM 2013. If any of your users have computers still running Windows XP with Office 2003, upgrade them prior to going to 2013. Other items that are no longer supported with 2013:

- Exchange 2003 (for the email router)
- Internet Explorer 7

Be aware of changes to the database structure in CRM 2013.

In CRM 2011 and previous versions, entities data was stored in two tables: a base table, holding the record ID and core system entities, and an extension base table, which stores non-core system entities, as well as custom entities. This structure was necessary in earlier versions of

Microsoft Dynamics CRM, but this design was also found to cause deadlocks under certain scenarios.

In Microsoft Dynamics CRM, the MSCRM database is updated to have a single table per entity. Note, even in CRM 2011, reading data directly from entity tables is not supported—for reporting and other sql data reading applications, only reading from the CRM Filtered views in the MSCRM SQL database is supported; however, given that some customers have built reports and integrations that read from the base or extension base tables, you will want to verify your implementation does not have any unsupported sql queries and update any of them to read from the Filtered Views prior to upgrading to CRM 2013.

The CRM 2013 upgrade process

In this section, we review how to upgrade to CRM 2013.

CRM Online

If you use Microsoft CRM Online, your environment will be upgraded to the new version automatically by Microsoft. You will receive an email from Microsoft notifying when your upgrade is scheduled to happen. As of this writing, all CRM Online environments are scheduled to be upgraded to CRM 2013 by early 2014, so by the time you are reading this, your upgrade has probably already happened.

CRM On Premise, version 4.0 or earlier

If you use CRM On Premise on a version earlier that CRM 2011, you will have to first upgrade to CRM 2011, then upgrade to 2013 using the normal CRM 2013 upgrade process.

CRM 2011 On Premise

If you use Microsoft Dynamics CRM 2011 On Premise, you choose when you upgrade, and the upgrade methodology that you will use. There are three different options that you can choose:

In-place Upgrade

In this option you will install CRM 2013 on an existing CRM 2011 server. During the installation, your CRM environment and database will be upgraded to Microsoft Dynamics CRM 2013.

Benefits of in-place upgrade

- Re-use existing CRM server architecture and SQL Server
- Preserve the existing URL and IP address for CRM
- Outlook clients do not need to be reconfigured.

Risks of in place upgrade

- Destroys CRM 2011 environment during installation
- No roll-back option
- Cannot be tried effectively prior to upgrade
- May leave artifacts of CRM 2011 application on the CRM servers

Point to existing database upgrade.

In this option you will install CRM 2013 on a new CRM Application server, but you point it to the existing CRM SQL Server. A clean copy of the application is installed, and during the installation the MSCRM SQL database will be upgraded to CRM 2013.

Benefits of "point to existing database" upgrade

- Re-uses SQL Server
- Fresh application server with no artifacts from previous version
- Can be rolled back by restoring a backup of MSCRM_Config and *_MSCRM databases

Risks of "point to existing database" upgrade

- While this option is less risky that an in-place upgrade, it still destroys the CRM 2011 environment during the installation, requiring more user down-time than an import upgrade.
- Given that the installation upgrades the CRM 2011 database during installation, this option cannot be effectively tried multiple times prior to upgrading.
- Since CRM 2013 is installed on a different application server than CRM 2011, the URL and IP address of CRM 2013 will be different than CRM 2011, which will require that Outlook Clients be reconfigured to the new URL, or existing URL DNS entries will need to be remapped, which will make CRM 2011 no longer available. Given that DNS entry changes can sometimes take several hours to take effect, this can result in multiple hours of CRM being unavailable.

Import upgrade

With this option, CRM 2013 is installed on a fresh set of CRM and SQL servers. A clean (empty) CRM installation is performed, then a backup of the CRM 2011 database is restored to the new CRM 2013 SQL Server, and the organization is imported via the deployment manager MMC console snapin.

Benefits of Import upgrade:

- Cleanest, least destructive upgrade option
- No artifacts from previous version on CRM or SQL Servers
- Since this option is nondestructive to your CRM 2011 environment, this upgrade option can easily be redone multiple times prior to your production environment. After installing CRM 2013, the database from CRM 2011 is imported and upgraded. If the import upgrade fails, you can drop the imported organization, resolve the issue, take another production backup, and try it again. At no point does the CRM 2011 production environment get disrupted, until the upgrade is complete and verified, and CRM 2011 is turned off.
- Less downtime for CRM users, as you can complete the CRM installation on the new CRM 2013 servers well in advance of the actual upgrade. This allows you to test and upgrade your customizations prior to the production upgrade, then when ready to go-live on CRM 2013 in production, import the final upgrade into your environment. This results in the users being out of the CRM application for a significantly shorter period of time.

Risks of in-place upgrade

- Added expense from having to provision new servers or virtuals for CRM 2013.
- CRM is installed on a different server, so Outlook clients will need to be reconfigured, or DNS entries will need to be remapped.

The import/upgrade option is Microsoft's recommended approach for upgrading to Microsoft Dynamics CRM 2013. In the remainder of this chapter, we assume that the reader will be taking this upgrade approach.

Planning your CRM 2013 Architecture

The system requirements for CRM 2013 remain unchanged from CRM 2011. This means that if your CRM 2011 environment is performing adequately, you can model your CRM 2013 server architecture similarly to you CRM 2011 servers. The full system requirements are covered in the Planning section of the CRM 2013 Implementation Guide from Microsoft.

If your CRM 2011 environment seems to run slowly or does not give you adequate performance, consider making some changes in your architecture design for CRM 2013. The following are some good places to begin:

- SQL Server performance is key to good CRM performance. If your SQL Server is resource constrained, your CRM performance will suffer. Adding memory and increasing SQL disk speed are good ways to increase CRM performance. Also, to avoid disk contention, SQL data, transaction logs, and tempdb should be located on separate physical partitions. For the best possible performance, consider implementing Solid State Drives (SSD).
- If you don't regularly service your SQL indexes, CRM performance will degrade over time. Regularly defragment and rebuild indexes and rebuild statistics to maintain optimal performance.
- For high availability performance, if you have more than 100 users, you should consider network load balancing the application servers. This will add availability for the application and all CRM services, as well as redundancy in the case of a disaster. Also, this will give you flexibility when installing update rollups, as you can install and reboot each node independently, without knocking users out of Microsoft Dynamics CRM.

From the outside

Dynamics CRM 2013 introduces some exciting new features, such as mobile applications and the ability to use the full CRM application from a tablet browser, such as Chrome on Android and Safari on iPad. Consider how users will have access to these great new features, as these types of devices are not connected to your Active Directory network. The answer is Internet Facing Deployment (IFD).

IFD is one of the best things that you can do to increase usage of CRM, by making CRM work anywhere, from wherever your users are, and IFD will be required to use these features for CRM On Premise.

The IFD deployment option is covered in the Installing section of the Microsoft Dynamics CRM 2013 implementation guide. The process is basically unchanged from Microsoft Dynamics CRM

2011, so if you already have IFD configured for 2011, you can use your existing Active Directory Federation Server (ADFS) deployment, and add a new relying party trust for your CRM 2013 installation.

While the IFD option is unchanged with 2013, many more users will want to implement IFD to take full advantage of the new mobile features in CRM 2013.

Pre-installation checklist

Before proceeding with the installation of CRM 2013, take a few minutes and verify that the environment is ready. The following is a simple pre-installation checklist that will help you verify that you are ready to install. If all of these conditions are true, the installation should proceed smoothly.

SQL Server

☐	64–Bit SQL Server 2008 R2 or 2012 Bit installed
☐	Installing user granted sys admin privileges in SQL Server
☐	SQL Agent running
☐	SQL full text indexing component installed
☐	Installing User granted local admin rights on CRM Server (and the Reports Server and Email Router Server so that reporting extension and email router can be installed)

CRM Server

☐	CRM Server Provisioned with Windows 2012 or Windows 2008 R2
☐	Web Server Role enabled on CRM server (with ASP.Net, Windows, and Anonymous Auth)
☐	If on Windows 2012, Windows Search Service enabled on CRM Server

☐	If on Windows 2008 R2, Indexing Service enabled on CRM server
☐	.Net 4.0 runtime installed on CRM server[1]
☐	Installing User given local admin rights on CRM Server
☐	Wildcard SSL certificate (or SAN certificate) procured and installed on the CRM application server

Service Account(s)

☐	Network service account created that meets the requirements in the implementation guide
☐	Service account is NOT the same account as the installing user (or any CRM user)

Active Directory (**Choose only one**)

☐	Organization Unit (OU) created to hold the CRM security groups, and installing user given permission to create and manage groups inside that OU
☐	Security groups pre-created by Active Directory administrator and installation configuration file created that includes the names and GUIDs of the pre-created groups

CRM License

☐	License key obtained from Microsoft
☐	Software installer downloaded to CRM application server

---

[1] If you don't install .Net framework prior to running the installation, it will be installed by CRM automatically; however, if this happens, the server will require a reboot, which will stop your installation, and you will need to start over. It is strongly recommended that you install .Net prior to installing Microsoft Dynamics CRM 2013.

Reporting Services

☐	64-bit reporting services installed and configured, either on separate reporting server, or on SQL database server
☐	SRSDATACONNECTOR subfolder of CRM installation media copied to the SSRS server, or available from a network location
☐	The reporting services URL (typically http://servername/reportserver) can be accessed from Internet Explorer on the CRM server

Installing CRM 2013

Now that you have prepared your new CRM 2013 servers and you have verified that all of the prerequisites are ready to go, you are now ready to install CRM 2013.

The full installation process is documented in the installing section of the Microsoft Dynamics CRM 2013 implementation guide.

1. Install CRM 2013 following normal installation procedures. During the installation, you will be asked what you want to name your organization. Remember that this installation will create an empty organization database—this is not what will be your upgraded organization, you do not want to enter the name that you want to ultimately use for your production CRM organization—we will do that when we import and upgrade the organization database from CRM 2011. I suggest using a name like "blank" or "temp," which you will not easily confuse with your production organization.
2. Configure the SSRS Data Connector and Email Router (if applicable).

Importing and upgrading an organization

Back up the database for your CRM 2011 organization on your CRM 2011 SQL server. This database will end with "_MSCRM." Restore the database to your CRM 2013 SQL server in SQL Management Studio, giving it the name of the organization you wish to use for 2013. Be sure to append the database name with "_MSCRM," as the organization import process will expect the name to be in that format.

In SQL Management Studio, expand the security node by the *_MSCRM database during the 2013 installation (not the database restored in step 2). Click the + button next to the database name and expand Security/Users.

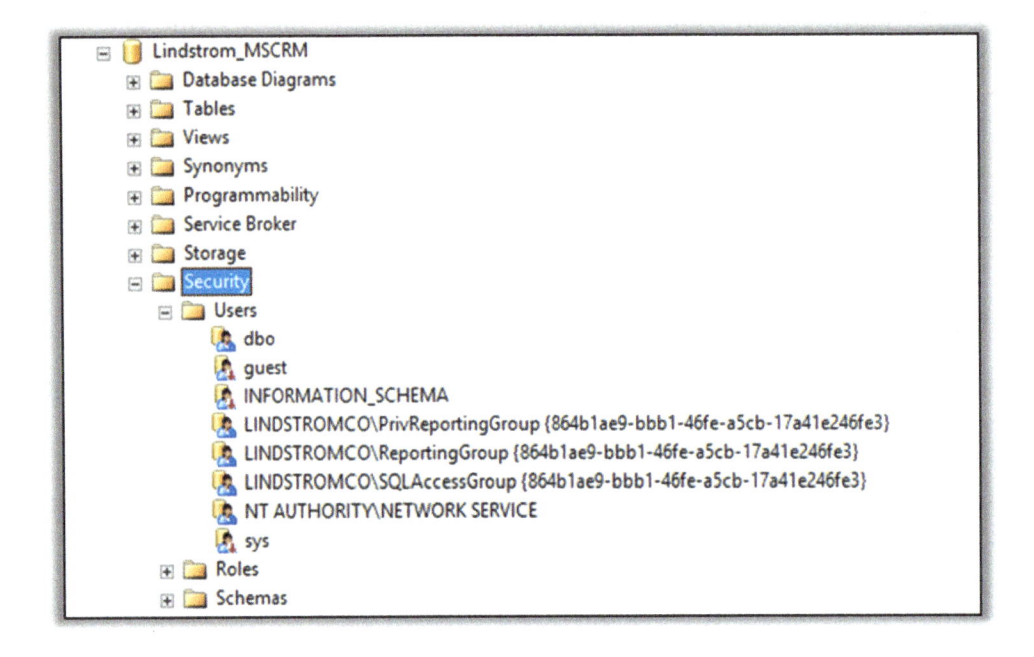

```
□ Lindstrom_MSCRM
    ⊞ Database Diagrams
    ⊞ Tables
    ⊞ Views
    ⊞ Synonyms
    ⊞ Programmability
    ⊞ Service Broker
    ⊞ Storage
    □ Security
        □ Users
            dbo
            guest
            INFORMATION_SCHEMA
            LINDSTROMCO\PrivReportingGroup {864b1ae9-bbb1-46fe-a5cb-17a41e246fe3}
            LINDSTROMCO\ReportingGroup {864b1ae9-bbb1-46fe-a5cb-17a41e246fe3}
            LINDSTROMCO\SQLAccessGroup {864b1ae9-bbb1-46fe-a5cb-17a41e246fe3}
            NT AUTHORITY\NETWORK SERVICE
            sys
        ⊞ Roles
        ⊞ Schemas
```

Note the security group assignments associated with the database and their roles. Add these same security group assignments to the restored MSCRM database. This will guarantee that the organization will have appropriate SQL permissions after it is imported.

Now that appropriate SQL permissions are set, we are ready to import and upgrade the organization.

On the CRM Server, launch the CRM Deployment Manager. To run the Deployment Manager, you will need to be a Deployment Administrator. If you installed CRM 2013 in step 1, you will have this role. If someone else installed CRM 2013, they will need to log in to the Deployment Manager and add you as a Deployment Administrator. The process for adding Deployment Administrators is detailed here: http://msdn.microsoft.com/en-us/library/gg197633.aspx.

In the Deployment Manager, select the "Organization" node, and on the right side, click "Import Organization.

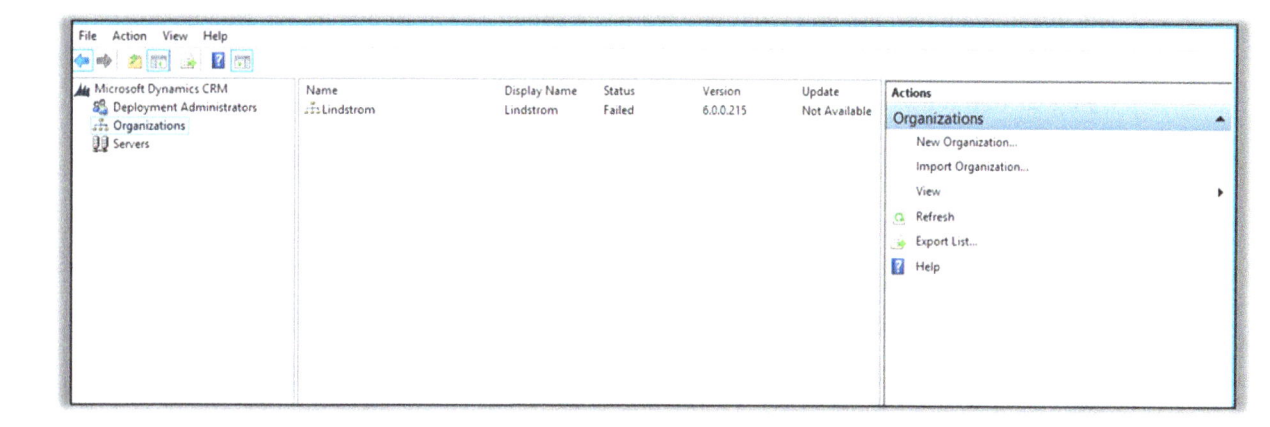

The Import Organization wizard will launch, and the restored MSCRM database should automatically be selected. Verify that the correct (restored) database is selected, then click "Next."

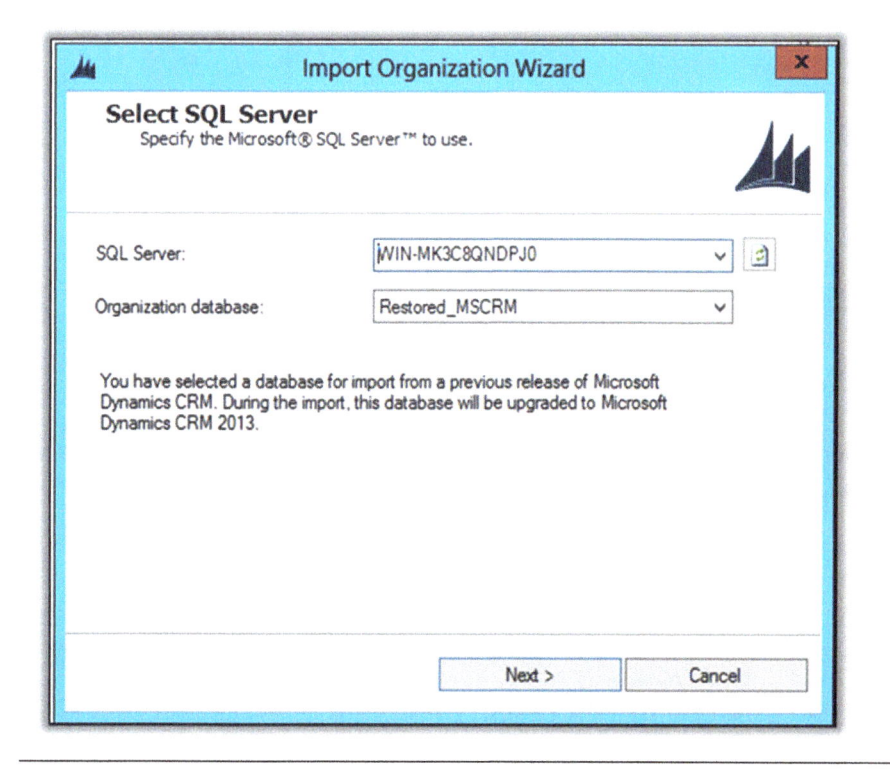

The wizard will then ask you what you want the organization to be named. I suggest using the same name as you chose when you restored your database, to eliminate confusion when later trying to match the organization to its SQL database. Enter the organization names, then click "Next."

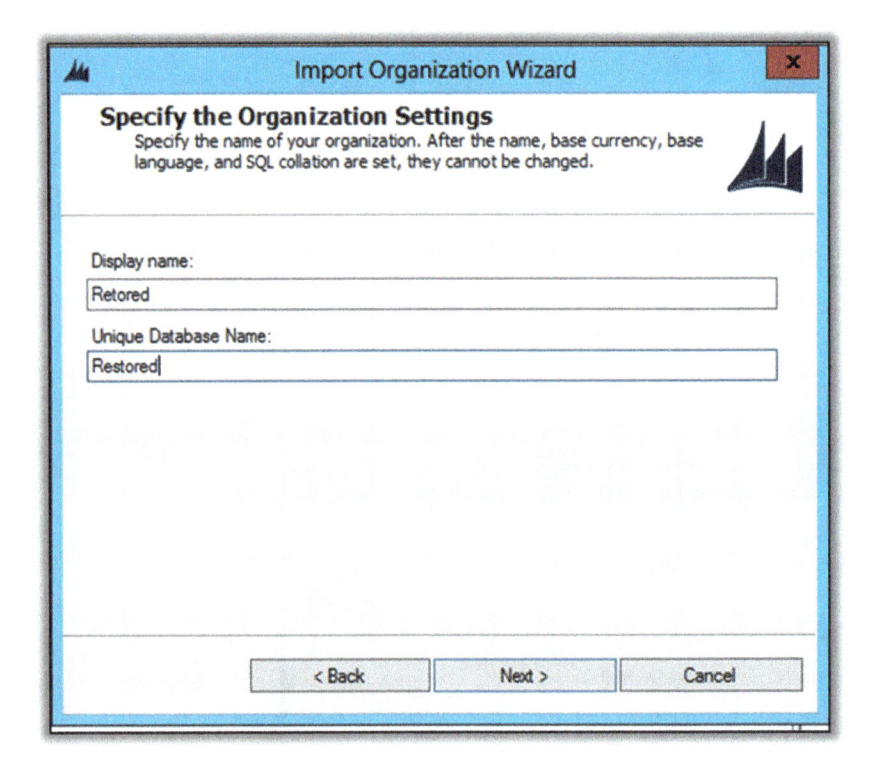

Select the desired reporting services URL. The wizard will default to whatever reporting services URL was selected during the CRM 2013 installation.

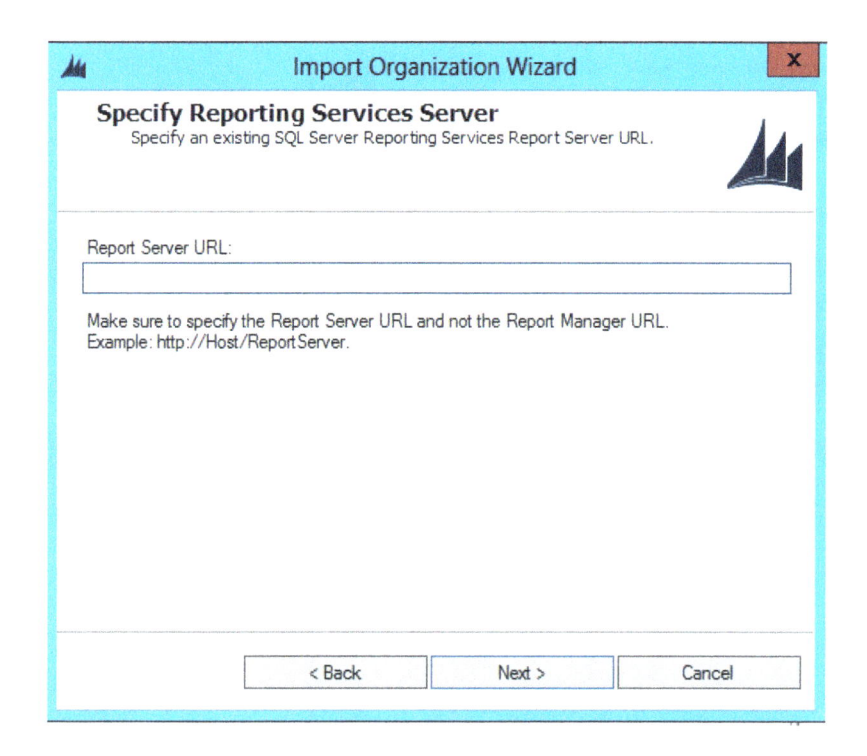

On the next step, select Automatically Map Users if deploying within the same Active Directory network as your CRM 2011 environment. Click Next

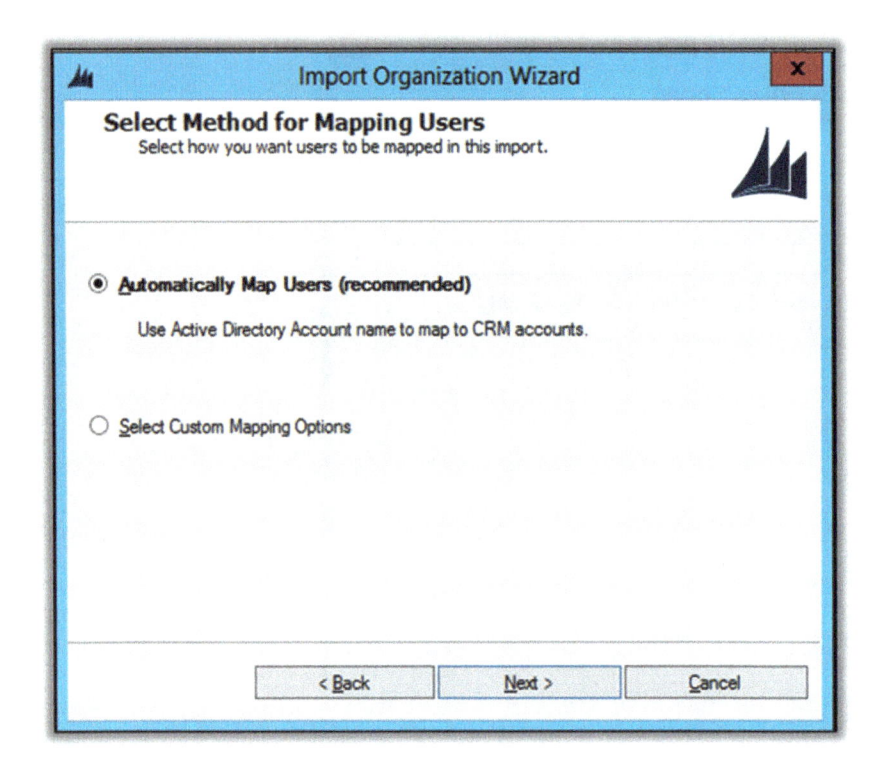

You may see an error message telling you that an error occurred during the mapping of users. This typically happens if you have disabled users in your CRM 2011 environment that no longer exist in your Active Directory.

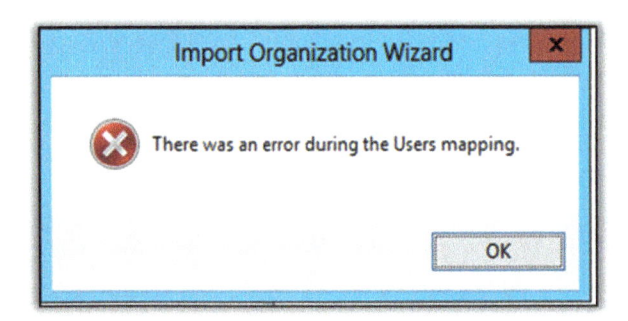

For example, if you have users who have left the company and they no longer exist in Active Directory, those users will not be able to be mapped when you import the 2011 database. This is expected behavior. On the next screen, you will see the list of mapped users. Any users that could not be mapped will be blank under the "New User" column.

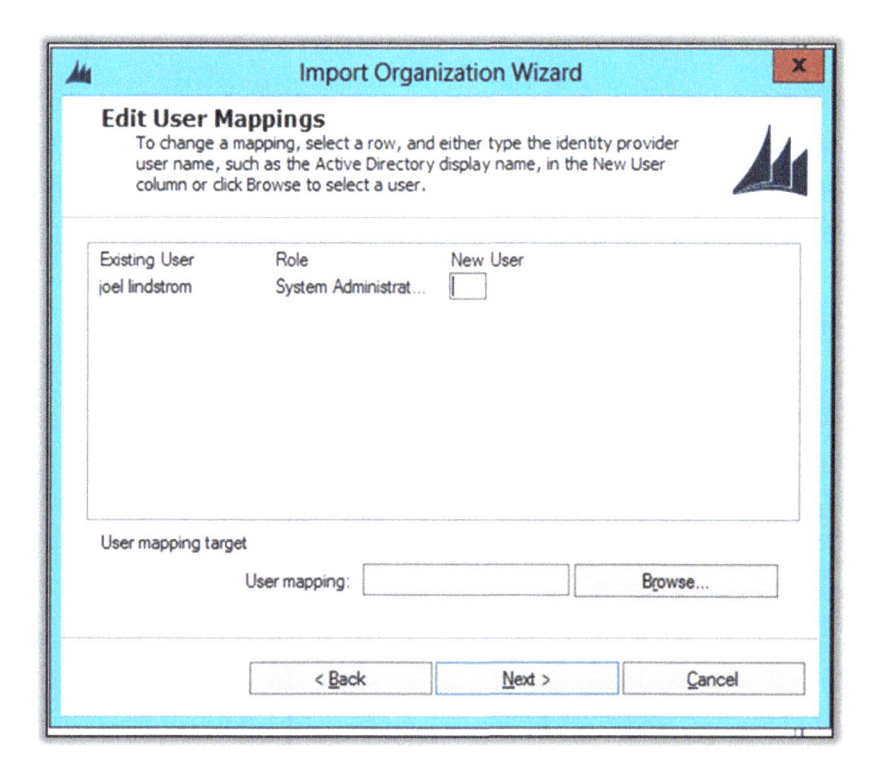

You can type in new user credentials for any unmapped users, select them and click the "browse" button to browse for the user credential, or just leave it blank to leave the user unmapped. If you choose not to map an unmapped user, the disabled user record will remain in CRM, all record assignments and activity party records linked to the user will remain, but nobody will be able to log in as that user while the user record is unmapped.

If you choose not to map a user during the import/upgrade, you can manually map the user record later, by opening up the user record and changing the user ID field to a current AD user credential.

Once you verify all user mappings are correct, click "Next."

The import organization wizard will then verify that the organization is ready to be imported and upgraded. If there are any errors or warnings, the system check page will display the error message, and you can select the error and click "Help" to get details about the error condition. Click "Next" to proceed.

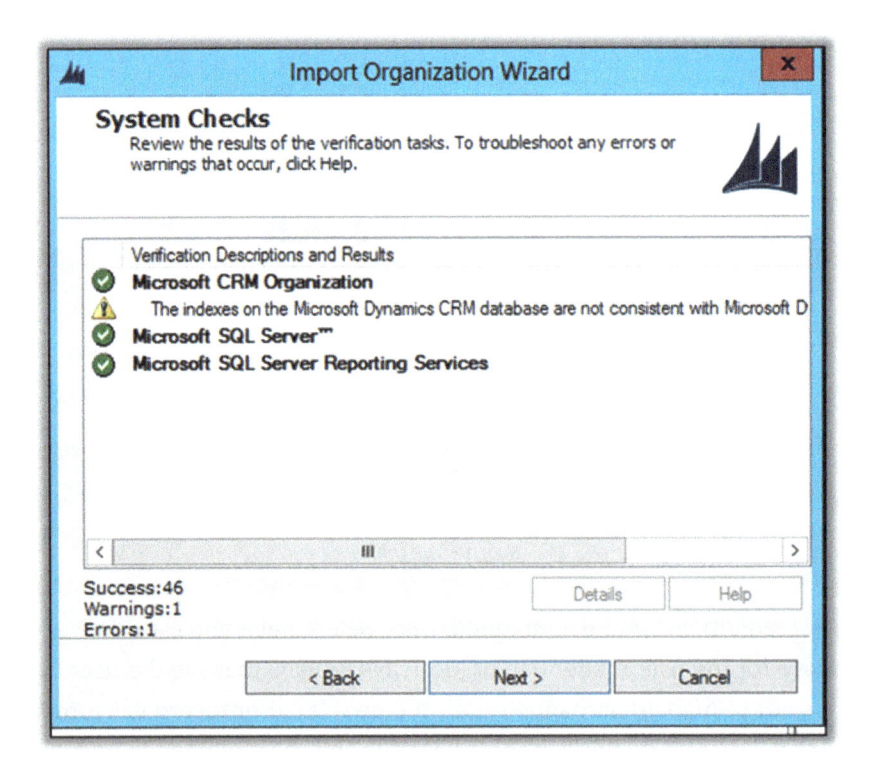

The error displayed in this picture is very common, especially when your CRM 2011 database contains custom indexes. You can still proceed with the upgrade, and the indexes will be rebuilt.

The last step of the import organization wizard lets you review the values entered as a final verification. If you wish to change anything, click the back button, otherwise, click "Import" to complete the import.

Rules of thumb for a successful import/upgrade

- The most common cause of organization import failure is lack of sufficient resources on the SQL server. The organization import/upgrade process is transaction log heavy, and I recommend that you have at least as much space available on your log partition (2x is even better) as the size of the organization database that you are upgrading.
- Another common cause of import/upgrade failure is unsupported SQL customizations. If you have SQL triggers or custom tables that you have added directly in SQL, chances are that your upgrade will fail. Replace any unsupported SQL customizations with supported customizations. For example, replace SQL triggers with workflows or plug-ins.
- As mentioned earlier in this chapter, during the upgrade, the entitynamebase and entitynameextensionbase tables will be merged. This process may take a long time in very large organizations. You can run the table merge process separately from the upgrade process by adding the following registry key:

HKEY_LOCAL_MACHINE\SOFTWARE\Microsoft\MSCRM\MergeBaseAndExtensionTables

DWORD (32-bit)

Value: 0

Then import the organization database as described above. Once you import the organization, during a scheduled maintenance window, you can then run the table merge process. Set the MergeBaseAndExtensionTables registry key back to 1, then make the following registry change:

HKEY_LOCAL_MACHINE\SOFTWARE\Microsoft\MSCRM\MergeBaseAndExtensionTables

DWORD (32-bit)

Value: 0

Disable the imported organization, then run the CRMMergeBaseAndExtension.exe tool. Then enable the organization. For full instructions on how to run the tool, see the planning section of the Microsoft Dynamics CRM 2013 implementation guide.

What if something goes wrong during the upgrade?

If the upgrade fails for some reason, the first thing to do is to figure out what the problem was. If the upgrade fails, you will receive a notification that it fails, along with a hyperlink to download the log file. You can always find the log files located in c:/program files/Microsoft Dynamics CRM/Logs. Look toward the end of the log file, and you should see an error message that gives you details of why the upgrade failed.

Address the cause of the failure, and then repeat the import process. For best results, I recommend that you restore a new copy of your CRM 2011 database (keep the original backup handy, in case it fails and you have to restore again).

This is the beauty of the import/upgrade. It is nondestructive. If you fail, you can easily start over. You do not need to re-install CRM 2013. Just restore a new backup and re-import.

Post upgrade

Now your CRM organization is upgraded to CRM 2013, we will now focus on updating the customization, forms, and user experience to take full advantage of CRM 2013. Microsoft has taken a nondestructive approach to upgrading CRM 2011 to 2013, which means that current form layouts and sitemaps will be preserved; however, you will want to make some adjustments to your configuration to fully benefit from the new user experience in CRM 2013.

Review and update the sitemap

The first thing that you may notice coming from CRM 2011 to CRM 2013 is that the application navigation is significantly different than it was in previous versions. Users of CRM 2011 and earlier are used to this sitemap layout:

CRM 2013 Quick Start

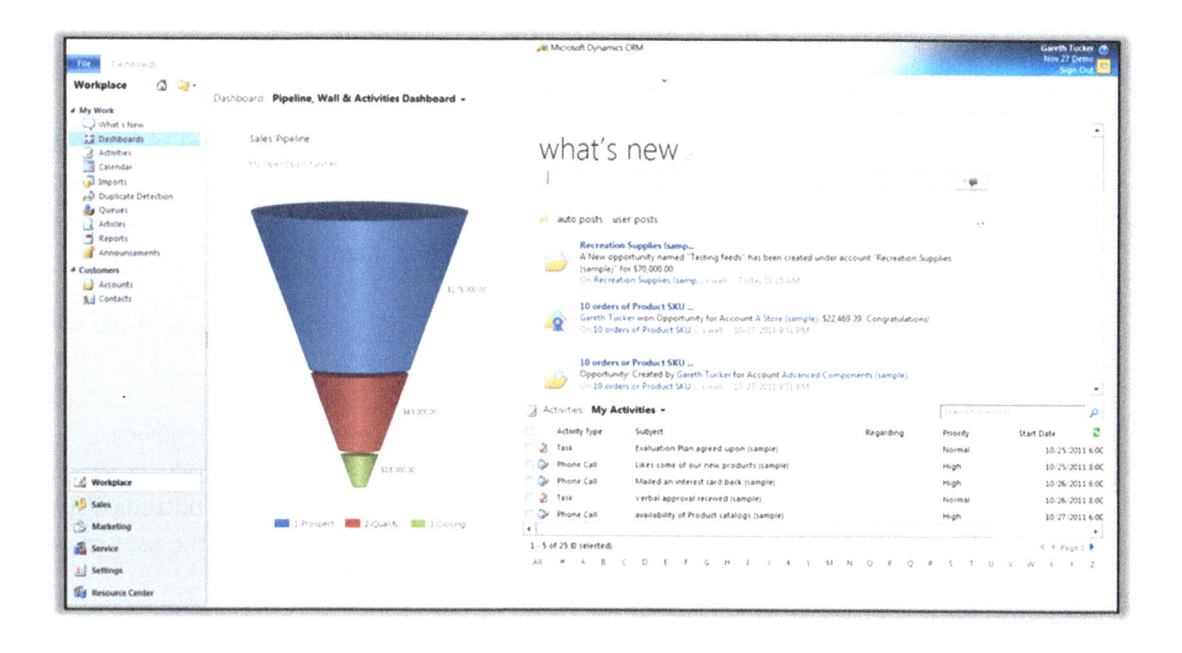

CRM 2013 radically changes this layout. Several things jump out when you see the new CRM 2013 user interface:

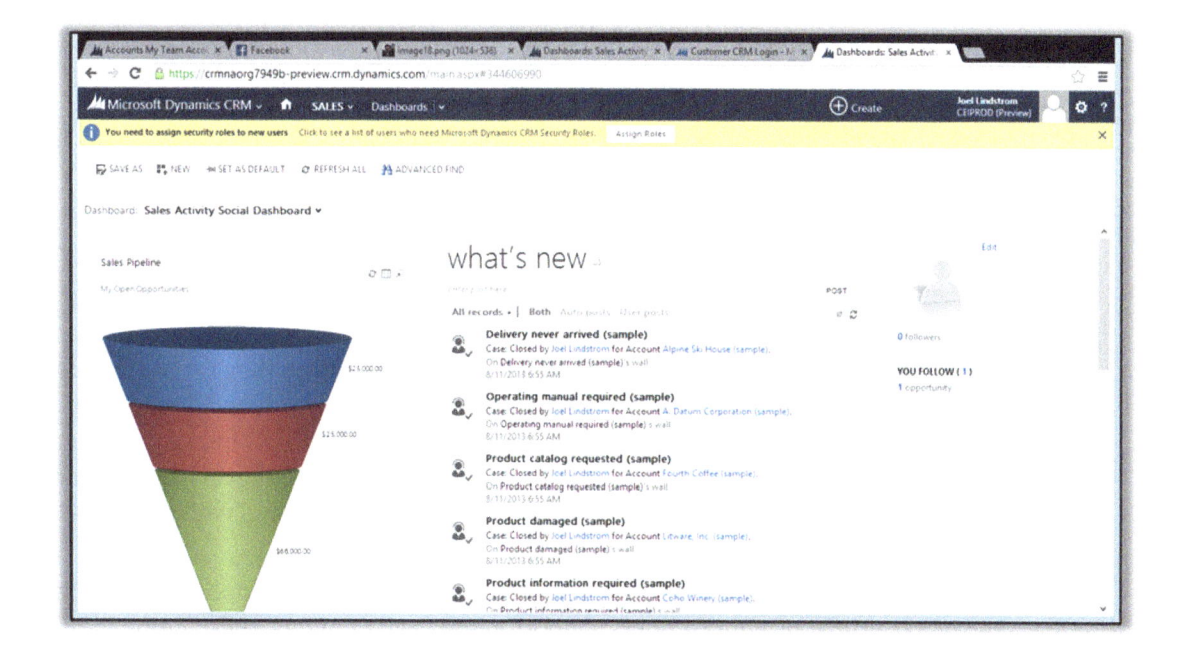

~ 233 ~

- The sitemap is hidden unless explicitly called by the user (by clicking on the arrow by "Microsoft Dynamics CRM".

- The sitemap areas (such as sales, marketing, service) are separated from the sub-areas (accounts, contacts, opportunities). The sub-areas are still organized by areas, but to select a link within the sales area, you have to first select the area with the first down arrow, and then select the sub-area under the second down arrow.

- Since menus are minimized, users have significantly more screen real estate, allowing more details to be displayed in a cleaner user interface.

- When exposed, the sitemap buttons are larger, to be useful from touch devices.

- Depending on the resolution of your screen, the maximum number of buttons displayed in the menu at one time is 5-7. To move further down the list of links, the user scrolls to the right.

With these changes in mind, there are several changes you will want to make to make your sitemap provide maximum usability to users in CRM 2013:

- In CRM 2011 and earlier, the common practice was to group every group's most common links in the "Workplace" area of the sitemap. It was not uncommon to see the workplace area have 20+ links in it. When you upgrade to CRM 2013, you will still see the workplace area at the top; however, this area has been deprecated for new 2013 environments.

- Given the limitation of how many links are simultaneously displayed, rather than having a very large "workplace" area that contains every group's links, a better approach is to use a separate area for each group. Out of the box you have sales, marketing, service, and you can add other groups.

- Each distinct group should have their own sitemap area, which they set as their default area in user settings. All of the links they use should live there, even if the same link (such as account) is duplicated in multiple areas. CRM 2013 works best when users do not have to frequently switch between multiple sitemap areas. If everything I need is contained in my default area, I can quickly navigate to what I need with minimal clicks.

- The sub-area links in each sitemap area should be prioritized by importance. If a sales rep works primarily with Accounts, Opportunities, and Contacts, these items should be positioned near the top of his group's sitemap area.

- If you look at a new CRM 2013 environment, you will see that each sitemap area has its own dashboard link—this allows each group to have their own unique dashboard, specific to their work. If you upgrade you will not have these links; however, you can copy them from a sitemap from a new organization (such as the one that was created by default when you installed Microsoft Dynamics CRM 2013), and paste them into the appropriate spots in your sitemap.

- It is very common in CRM 2011 and earlier for customizers to put links to every custom entity in the "Settings" sitemap area. In 2013 you will want to re-think this practice. Too many links in settings will make system administration more difficult, and custom entity links should at a minimum be positioned underneath the links for customization and administration.

- Don't edit the sitemap XML directly. There are several convenient sitemap editors that make sitemap surgery easy. I recommend Tanguy Touzard's sitemap editor that is part of his XRM Toolbox http://xrmtoolbox.codeplex.com. It works with CRM 2011 and 2013, and makes adding, removing, or editing Sitemap areas and sub-areas very easy, and also allows you to quickly rearrange the order of the subarea links.

- Consider which interface your users will be using. The new navigation primarily applies to the web interface. If users are using the Outlook client, sitemap navigation will still be rendered as it is in CRM 2011 for Outlook, in alphabetically arranged folders. If users primarily use CRM for Outlook to access CRM, you may not need to modify your sitemap layout.

Re-evaluate your dashboards.

Without the sitemap and ribbon displayed by default, you will have approximately 25% more visible space. To take full advantage of this real estate, you may want to reconfigure your system dashboards. A two-column CRM 2011 dashboard may look somewhat sparse in 2013.

In CRM 2011, due to the limitation on visible space, CRM users frequently configured multiple dashboards designed for the same group. This sometimes lead to "dashboard overload" with 20-30 dashboards, and diluted the usefulness of dashboards as a feature in CRM. A chart on a dashboard that nobody sees is no better than no chart at all.

Also, CRM 2013 adds some components, such as the social pane web resource, which allows you to add the "what's new" wall to a dashboard, rather than displaying it in a separate tab.

Update your forms.

Probably the biggest part of your upgrade will be updating your forms. Unlike the move from CRM 4 to 2011, most of the "under the covers" components remain the same, such as JavaScript, plug-ins, web service end points. If these things work in 2011 in a supported way, they should continue to work in 2013.

The bulk of the changes are going to be related to the new UI—flat forms that hide the navigation bar and all but the first five ribbon buttons, giving the user a wider canvas for the form layout.

When you upgrade your CRM 2011 environment to 2013, your existing forms will be preserved. The tabs, section, layouts, and form scripts will remain the way they were in 2011. However, to optimize usability, you will not want to leave your layout in the conditional two-column "long" form.

If you are upgrading an On Premise CRM environment, or if you are using CRM Online and never enabled the Polaris enhancements, your main form will be called the "information" form, and will be the active form in CRM for all entities. There will also be a new form, which typically has the name of the entity.

> **NOTE**
> *Dynamics CRM 2013 forms automatically save changes every 30 seconds by default. This can cause issues if you have on save scripts, as the scripts may fire repeatedly. Auto-save can be disabled in Settings →Administration →System Settings. By disabling auto-save, users will save the record after updating it, just like in Dynamics CRM 2011.*

CRM 2013 Quick Start

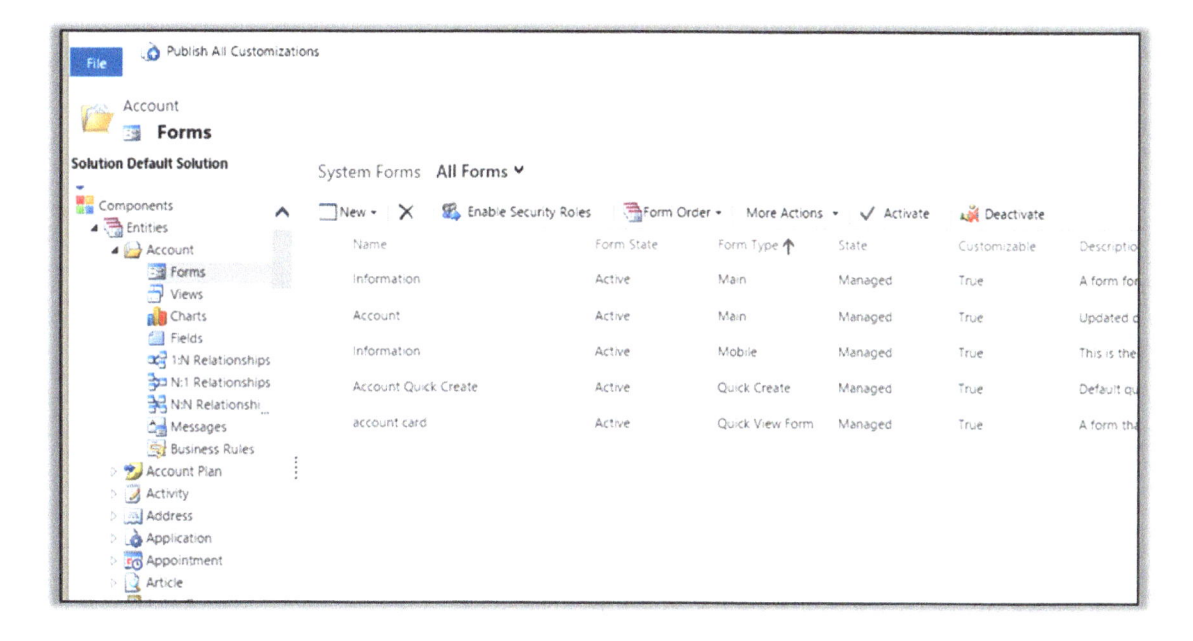

After the upgrade, system entities will include the "Information" form, which is the classic form from CRM 2011, and the new form with the name of the entity.

The "Information" form will contain your existing CRM 2011 form customization. It will be rendered in the new UI, with the ribbon and navigation bar, but any tabs, sections, and fields will be rendered in the same layout as they were in 2011, and any JavaScript form events that were on the form in CRM 2011 will be there in 2013, and if they are written in a supported way per the CRM 2011 SDK, they should still work with CRM 2013.

Just like the sitemap, the form customization is preserved so as to not destroy your customization; however, you will notice that it doesn't take full advantage of the new user interface. The traditional layout requires scrolling vertically, and having only two columns in the display, there is a lot of wasted white space on the form. You will want to update the form to take full advantage of the new user interface.

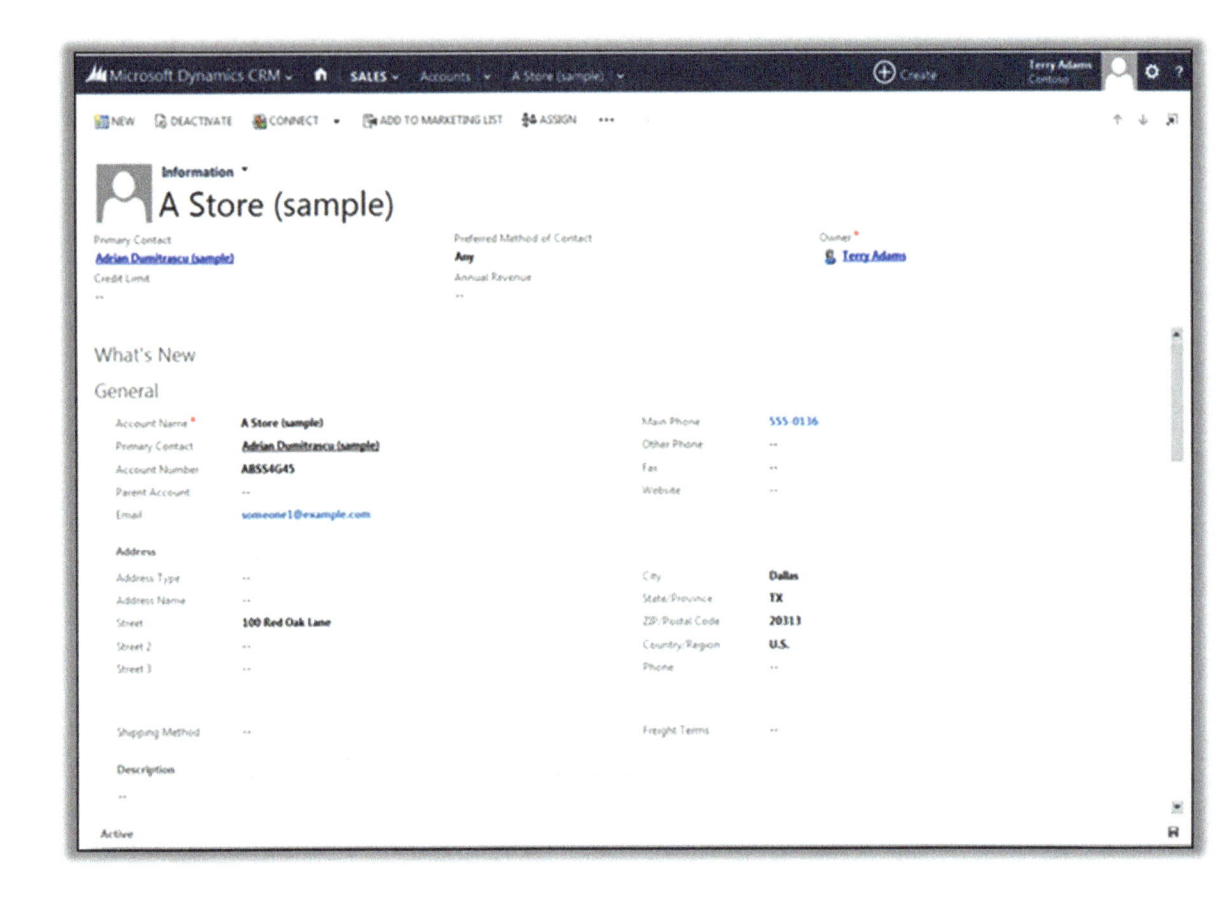

The Account "Information" form illustrates how the "classic" 2011 forms will be rendered in CRM 2013.

There will also be a new form, with the name of the entity. This form will be the new "refreshed" form for the entity. These forms are the out of the box forms for new deployments, and they show Microsoft's best practices for designing forms for 2013:

- Instead of two column full form width sections, use more single column sections
- Vertical scrolling is minimized.
- New components like combination address field block are more in-line with other Microsoft Applications, such as Outlook.
- Notes, activities, and posts are central to the record, but are displayed in a tabbed pane, taking up much less total space.
- Subgrids are emphasized over navigation bar links

CRM 2013 Quick Start

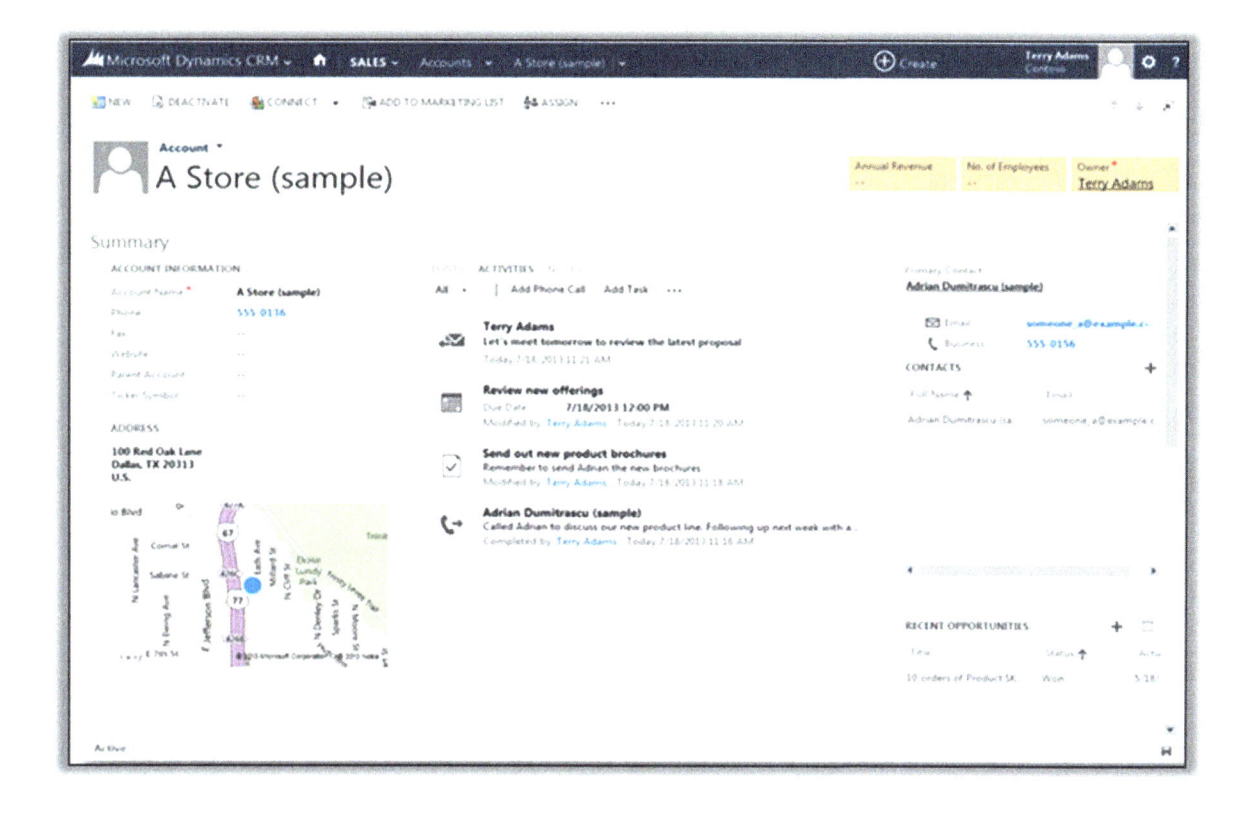

The "refreshed" form for the Account entity includes new features and is optimized for the CRM 2013 user interface.

To take full advantage of the new functionality of the refreshed form, you will want to update your form customization. However, you don't have to get rid of your existing form to do this. Microsoft Dynamics CRM 2013 includes a new merge form function that makes bringing your existing form customization into the refreshed forms.

1. Go to Settings→Customization→Customize The System
2. Select the entity that has the form you wish to customize and expand the "Forms" section.
3. Open the refreshed form for the entity (usually this form will have the same name as the entity.

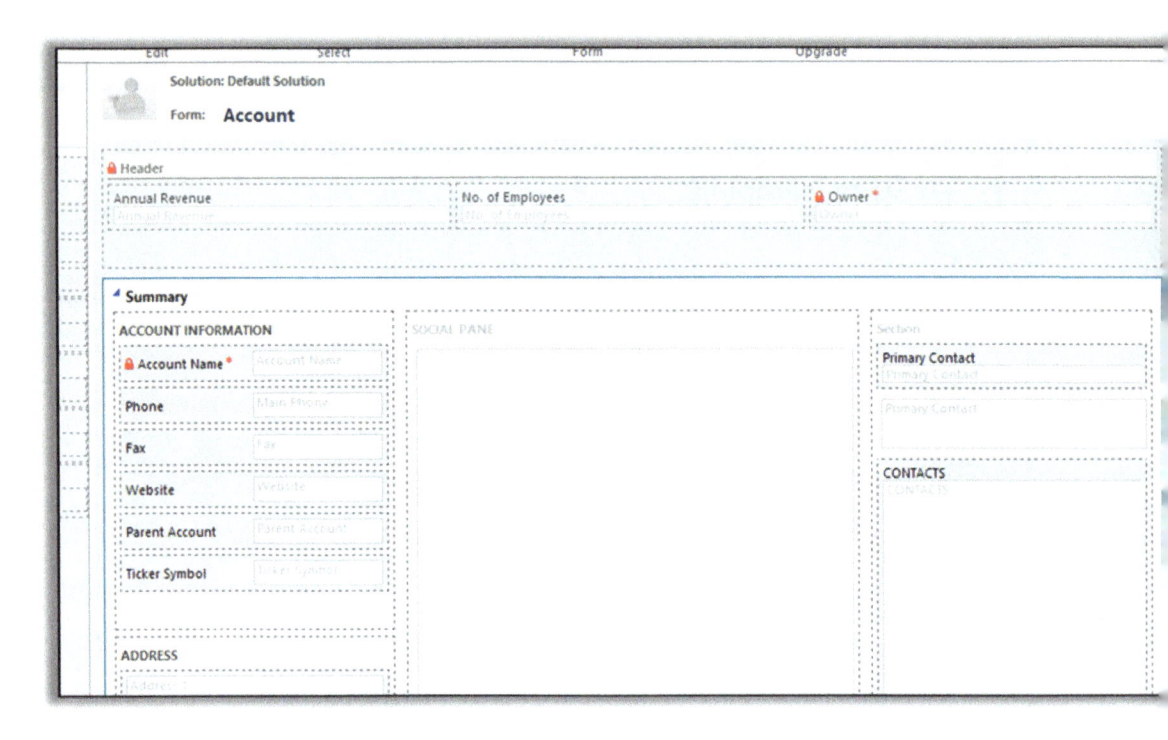

4. Back this form up—we will be modifying it, so we will want to make a copy as a backup, just in case something goes wrong. On the ribbon, click "save as", and save a copy of the form with a new name.

    Save As

5. On the far right side of the ribbon, there is a button called "Bring in another form."

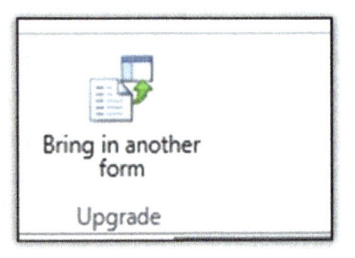

When you push the "Bring in another form" button, you will have the option to merge the new form with the contents of the selected form. Select the "Information" form, and the contents of the information form will be brought in to the new form, below the existing form sections. The new form will now contain all of the contents of the new form, as well as the contents of the legacy form.

You can now update and rearrange the contents to update your form to the desired configuration.

1. Remove/update redundant sections and fields. For example, on the account form, you will now have name and address sections duplicated. If you want to take advantage of the new combined address control, remove the legacy address section.
2. If you want to use the new social pane with combined notes and activities, remove the legacy activity and notes section.
3. Rearrange and resize remaining legacy sections to match the new layout. Existing legacy tabs will be single column tabs. You can select them and change to two or three columns, then edit the sections to modify their width.
4. You can also change the label placement to appear over the field to free up screen real estate.
5. Publish changes, then test the form. When you open a record, you will probably get the old "Information" form. You can test the new form by clicking the form selector arrow by the entity name on the upper left of the form.

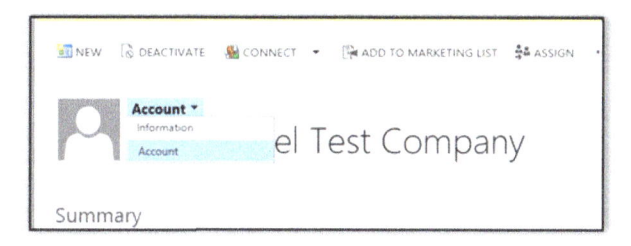

6. Once you get the form layout updated and tested, deactivate your old form by going to settings→Customization→Customize the System. Select the old entity form, and from the ribbon click "Deactivate."

7. Evaluate your form scripts. If your JavaScript is written in a supported way for CRM 2011, it should work in CRM 2011. However, you will still want to re-evaluate your form scripts to verify that they are optimally written, and that they are still needed for CRM 2013. One very nice new feature of CRM 2013 is Form Business Rules. These rules allow customizers to create conditional business rules for CRM 2013 forms by using a user-friendly rule engine, as opposed to writing JavaScript.

From the form customization ribbon, you can click "Business Rules" on the ribbon to expose the Form Business Rules pane, then click "New Business Rule" to create a new business rule.

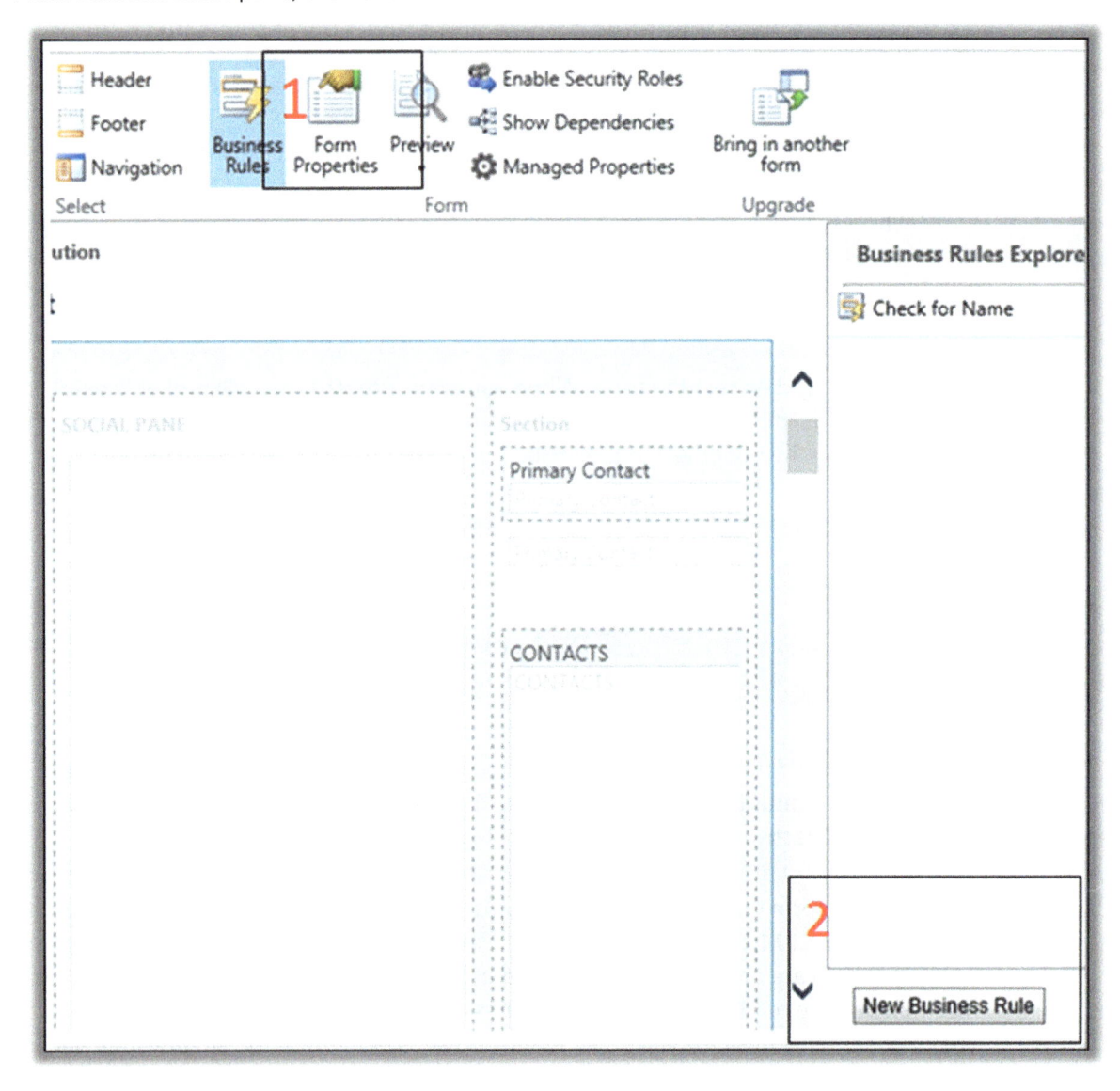

Business rules allow you to easily configure form business rules, which allow you to create dynamic rules that happen real-time on a record's form. In previous versions of CRM, form business rules required JavaScript. Business Rules run real-time on the form and load client side, just like JavaScript, but are created and maintained in an easy-to-use wizard.

Some common examples of things that you can do with business rules:

- Validate that fields are populated correctly
- Compare two fields
- Use the same expressions as you do with advanced find or workflow wizard, such as greater than, less than, equals, contains data, does not contain data
- Perform calculations
- Set visibility
- Set requirement
- Set field values

When upgrading, you should evaluate your existing form scripts. Can these functions be performed by business rules? If they can, you should strongly consider replacing JavaScript with form business rules.

Why should I replace JavaScript with form business rules?

1. Moving scripts to business rules puts them in a format that can be easily extended or updated by users who are not script experts
2. Reducing custom script will make forms load faster
3. Form rules will more easily move through future upgrades. Custom scripts can complicate upgrades, especially if the JavaScript endpoint changes. Form rules are more out of the box, like workflows.
4. Form rules can help ease the transition to auto-save. The new auto-save feature in CRM 2013 will make forms save every 30 seconds. This can be a problem if you have scripts that run on save of the form.

   Frequently, OnSave events are used to validate data completion before saving the form, and pop up an alert if the data entered is not valid.

   Form rules can move this functionality out of the OnSave form event, by creating a form rule that verifies that when each field contains data, if the condition is not valid, pop up an error dialog.

Other post initial upgrade tasks

- Configure process flows for any process driven entities. The new process flow control will be exposed on several out of the box entities, such as leads, opportunities, and cases; however, you can also add process flows to any custom entity that is process driven.

Review your user's business processes. What are the steps that they go through to close a sale, resolve a case, and complete a project? How is this currently configured in CRM? Do you have a bunch or required fields on the form? Do users have to know how to navigate the process?

Take your processes and break them down to their main steps. Identify fields or actions that must be completed during the process, and build that into the new process flow feature. For more information about the process flows, see that chapter.

- Package your customization changes into an unmanaged solution. This is what we will export to production.

- Update your documentation. If you have training and user documentation from when you implemented CRM 2011, you will want to update the documentation to reflect the changes in 2013. While Dynamics CRM 2013 looks dramatically different, most of its core functionality has not changed. For example, the process to create a chart, perform advanced find, or navigate to an Account all remain the same steps; however, the look and feel of how to get to these items has changed significantly. Most of the documentation update will be changing screenshots and adding content about new functionality, such as process flows. One big benefit of the new forms (if properly configured) is that they are not nearly as "long" as 2011 forms, so they should more easily fit into a single screenshot.

- Train your users. Many people did the CRM 4 to 2011 upgrade with minimal user training. For the 2013 upgrade, this is not a great idea. The look and feel has changed so significantly that existing users may be surprised when they first see it. User training for existing users should cover navigation and working with the new forms.

We also now have three different user experiences: Web client, Outlook client, and mobile app. For best results, plan your training around the client that your users will primarily use. It is a bad idea to train most users on the web client and the Outlook client if they mainly use Outlook—it can confuse the user and create the perception that CRM is overly complicated. Each user experience takes advantage of its environment's unique characteristic: Web client is a touch friendly web application, Outlook client is deeply integrated into Outlook, so views and navigation follow the same metaphor as other Outlook areas (like mail) and take advantage of Outlook functionality (like tagging records, conditional formatting, Outlook views). If users will be using CRM for Outlook, I recommend conducting their training in the Outlook client.

- If you have any integrations with any other systems, you will want to update and test these integrations. Check with your ETL tool provider to see if they have an update for their CRM adaptor, then test the integration in a dev environment.

The expectation is that your integration (if done in a supported way) should work with 2013 like it does with 2011. Given that the web service endpoints are not changing with 2013, and in the upgrade process we have not deleted or modified any existing entity structure data (just changed how it is presented on the front end), your integration should work with 2013. The 2011 version of CRM ETL tools such as Scribe Insight, Cozyroc, and KingswaySoft all work with 2013. If you do anything unsupported, such as reading or writing from the base CRM tables, the integration will most likely need to be updated.

Take pressure off of your production upgrade.

We all know that upgrades can be stressful—users are knocked out of the system, and there is a risk that something might fail. The good news is that you can take a lot of the pressure off of your production upgrade by doing several things prior to the actual cut-over.

1. Document the upgrade steps. The upgrade steps will need to be performed in a certain order. For example, if you are upgrading a solution that has an ISV add-on such as Inside View, you will have to install the Inside View solution update prior to importing your upgrade solution package. Document the order in which these need to be applied so the production upgrade goes smoothly. Be sure to include all steps, including things like repointing the integration DTS to the new CRM 2013 URL.

2. Install your production environment early. Many people wait until the actual production upgrade date to install the production environment. A better idea is to install your production environment early, maybe as soon as you install your development environment. Remember that since we are following the import-upgrade methodology, the installation of the server and the upgrade of the environment are two separate steps. By installing production early, you have plenty of time to verify that the installation is right, set up and test IFD, and test performance.

3. Test your upgrade. For moderately complex customizations, it can be a good idea to do a test run of the production upgrade prior to the final production upgrade. Since we are following the import upgrade methodology, we can upgrade multiple times on the same server. Once your dev upgrade is done and you have your upgrade solution package built,

schedule a test upgrade in your production environment. I like to do a test run into the production environment, because it will show exactly how it will work in production. A test upgrade also will test our steps documented in #1, and will show if there are any missing steps. Also, by doing a test upgrade in production, the people who are performing the production upgrade will be familiar with the steps (and their expected duration) and the production upgrade will go faster.

4. Do not combine the upgrade with a new project phase. Upgrades are stressful enough. This is not the time to introduce new entities or groups into your environment. Keep upgrades for upgrades. It is ok to turn on the new features and change existing form layouts as part of the upgrade process, but I would not recommend introducing new entities during the upgrade process.

The production upgrade

Now we have our customization upgraded to 2013 and we have tested the upgrade, we are ready for the big day. If you have followed the recommendations in this chapter, the production upgrade will go smoothly.

At the scheduled time (hopefully after hours or on a weekend), disable the CRM 2011 website. You can do this by turning off the CRM 2011 application server or by disabling the organization in the CRM 2011 Deployment Manager.

Then restore a copy of the MSCRM database to the CRM 2013 database server and import it in through the CRM 2013 Deployment Manager. When finished, import your upgrade solutions.

When you import your organization in the Deployment Manager, you will have the option to select the organization name. Most CRM customers will want the URL for their upgrade environment to match the URL for CRM 2011, so users will not have to change their shortcuts or reconfigure their Outlook clients. By selecting the same organization name for 2013 production as you had for CRM 2011 production, the IFD URL for the organization can be repointed to the 2013 environment. Once you are finished importing the org, go in to the properties of your deployment and set the web addresses to match what they were for 2011, then make sure you repoint your DNS entries (external and internal) to point to the 2013 server.

What about the Outlook client?

CRM 2013 introduces a new version of the Outlook client; however, you are not required to upgrade the Outlook client at the same time as you upgrade your servers. As long as you are on

Update Rollup 14 of the 2011 Outlook client, it will work with CRM 2013. Upgrading multiple Outlook clients can be painful, especially in large organizations. Since the Outlook client for 2011 works with 2013, this allows users to separate the server upgrade from the client upgrade. You can upgrade your server, be sure that it works, then at a reasonable future date upgrade the clients. You can upgrade the clients in batches, or by group, rather than having to upgrade everybody simultaneously.

For more information on the Outlook client deployment and upgrade process, see the installation section of the Microsoft Dynamics CRM 2013 Implementation Guide.

Upgrades don't have to be painful

If you plan for it, upgrades can be an enjoyable process. Prepare ahead of time, perform your upgrade in a non-production environment, turn on new features, remove old customization, replacing it with improvements like form business rules and process flows. Don't just keep your "classic" form layouts and perform just a technical upgrade. This is your chance to shed the limitations imposed on you by earlier versions. There will never be a better time than an upgrade to change your forms to a modern configuration. Yes, users are used to a certain configuration; however, keep in mind that the new UI has different characteristics than the old one. A "classic" configuration in the new UI will be less productive in 2013 than it was in 2011. A "modern" form configuration that presents more information and takes full advantage of the new user experience will be more user friendly and allow your users to get more done faster, and make your configuration work with the new world of "post PC" screens.

9

Solutions going forward

A Brave New World

Life in the software world is changing rapidly as we now find ourselves in a paradigm driven by approaches like "Cloud-First" or "Online-First", these approaches are being adopted by software vendors both large and small. The benefits of these strategies are vast, not least of which is the ability to be far more agile with product enhancements, in order to adapt and survive in today's competitive landscape.

Microsoft has been clear for some time now that "Cloud-First" is their approach of choice with Dynamics CRM Online leading the charge. The 2011 release of Dynamics CRM Online was the beginning, with a number of "Cloud-First" releases between then and Dynamics CRM 2013 release in October 2013.

Dynamics CRM 2013 marked the point where this strategy reached full steam, being the first of eight releases planned between October 2013 and the end of 2014. What does this mean for us? It means we need to have a clear understanding of what is required to build and package Solutions in such a way that they can keep up with this rapid release cadence, as well as an understanding of what has changed to date in the Solution framework and what might change in the future, as the framework itself evolves to better handle the deployment of these changes.

> **TIP**
>
> **Regularly check for updates to the Dynamics CRM SDK**
> The Software Development Kit (SDK) for Dynamics CRM is typically updated at minimum with each release of Dynamics CRM Online and contains a "Release History" and "What's New for Developers" section that should be your first port of call for information. All the latest updates and Information can be found on the CRM Team blog.

Dynamics CRM 2013 – The Beginning of a Paradigm Shift

What has changed in Solutions today with Dynamics CRM 2013

Let's start by taking a look at Solutions today and the changes that have been made to start providing us with better capability moving forward.

The Dynamics CRM 2013 release hasn't brought about much change to the Solution framework but has started laying the foundation required in order to build a more robust Solution framework going forward. The fundamental change is the introduction of Solution versioning. Now you may be asking, hasn't versioning been there since CRM 2011?

While there was the capability in CRM 2011 (as well as CRM 2013) to specify a version number in the Solution Editor, this version number is purely for you to track which version of your Solution is installed in a CRM environment.

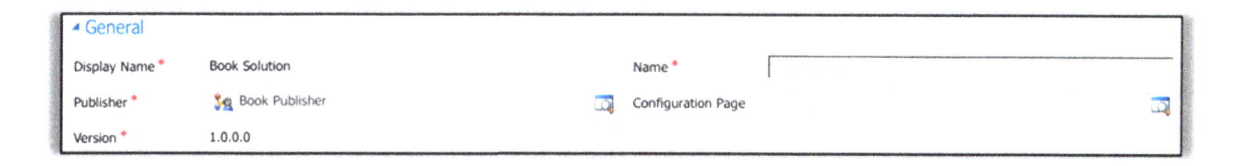

The versioning introduced in Dynamics CRM 2013 is hidden away a little deeper, inside the actual Solution file, and managed by the platform itself.

```xml
<entity Name="Contact">
        <IsBusinessProcessEnabled>1</IsBusinessProcessEnabled>
        <IsRequiredOffline>0</IsRequiredOffline>
        <OwnershipTypeMask>UserOwned</OwnershipTypeMask>
        <IsAuditEnabled>0</IsAuditEnabled>
        <IsActivity>0</IsActivity>
        <IsVisibleInMobileClient>1</IsVisibleInMobileClient>
        <IsReadingPaneEnabled>1</IsReadingPaneEnabled>
        <IsQuickCreateEnabled>1</IsQuickCreateEnabled>
        <IntroducedVersion>5.0.0.0</IntroducedVersion>
</entity>
```

You will notice in the above XML Snippet that there is a tag <IntroducedVersion>5.0.0.0</IntroducedVersion>, this is added to every Solution component (Form, Entity, Attribute, View etc.) in a Solution file exported from Dynamics CRM 2013 (Dynamics CRM v6.0.0.0) onwards.

If a component was part of CRM already in CRM 2011 then its *IntroducedVersion* will be 5.0.0.0, any component introduced as part of the Dynamics CRM 2013 release will have an *IntroducedVersion* of 6.0.0.0 and any component introduced in a subsequent release will have the version number of that release.

> **NOTE** *For Metadata added in custom Solution components, the IntroducedVersion will be the version number of CRM in which the component was **created**.*

Additionally there was an overall Solution versioning component (which existed in CRM 2011) called *MinimumVersion* that has now been replaced in CRM 2013 with *SolutionPackageVersion*.

The capability that these new versioning components enables today is that they prevent Solution files from newer versions of CRM being imported into previous versions, this includes both major and minor versions.

Before continuing with examples of what this means it may be prudent to clarify how CRM version numbers are being applied from Dynamics CRM 2013 onwards. The version numbers will now conform to the *major.minor.update.build* format, with the original Dynamics CRM 2013 release having a version number of 6.0.**0**.809 and Update Rollup 1 for Online having a version number of 6.0.**1**.61

To check the version number of your CRM environment click the settings ⚙ icon and select *About*.

Microsoft Dynamics® CRM Online Fall '13
(6.0.1.462) (DB 6.0.1.462)

Coming back to the Solution file and its versioning, I mentioned earlier that the Solution import will now prevent newer versions of Solutions being imported into previous releases of CRM (including both major and minor versions). As you will have seen from the version numbers before Update Rollups only affect the *build* number part of the version, so are not considered *minor* versions, therefore you **will** be able to import Solutions between Update Rollups. The reason for this is that Update Rollups will no longer contain feature releases but will only include fixes for existing functionality.

> *Remember: Update Rollups will only include fixes for existing functionality. There will be no feature releases with the Updates.*

Feature releases for CRM (which typically happen bi-annually for Online and annually for On-Premise) will result in the *minor* (or *major*) revision number changing and preventing Solution imports to the prior release.

In the CRM Online world, this restriction is likely of little consequence as the entire online platform is typically updated at the same time which means that you would not have a mixture of current and previous versions. Where this does have a significant impact is in the On-Premise space, as well as for Independent Software Vendors (ISVs), that are building Solutions to target both Online and On-Premise deployments of CRM. I will talk more about this and some of the approaches you can use later in this chapter.

What will Versioning Allow?

So what will this versioning of individual Solution components allow? Aside from the currently obvious prevention of deploying to a previous version of CRM.

With the *IntroducedVersion* flag existing on just about every Solution component it would be very likely that in the future the Solution Export capability would be able to export a Solution file targeted for any specific version of CRM (Only from v6.0.0.0 onwards) by having the ability to exclude components at a more granular level as it will be easy to identify components that were introduced in later versions.

We already saw something similar introduced with CRM 2011 in the 5.0.14 version of its SDK. A tool was released as part of this SDK called the Solution Down-Level tool, which enabled you to take a Solution file from an Update Rollup 12 (December 2012 Service Update for Online) or later environment and remove the dependencies created by this update, creating a new Solution file targeted for Update Rollup 6 or later.

The Future's Past

Upgrading CRM 2011 Solutions

While you are unable to import newer Solutions into previous versions of CRM you can import Solutions from a previous version of CRM into a newer release, this is commonly referred to as backwards compatibility. This backwards compatibility even traverses across the *major* version boundary by allowing you to import Solution files from CRM 2011 directly into a CRM 2013 environment (Both Online and On-Premise)

> **NOTE** *While the supported versions for upgrading a CRM 2011 system to CRM 2013 are Update Rollup 6 or Update Rollup 14+ you can import Solution files created in any version of CRM 2011 into CRM 2013.*

Legacy Features

A number of changes in CRM 2013 mean that there are certain considerations that need to be taken into account when importing a CRM 2011 Solution file into CRM 2013.

A Number of Dynamics CRM 4.0 features will no longer be supported:

- CRM 4.0 plug-ins
- CRM 4.0 client-side scripting
- CRM 4.0 custom workflow activities
- CRM 4.0 web service API (also known as the 2007 web service endpoints)
- ISV folder support for custom web applications

The first four items above are components that would typically exist in your Solution file, unlike the CRM 2013 upgrade process (which will actually prevent the upgrade if these components exist), the Solution import will still import the Solution file which means that you could introduce "broken" components into your environment.

The best way to ensure that you don't have any of these legacy components is to make use of the tools provided to check a CRM 2011 system and identify unsupported upgrade components.

Microsoft Dynamics CRM 2013 Custom Code Validation Tool

The custom code validation tool will examine your web resources and show you where there might be problems. The issues that are flagged are either using unsupported coding processes or using the CRM 4.0 objects and functions. Download this tool and extract the contents. Within the contents you will find instructions about how to install and use the tool.

> **NOTE** *You can download the Custom Code Validation tool from http://www.microsoft.com/en-us/download/details.aspx?id=30151*

Legacy Feature Check Tool

The legacy feature check tool detects and reports on server extensions in your organization that use the 2007 endpoint and legacy Microsoft Dynamics CRM 4.0 features. These checks are also performed when you upgrade your server. For more information about this tool, read the topic in the CRM 2011 SDK: What's Changing in the Next Major Release

> **NOTE** *You can download the Legacy Feature Check tool from http://go.microsoft.com/fwlink/p/?LinkID=309565*

CRM 2013 Quick Start

Importing your CRM 2011 Solution - Forms

In Chapter 3 – Customizing CRM Forms it was covered that all entities in an upgraded environment (from either a system upgrade or a CRM 2011 Solution file import) have both a CRM 2011 and a CRM 2013 form available to them in CRM 2013. If you import a CRM 2011 Solution file that contains any form customizations, these customizations will be applied to the 2011 form only and in order to make use of them on the CRM 2013 form you will need to upgrade the 2013 form to make use of them.

Form list showing CRM 2011 (Information) and CRM 2013 (Account) form

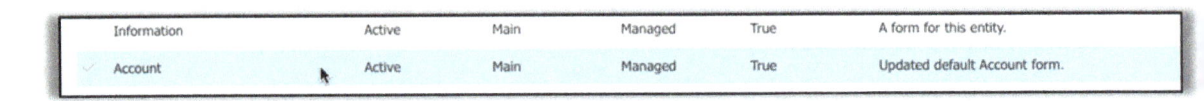

Information		Active	Main	Managed	True	A form for this entity.
Account		Active	Main	Managed	True	Updated default Account form.

The Form called "Information" will be the original CRM 2011 form and the form with the entity name, in this case "Account" will be the default CRM 2013 form layout.

> **TIP**
>
> **Use the "Merge Forms" button**
> This tool, available on the Form Designer, allows you to import elements from another CRM Form.

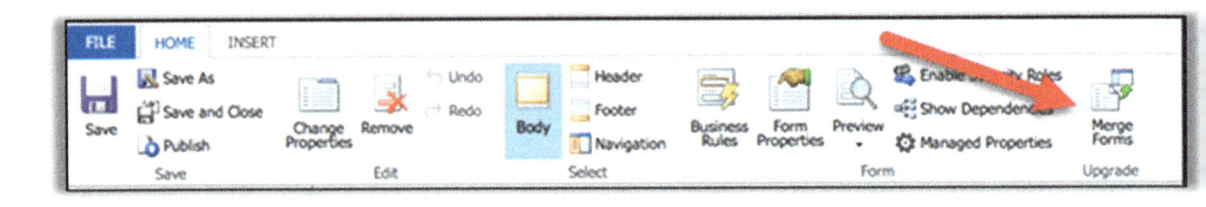

Importing your CRM 2011 Solution – Sitemap & Navigation

The other element that you should pay special attention to when importing a CRM 2011 Solution into your CRM 2013 environment is the Sitemap. The one key change to the Sitemap in CRM 2013 is that there is no longer a "Workplace" area. This however only applies to any New CRM 2013 organization. If your organization has been upgraded or you import a CRM 2011 Solution file where the sitemap has been customized, then you will still see the "Workplace" area in the Sitemap.

The reason you will see "Workplace" in these scenarios is because if CRM 2013 detects changes in the Sitemap then it preserves the sitemap from before the upgrade. The downside of preserving the sitemap is that the new sitemap elements from CRM 2013 will not be present, so if you would like them visible then you will need to add them back manually at present.

> **NOTE**: *CRM 2013 considers the Sitemap as changed if any element is explicitly changed as well as if a custom entity is set to be displayed under any of the standard areas, like "Sales", "Service" and "Marketing" etc.*

Sitemap from an Upgraded CRM 2011 environment

Sitemap from a New CRM 2013 environment

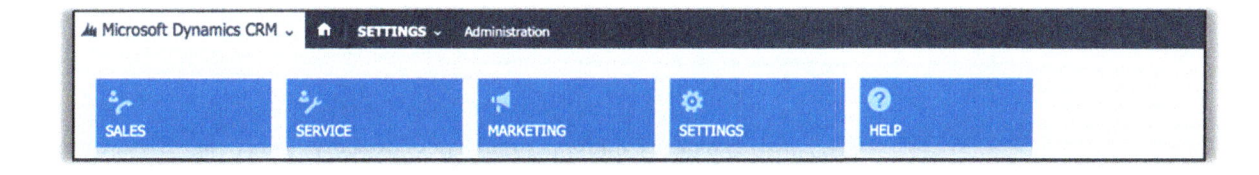

The sitemap elements added in CRM 2013 under each area are as follows:

Area	Sub Area	Element
Sales		
	My Work	
		What's New
	Tools	
		Alerts
Service		
	My Work	
		What's New
	Tools	
		Alerts
Marketing		
	My Work	
		What's New
	Tools	
		Alerts
Settings		
	System	
		Email Configuration
		Post Configuration
		Post Rule Configuration
Help		
	Help	
		Customer Center

NOTE: *If you are using CRM On-Premise and did not previously have the "Activity Feeds" Solution installed, you will need to manually add "Post Configuration" and "Post Rule Configuration" in order to be able to configure Activity Feeds or Yammer Integration.*

It is important to note however that although pre-existing workplace areas are maintained, users will no longer have the option to personalize what is displayed there within the Personal Option menus. Whatever personal option settings users had at the time of the upgrade will persist. The *<Group> (SiteMap) IsProfile* attribute will no longer allow groups to be options that users can select to include in the workplace.

There are two approaches you can take to add missing elements back to the sitemap, you can make use of a tool to edit the sitemap and insert the elements back in. One of my favorites is included in the Toolbox for Dynamics CRM 2011/2013 which is available for download at http://xrmtoolbox.codeplex.com/

Alternatively you can manually edit the Sitemap XML and insert the elements back in. Below is an example of the type of XML you would need to add.

```xml
<Group Id="Tools"
       ResourceId="Area_Tools"
       IsProfile="true"
       DescriptionResourceId="Area_Tools_Description">
  <SubArea Id="nav_traces"
           Icon="/_imgs/area/18_alerts.png"
           Url="/_root/tracewall.aspx"
           ResourceId="Homepage_Alerts"
           AvailableOffline="false"
           DescriptionResourceId="Alerts_SubArea_Description">
    <Privilege Entity="tracelog"
               Privilege="Read"/>
  </SubArea>
</Group>
```

You can find detailed instructions on how to add back all the missing elements on Microsoft TechNet at http://technet.microsoft.com/en-us/library/dn486920(en-us,CRM.6)

TIP: *There is also a managed Solution file available for download at the above TechNet site which you can import to bring back the "Post Configuration" and "Post Rule Configuration" Sitemap entries.*

Reaching for the Stars

Building Solutions to Target the Appropriate Platform

While Microsoft truly are reaching for the stars, with release names like "Orion", "Mira", "Leo" and "Vega" and all the new functionality they will bring, the net result is that we have to make sure we follow the correct approach to Solution development in order to ensure that our planets continue to align.

Until we reach a point where the Solution export will be able to target a specific version of the CRM platform, there are a number of design considerations you will need to take into account when building your Solution. Do you want a Solution that is compatible with as many versions of CRM as possible? Do you want a Solution that leverages the latest features of CRM? Should your Solution work On-Premise, Online or Both.

The Lowest Common Denominator

If you are wanting to create a Solution that can be imported into as many versions of CRM as possible then you are likely best off determining the lowest common denominator of functionality that you would like to leverage and start building with the lowest version of CRM 2011/2013 that contains that functionality. It is likely then that your Solution would start its life in a CRM 2011 environment, as this will allow your Solution to be imported into both CRM 2011 and CRM 2013 systems.

Once you have built your baseline Solution in CRM 2011 you could also import it into a CRM 2013 environment and then tailor it further to leverage the new form layout design and capabilities available in CRM 2013.

You can then have both a CRM 2011 and CRM 2013 Solution available and targeted to those specific releases of CRM.

Adopting a Version Dependency

Another approach you could take is to decide to make your Solution dependent on a specific version of CRM, of course you may need to do this if you wish to leverage functionality that was only introduced in one of the later releases. The key thing you need to think about in this instance is the potential differences between Online and On-Premise versions of CRM. At the time of writing this book CRM Online was at Update Rollup 2 of the Dynamics CRM 2013 release, which means that there is feature parity between Online and On-Premise, so it makes it a little easier to build Solutions targeted to both platforms. However as each year progresses, the scheduled mid-year release on CRM Online will typically introduce new features that won't be available in On-Premise until the following annual release. When this arises, unless you plan to make use of those new features in your Solution, you would be best placed to build your Solution in an On-Premise version of CRM so that it can be imported into both On-Premise and Online environments.

The Multiple Solution Approach

Depending on the type of components that your Solution makes use of, you could consider an approach of using multiple Solution files and breaking your Solution down, delineating between elements that are currently version independent (Plug-ins, Web Resources, Asynchronous Workflows, Templates etc.) and those that might not be, like Entities, as they might include Form changes that leverage newer Form components. This approach would need to follow the concepts defined in the section "The Lowest Common Denominator" as each Solution should be built on the lowest possible version of CRM 2011 or CRM 2013 to support the functionality required.

> *When exporting a Managed Solution, if you have not made any changes to the entity forms, they will not be included in the Solution file.*

Not for the Faint Hearted

The final approach you could take is some manual manipulation of your Solution file XML to determine what should be included and what should not. This is obviously the least favorable approach and not recommended. If you plan to follow this approach you should make sure to adopt a proper ALM strategy and use scripted processes to package your Solutions in a structured and repeatable manner as well as to store all your components in Source control for access and the ability to easily revert changes back.

The first tool you will need is the Solution Packager tool that is included in the Dynamics CRM SDK download. This tool takes an exported Solution file (both Managed and Unmanaged) and extracts it into individual XML elements.

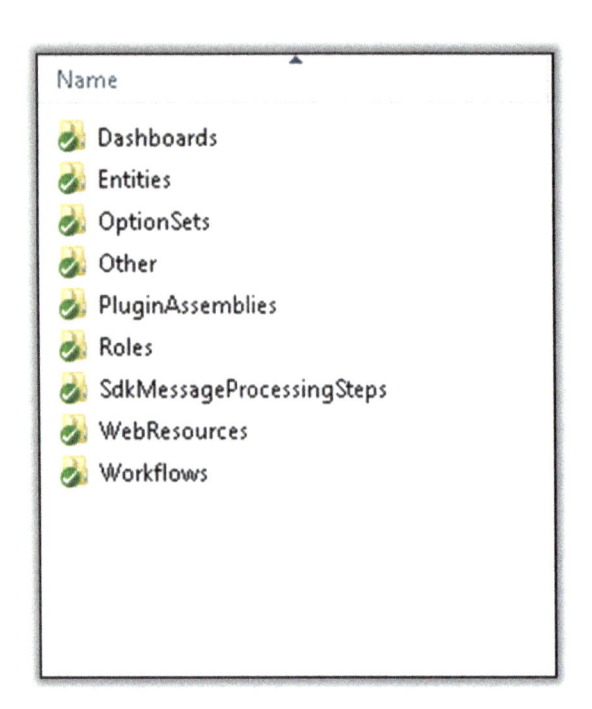

```
Name
   Dashboards
   Entities
   OptionSets
   Other
   PluginAssemblies
   Roles
   SdkMessageProcessingSteps
   WebResources
   Workflows
```

From there you can manipulate and / or remove XML files (like Forms) that you don't want to be included in your Solution file and then use the Solution Packager to repack the Solution file as either a Managed or Unmanaged Solution file. Be sure to test your Solution thoroughly to make sure everything imported as expected.

NOTE *For full details on how to use the Solution Packager tool as well as details of the Folder Structures and their contents, please see the sections "Use the SolutionPackager tool to compress and extract a Solution file" and "Solution component file reference (SolutionPackager)" in the latest CRM SDK.*

Wrapping Up

While there are many possible approaches to working with Solutions, and you will no doubt adopt some of your own, it is always a good idea to keep up to date with the latest developments in the Solution Framework within CRM. Always ensure you have the latest version of the Dynamics CRM SDK and review the best practices defined in the SDK documentation. By following the guidelines set out by the CRM Product Team you are less likely to find yourself in a situation where your Solutions are not supported in future releases of Dynamics CRM.

I believe we should watch this space closely as I am sure we will see some great improvements to the Solution framework in the future.

10

Taking CRM on the Road

Microsoft Dynamics CRM has seen quite a transformation over the past few years. It used to be that Dynamics CRM was wearing a business suit and used only the inside of an office. Then with CRM 4.0 and 2011 it took off its necktie with IFD, but you still had to use it on a laptop or desktop computer. Now with Microsoft Dynamics CRM 2013, it can be used on virtually any device, including computers, both Windows and Mac, tablets like iPads and Microsoft Surface, and smartphones. CRM has traded its business suit for hiking boots and has hit the road. You can now use it from wherever you work and on virtually any device.

In this chapter we are going to explore the ways to use Microsoft Dynamics CRM on modern devices, and what you should do to get the most out of CRM on these devices.

Each of these interfaces take advantage of the unique characteristics of the environment, and each is best suited for a certain use case. Keep in mind as you read this chapter that these are all different options for getting to CRM, and they are not mutually exclusive. A user may use CRM for Outlook, CRM in a mobile browser, and the new Microsoft Dynamics CRM mobile clients at different times, depending on where they are and what they need to do. There is no additional cost to implement another interface—with your CRM user license, you get all user clients on as many devices as you want. The power of choice is multiplied.

CRM for Outlook

The venerable Outlook client is still available in Dynamics CRM 2013. It has been enhanced with a new version.

When you start CRM for Outlook 2013, you will notice that it looks very similar to CRM 2011 for Outlook and takes advantage of the unique characteristics of Microsoft Outlook. For example, the views (such as "My Accounts") are actually rendered as Outlook views, just like your inbox and other Outlook Views. This brings several advantages to Outlook heavy users:

- Users who spend a lot of time inside of Outlook can get to CRM from where they work.
- Users who send emails and schedule appointments with customers can instantly track a copy of the activity in Outlook by clicking one button.
- Since CRM views are rendered as Outlook views, functionality such as flagging, categorizing, and conditional formatting can be used on CRM records and views, just like other Outlook views.
- The consistency of interface with other Outlook views simplifies training for those who are experienced Outlook users.

What does this have to do with mobile?

Microsoft Windows 8 and 8.1 have reinvented what the word "tablet" means. Devices such as the Surface Pro have full Windows capabilities, and can use the full version of Outlook and CRM for Outlook. This means that many users in Microsoft centric environments are carrying tablets that run the full version of Outlook, enable them to track their emails and appointments, and use fully suite of Microsoft Office applications and functionality.

Who should use CRM for Outlook?

The CRM Outlook client is designed to give Microsoft Outlook users full access to Microsoft Dynamics CRM without leaving Outlook. Next to the Outlook navigation areas for email, contacts, and calendar, you will see a button for your Microsoft Dynamics CRM organization. This brings you to a folder-like navigation used throughout Outlook.

CRM folders are presented as Outlook folders, and views are rendered as Outlook views. This results in a very familiar navigation for Outlook users, and allows for native Outlook functionality, such as categorization, filtering and conditional formatting to be used on CRM views, exactly the way that they are used for other Outlook views, such as the inbox.

CRM for Outlook also provides other unique features not included in other Dynamics CRM user interfaces:

- **Offline access:** CRM for Outlook is the only interface that provides offline data synchronization. Users set configurable filters that specify what data synchronizes offline. When offline, users have full access to the application with the data that is synchronized offline. Offline synchronization can happen manually or automatically in the background.
- **Tracking activities and contacts**: Many people use Microsoft Outlook to send email, manage calendar appointments and tasks. This makes CRM for Outlook a natural

extension of users existing daily work flow. Since you are going to send an email through Outlook anyway, having the ability to click a button and have the email promoted (tracked) in CRM is a great way to help ensure that activities are accurately captured and CRM users adopt it, all while allowing users to keep working the way that they already do. When someone replies to the email or the appointment is updated, the changes will automatically be reflected in both CRM and Outlook.

Also, consider the scenario where you are at a meeting and a potential client hands you their business card. What are you going to do? Many users will add the person to their Exchange contacts, either through their smartphone or by entering them into Outlook contacts. The contact synchronization in CRM for Outlook makes it very easy to get these contacts into CRM. Users can click a single button and track the contact, just like the way that emails, appointments, and tasks are tracked. You could manually create the contact in CRM, but for busy users, this step often gets skipped if a lot of manual work is required. If contact management is important to your business and users use Outlook, CRM for Outlook will make it easier for users to enter contact information and capture more complete contact information, all without changing your user's existing work flow.

So CRM for Outlook should be considered for users who are using Windows based computers and tablets that run Microsoft Outlook. Users who manage email, calendar, and contacts in Outlook will appreciate the consistent user experience that gives them ready access to CRM functionality from within the familiar Outlook interface. They will be able to quickly add activities and contacts to CRM while doing things the same way they do now.

What is new in CRM 2013 for Outlook?

At first glance, the Outlook client looks very similar to CRM 2011 for Outlook. Record views look and work in the same way. However, once you get to a record, you will immediately see the difference. Record forms and ribbons now reflect the enhanced user experience of CRM 2013, including the new "flat" user interface and minimized form ribbons and menus.

Server sync is a major change in Dynamics CRM 2013, and if enabled in your environment, has a major impact on CRM for Outlook. When server sync is enabled for a user, the Outlook client no longer is tasked with synchronization, as CRM directly synchronizes with the user's Exchange. This makes synchronization happen outside of the Outlook client.

The impact of this change is very significant for the Outlook client. By removing sync from the client, it makes the client much lighter, as the contact and appointment synchronization no longer hits the client, so performance should be better. Also, since sync happens independently of the client, synchronization is no longer dependent on the client running.

With earlier versions, contact and appointment synchronization only happened when the users were logged in and Outlook was running. This meant that if a user was not logged on to Outlook, no changes would synchronize to his calendar until he next opened Outlook. If someone went on vacation for a week, and during that week one of his appointments was updated in CRM, that change would not synchronize to his Exchange calendar until the next time he opened Outlook.

With server sync enabled, these changes will now synchronize from CRM to Exchange without Outlook being open and with no impact on the user's computer performance.

These and other topics are covered in more detail later in this chapter in the Server Sync section.

Installing CRM 2013 for Outlook

When you deploy the client, there are two main options:

1. Manual installation. Like any other Microsoft Office product, a user can download and install the client on any supported Windows computer. The download can be found in the Microsoft download center by searching for "Download Dynamics CRM 2013 for Outlook," or by logging in to Dynamics CRM in a web browser and clicking the download link from the yellow notification area at the top of the screen (the "Get CRM for Outlook" button).

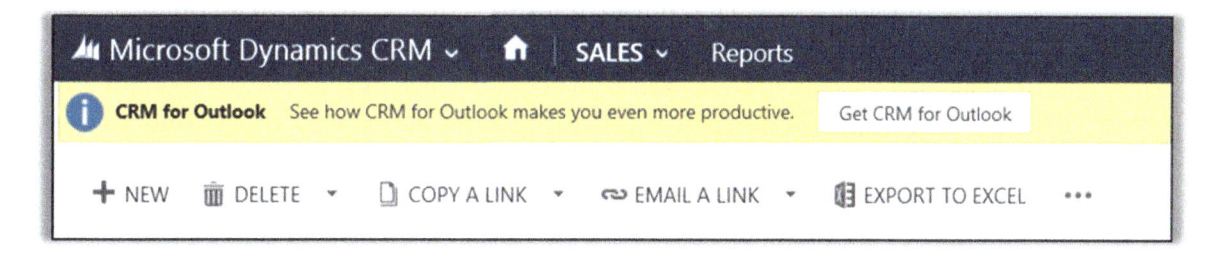

2. For larger environments, Dynamics CRM for Outlook may be deployed via Microsoft System Center Configuration Manager (SCCM). This option allows an administrator to silently push out the installation of the client to multiple users. For detailed instructions on pushing out the client installation via SCCM, see the Microsoft Dynamics CRM 2013 Implementation Guide.

Upgrading to CRM 2013 for Outlook

As discussed in the upgrading chapter, the 2011 version of CRM for Outlook will work with CRM 2013. Microsoft designed the upgrade process to minimize the pain of upgrading by not forcing clients to be upgraded at the same time as the server. That way, you can upgrade your server and users can continue to use CRM 2011 for Outlook. Then, once the upgrade is successful, you can schedule your client upgrades. You do not have to upgrade every client at the same time. If you have a large quantity of users, another approach is to roll the client upgrade out by group. This will allow you to systematically upgrade your client installations, train users on new client functionality by group, and allow you to optimize the process. For example, if you find that when you push it out to the first group that the installation fails for some of the users, you now have the flexibility to troubleshoot the issue and make changes to your settings and group policies so the next group goes smoothly.

If you choose to delay the client upgrade until after the server upgrade, there are several special considerations you need to remember for your upgrade:

1. **Connected only:** The 2011 Outlook client is compatible with 2013, but only for non-offline use. If you have users who actively use CRM for Outlook offline, you will need to upgrade them immediately for offline functionality to work.
2. **Server Sync**: The CRM 2011 client is designed to handle synchronization with Exchange. If you are going to enable server sync, you will want to first upgrade the clients for the users who will be using server sync.
3. **Keep your URL the same**: If you are using CRM Online, the clients will automatically continue to work post upgrade, because your environment URLs will remain the same thing that they are now. If you are on premise, if you upgrade and change the URL to the URL of your new server, you will break the configuration of all of your Outlook clients, and all clients will need to be reconfigured. If you are going to do that, you probably should just go ahead and install the 2013 client.

Many on premise users are unaware that you can specify an alias (such as http://crm) in the web settings in deployment manager. If you take this option, and then when you upgrade the server repoint the DNS entry for that alias to the new server, existing client configurations will not break. By repointing the existing URL for CRM 2011 to CRM 2013, existing users of Microsoft Dynamics CRM 2011 for Outlook can continue working in the 2011 client without having to reconfigure the client.

Upgrade Options

When you are ready to upgrade your clients, there are a couple of options:

1. In place upgrade—this option installs the 2013 client over the 2011 client, and all files and settings are upgraded in the process.
2. Clean installation—with this option, you first uninstall the 2011 client, then install and configure the 2013 client.

Benefits of in-place client upgrades

When performing an in-place upgrade to Microsoft Dynamics CRM 2013 for Outlook, all client settings and configurations are preserved. All contact synchronizations will remain intact, so contacts will not be duplicated after the upgrade. When you install CRM 2013 for Outlook on a computer currently running CRM 2011 for Outlook, you will be given the option to upgrade now.

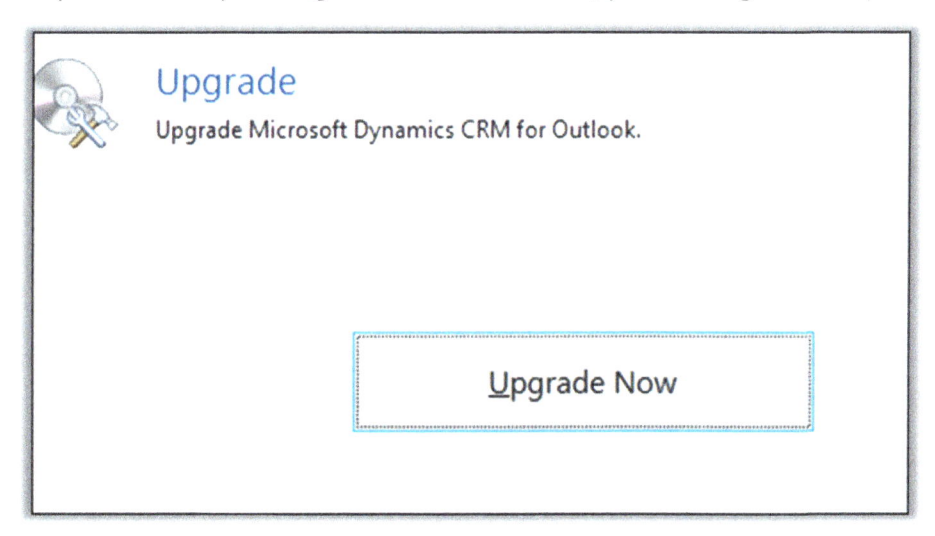

Disadvantages of in-place client upgrades

Like upgrading any Microsoft Office application, sometimes artifacts from the previous version get left behind.

Advantages of a clean client installation

A clean installation totally removes the prior version of the client before installing and configuring the new version of the client. Traditionally, users whose clients are freshly installed have the best experience, as no file or settings artifacts from previous versions are present on their computers.

Disadvantages of clean client installations

The clean installation upgrade approach can be more time consuming than an in-place upgrade, because it requires that the existing client be uninstalled first, then the new client installed. Removing the old client will break the current configuration, so the client will need to be configured post installation. Also, consider contact synchronization. The user's synchronization rules determine which contacts are synchronized with Outlook contacts. When the 2011 client is uninstalled, all non user-owned contacts will be removed from Outlook contacts, and the contacts that the user owns will remain in their Outlook contacts. Then, when the new version of the client is installed, the local synchronization database will be rebuilt, and contacts will be resynchronized. In some cases, this results in duplicated contact records in the user's Outlook contacts.

Which approach should I use?

As you can see from reading the advantages of each approach, client upgrades are not as clear cut as to which is the best option. However, the recommendation is that you test an in-place upgrade in your environment. If it goes smoothly, that may be the best option for you, especially if you make heavy usage of the contact synchronization.

If you find that the upgrade fails when you test it, or if users have problems post upgrade, you will want to perform a clean installation upgrade.

Why upgrade?

OK, earlier in the chapter I said that there isn't that much difference in the 2011 and 2013 Outlook clients. If the 2011 client works with 2013, why should I upgrade?

1. Natively supports Outlook 2013 (and by extension, touch). CRM 2011 added support for Outlook 2013 in later update rollups, but it wasn't designed for it. CRM 2013 for Outlook is designed with Outlook 2013 in mind. If you are using a Windows 8.1 Surface with Outlook on it, you will want to run Outlook 2013. Like the other Office 2013 applications, Outlook 2013 includes a touch friendly mode, which makes it much more usable on a touch screen. You will also want to use CRM 2013 for Outlook to have maximum compatibility with CRM 2013 (and the touch friendly mode). Don't limit your modern device with a version of Office that is not designed for touch.

2. Offline synchronization with Dynamics CRM 2013 requires CRM 2013 for Outlook
3. CRM 2013 for Outlook fonts and colors are consistent with CRM 2013.
4. If you use Server Sync, you will want to upgrade to the 2013 Outlook client.

NOTE: *In the following sections we cover options for accessing Microsoft Dynamics CRM via smartphones and tablets. These options assume that your CRM environment is available from your device. Given that these devices are typically not on your Windows domain, they require an internet available connection. For CRM Online, this will work, because CRM Online is always Internet available. For On Premise CRM deployments, the Internet Facing Deployment (IFD) deployment option is required to use the mobile options detailed later in this chapter.*

CRM for Phones

For many users, a smartphone is their most accessible computer.

It is amazing to think how things have changed in the past few years. We have gone from a phone being mainly a telephone to a phone being a powerful computer in our pockets. For many people, a smartphone is the most accessible computer they have—during lunch, at night, on weekends. People always have their smartphones with them. When they are driving in their car and need to stop and look up an address for a meeting or find a phone number to call a client, they are not going to boot up their computer or turn on their iPad and connect to the internet. They are going to use their smartphone.

CRM for Phones is the new smartphone interface for CRM. In previous versions, CRM for Phones was called *Mobile Express*. Every CRM environment has Mobile Express available to them as long as the environment is accessible from your phone, such as with the Internet Facing Deployment (IFD) option. To access Mobile Express, you can add "/M" to the end of your CRM URL.

Mobile Express was originally designed to work well in Blackberry-era phone web browsers. These browsers were very limited, and mainly displayed text. Modern smartphones, such as iPhone, Android and Windows Phone, have much better mobile browsers, but Mobile Express had not been updated to take advantages of modern browsers—until now.

CRM for Phones is available as free app for Windows Phone, iPhone, and Android smartphones, as well as via mobile browser.

Should I use the app or the mobile website?

The user experience of the app vs the mobile website is very similar. The app gives users quicker access to CRM for Phones at the touch of a button, so they can more easily launch the app.

What is included in CRM for Phones?

Several entities are enabled out of the box for mobile applications, including Contact, Opportunity, Lead, Appointment and Account. Other system entities and custom entities can be enabled for CRM for Phones. See the section "How to enable and configure CRM for Phones" later in this chapter for more details.

CRM for Phones has been significantly updated with CRM 2013. If you evaluated Mobile Express in the past and found that functionality was too limited, it is worth taking a second look with CRM 2013. Some of these enhanced features include:

1. **Application fonts are consistent with CRM 2013.**
2. **Entity Icons are displayed, increasing navigation usability.** Fonts and icons in CRM for Phones are now consistent with Dynamics CRM, providing a clean modern user experience.

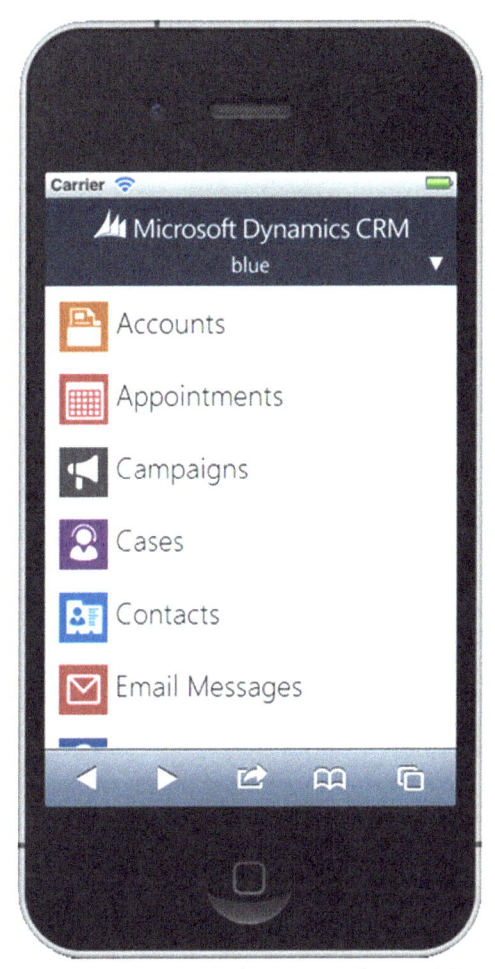

3. **Appointments can be created**. Consider this scenario—you are at a meeting and need to schedule the follow up meeting. You could create it on your phone calendar, but that appointment will not synchronize to CRM unless you start your computer, go to Outlook, select the appointment, and track it. You can now use Mobile Express and create the appointment, add meeting attendees, and schedule the meeting in CRM. CRM server sync will then synchronize the appointment with your calendar.
4. **Support for lookup fields, date selectors, and option set drop-downs**. Traditionally these have been presented in Mobile express as text fields. If you needed to populate the lookup for account on an opportunity, you would have to type it in precisely and then it was validated when the record was saved. In CRM 2013, these controls are presented as you see them when working in the full application, which significantly improves usability when creating or updating records.
5. **The consolidated address block can be displayed on the CRM for Phones form**. This new control allows the full address to be displayed in a single text field, saving significant

space on the form. In Mobile Express, this address block can now be displayed, however, it cannot be edited. Many companies validate their addresses and, as a result, probably do not want users updating the address from Mobile Express. However, if your users will be adding accounts and contacts and editing addresses on the go, you will probably want to display the individual address fields on the mobile form.
6. **Support for Bing Maps and Activity Feeds (on Windows Phone).**

How to enable and configure CRM for Phones

To be included in CRM for Phones, an entity must be enabled for CRM for Phones. Go to Settings → Customization→Customize the System and then select the entity you wish to expose in CRM for Phones (Mobile Express).

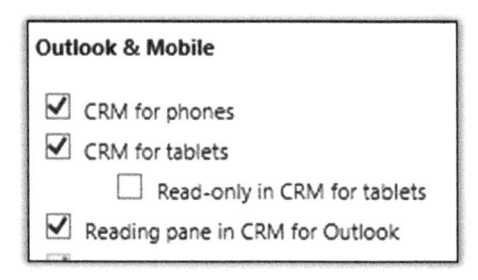

Under "Outlook & Mobile" check the box by "CRM for phones" and then publish the entity.

Next, configure the phone form. Go to Settings→Customization→Customize the System and then expand the forms section.

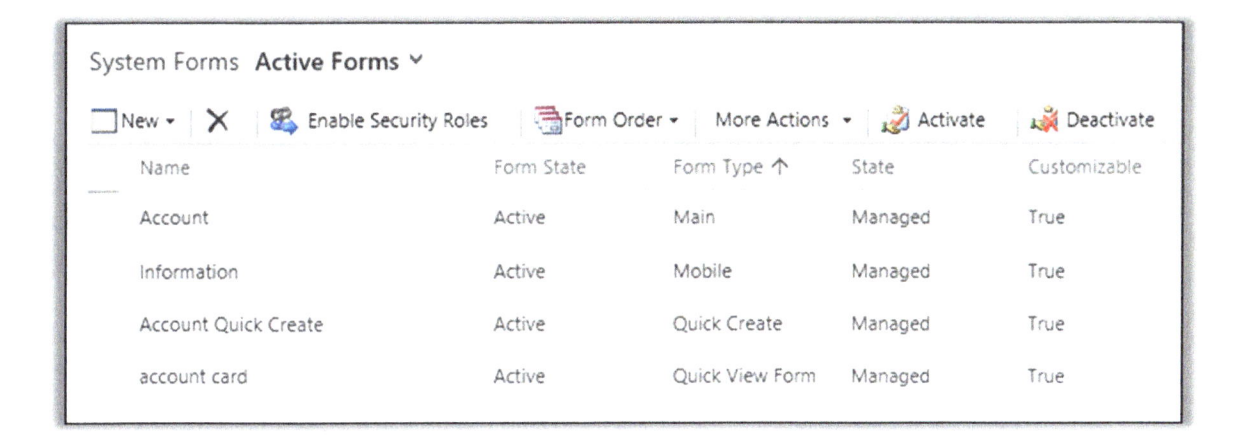

Name	Form State	Form Type ↑	State	Customizable
Account	Active	Main	Managed	True
Information	Active	Mobile	Managed	True
Account Quick Create	Active	Quick Create	Managed	True
account card	Active	Quick View Form	Managed	True

Edit the mobile form to configure the fields that appear on the entity in Mobile Express. You will notice that there are some limitations when compared to full form configuration.

1. You can specify the fields and their order, but you cannot change column layouts. This is by design, as a phone is a much smaller size, so multiple columns and tabs wouldn't work as well as on a tablet or PC. This also means that you will want to limit the number of fields that you display on the mobile form. You probably don't want every field you see on the full form to appear on the phone screen.
2. No form scripts or iframes. If you have a dynamic process that requires form scripts for a user to correctly complete the process, you will probably not want to expose that entity form via CRM for Phones, or maybe go with a more limited, read only implementation when viewed in CRM for Phones. Workflows do support CRM for Phones, including the new synchronous (real time) workflows, so it is possible to have real-time business rules triggered by changes in CRM for Phone.
3. No subgrids however, related entity record views are available from the CRM for Phones form, as long as that entity is enabled for CRM for Phones.
4. Views only display the first two columns of the view.

Tablet Browser

With the release of Dynamics CRM 2013, CRM now fully supports mobile tablet browsers, such as iPad Safari and Google Chrome on Nexus tablets.

This means that CRM fully works on non-PC browsers for non-administrative functions. This means that a user can leave his PC, open CRM in browser on his iPad, and see the same forms and dashboards that he used on his computer. Below is an example of CRM in Chrome on a Google Nexus 10. All entities and dashboards are available, other than links in the settings area.

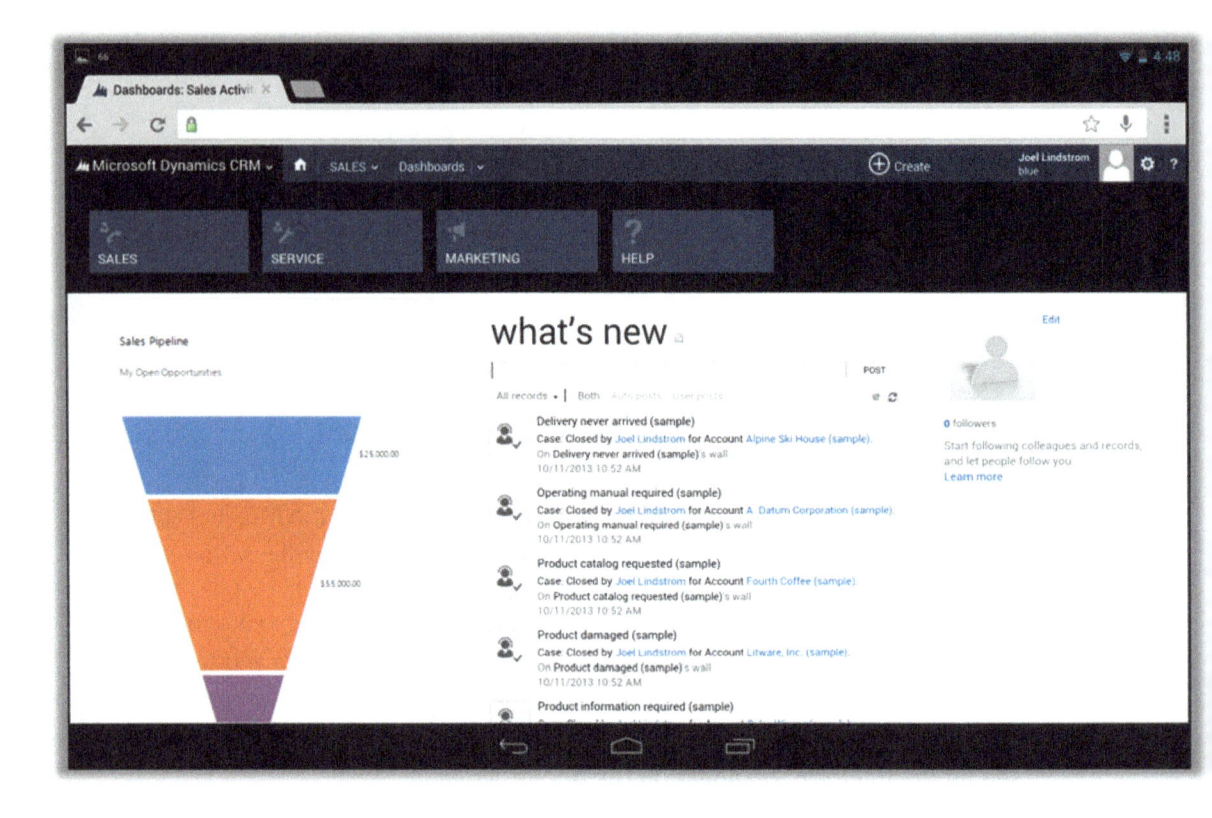

CRM in mobile tablet browser supports JavaScript, web resources, subgrids, and iframe content, as long as the content displayed in the iframe supports the browser you are using (for example, Silverlight content won't work on iPad Safari, because Silverlight is not available for IOS).

Who should run CRM in browser on tablets?

CRM in tablet browser is a good fit for power users, they can create all activity types, create cases, send emails, manage marketing lists, and do almost everything that they do in CRM on PC from a tablet. It provides continuity of functionality between computer and mobile, since the user's default dashboards and views will be available, and the forms will appear identical to the way that they look in the traditional environment.

What browsers are supported?

- **Windows PC:** Internet Explorer 8-10, Firefox, and Google Chrome
- **Mac OSX:** Safari
- **iPad:** Safari
- **Android:** Chrome on Nexus 10

What does it mean if my browser or device is not supported?

If your browser or device is not listed above, it does not mean that it won't work. Microsoft cannot test every browser and certify compatibility, so they limit their tests to the most common browsers, based on market share. If your browser is not part of the supported browser list (such as Safari on Windows or Chrome on Mac OSX), chances are that it may still work.

> **NOTE**: *The list of supported browsers changes frequently. The browsers listed in this chapter are the currently supported browsers as of the writing of this book.*

If you log into CRM from a non-tested browser, it most likely will default to the CRM for Phones user interface. However, you can make it default to "full" CRM by appending "/main.aspx" to the URL.

CRM for Tablets

Other than accessing CRM from a browser, Microsoft Dynamics CRM users on Windows 8/8.1/RT and iPad also have another option for accessing CRM from their tablet: the new Microsoft Dynamics CRM tablet app.

The Dynamics CRM Mobile app is designed to provide a more immersive experience on a tablet than running CRM in browser, and take advantage of native OS functionality:

- Bing maps on account and contact records take advantage of GPS.
- Accelerometer smartly resizes screen when rotated.
- In Windows 8/RT, records can be pinned to the start screen

How do I make an entity appear in CRM for Tablets?

To be included in CRM for Tablets, an entity must be enabled for CRM for Tablets. Go to Settings → Customization→Customize the System and select the entity you wish to expose in CRM for Tablets.

[Outlook & Mobile settings screenshot showing checkboxes: CRM for phones (checked), CRM for tablets (checked), Read-only in CRM for tablets (unchecked), Reading pane in CRM for Outlook (checked)]

Under "Outlook & Mobile" check the box by "CRM for Tablets." If you want the entity to be read only in Tablet client, check the box "Read-only in CRM for tablets" and save the entity customization, then publish the entity.

How is the CRM for Tablets deployed?

Microsoft Dynamics CRM for Tablets is available from the Windows and IOS app stores. On the device, search in the app store for "Microsoft Dynamics CRM." You may see several different apps returned by your search, including third party apps, such as Resco. Look for the app that has the official blue Dynamics CRM icon.

After the app finishes installing, launch the app. The user will be presented with a setup screen.

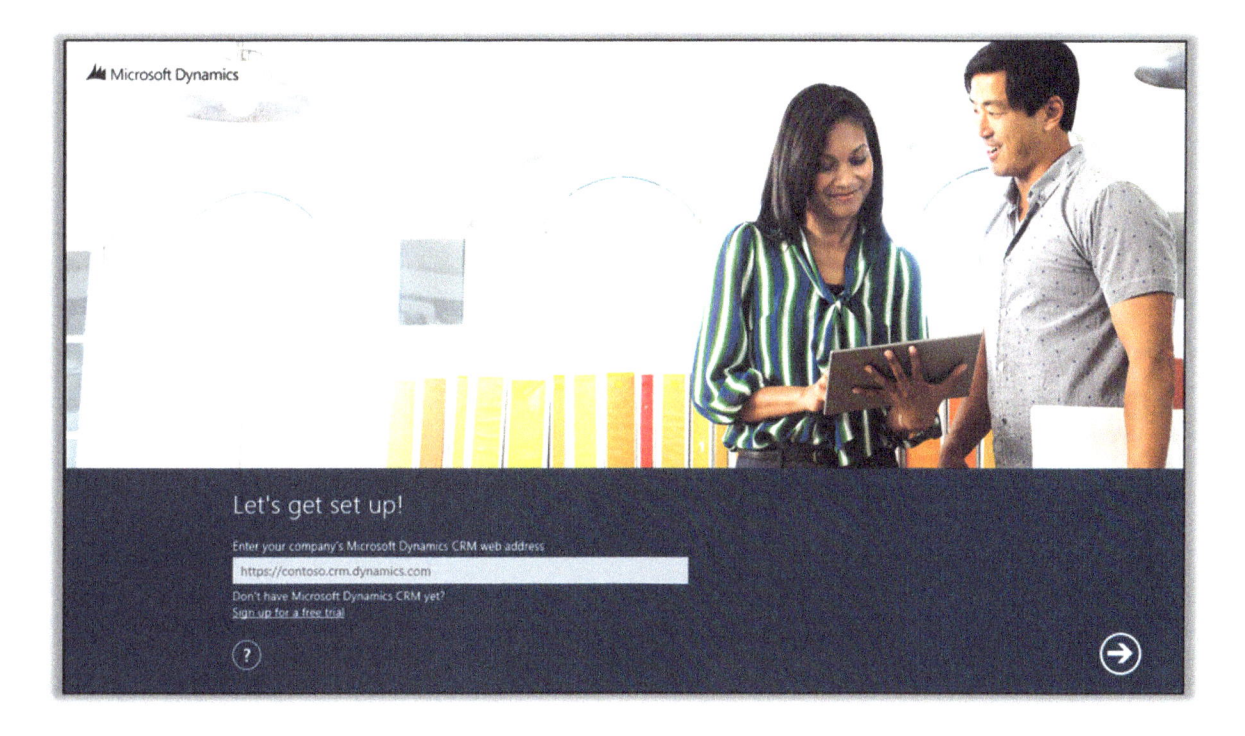

The next screen will prompt for user ID and password, and once authenticated, the tablet app will be configured.

CRM for Tablets Functionality

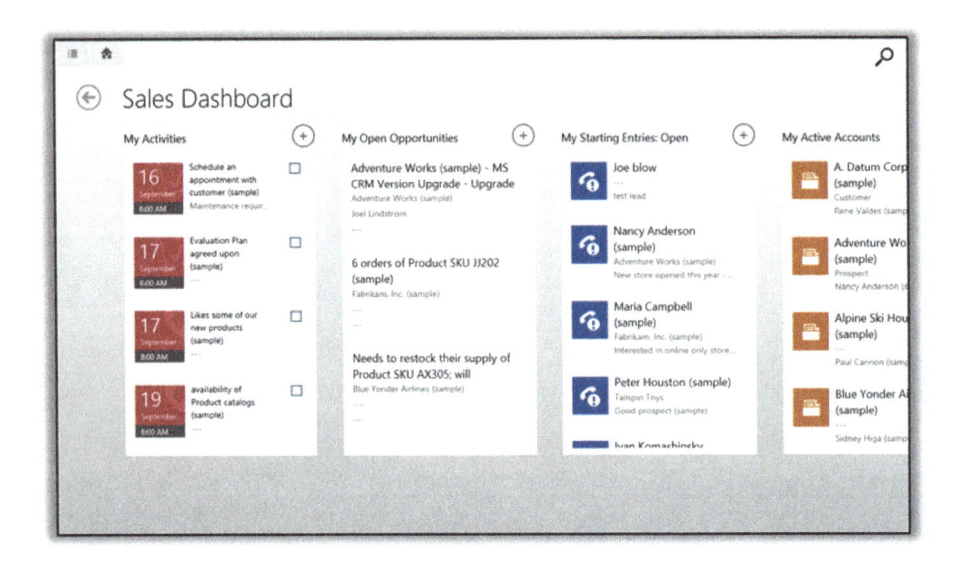

Navigation menu can be accessed by clicking/touching the menu button in the upper right corner.

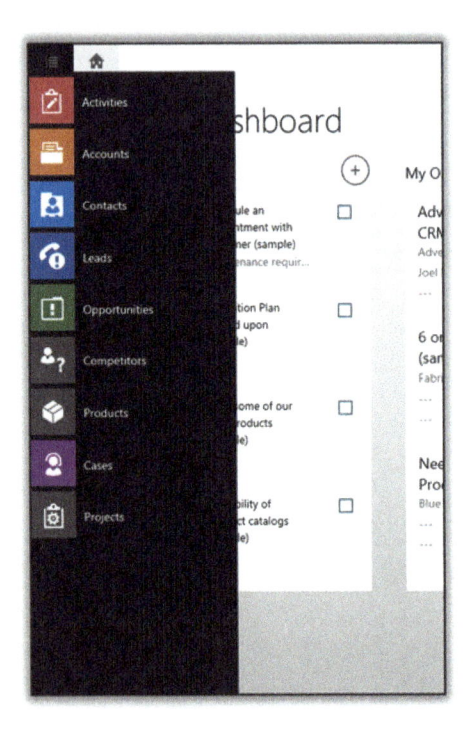

Users will see their default view for a selected entity, but can easily select another view.

When viewing a view or record form, the options menu allows the user to easily change views, pin to the start menu (in Windows 8), or launch the view or record in browser in the "full client."

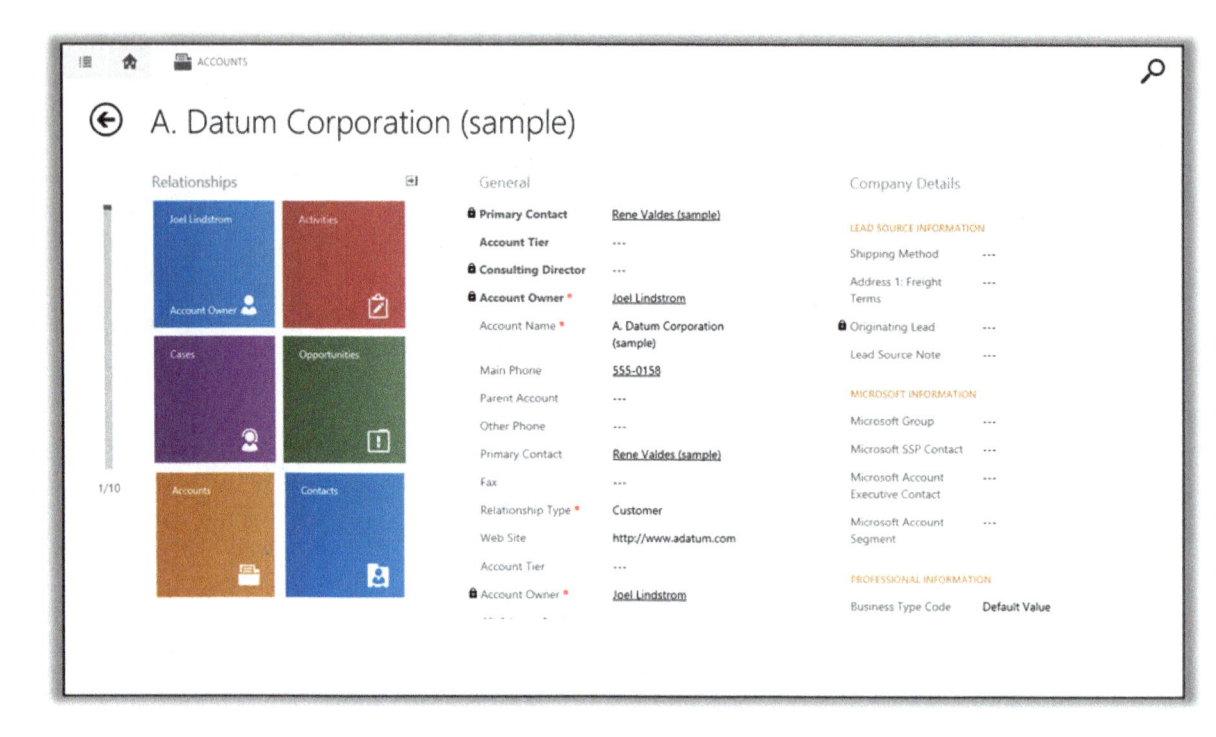

[Screenshot of A. Datum Corporation (sample) account form in CRM for Tablets]

The forms in the mobile client reflect the layout of the user's default form for the entity in CRM. Tab and section layouts are preserved, subgrids are rendered, and related records are easily accessible via the relationship tiles on the left of the form, if they have been enabled for this environment. The user can swipe to the left to scroll through the form. Dialogs, JavaScript form events, and Portable Business Logic (PBL) rules are rendered on the form, just like in the web client in browser.

> **NOTE**: When a user creates a record in CRM for Tablets, she will be presented with the entity Quick Create form. If you allow users to create records from CRM for Tablets, be sure that you configure the Quick Create form to include all important fields and required business logic for validation to prevent incomplete data from being created via CRM for Tablets.

Advantages of CRM for Tablets

CRM for Tablets provides several unique advantages when compared with other Dynamics CRM user experiences:

- **Simpler user interface** – Since CRM for Tablets does not include the full application, just the entities exposed via CRM for Mobile, it is an easier interface for users to learn how to use.
- **Designed specifically for tablets**. The full web UI of CRM has been redesigned to be touch enabled, but it is designed to be device independent. CRM for tablets is designed specifically for tablets to take advantage of the unique capabilities of a tablet device, such as navigation that is similar to tablet apps, providing updates via the OS app store, disconnected access, pinning records, gps, and accelerometer.
- **Faster form performance** – CRM for Tablets renders forms in HTML5 and caches forms and common views, resulting in very fast performance and form load time.
- **Multi-entity search** – CRM for Tablets is the only interface that provides the ability to search across multiple entities simultaneously. When you search in the web or Outlook client, it searches one entity at a time. If you do quick search in CRM for Tablets, the tablet app will search across all entities.

A System Administrator can enable up to ten entities to be used for multiple-entity search in CRM System Settings.

- **Disconnected record access** – CRM for tablets caches the last 500 records viewed for disconnected access. This means that if your tablet does not have a connection to the internet, you can view the last 500 records in read only mode. This is a lighter alternative to CRM for Outlook offline access.
- **Forms are rendered based on the user's default form configuration**, and JavaScript, Portable Business Logic rules, Business Process Flows, dialogs, and workflows are

supported, so business logic from CRM is maintained in CRM for Tablets, without having to configure a separate mobile form.
- **Most system entities and all custom entities can be exposed via CRM for Tablets**.

Limitations of CRM for Tablets

CRM for Tablets presents the functionality most commonly used in Microsoft Dynamics CRM in a fast, simple mobile app. However, there are some limitations to CRM for Tablets when compared with the full Microsoft Dynamics CRM application. Note—these limitations are current as of RTM (October 2013). Microsoft will be enhancing CRM for tablets independently of the update cycle for CRM, so these limitations may change.

- **Forms in CRM for Tablets are limited to 5 tabs OR 75 fields and 10 lists**. This limit includes hidden fields. This means that very complex forms may not completely render in CRM for Tablets. Configurators should prioritize sections and tabs to put the most commonly used fields within the top 75 fields on the form.
- **CRM for Tablets will not render web resources (other than form script web resources).**
- **CRM for Tablets will not render iframes.**
- **CRM for Tablets will not render reports.**
- **No customization can be performed in CRM for Tablets**. Customization is performed in the full CRM application.
- **CRM for Tablets has a single dashboard (called the Mobile Dashboard)**. Multiple dashboards are not supported in CRM for Tablets.
- **The case entity is read only in CRM for Tablets.**
- **Emails are read only in CRM for Tablets**. You can select an email address in CRM for Tablets to send a customer an email, but this will launch your tablet's default mail client, not send a tracked email through CRM.

Which interface should I use?

Now that you are familiar with all of the new ways that you can access Microsoft Dynamics CRM from a tablet, you may feel a bit overwhelmed in trying to decide which client you should recommend that your CRM users use on their tablets. The following are common scenarios that should help you make that decision:

Scenario	Recommended tablet client
End users accessing system or custom entities	CRM for Tablets

Users quick searching across entities	CRM for Tablets
Mobile sales representative working from an iPad or Microsoft Surface	CRM for Tablets
Android users	CRM in tablet browser
Users creating appointments, tasks, and phone calls	CRM for Tablets
Users sending tracked emails	CRM in tablet browser
Mobile customer service reps creating and updating cases	CRM in tablet browser
Users accessing records while disconnected from the internet	CRM for Tablets
Users needing to do advanced functions like bulk email, merging or deactivating records, quick campaigns, or run reports	CRM in tablet browser

The answer may be "All of the above"

Keep in mind that you don't have to pick just one. Your CRM license entitles a user to use CRM on multiple screens and devices. For many users, the interface that they use will depend on where they are and what they are doing.

Consider the following scenario:

Debbi is a Client Advisor working for a Wealth Management company. She works mainly from her iPad. During the day she schedules appointments with clients, updates client information, and checks portfolio performance.

She mainly uses **CRM for Tablets**. This allows her to easily open CRM on her iPad, create contacts, and update client financial account information, and schedule meetings and phone calls with clients. She frequently uses the multiple entity quick search to search across clients and activities.

Occasionally she needs to use some advanced functionality that is not exposed in the tablet client. She has a view of clients whose birthday is in the current month, and once a month she uses the CRM bulk email functionality to send happy birthday emails to her clients. While she cannot do this from the tablet client, she can select that view from the client and click the view in browser button and launch that view in a browser, from where she can create her bulk email or quick campaign in **CRM in Mobile Browser.**

If she had a Microsoft Surface Pro rather than an iPad, she probably would use Microsoft Outlook to manage email and calendar. She could then also run **CRM for Outlook** on her tablet, and as she creates emails and other activities, she can use the Outlook client to track those emails in CRM.

This scenario illustrates how each CRM client takes advantage of its unique capabilities, and, depending on the use case, a user may use more than one interface for CRM.

Use CRM for Tablets when you need a simple, fast tablet experience. Use CRM in browser when you need to use advanced functionality. Use CRM for Outlook when you are in Outlook.

Server Sync: connecting it all together

For many companies, contacts and activities like email, tasks and appointments are a very important part of CRM. Traditional CRM systems have had barriers to effectively managing contacts and activities, because the CRM system was separate from common mail and calendar applications, like Microsoft Outlook. Microsoft Dynamics CRM revolutionized contact and activity management by integrating to Microsoft Outlook, allowing users to continue to use Outlook for email, calendar, and personal contact management, while providing the ability to easily synchronize with CRM.

With the post-pc revolution, a growing number of users are moving away from traditional computers and Microsoft Outlook, or using Outlook less frequently, and managing their calendar, email, and personal contacts on mobile devices. To be able to continue to integrate user's calendar, inbox, and contacts with CRM when the user is not using a traditional personal computer, additional synchronization options were necessary beyond the traditional Outlook Client synchronization.

This section explores the impact of Server Synchronization in Microsoft Dynamics CRM on mobile users. In this chapter we don't go through how server synchronization is configured. In this section we cover how server sync keeps mobile users calendars synchronized with CRM, without using Outlook.

Traditional Sync Process

In earlier versions of Microsoft Dynamics CRM, synchronization of activities and contacts was performed by CRM for Outlook. This means that if you were logged in to Outlook with the CRM client configured, CRM appointments, tasks, phone calls, and contacts would synchronize with your Exchange calendar and contacts via Outlook. If I created an appointment, email, or contact in Outlook and hit the track button, the record would be promoted to CRM, and if someone made a change to that record, either in CRM or Outlook, the changes would be synchronized in both CRM and Outlook.

While this synchronization worked well for people who were always in Outlook working from the same PC, it did not work well for some scenarios:

- People working from non-PC devices like tablets and phones, as Outlook doesn't run on many of these devices
- People who use one computer in the office, another on the road, as the synchronization could only be actively configured with one PC.
- People who have an assistant create appointments on their calendar for them (delegates). In this scenario the delegate could create and track an appointment on the shared calendar, but it would not synchronize until the owner of the calendar logged in to Outlook. If the owner is out of the office for a week traveling with just an iPad, the appointment may not show up in CRM until after the meeting happened.
- People who rarely log in to Outlook. Consider the scenario where a sales rep is on the road for days at a time and infrequently logs on to his computer. The traditional CRM for Outlook synchronization would not run until the user logs in to Outlook, so if someone updated a meeting details in CRM, the change will not appear on his calendar if he doesn't log in to Outlook.

These scenarios illustrate the value of server sync for mobile users. It makes the synchronization independent of the Outlook client, and means that whatever device I'm using (or even if I'm not in CRM for a while), I can be confident that my calendar, contacts, and tasks are up to date, and that responses to tracked emails are synchronized automatically to CRM.

How Server Sync Works

CRM 2013 Quick Start

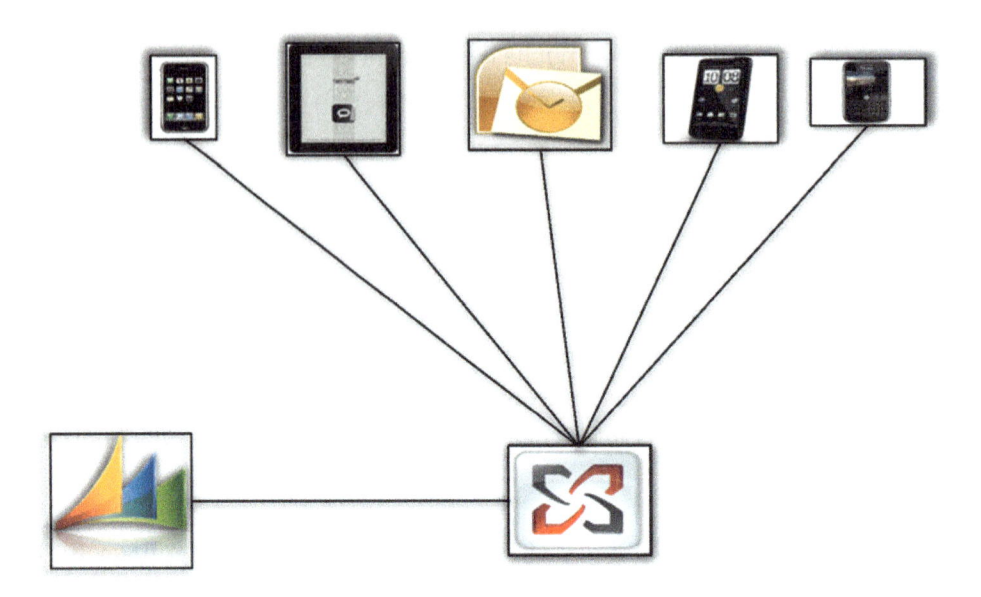

When server sync is enabled, the synchronization happens at the server level. Even if the user goes a week without logging in to CRM, or if they never use Outlook, their records still stay in sync. When they view their calendar or contacts on any device, they will be up to date with what is in CRM.

- Synchronization is controlled by the same synchronization filters used by CRM for Outlook. Just like in the Outlook client users have sync filters that determine what contacts, appointments, tasks, and phone calls are copied from CRM to Outlook, the same filters will determine what synchronizes to CRM with server synchronization.

    To see your current user synchronization settings, in CRM click the options gear in the upper right hand corner and select "Options."

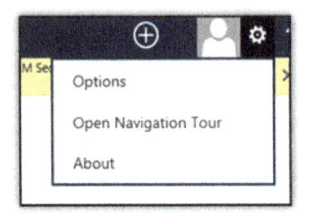

    In the personal options, go to the "Synchronization" tab and click the hyperlink for Filters to view and modify the default synchronization filters.

![Set Personal Options screen showing tabs: General, Synchronization, Activities, Formats, Email Templates, Email, Privacy, Languages. The Synchronization tab is shown with "Synchronize Microsoft Dynamics CRM items with Outlook or Exchange" and text "Your Filters determine the data that is synchronized with your Outlook or Exchange folders."]

- Server Sync also will automatically track emails in response to tracked emails (just like the Outlook client). This is based on the user's email preferences in CRM Personal Options.

    In CRM Personal options, go to the "Email" tab.

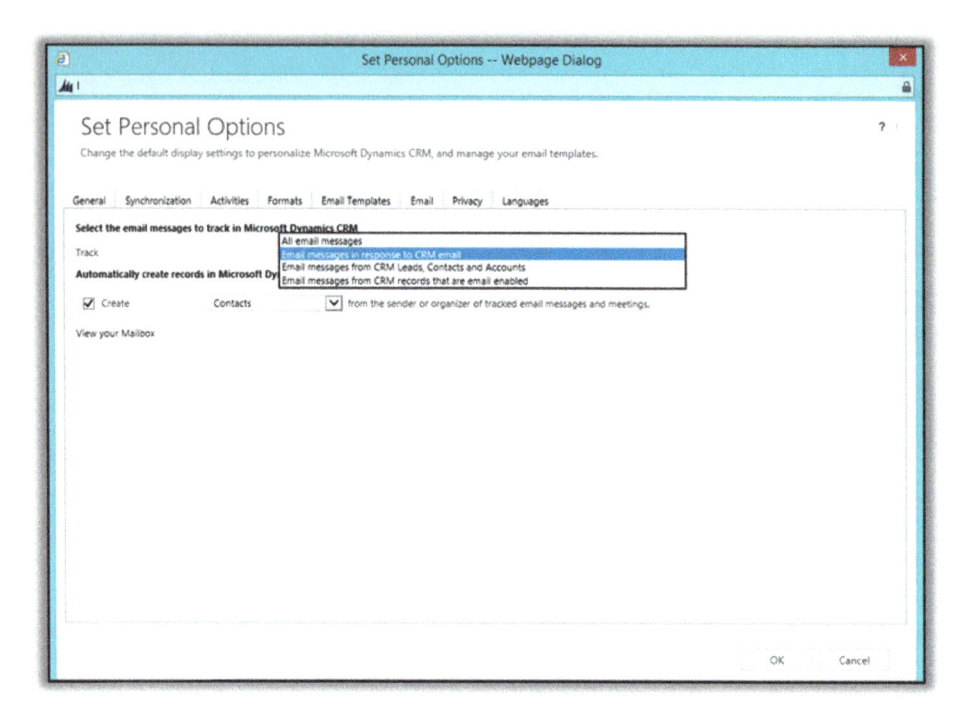

The top option determines which incoming emails are tracked to CRM automatically. The default choice is "Email messages in response to CRM email." This is the most commonly selected option. It means that if an email is created in CRM, any response to that email will automatically be tracked in CRM. This helps ensure that you capture complete conversations, without tracking emails that you do not want to automatically be tracked.

Other options include:
- All email messages: this means that all incoming email received by the user will be captured. This option can be dangerous, because it will track all email the user receives, including spam/junk email, as well as private conversations, but it can be useful if you have a business case for every message being captured.
- Email messages from CRM Leads, Contacts and Accounts—this automatically will capture the message if the email is from an address associated with one of these entities.
- Email messages from CRM records that are email enabled—this is like the previous option, but it also will capture emails that are related to custom entities that are set to be email enabled.

- Server sync does not automatically track the user's outgoing messages. For example, when I send an email to a customer in my tablet mail app, server sync is not going to automatically promote the message to CRM. This is by design, because tracking an outgoing email is meant to be a deliberate action—we typically only want to track the emails that are business relevant, and we also want to intentionally link the email to the appropriate record. CRM can automatically resolve records to associated contacts or companies via the email address used, but frequently it is a best practice to specifically relate the email to a specific opportunity, lead, case or custom entity. This is what the Outlook "set regarding" button does. That way the email shows up in the activity history of the recipients as well as related to the regarding record.

This means that server sync does not handle the tracking of initial emails in a conversation. If a user needs to track outgoing email on a tablet, the recommended approach is to send the email from CRM. By sending the email directly through CRM, it associates the record with the appropriate regarding object, then any future responses to the email will automatically be tracked via server sync.

This approach may also save some effort for the user. If the user navigates to the contact record in CRM in his iPad browser and click the email button on the contact, an email form will pre-populate the contact email address in the "to" field, so the user can quickly send the tracked email from his tablet. Server sync will then send the email through the user's Exchange account, and the sent email will appear in the user's sent folder in Exchange and Outlook.

So do I still need to use CRM for Outlook?

Now that server sync is in place, you may wonder if users still need to use CRM for Outlook? If the Exchange synchronization happens directly between CRM and Exchange, does the Outlook client still add value for users?

While users no longer will need to use the Outlook client to synchronize their contacts, calendar, and incoming email with CRM, CRM for Outlook may still provide a tremendous value, if users are using Microsoft Outlook.

- CRM for Outlook is the easiest way for Outlook users to track outgoing email or track personal contacts to CRM. Since server sync does not automatically track outgoing exchange messages or promote personal Exchange contacts to CRM, users still need a way to get these into CRM. If a user uses Outlook, this is the easiest option.
- Offline synchronization is not server-based. If you need to use offline CRM access, you will still need CRM for Outlook

- With Server Sync enabled, the Outlook client is a much lighter application. Many of the perceived performance issues with CRM for Outlook are driven by large synchronizations hitting the user's computer. Since these synchronizations will all be server side (when server sync is enabled), CRM for Outlook carries a much lighter load.
- CRM for Outlook makes Outlook user's lives easier by providing access to CRM functionality while they are in Outlook. Even if a user is only in front of Outlook part of the time, and working from a tablet the rest of the time, having CRM accessible from Outlook makes CRM available from where he is working while in Outlook. As mentioned earlier in this chapter, a user can access CRM in different ways from different devices for no additional cost.

Bringing it all together

Seeing Microsoft Dynamics CRM go from a Windows only application to a cross platform mobile friendly application can be summarized in the word "freedom." Freedom to use the application where you want, when you want, and how you want—on a pc, on a tablet, on your phone. Freedom to move from your iPad to your Android phone to your Windows PC, all without losing connectivity to CRM or calendar and contact synchronization with Exchange.

Users have the ability to use CRM on any screen, and they don't have to choose just one interface. They may use Outlook on their computer, CRM for Phones on their smartphone, and CRM for Tablets or CRM in tablet browser on their tablet.

Wherever they are, whatever device they are using, users have access to the same data. By freeing your users to use CRM on modern devices, users will have fewer barriers to using CRM, your data will be more up-to-date (because users can add or edit records while not in front of their computer), and user adoption will be greater, because users will have greater access to the system.

11

Developers, developers, developers

Developers are integral engineers of the Dynamics CRM landscape. When our job is done best we are invisible. Users that frequent the vistas for which we lay the foundation should rarely be able to discern that a developer had in fact been there. To maintain the marvel at our work, we tuck our tools and scaffolding away, and never obstruct the user's experience. Our purpose is to provide the capabilities necessary to sustain and support the higher orders of systems and features that the users *will* see, and hopefully maintain without us.

To this end, Dynamics CRM 2013 has improved greatly over previous iterations. Fantastic new features allow developers to focus more on the substrate layers, and less on the surface. These improvements allow for business analysts, consultants, and the new breed of User Experience (UX) agent to rule the user's domain. Features like Business Rules, Real-time Workflows, and Business Process Flows enable these surface-dwellers a level of control that could previously only be obtained via development.

> **NOTE**
>
> *Definition:*
> **de·vel·op·er**
> *[dih-vel-uh-per] noun*
>   1. *A person that develops.*
>   2. *"Code monkey", who may or may not like you*

Do not despair, my fellow developers! It may seem as though our territory has shrunk, and our necessity forfeit. However, not only are the aforementioned changes complimentary to our role, they help us engage Dynamics CRM at a level that is more satisfying *and* important. An evolution of the symbiotic relationship between developers and other roles is taking place, and while it can be uncomfortable or awkward, rest assured that it's also rewarding. This chapter will demonstrate how these changes are simultaneously beneficial to developers and their colleagues.

I, Developer

The role of the developer changed very little between CRM 1.2 and CRM 2011. While many pivotal extensibility features were introduced along the way, developers have regularly been involved with inscribing business processes into code, often alongside functional and technical enhancement. Unfortunately, the impetus for this process-driven scope tends to produce code that is difficult to reuse. Dynamics CRM 2013 offers several new remedies to appeal to the exhausted developer masses who perish the thought of hiding another field within a Form or writing a Plug-in to synchronously update related records.

These remedies will liberate many developers from looming mountains of customer-specific code and free them from the role of "process implementer". For developers who have rigorously applied test-driven API-centric development, Dynamics CRM 2013 is a vindication of that effort. Yet, all of the promise for change remains in how the new features are adopted, and what involvement other roles may have. In my experience, a Dynamics CRM developer needs experience in architecting solutions that embrace the whole platform.

xRM → Extensions Development → Business Processes

Throughout this chapter, I will make distinctions between "business processes" and "extensions". These are two modes in which Dynamics CRM customizers have traditionally produced code. In my experience, non-developers would find themselves getting into code, and when working simultaneously with a developer doing the same, the results could be volatile. This often arose in the implementation of business processes.

Developers need independent space to build extensions, and business experts need tools to erect and maintain business processes. When properly isolated, these discrete domains leverage their respective strengths and weaknesses to deliver a product that minimizes on-going development needs, and gives Dynamics CRM users unparalleled control over maintenance and evolving business requirements.

So it is that I seek to embrace the new features in the best interests of my growth, efficiency, and effectiveness. I, Developer will provide a map of Dynamics CRM 2013's extensibility framework, incorporating the new and old together for optimal execution and evolution.

Because the strength of these features is derived from collaborative efforts, I encourage you to embrace change to build the best product for your customer.

The Non-Developer on My Back

Major changes to Dynamics CRM provide non-developers with tools to accomplish tasks that previously required JavaScript experience, .Net experience, or licenses for heavy-lifting 3rd-Party frameworks. While the latter would relieve developers of certain responsibilities, they aren't as attractive to smaller projects, and aren't always economical. Addressing a full business process may span multiple extensibility areas, and therefore could require multiple 3rd-Party utilities.

Two exciting, new features for non-developers are Business Rules and Real-time Workflows. Of course, while a developer understands that "real-time" simply means "synchronous", we must remember that these features are not intended for us, even if we understand them better than our counterparts. While we have been given the ability to extend the platform, Business Process Flows and Workflows of synchronous and asynchronous varieties are intended for non-developers, as a way to visually and easily construct behaviors that address business needs.

Business analysts and functional consultants generally try to optimize a project's budget by minimizing costly development cycles, and may take on customization tasks that can be performed through Dynamics CRM's customization interface. Developers, in turn, may not be involved in a project until significant schema changes have been applied. Non-developers may not see the xRM platform through the eyes of a developer, and accidentally produce a schema that implements poor data structure.

This minimization factor can make in-house library building difficult without generous R&D time, and justifying the expense is all but improbable in lean and understaffed departments. Value-added resellers (VARs) and Independent Software Vendors (ISVs) differ greatly in this regard, and few bridge the gap successfully. Still, a developer can add a significant amount of value and budget control to future projects by constructing libraries of features. When a VAR can involve insightful and experienced software architecture early in the design process, an exciting evolution in the relationship between developers and non-developers will successfully meet the rising tide of Dynamics CRM adopters.

To accomplish that, each party should focus on distinct, yet shared frameworks. The non-developer roles will find higher utilization in implementing business processes, while the developer can leverage any slack in improving them.

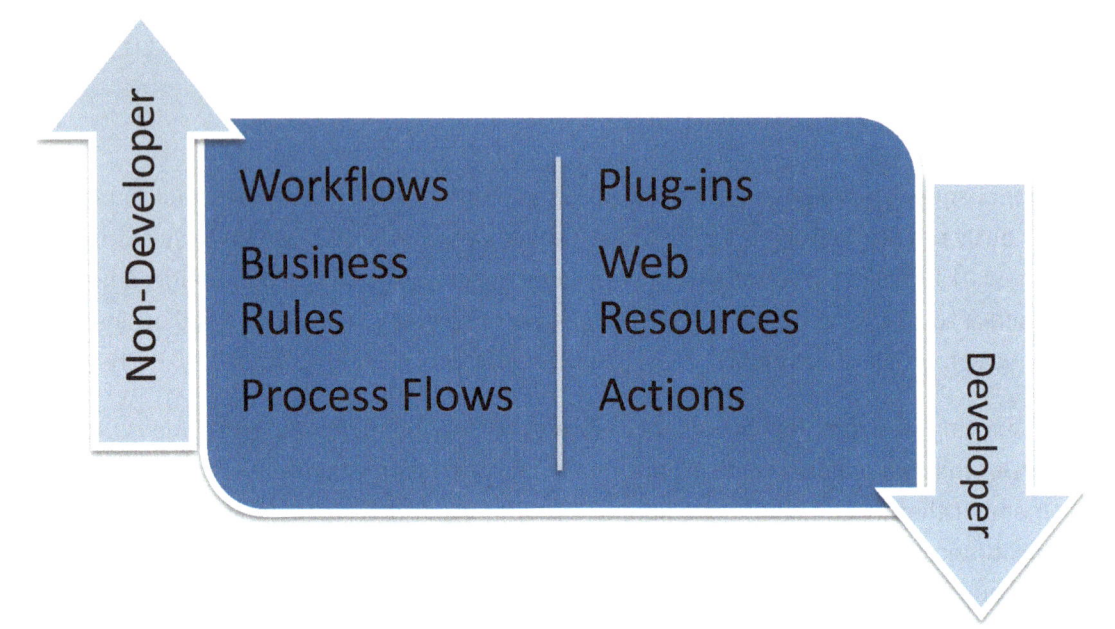

Non-Developer ↑

Workflows	Plug-ins
Business Rules	Web Resources
Process Flows	Actions

Developer ↓

My Friend, the Non-Developer

Non-developers are an ISV's bread and butter. By warehousing development talent, these framework- and feature-driven companies churn out remarkably rich enhancements to any Dynamics CRM deployment. Business analysts and other consultants are keen to adopt extensions that relieve the need for custom development and also reduce completion times. A trusted, stable, and well-supported extension can outlast, adapt, and improve where client-specific code might otherwise stagnate.

There will always be limitations and opportunities to improve on Dynamics CRM features, regardless of whether Microsoft introduces a native function that previously only extensions provided. Divergent and convergent evolution will provide space for ISVs to distinguish their products from the platform's default feature set. That said, Microsoft has built-in economically compelling alternatives. Perhaps, in reviewing the features in-depth, we can determine where product weaknesses can play to ISV strengths.

Regardless of the impact to existing ISV products, these new features offer few API changes to the platform of Dynamics CRM 2011, so this makes the product lines easier to bridge. With the capability to develop custom APIs, ISVs now have a potent opportunity to broaden horizons. New features like oAuth will also give ISVs potential to bridge Dynamics CRM with many new platforms and build convenient APIs for VAR developers to utilize.

Customizers Assemble!

A premier customer experience is delivered by the collaboration and distinction of domains in Dynamics CRM customizations. I'm confident that the divisions of responsibility will become cleaner with each new version of Dynamics CRM, and I for one appreciate Microsoft's effort to this end. It makes my job more rewarding and gives non-developers opportunities to produce high-quality results.

Developing for xRM, Evolved

This section is dedicated to the features which have evolved from predecessors in the Dynamics CRM family line. The greatest contributions to non-developers and developers alike will be covered here. Non-developers will gain significant advantages when implementing to specifications, by encouraging developers to create atomic extensions, and reusable features.

With the newfound popularity of Windows Workflow Foundation in every corner of Dynamics CRM, VARs should find they will rely less on Plug-ins. While Plug-ins will still remain a powerful

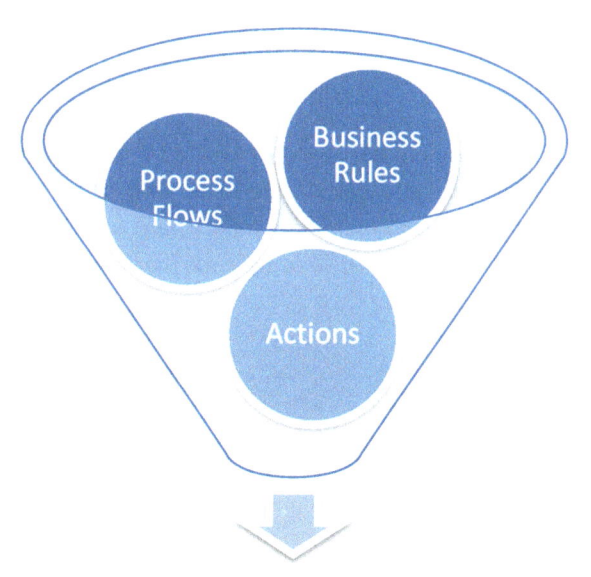

Windows Workflow Foundation

extensibility tool, especially for ISVs, developers should focus on improving the available tools for other roles in a Dynamics CRM implementation. As an added benefit, the client can train their power users and administrators to customize and adapt workflow logic to changes in business processes—an attractive incentive for clients.

You rule, I rule, we all rule for Business Rules!

Business Rules are currently a token advance in the area of dynamic form manipulation, departing from the JavaScript-heavy customizations of the past. Business Rules are simple, in scope and flexibility, and may not fully enable every desired scenario. So, there remains a great deal of room for improvement. This does not make them worthless, nonetheless.

In their current iteration, values may only be influenced by static values, or other fields within the same record. However, their triggers *are* optional—and "always on" Business Rules can be useful for many scenarios.

Business Rules have been referred to as "Portable Business Logic" in some cases. I believe this term is in reference to the format in which Business Rules are serialized for transport in Solutions. Portable Business Logic is expressed in XAML, as Windows Workflow Foundation activities. Because they are Solution-aware, when extracting CRM Solutions with the SolutionPackager.exe utility from the SDK, all Business Rules can be found in the decompressed "Workflows" folder.

> **NOTE** *A component of the Dynamics CRM SDK, the Solution Packager was first introduced in CRM 2011. Allows for the expansion of a Solution file into distinct customization areas for the purposes of Application Lifecycle Management. Can also be used to recombine the expanded product back into a Solution file.*

What's good about Business Rules

Business Rules can be form-specific or form-agnostic. The latter type may also be called "universal Business Rules." This can greatly simplify implementing universal behaviors upon fields, without requiring one to register JavaScript methods upon each form, or to supplement such registration with a form-cloning strategies.

One scenario, in particular, that often troubles workflow authors and maintainers: read-only fields. Fields that are specified as "read-only" on an entity's default form cannot be set with the

Update or Create actions of Workflows, Dialogs, or with the newly minted, custom Action feature (collectively: Processes). As a consequence, two options have been traditionally available to circumvent this limitation:

- Toggling the published "read-only" state of the field, for the duration of Process authoring; or
- Using an "OnLoad" JavaScript method to lock the fields on every Form load.

Fields that are often manipulated with workflows—but require a read-only state on the form while in use—could rely on a universal Business Rule to lock them down. This would offer Workflow authors the ability to work with the fields, and superficially protect them from users. Field security can also be used to fill this gap, however that feature remains unavailable to "out of box" fields.

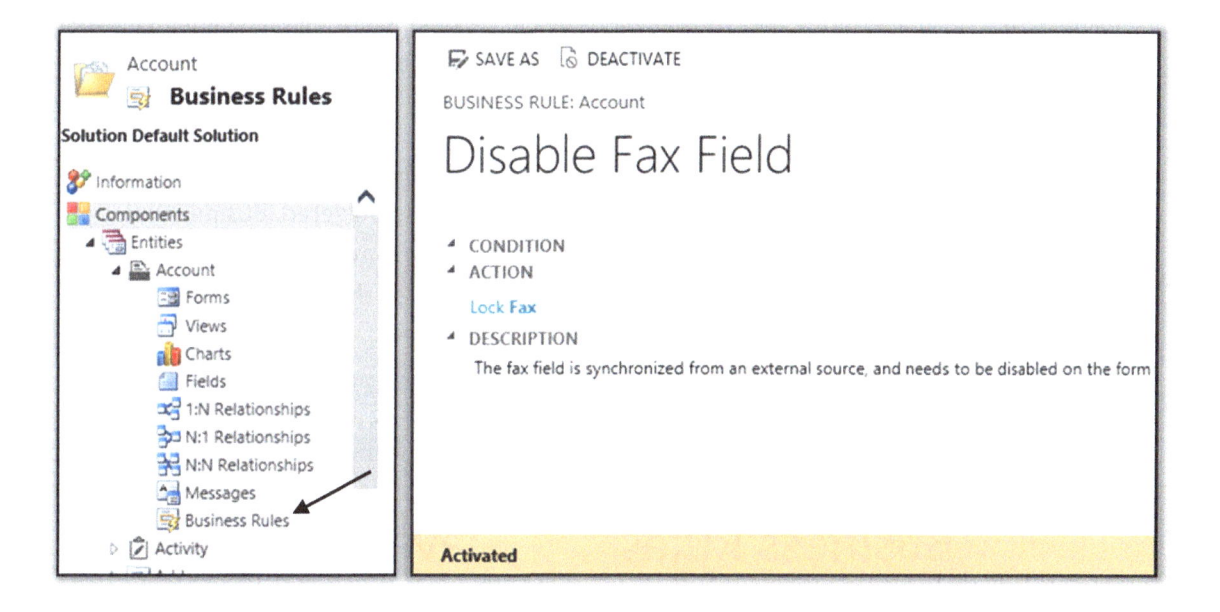

What could be better about Business Rules

Business Rules do not support branching logic, or the use of "OR" evaluations in conditions. This is perhaps one of the more noticeable deficiencies with their use. Already, early in the product's lifecycle, Business Rules adopters are noticing an explosion of definitions in order to accommodate relatively simple scenarios. Because of the added administrative effort to manage all the permutations of logical conditions, customizers find refuge in 3rd Party products (or have returned to them after uncovering this functional deficiency).

Business Rules also cannot look through relationships to evaluate fields from a related record. Many processes for child records tend to be dictated by the values held by their parents—relationally speaking. As a fallback, JavaScript makes for an eager participant in these situations.

Unfortunately, Business Rules cannot be authored in Visual Studio. To the best of my investigation, this appears to be because their internal components require use of the "Microsoft.Crm.Workflows" namespace—for which no SDK library is provided. However, because of this framework, there exists an exciting amount of possibilities for the evolution of this feature. Be sure to look at the No Code Business Rules Chapter 6.

When Business Rules Attack

When intermixing JavaScript and Business Rules, it's essential to note that they take different places in the sequencing of event handlers, depending on which event you're concerned about. Business Rules execute during the OnLoad event of the Form, and during the OnChange events of fields that are selected in their Conditions list. (Incidentally, this may be why the scope for Condition evaluation is so limited.)

When the OnLoad event is triggered, Business Rules are evaluated *first*, followed by registered JavaScript methods. However, when a field's OnChange event is triggered, Business Rules are evaluated *last*, after all JavaScript methods have returned. This may be because JavaScript could be designed to alter fields that are specified in a Business Rule, so the Business Rule may not be applicable.

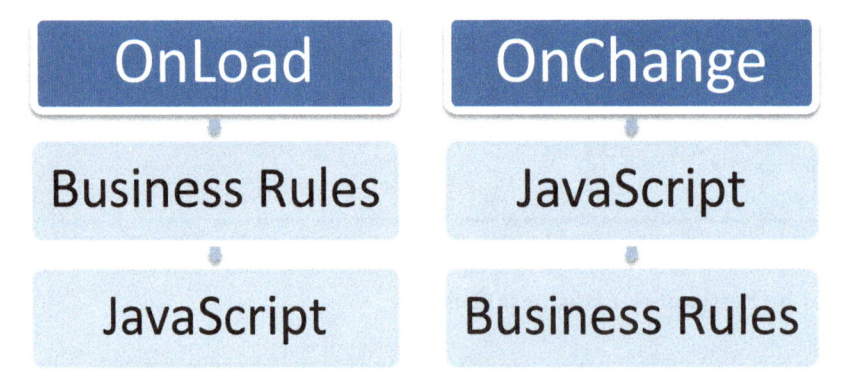

OnLoad	OnChange
Business Rules	JavaScript
JavaScript	Business Rules

Business Rules do not trigger OnChange events with their "Set value" actions. This means you don't have to worry about creating a feedback loop between a Business Rule and JavaScript (or other Business Rules). This behavior can be useful for slipping values into fields without waking their OnChange demons.

How to Use Business Rules Effectively

Business Rules work wonders when engineered around record states. Developers and non-developers can utilize the "state" and "status" fields of an entity to drive the various states of fields. This assists with establishing an over-arching design via phases through which a Form can pass. This approach can help leverage Business Rules in their current form, and provide a foundational framework upon which to design granular controls and behaviors.

For example: by storyboarding the lifecycle of a record into distinct states, a field-behavior foundation can be applied to each state, through separate Business Rules. Isolating complex field control within JavaScript. This will grant you foothold in an evolving feature's territory, and reward the investment with experience, leveraging the strengths of both Business Rules and JavaScript.

Alternatives to Business Rules

Several vendors have long operated in the market of dynamic forms, and have mature and stable offerings that are compelling alternatives to the new Business Rules feature. They are worth investigation and familiarity by any Dynamics CRM customizer.

- Visionary Software Consulting
  CRM Rules
  http://crm-rules.com/
- Sonoma Partners
  Dynamic Forms
  https://community.sonomapartners.com/content/dynamic-forms-for-crm-2013/
- North52
  Formula Manager
  http://www.north52.com/business-process-activities/formula-manager/

Business Process Feng Shui

Sales Processes in Microsoft CRM 3.0 were an ugly, primitive thing. Be that as it may, they were inexorably the progenitor of Business Process Flows for Dynamics CRM 2013. Long-time customers of CRM have often used the feature as it evolved through versions. To many, its maturation into a universal tool was inevitable. Microsoft has finally realized the vision started so long ago.

However, first I would like to clarify some terminology use for the purposes of this section:

Business Process Flow	The Microsoft-given name of the feature, and generally considered to be the name for individual sequences.
Flow	The name I use to indicate individual Business Process Flow sequences.
Stage	Refers to the individual stages within a Flow; originally, "Process Stage".
Process Ribbon	Refers to the header-interface displayed on record forms.

What's good about Business Process Flows

Business Process Flows are another feature driven by the Windows Workflow Foundation. They are solution-aware, and will extract into the "Workflows" directory of a SolutionPackager-expanded Solution file. Like Business Rules, they cannot yet be authored in Visual Studio, however they are authored in the same "Processes" area of Dynamics CRM with all other Workflow components.

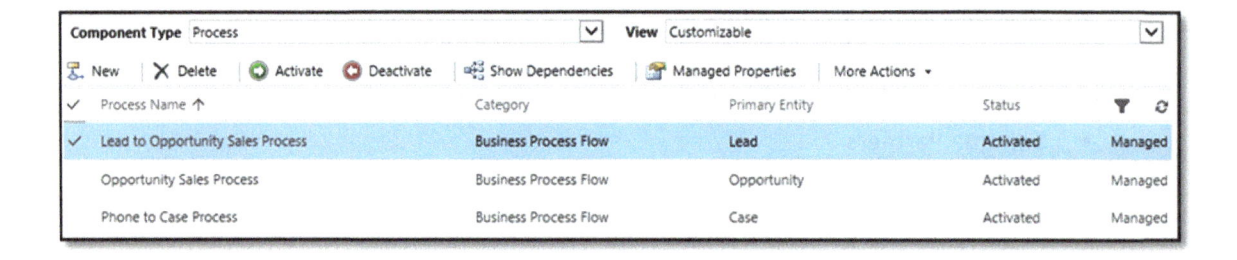

For a developer, Flows offer few extensibility scenarios. Flows are available to be run on any "refreshed" or custom entity. Notably, a record's progression through Flow stages can trigger Plug-ins and Workflows. This is enabled through quasi-relationships with the Process entity, and the new Process Stage entity.

These unique relationships can be monitored for changes, enabling other Process models to hook into the progression of a Flow. For example: in order to leverage Business Rules and Business Process Flows together, Workflow can step in as an intermediary, and change a record's state.

What could be better about Business Process Flows

Being able to reference an Entity's Flow and Process Stage fields from Business Rules would be nice. However, due to the distinctive nature of the relationship between entities and Flows, this breaks from with the underlying dependency logic. Either way, it forces a need to bridge the gap with Workflows or other code.

One might argue that automated progression through Process Stages is a "must-have", but they're missing the point of Business Process Flows: to help drive progression and management of records via user interaction. There may, at some future time, be a sensible way to enable automated stage progression.

A major deficiency in the current Process Ribbon implementation is that custom scripts, Lookup filtration, and field state management are not applied to fields within the ribbon the same way they're applied on the form. This has been determined as by design, and for performance reasons. Whether this behavior will be corrected in the future is unknown at the time of this writing, but I believe that customer feedback stands the best chance of effecting change.

How to Use Business Process Flows Effectively

Business Process Flows are almost too simple and flexible to go wrong. A record can be associated with only one Flow, and occupy a single Stage, at any given time. Combining these relationships with automated transition through State and Status values, through the use of Workflows or Plug-ins, can lubricate inter-Entity processes as well.

Changes to the current Flow or Stage will be reflected in these fields, and can be monitored for change by Workflows and Plug-ins. However, these are *not* normal EntityReference fields. In the Metadata, they're listed as "UniqueIdentifier", which is synonymous with "Guid". This special field establishes no foreign key constraint, and therefore cannot pre-empt the runtime adjustment of the associated Flow or Stage. There are probably other benefits as well, but the downside is they're not easily targeted by Workflow "check" conditions, and impossible to target by Create or Update steps.

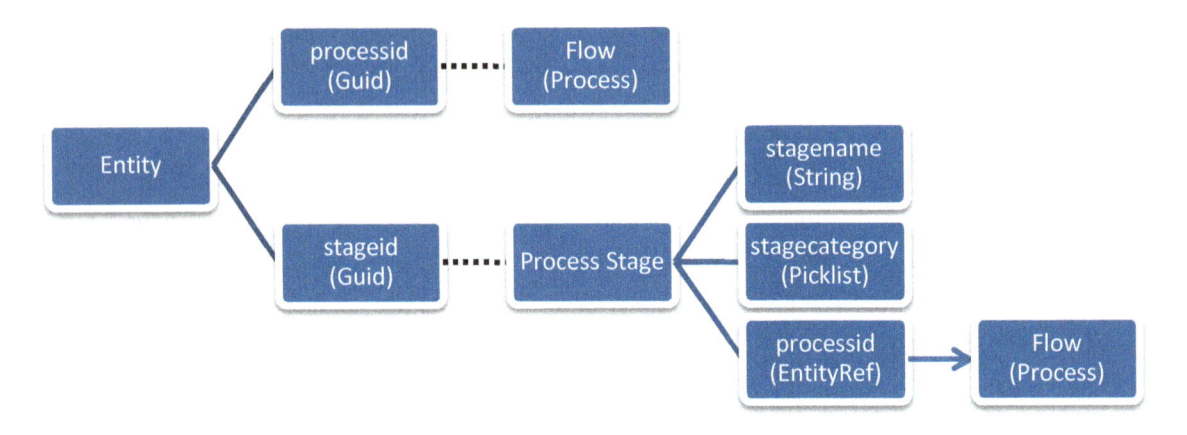

```
Entity ──┬── processid (Guid) ······ Flow (Process)
         │
         └── stageid (Guid) ······ Process Stage ──┬── stagename (String)
                                                   ├── stagecategory (Picklist)
                                                   └── processid (EntityRef) ──→ Flow (Process)
```

The relationship for Process Stage is exposed for Workflow conditions and any views, including Advanced Find. Through it, another relationship to the Flow can be traversed. Use the Stage's name or category to identify it; it's then possible to craft a reference to the specific Flow. This can help you build views, and adequately build Workflow conditions.

The real problem for Workflow conditions is that, at the deepest, only the Stage's name will distinguish it from others. This is reasonably satisfactory when the names are unique; but unlikely to satisfy a desire to utilize a stronger reference. This is because Flows are intended to be volatile; and, as I indicated before, a Workflow creates dependencies on records specified within its steps. Using a custom Workflow activity to fill in some of the functional gaps can come in handy. On the other hand, FetchXML can be used with great success for getting under the covers with Flows and Stages. So, let's get into that.

Querying for Business Process Flow

To identify the unique identifier for a Flow, open it with the editor, and cut out the Guid in the URL. Alternatively, you can query against the Workflow entity. Each Flow is a Workflow instance (schema name: workflow), with a *category* (OptionSet field) value of "4". The *workflowid* (primary key field) value from these Workflows is the value to look for in the *processid* field of Flow-enabled entities. Select and copy the GUID from between the %7b and %7d character boundaries.

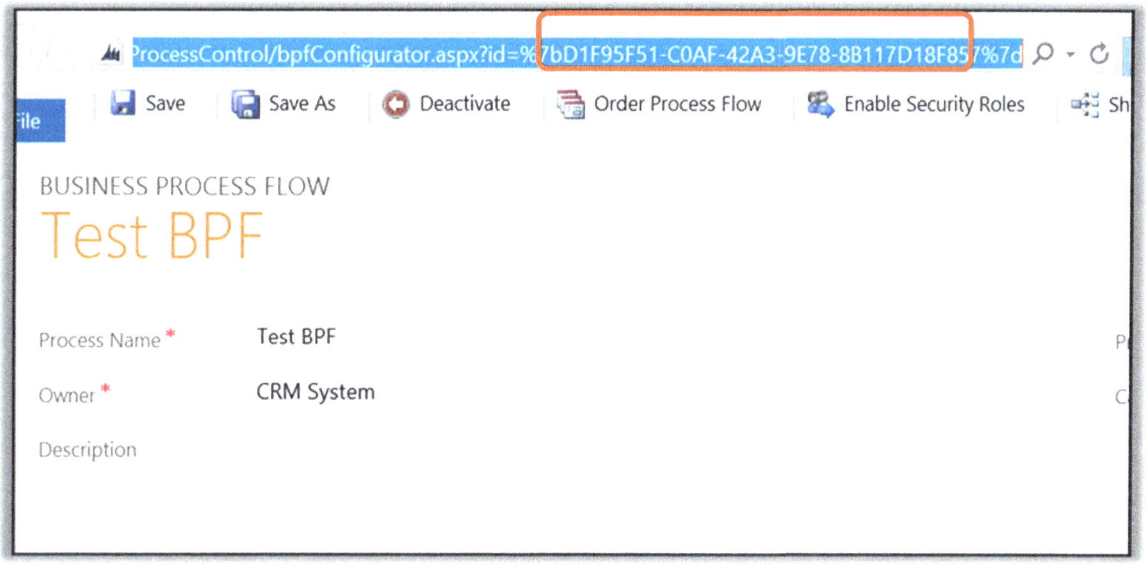
ProcessControl/bpfConfigurator.aspx?id=%7bD1F95F51-C0AF-42A3-9E78-8B117D18F857%7d
Save
Save As
Deactivate
Order Process Flow
Enable Security Roles
BUSINESS PROCESS FLOW
Test BPF
Process Name
Test BPF
Owner
CRM System
Description

Stages (schema name: processstage) also have a *processid* field, which can also be linked back to the Flow. Naturally, the *processstageid* (primary key field) value is used within Flow-enabled entity's *stageid* field. Apart from this, the only other interesting or useful fields from a Stage are *stagename* (string field) and *primaryentitytypecode* (a "typecode" field), which you can learn the values for here: http://msdn.microsoft.com/en-us/library/bb928150.aspx.

My best guess is that the integer reference is faster for indexing and query operations at SQL, so rather than using the schema name of an Entity, the "typecode" still finds use, buried in areas that only the intrepid dare explore. Because "typecodes" are auto-incrementing, no two deployments can be expected to assign the same value to identical entities—even if they're shipped in a Solution. This makes the *stagename* and *processid* fields prime candidates for Process Stage queries.

Flow-driven automation can be achieved by understanding how the Business Process Flow feature works, and leveraging existing behaviors to your advantage. When automated processes are driven and signaled by Flows and Stages, the volatility of the feature needs to be mitigated. This can be accomplished with care and training, however I strongly suggest looking to Managed Solutions. For both VARs and ISVs, this protects Flows which must not be changed, lest doing so impedes the automation.

Sample FetchXML result querying "workflow" for Flows:

```xml
<result>
    <processorder formattedvalue="100" >
        100
    </processorder>
    <triggeroncreate name="Yes" >
        1
    </triggeroncreate>
    <ismanaged name="Unmanaged" >
        0
    </ismanaged>
    <workflowidunique>
        {286E9CEE-7FE9-4A6A-ABCD-302BCD6E8D51}
    </workflowidunique>
    <workflowid>
        {D1F95F51-C0AF-42A3-9E78-8B117D18F857}
    </workflowid>
    <solutionid>
        {FD140AAE-4DF4-11DD-BD17-0019B9312238}
    </solutionid>
    <subprocess name="No" >
        0
    </subprocess>
    <statecode name="Activated" >
        1
    </statecode>
    <runas name="Calling User" formattedvalue="1" >
        1
    </runas>
    <iscrmuiworkflow>
        1
    </iscrmuiworkflow>
    <name>
        Test BPF
    </name>
    <category name="Business Process Flow" formattedvalue="4" >
        4
    </category>
```

```xml
        <statuscode name="Activated" >
            2
        </statuscode>
        <type name="Definition" formattedvalue="1" >
            1
        </type>
</result>
```

Sample FetchXML results, querying the "processstage" entity:

```xml
<result>
    <processid name="Test BPF" type="4703" >
        {D1F95F51-C0AF-42A3-9E78-8B117D18F857}
    </processid>
    <processstageid>
        {E43764C3-19EA-A851-93ED-0BD1408D582D}
    </processstageid>
    <ownerid type="8" >
        {A21789B7-171B-E311-81F9-00155DFD0307}
    </ownerid>
    <stagename>
        New Stage
    </stagename>
    <primaryentitytypecode name="" formattedvalue="112" >
        112
    </primaryentitytypecode>
    <owningbusinessunit>
        {370189B7-171B-E311-81F9-00155DFD0307}
    </owningbusinessunit>
</result>
```

Working Together

Tying Flows and Stages together with record states (or other) automation might limit the Business Analyst's ability to modify the established processes after the fact, therefore the developer must remain engaged in the design and implementation of such business processes. Business Process Flows are designed to be soft overlays, and impermanent rails to guide a record through its own life-cycle. Driving automation with them is certainly less practical than using a

Dialog, for example, but offers a nice visual plot and linear progression that automation is keen to utilize. With careful planning, implementation, and management, developers and non-developers alike can maximize the benefit of using Business Process Flows.

The Weird, Wide, World of Workflows

The Windows Workflow Foundation has taken xRM by storm with a bevy of new features, but it's nice to see an old friend get an upgrade too. I'm talking of course, about Real-time Workflows. Since the developer in me begs to call them "Synchronous Workflows", I think I will. Now—finally—business analysts, power users, administrators, and managers can extend Dynamics CRM in ways that only Plug-in developers could. What's more, is that investments into custom Workflow assemblies and extensions have been rewarded tremendously.

What's good about Synchronous Workflows

Over the years, Dynamics CRM developers have learned how to leverage asynchronous and synchronous process architecture in business process modelling. The line between Plug-in and Workflow was drawn very strongly at the borders of synchronicity. Although Plug-ins can be implemented asynchronously, I wager that developers like me would prefer to look to them for feature implementation, rather than business process implementation. Workflows have remained the premier vehicle for non-developers to get *into* business process automation.

Synchronous and Asynchronous Workflows can work together to perform process-validation and event-driven automation across the following xRM events:

| Create | Assign | State Change | Update | Delete |

Synchronous Workflows operate within the database transaction, and may also be executed before the system operation is called. This is similar to Plug-in behavior, and is a concept that non-developers may struggle with. The SDK has a great article to explain the "Event Execution Pipeline."

What could be better about Synchronous Workflows

Because Workflows use "entity images" behind the scenes for context, Synchronous Workflows cannot be executed Before Create or After Delete.

> **NOTE**: *An Entity Image is a snapshot of the record receiving an xRM operation. Plug-ins have access to "pre" and "post" entity images. A "pre" entity image is generated before the platform performs its operation, and a "post" entity image is generated after the operation completes. Synchronous Workflows use only "pre" images, and Asynchronous Workflows use either "pre" or "post" images.*

Because this context is derived from the use of images, rather than from the operation's invocation, updated values will only be available in the "After" stage, but the previous values only available in the "Before" stage.

A Plug-in maintains an edge in situations where a snapshot of the record before the operation needs to be compared to the snapshot of a record afterward, and for any pre-operation validation on changing values. This is important, because the operation, and the things it might trigger inside the database transaction, could incur wasted time and overhead.

> **TIP**: *Just to be clear: Workflows cannot evaluate the new values of fields that have changed in the "Before" stage, and are poor data validators.*

How to Use Synchronous Workflows Effectively

Any good Workflow's purpose is to easily implement business process and provide a manageable surface area for business analysts and the gamut of non-developer assets. That said, there are performance considerations to be made. Plug-ins don't incur the overhead costs of the Windows Workflow Foundation, or interpretation from XAML. Consider strongly the processes that must be synchronous, and make an effort to leverage asynchronous modes where possible.

When performance doesn't meet expectations, and Synchronous Workflows are found to blame, consider refactoring in Plug-in. If migrating data into entities with Synchronous Workflows, consider disabling them and transforming data beforehand. Otherwise, import speeds may not meet expectations. The Dynamics CRM 2013 SDK specifically cautions against this scenario.

For data validation needs, a Plug-in remains the reigning champion, with JavaScript a close second. JavaScript will obviously be unable to perform validation on data passed directly to the platform, circumventing the UI altogether. Business Rules have few options for validation, but are worth mentioning, because they require no code—even though they're also limited to UI operations.

Working Together

Developers should approach deficiencies in Workflows for a particular process as a challenge to extend the Workflow with custom components. Bridging functional gaps with custom workflow assemblies will reward the investment of time by allowing non-developers the ability to mesh those components at-will, and dynamically. It's no secret that business processes change unexpectedly, so empowering the customer or consultant depends on Workflow-centric development efforts.

Lights, Camera, (Custom) Action!

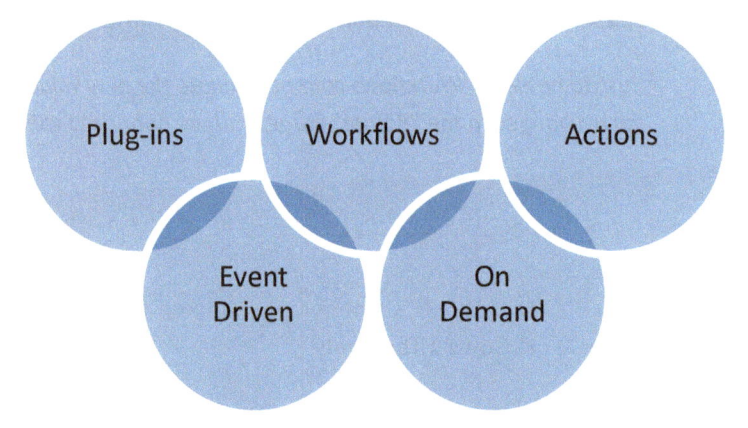

Microsoft delivered a massive wallop of extensibility for xRM with the Actions feature. As Entities are building blocks for data structures and relationships, Actions are building blocks for processes. Actions can be Entity specific, or agnostic (also called "global"), and provide developers and non-developers the tools necessary to create simple or complex operations that are not tied to record-centric events—in contrast to Workflows and Plug-ins both.

What's good about Actions

There are three significant differentiators between an Action and Workflows or Plug-ins. First, Actions are summoned through CRM's own Web Services as first-class citizens on the line. This is an exciting extensibility model by its own right. Second, input and output for an Action are derived from configurable parameters. Finally, the Plug-in framework can attach to the Action through assembly registration, thereby skyrocketing the extensibility value of the feature.

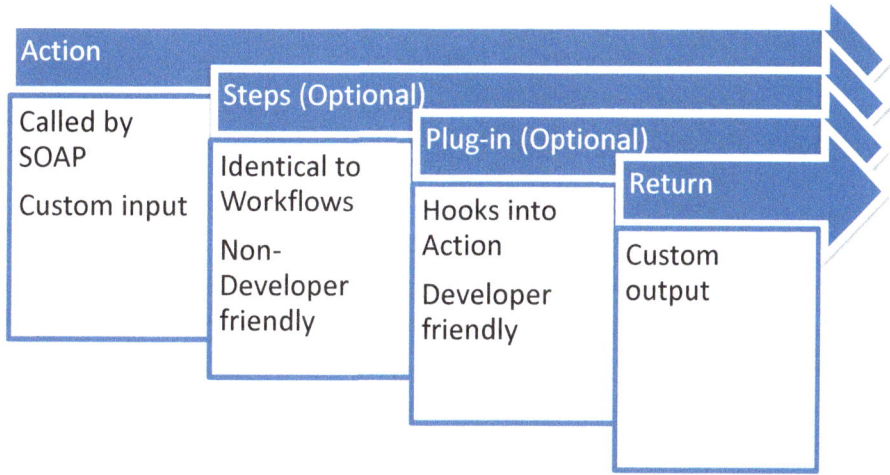

Action	Steps (Optional)	Plug-in (Optional)	Return
Called by SOAP Custom input	Identical to Workflows Non-Developer friendly	Hooks into Action Developer friendly	Custom output

As extensions to Web Service messages that also implement Workflow architecture, Actions will be indispensable to platform and interface extensibility. Gone are the days of using specialized sets of Entities to behave like methods. Even configuring simple Actions to respond with output that's set with "Assign Value" step can eliminate the use of an Entity to store configuration data.

Parameters on an Action establish a contract for the method, and can implement some convenient data-types not found in any other Workflow-derived feature. These are:

1. Entity
2. EntityReference
3. EntityCollection

Plug-ins can attach to Actions as easily as any other available web service message, and access the parameters from the context's InputParameters and OutputParameters collections. Even "global" Actions require an input on the "Target" parameter, which will be familiar to developers used to extending the Create and Update messages. The execution pipeline applies the same, with (for the first time ever), the core operation defined as the steps configured in the Action definition. No steps are required, if an Action will serve only as an interface to Plug-in code.

What could be better about Actions

Since Actions are authored in XAML, as a Windows Workflow Foundation component, it would seem logical to execute them from within Workflows and Dialogs. However, that is certainly not the case with this iteration of the feature. I hope whatever is blocking these scenarios is removed in the next version of the product, but I'm happy enough with the feature as-is, that I can scarcely muster the disappointment to miss it.

Custom workflow assemblies are the fastest way to invoke Actions from within Workflows and Dialogs, as a stop-gap. This is important, because Actions can operate in an entity-agnostic fashion, and can represent logic applied to multiple entity types. Actions can also summon "child Workflows", for spawning simple asynchronous, business-process offshoots.

How to Use Actions Effectively

Actions must be called as Web Service messages, so building shims between Workflows and Actions may be a tedious and unavoidable compromise. Calling them from JavaScript and Plug-ins is trivial, however, and can be richly leveraged from those frameworks. Ideally, they should be used to provide triggers for operations that aren't tied to an event, creating rich extensions with Web Resources, or enabling complex integration scenarios.

As a developer, I try to abstract an Action as much as possible to fit many situations. Parameters are a powerful tool, and in particular the EntityCollection's independence from an entity type configuration, means that you could use it as a wrapper for polymorphic input. EntityCollection also allows you to apply an operation to records in bulk; for aggregation, updates, or iterative evaluation. This could, for example, enable a scenario where creating a "Customer" operation—for both Account and Contact entities—is finally easy.

Non-developers can create client-maintainable logic that is summoned by areas that only a developer could maintain. This powerful collaborative facet of Actions that should not be overlooked. In projects with limited development resources, non-developers can step in to a certain degree. This is one area where "functional" and "business process" lines blur again, but into the non-developer's court.

Working Together

Actions offer another strong opportunity for non-developers and developers to collaborate, or allow a developer to birth powerful features for internal and external consumption. Integrations that can leverage Actions may be strengthened and advanced beyond simple CRUD operations. ISVs in the integration space should take special effort to cater to them.

Plug-ins Unplugged

Plug-ins are by no means deprecated by any of the aforementioned features. If anything, their purpose should become more focused on functionality over business process. For example, if I were to design a product configuration feature, I would not look to Workflows to import hierarchical product structures, but I might look to a custom Action, with a Plug-in component to do the heavy lifting. By intermixing Actions and Plug-ins, in this way, I've created a "hook" for non-developers to extend the Action's internal steps with business process automation—for example, changing the state of the record with newly configured products, which my Plug-in imported.

Plug-ins are also the performance mainstay of the xRM customization stack. In some situations, Synchronous Workflows will be too burdensome on resources or performance, and Plug-ins may be necessary for business processes. Hopefully, these situations will be rare enough that Plug-in development can remain focused and encapsulated to feature behavior.

I'm not going to breakdown Plug-ins, because they're a mature and established feature with tremendous amounts of information and guidance available all over the Internet. For Dynamics CRM 2013, the best perspective I can give is to avoid Plug-ins for business processes wherever possible, and consider Actions as the entry-point for Plug-in code, where it makes sense. This approach helps compartmentalize purpose and implementation, fostering collaboration over task management.

Just JavaScript

JavaScript has claimed territory, by-and-large, over Silverlight's hemorrhaging circulatory system. While I still believe Silverlight has a role to play, my opinion of late is that it's mostly by way of post-sunset support. HTML 5 has taken web browsing by storm, and as well it should, being the most harmoniously implemented and rapidly deployed cross-device, cross-platform, and cross-browser framework for interconnected applications.

What about Silverlight? Microsoft should straddle the uncertainties of Silverlight's fate in their own best interests. As with any technology, if there are enough customers, there will be a product to sell. In this light, Silverlight is certainly wounded. This is most true in the general consumer demographic. However, enterprise uses will continue to enjoy a long support cycle.

From a technology standpoint, XAML is a powerful application language and is very prevalent in Silverlight. Modern Microsoft developers will encounter it when designing applications for the Windows Store, or Windows 8.x tablets.

Code which previously altered the UI in unsupported ways, such as with colorization, should not be expected to upgrade well. Dynamics CRM 2013's DOM has been completely overhauled, and new inroads must be discovered to deliver experiences to which CRM 2011 customers may be accustomed.

Concerns about compatibility also applies to code written exclusively for earlier versions of Internet Explorer (intentional or not). Cross-browser functionality, through the implementation of stricter HTML standards, was delivered later in Dynamics CRM 2011's lifecycle, and many differences in JavaScript APIs are smoothed over by Internet Explorer's "compatibility mode" rendering capabilities. With the push to bring Dynamics CRM to broader device selections, cross-browser libraries and development patterns are more important than they have ever been. Which brings us conveniently to the next topic.

jQuery is Baked In

Nearly four years ago, Microsoft pledged to support the jQuery project with resources and development, and this is evident in Dynamics CRM 2013 with jQuery at its core. As a library for cross-browser development, it is both effective and compelling. The simplification it lends to traversing DOM structures, parsing XML strings, interfacing with Web Services, and managing event handlers, is indispensable.

The SDK doesn't document it, so the following information is certainly unsupported, but the location of the jQuery script file is at this root location:

```
/_static/_common/scripts/jquery1.7.2.min.js
```
Use of this URL is unsupported.

This relative URL can be consumed by Web Resources, or other places where jQuery is not loaded by default; but again, this is unsupported, and should be watched carefully for updates in the future. Did I mention that it was unsupported?

So why consider it? Well, with each solution publisher that integrates jQuery, 90+ KB is added to the browser's cache, and impacting load times as the library is processed. The jQuery Foundation does not recommend using multiple versions in parallel, however it is necessary to follow Microsoft's guidance on jQuery use.

The SDK warns against the use of jQuery, in both entity forms and command bars, and states quite clearly that DOM-manipulation in these areas is an unsupported form of customization. However, jQuery.ajax() makes for a natural, cross-browser option for rapidly implementing client-side consumption of REST endpoints, and *is supported*. jQuery implements promises across its ajax handlers, which I find easier to read and manage. The SDK implies that importing a custom version of jQuery is not necessary to use $.ajax(), and indeed, it is not—unless you require features beyond version 1.7. In my experience, "$" is available by the time any of my scripts are called by CRM, either from the command bar or entity forms.

Regardless, there are considerations to make when running two versions of jQuery side-by-side. The jQuery project advises side-stepping namespace collisions with the *noConflict()* method. When I must use a different version of jQuery, I put this statement at the end of the script file that contains it:

```
window.abc_jQuery = $.noConflict();
```
"abc" represents the Solution publisher's customization prefix

This is in accordance to the SDK's best practice recommendations because CRM's jQuery occupies the traditional "$" namespace. I can tell you from experience that crossing the jQuery streams produces ill effects, not the least of which is total protonic-reversal. Mind your jQuery where you must, and leverage common resources wherever possible.

Defer to Reactive Experiences

Dynamics CRM 2013 tries to make great strides in managing the impact to page load times, but can be trumped by inconsiderate design. Some practices and designs come from much earlier versions of Dynamics CRM, where they were comfortably established as "best practice" from a development and deployment perspective.

In CRM 2011, Microsoft introduced the concept of "Read Optimized Forms". The purpose of the feature was to strip all JavaScript from the regular forms, and present information in a read-only state. The user could toggle away from this skeleton form when edits were required, but the process was cumbersome, and most deployments simply disabled the feature altogether. The feature was transformed into "Quick View Forms". Instead, the CRM product team doubled-down efforts to improve JavaScript behavior, loading and execution.

Wherever possible, xRM will defer the loading of Web Resource and Iframe controls when their container tabs are collapsed by default. Of course, this renders the information within them unavailable until the user (or another bit of code) expands the tab, so the trade-off in performance is for availability.

Library Support and Use

The SDK cautions against the use of many and large JavaScript libraries. I think the solution instead is to approach them sensibly with a deep understanding of xRM's loading and execution model. To that end, I can think of no better resource than an article by the esteemed Scott Durow, a Dynamics CRM MVP, and developer behind the wildly popular Ribbon Workbench tool: http://www.develop1.net/public/post/CRM-2013-Script-Loading-Deep-Dive.aspx

In this article, Scott covers the parallel and sequential loading behaviors of the interface at several extensibility points, and offers helper code to establish ordered loads at every point. I think this breaks away from one of the premier features of HTML 5: asynchronous, parallel script loads. Since forms were the only feature designed to implement "libraries" of JavaScript code, this is the only place where they load asynchronously. By contrast, JavaScript libraries referenced in "Enable Rules" for the Command Bar are loaded sequentially, as each rule is evaluated, and preempt the loading of libraries on the form—thereby preventing duplicate loads. This is slow, and inefficient.

Not only does the HTML 5 model improve interface responsiveness, it encourages module-driven development, and the use of event-driven architecture to make the determination as to the readiness of the application's resources. I'm not so quick to shrug it off, but I understand that without knowing why it's a good thing, I can't write code that works well with it.

My advice is to leverage purpose-built and streamlined code resources in the Command Bar, and avoid the use of libraries. This was generally accomplished with a well-documented "isNaN" hack. It's important to note that Command Bar actions executed the Form will benefit from libraries loaded by that Form, so this alternate approach is really only necessary for Command Bars outside the form, or for "Enable Rules".

> **NOTE** *Command Bar or Ribbon? "Command Bar" is the name of menu bar atop Dynamics CRM pages, and adheres to RibbonXML definitions for customization. It's an evolution from an Office-style "Ribbon" menu that was first introduced in Dynamics CRM 2011. The monikers are used to identify the same feature.*

How to Use JavaScript Effectively

I think that rich and large JavaScript libraries are useful for form and HTML Web Resource features, but at all turns, we should look to Actions as a relief valve for tangled and sensitive areas, such as the Command Bar. This is especially true for Command Bar "Enable Rules", which could serve to be streamlined tremendously with simpler JavaScript. If we play to the strengths of features by understanding their individual weaknesses, we can deliver rewarding results.

Caution: Fun Times Ahead

While many existing features have not changed, and are largely backwards compatible with CRM 2011, the completely redesigned UI has introduced some challenges and inverted long-held assumptions about how the UI drives process design. Previous versions of Dynamics CRM were heavily windowed, click-intensive, and dependent on explicit user behaviors. Now, Dynamics CRM 2013 provides a unified, touch and click friendly, implicitly automated interface that is wholly alien to design concepts of the past.

As a consequence of many radical UI changes in confluence, even *compatible* customizations from CRM 2011 are only technically so. Features like automatic saving can introduce a race-condition minefield, limited inline editing capability and selectively available composite controls can impact the perception of what can be customized, and widespread availability of the Mobile Client Application for Dynamics CRM will propel desktop-designed components into the mobile space whether they're prepared or not. In short, it is disingenuous to state that Dynamics CRM 2013 is little more than Dynamics CRM 2011 with fresh paint and a handful of cool extensibility additions. It may appear that way on paper, but in practice, this is a new application that used arguably the best parts of previous versions, and built the rest from the ground up.

Many of the concepts introduced to xRM in this version have already pervaded other areas of our lives, whether we recognize them or not. As a developer, it's difficult not to get upset at having to redesign according to new expectations. To Microsoft's credit though, they've included tools and workarounds for the future and interim respectively. I'm of the opinion that we should embrace these changes, for the improvements they offer in efficiency in the long run.

Auto-Save Me

> **NOTE**
>
> *Automatic Saves*
>
> *Modern applications on the web, on phones, and tablets are adopting a policy of eliminating the explicit save operation. Modern office applications even continuously save in the background. The intent is the same: protecting new data from inadvertent loss.*

Perhaps the most controversial, and least appreciated change—among seasoned xRM developers—is the form's move from explicit saving, to implicit saving. Any change on the form starts a countdown timer (default: 30 seconds), at which point the form will be automatically saved. As some business processes depend on receiving multiple changes simultaneously, or are intolerant of receiving unsynchronized field changes, greater attention must be paid to impeding the save operation at the UI.

Pictured: a dinosaur finally going extinct

Dynamically altering the requirement of a field can abort an automatic save, so long as the field is empty. Saves cannot be avoided by using Business Rules or JavaScript to produce field-level or form-level error notices. Additional validation efforts can be implemented in "OnSave" event handlers, where the action can be aborted first. Business Rules can assist, but Synchronous Workflows can step in and perform codeless validation too. Any failure to complete the transaction will be reported back to the form; terminating a Synchronous Workflow with a status of "Cancelled" will do just that.

Microsoft extended an olive-branch to detractors and overworked developer masses who perished the thought of refactoring code as a barrier to upgrading. In the "System Settings", the auto-save feature can be partially disabled. For many upgrade scenarios, this should be an acceptable compromise. Prior to Update Rollup 2, the act of navigating away from a record will still perform an implicit save operation.

By making the act of saving a record the implicit result of making a change or navigating away from the record, Microsoft has adopted the behavior found across many mobile platforms and applications, and expressed throughout their current Windows product lines. Office365 treats whole documents this way! By reacting more to independent changes, we can steer users and avoid troublesome save actions, while capitalizing on a gentle, innate behavior—and recovering precious command bar real estate.

I openly encourage developers to embrace automatic saving as a feature, without disabling it for convenience or adherence to older architectural patterns. This will challenge our planning abilities, but the pay-off will be worth it. If data fidelity is a concern, and it should be, the ability to rollback a save operation might be essential. To that end, I recommend looking into the "CRM 2013 Audit Undo" project, developed by Dynamics CRM MVP Jason Lattimer:

> https://crm2013auditundo.codeplex.com/

Ribbon Dance-Off

Dynamics CRM 2011 offered a radical new menu system designed to match the Microsoft Office experience. It introduced an ever persistent Ribbon interface. Extending the Ribbon interface was performed via XML, and it still is in Dynamics CRM 2013—however the Ribbon was commuted to a shadow of its former self. This feature has been rechristened as the "Command Bar".

The Command Bar transformed into a dynamic menu, with a default limitation of 5 visible commands, while the rest are concealed by an ellipsis command. The principle guiding this design is to keep a less busy interface, by encouraging more effort taken in the customization and context to deliver a dynamic interface. As a side-effect of this change from the Ribbon is that the enabled state of a command also controls its visibility on the bar. Whether one mode of command hiding will end up deprecated, in favor of the other, remains to be seen.

If guidance I've already offered in this chapter is any indication, I prefer JavaScript-light command bars for performance and responsiveness, so consider using "Enable Rules" that evaluate field values simply, rather than call complicated validation scripts. Like Business Rules, I look at states and status reasons as the principal engine for determining the commands I want to be available.

"Display Rules" and "Enable Rules" are treated the same way by Dynamics CRM 2013. The latter is a vestigial expression of Dynamics CRM 2011, and I be consider it deprecated—however, Microsoft has not stated so for either. What is known is that the Command Bar will only display a button that is both enabled and displayed, as evaluated by its rules. Since there's no effective difference between the treatments of these representations, I have chosen "Display Rules" as the winner, since it most aptly describes what is happening at the UI.

Composite Field Theory

Composite fields have a very large role in demonstrating a new approach to the distinction between presentation, and administration. Found on address and name fields for Account and Contact forms, these fields pack many fields into a single frame of reference, and fly-out the individual controls for data entry. They're a preview of the possibilities in the UI foundations, and limited to these particular instances for Dynamics CRM 2013. This means that they do not provide for any customization, and cannot be applied elsewhere.

Leveraging this unique feature should not come at the cost of productivity, or the expense of working around it. I believe it would be simply enough to thank Microsoft for the concept, and express our excitement for its potential. If it is not simply enough to redeploy the composited fields into a hidden section, to bridge gaps in the event model, then it may be more effort than its worth. It's easier to let go of a feature that never got close to our hearts, than to deal with the pain and heartache of insufficient reciprocity.

Mobile to Go, Please

The Mobile Client Application demonstrates Microsoft's commitment to bringing the Dynamics CRM application to the field by supporting "Bring Your Own Device" initiatives. The cross-browser investments of Dynamics CRM 2011 Update Rollup 12 provided the foundation for Dynamics CRM 2013's Android, IOS, and WinRT clients. These clients are produced and executed in HTML 5, which means that a great deal of JavaScript is compatible for use.

The caveat is, however, that the further you stray from the Xrm.Page API, the greater the risk of running afoul of compatibility assurances.

The mobile clients are a fantastic bridge into the mobile space, without the high cost of ISV platforms. Still, ISV platforms are well established and offer better integration with platform-native apps, and a stronger offline synchronization experience. Whatever the case, there is enough mobile to go around, and a large customer base eager to leverage it.

From a development perspective, this can present some challenges. Web Resource and Iframe controls are unsupported. *Xrm.Utility.openWebResource()* will therefore fail. Because of this, client-context APIs have been added to Xrm.Page.context.client by way of *getClient()* and *getClientState()*. Using them will allow developers to develop for mobile and desktop environments.

When it comes to developing with mobile in mind, it helps to confine efforts to features and interface components that display and work well. The limitations of the mobile client aren't many, but enough to stymie common workarounds for deficiencies in extensibility elsewhere. ISVs with mobile client alternatives should not be dismissed easily, as many are solid candidates for filling functional gaps.

> *Debugging the mobile client isn't easy, but can be achieved with tracing on both Windows 8 and iPad platforms with instructions from this Microsoft Customer Center article: http://www.microsoft.com/en-US/dynamics/crm-customer-center/enable-tracing-in-crm-for-tablets.aspx*

Wrapping Up

Throughout this chapter I've tried to illustrate the future I envision for Dynamics CRM developers. I strongly believe that Microsoft has delivered major enhancements across multiple surfaces, which enable developers and non-developers to collaborate more effectively. I'm personally excited that I get to follow yet another chapter in the history of Dynamics CRM, as it rises in popularity and emerges stronger with each iteration. The product team listens to us; all of us. Most of the features discussed in this chapter were birthed by feedback. So, make your opinions known and engage in the discussion about the future of the product over at Microsoft Connect: http://connect.microsoft.com

Index

A

address fields
  combined, 115-17
  consolidated, 114, 119
Asynchronous Workflows, 259, 306-7
Auto Number, 204, 209, 211-12
Auto Number Sequence, 208-10

B

background workflows, 13, 199-202, 206-7
business process automation, 306, 311
business processes, real-world, 8, 130
business process flow area, 133, 139
business process flow designer, 148, 167
Business Process Stage, 76-78
business rules, universal, 296-97

C

Case Process, 139, 148, 154, 156
CBRs (CRM Business Rules), 11, 25-27, 172-76, 180-81, 185, 187-90, 192-95
child records, 42-43, 57-58, 67-68, 152, 155, 157, 165, 207-8, 212, 298
client script, 12, 20, 25, 173, 188-90, 193, 195
client side, 173, 187, 205
client upgrades, 247, 266, 268
conditions, multiple, 184-85
CRM Business Rules. *See* CBRs
CRM Server, 218, 221-24
CRM users, 41, 46-47, 49, 69, 76, 142, 166, 222, 232, 235, 264, 282
custom code, 9, 12, 26, 132, 172-73, 203, 208, 211, 215
Customizing Business Process Flows, 11, 142
Custom Workflow Activities, 203-4, 206, 208-9, 212, 252

E

email router, 27, 216, 221, 223
Enable Rules, 314-15, 317
entity images, 82, 307
error message, 71-72, 165, 185-86, 190, 192, 228, 230, 232
execute, 172-73, 175-76, 180-81, 185, 187-89, 198-99, 205-6, 310

F

field display names, 62-63
fields

    default, 64-65
    image, 82, 95-97
    primary, 50-51, 65-67
    primary key, 302-3
    processid, 302-3
    stage category, 157-58, 167
fields column, 150, 154
field values, 67, 69, 71-72, 78, 132, 185-86, 317
formattedvalue, 304-5
form business rules, 111, 215, 241-43, 247

G

GUID field, 157-58

I

Image Type Fields, 95-96
import upgrade, 218-19
information form, 117-18, 236-38, 240-41
in-place upgrade, 217-19, 267-68
instruction fields, 77-78

J

JavaScript and Business Rules, 204-5

L

leverage Business Rules, 299-300
logic, conditional, 155, 157, 159, 167, 205
lookup fields, 50, 65-66, 68, 79, 84, 88, 90, 110, 153, 271

M

maximum number, 167, 234
Microsoft Dynamics CRM users, 81, 214
Microsoft Outlook, 115, 262-64, 284

N

name, primary Field, 177, 179
navigation bar, 17-18, 35-36, 44, 58, 60, 68, 102-3, 106, 236-37
new entities, 51, 81, 133, 201, 246
New Form Types, 11, 20, 84, 90

O

Outlook client, 37-38, 40, 218-19, 235, 244, 246-47, 264, 266, 268-69, 281, 284-85, 287, 289-90

Owning Teams, 11, 120-22, 128

P

PBL (Portable Business Logic), 8, 132, 280, 296
phone calls, 113-14, 119, 141, 148, 152-53, 162, 283, 285-86
Portable Business Logic. *See* PBL
process entity, 24, 142, 165, 171, 193, 300
processes
  customizable, 160-61
  new, 26, 130, 145, 147-48, 153
processid, 302, 305
Process Sessions, 201-2
Process Stage, 73, 75, 78, 157, 169, 300, 302-3
process stage field, 156-58, 301
processstageid, 303, 305
production upgrade, 13, 219, 245-46

Q

Quick Create forms, 20-21, 29, 42-44, 53, 55, 90-91, 93, 280
Quick View Forms, 20, 57, 77-79, 84, 86-88, 90, 92-93, 313

R

Ready-to-Use Business Processes, 159, 169
real-time workflows, 68-69, 132, 171, 291, 293, 306
Real Time Workflows, 9, 12-13, 24, 192, 196, 200-208, 210-13
record types, 126, 134-35, 137, 157, 165
rules, 25, 44, 68, 71, 172-86, 188-91, 205, 208, 241, 280, 291, 296, 314, 317

S

SDK (Software Developer Kit), 28-31, 72, 96, 112, 237, 248, 251, 253, 296, 306, 308, 312-14
security roles, 37, 43, 91, 118, 121, 129, 142, 144-46, 165-66, 169
server, 59, 195, 205, 215, 217, 219-20, 222-23, 245-47, 253, 266
server sync, 9, 30, 264-66, 269, 284-90
sitemap, 34-36, 108, 232, 234-35, 237, 254-55, 257
Software Developer Kit. *See* SDK
SQL Server, 218-21, 223, 231
stage name, 134-35, 149, 158, 167
stagename, 302-3, 305
steps, custom, 137, 200, 206, 209
Switch Process, 135, 145
Synchronous Workflows, 306-7, 311, 316

T

tablet app, 84, 111, 277, 281

tablet browser, 220, 273-74, 283, 290
tablet client, 276, 284

U

Update Rollup, 216, 247, 250-52, 258, 268, 316, 318
Update steps, 203, 302
upgrade process, 13, 117, 214, 217, 231, 245-47, 252, 266
users, mobile, 284-85

V

version number, 249-50

W

Windows Workflow Foundation, 295, 300, 306-7, 310
workflowid, 302, 304
workflow processes, 11, 68, 79, 132, 155-56, 159, 165
   companion, 159, 162
   real-time, 78, 132, 156
   traditional, 132, 155